Morality and Self-Interest

Morality and Self-Interest

Edited by

Paul Bloomfield

OXFORD
UNIVERSITY PRESS
2008

OXFORD
UNIVERSITY PRESS

Oxford University Press, Inc., publishes works that further
Oxford University's objective of excellence
in research, scholarship, and education.

Oxford   New York
Auckland   Cape Town   Dar es Salaam   Hong Kong   Karachi
Kuala Lumpur   Madrid   Melbourne   Mexico City   Nairobi
New Delhi   Shanghai   Taipei   Toronto

With offices in
Argentina   Austria   Brazil   Chile   Czech Republic   France   Greece
Guatemala   Hungary   Italy   Japan   Poland   Portugal   Singapore
South Korea   Switzerland   Thailand   Turkey   Ukraine   Vietnam

Published by Oxford University Press, Inc.
198 Madison Avenue, New York, New York 10016

www.oup.com

Oxford is a registered trademark of Oxford University Press

Library of Congress Cataloging-in-Publication Data
Morality and self-interest / edited by Paul Bloomfield.
p. cm.
Includes bibliographical references and index.
ISBN 978-0-19-530584-5; 978-0-19-530585-2 (pbk.)
1. Ethics. 2. Self-interest. I. Bloomfield, Paul, 1962–
BJ1581.2.M65 2007
170'.42—dc22   2007016218

9 8 7 6 5 4 3 2 1

Printed in the United States of America
on acid-free paper

Acknowledgments

My professional interest in the relationship between morality and self-interest is due to an ongoing exchange I'm having with Richard Joyce, from which I have greatly profited and for which I am much obliged. The reader will soon see that Joyce has commented rather extensively on my own contribution to this volume. He read and commented on an early draft of "Why It's Bad to Be Bad," which I emended in light thereof. After, seeing his contributuion, I did not use my position as editor to reply. I begin to address his point of view in my review, in *Mind* (Bloomfield, 2007), of his latest book *The Evolution of Morality* (2006).

I thank Stephen Finlay and Michael P. Lynch for their early and continuous encouragement of my editing what has eventually become this book. Especial thanks go to Sonia Michel for finding the cover art, on top of all her help and support. I also had helpful early conversations on the topic in a graduate seminar with Erin Andrews, Robert Crum, Bo Ram Lee, and Daniel Massey. Christopher Morris has given excellent advice all along the way, all greatly appreciated.

Approaching the question of how to comprehend the issues involved in thinking about morality and self-interest was difficult. Insofar as the issues concern the meaning or semantics of "morality", or a conceptual analysis of *morality*, it is metaethics par excellence; insofar as it concerns the question "how should I live?", it is squarely an issue in normative ethics. Bringing together the justification and/or rationality of morality, with the sort of motivational or psychological issues involved in the question "Why be moral?" means the situation can become conceptually daunting. The distinction between self and other was a natural place for someone with my interests to begin, since it bears on both metaphysical and moral discourse. A bit of research showed that W. D. Falk had already invented the wheel on which I had begun working. His paper "Morality, Self, and Others" is a masterpiece, and is included here in full. I'd like to thank George Nakhnikian for his permission to reprint it.

There is one other contribution within not expressly written for this volume. Thomas Nagel's paper, "The Value of Inviolability" appeared first in French and appears here in English for the first time. I am grateful to the editors of *Revue de Métaphysique et de Morale* for their permission to publish a translation of "La valeur de l'inviolabilité".

The prospect of editing a volume is made most unattractive by the grim stories one hears about the process. Frequently, editing is said to be "a labor of love" and being an editor "a thankless position". In retrospect, I am very lucky to have had an experience that is an exception to the rule. I am most thankful and grateful to my contributors, each and every one, as well as to my editor, Peter Ohlin, and the production editor, Gwen Colvin.

Contents

C. Potential Congruence and Irreconcilability

PART II: MORALITY WITHIN SELF-INTEREST

A. Morality as Necessary to Self-Interest

B. Morality as Indistinguishable from Self-Interest

Contributors

JULIA ANNAS is Regents Professor of Philosophy at the University of Arizona. She has published several books and articles across a wide range of topics in ancient philosophy, and in recent years has concentrated on ancient ethical theories and also contemporary virtue ethics.

PAUL BLOOMFIELD is Associate Professor of Philosophy at the University of Connecticut. He has published on topics in metaphysics and moral philosophy, and he is the author of *Moral Reality* (2001).

W. D. FALK taught philosophy for more than forty years in Europe, Australia, and the United States, finishing his career at the University of North Carolina, Chapel Hill, in 1975. His collected papers are entitled *Ought, Reasons, and Morality* (1986).

STEPHEN FINLAY is an Assistant Professor in the School of Philosophy at the University of Southern California. His research focuses on the explanation of normativity and the metaphysical and semantic foundations of ethics.

T. H. IRWIN is Professor of Ancient Philosophy in the University of Oxford and a Fellow of Keble College. From 1975 to 2006, he taught at Cornell University. He has written on ancient philosophy and the history of ethics.

RICHARD JOYCE is a Research Fellow at the University of Sydney. His primary research areas are metaethics and moral psychology, and he is the author of *The Myth of Morality* (2001) and *The Evolution of Morality* (2006).

JOEL J. KUPPERMAN is Board of Trustees Professor of Philosophy at the University of Connecticut. His most recent books are *Ethics and Qualities of Life* (2007) and *Classic Asian Philosophy: A Guide to the Essential Texts*, 2nd ed. (2007).

CHRISTOPHER W. MORRIS is Professor of Philosophy at the University of Maryland, College Park. His research interests are moral and political philosophy, philosophy of law, and practical rationality, and he is the author of *An Essay on the Modern State* (1998).

THOMAS NAGEL is University Professor, Professor of Philosophy, and Professor of Law at New York University.

MATHIAS RISSE is Associate Professor of Public Policy and Philosophy at the John F. Kennedy School of Government at Harvard University. He works primarily in political philosophy, and his main research area there is global justice. He also has research interests in nineteenth-century German philosophy, especially in Nietzsche.

SAMUEL SCHEFFLER is Professor of Philosophy and Law at the University of California, Berkeley. He is the author of *The Rejection of Consequentialism* (1982), *Human Morality* (1992), and *Boundaries and Allegiances* (2003).

DAVID SCHMIDTZ is Kendrick Professor of Philosophy and joint Professor of Economics at the University of Arizona. He is author of *Elements of Justice* (2006) and *Person, Polis, Planet* (2008).

MICHAEL STOCKER is the Guttag Professor of Ethics and Political Philosophy at Syracuse University. His work focuses on moral psychology and ethics, dealing with such topics as emotions, affectivity, pleasure, friendship, and love. His writings include studies of classical and early modern moral theorists as well as critiques of contemporary ethical thinkers.

RALPH WEDGWOOD is Lecturer and Professor of Philosophy at the University of Oxford, and a Fellow of Merton College, Oxford. He is the author of *The Nature of Normativity* (2007), and many philosophical articles, especially on metaethics and epistemology.

Morality and Self-Interest

Introduction

There are two conceptions of "morality" currently at play in the philosophical literature and employing them differentially affects how the relationship of morality to self-interest is conceived.[1]

The first conception may be thought of as the social conception of "morality". It begins with the question of how one ought to behave toward others. Morality is seen as having a final authority over our lives and the interests of others play a necessary role in the decision procedures we ought to use. Where the interests of others are not at issue, morality does not come into play: there is no morality for an agent stranded alone on a desert island. Thus, on such a view, morality and justice, understood loosely to encompass all fair dealings between people, are often seen to have the same scope. Typically, on this conception, morality requires impartiality, such that agents must not see their own interests, or the interests of their families, communities, etc., as having any special standing whatsoever in the decision procedure that determines what ought to be done. Thus, we see Kantian deontology requiring the universalizability of maxims of action and utilitarianism, and consequentialism more generally, requiring strict impartiality in the evaluation of the outcomes of possible actions. On some accounts, the strict impartiality may be loosened somewhat by, for example, "agent-centered prerogatives", as discussed by Scheffler (1982), but this loosening must still be justified given standards according to which it would be acceptable for everyone to act in the same way; agents may, to some degree, favor themselves to avoid undue sacrifices that would be required by strict impartiality, but they may only do so according to rules that admit no exception.

---

1. The basic distinction here is developed in W. D. Falk's "Morality, Self, and Others," reprinted within, as well as in William Frankena's "The Concept of Morality," *The Journal of Philosophy* 63, no. 21 (Nov. 10, 1966): 688–96. My use below and throughout the volume of the names "Within" and "Without" are based on "In" and "Out" in the masterful opening dialogue of Falk's paper, which itself could serve as an excellent introduction to the volume as a whole.

The other conception of morality dates back to the ancient Greeks, and takes as its starting point the question, "How ought I to live?". It might fairly be called the "Socratic" conception of morality (see Plato's *Gorgias*, 500c; *Republic*, 344e). Answering this question will inevitably require one to consider how one will behave toward other people, but extends beyond that, to every significant aspect of a person's life, however private. Thus, someone stranded alone on a desert island may be faced with moral questions, given the possibility of living as well as possible in those trying circumstances. Like the social conception of morality, the Socratic conception of morality will have final authority over the agent's life, representing the agent's "rule of life". As such, the Socratic conception may be seen as formally egoistic, since one begins by aiming at living well, though it need not be substantially egoistic if one determines that one must treat others well in order to have a well-lived life. (For more on this distinction between "formal" and "substantive", see Annas' contribution within; see also Williams, 1985, p. 32.) Given the Socratic conception of morality, however, and in contrast to the social conception, rabid, selfish egoism still represents a form of morality, however mistaken it may be.

As noted, these two conceptions of morality will represent the relationship of morality to self-interest differently. Given the social conception, morality is defined without reference to self-interest, and for the purposes of this introduction and the structure of the volume as a whole, we may refer to a defender of such a view as "Without". Given the Socratic conception, morality is defined within the terms of self-interest, given that it is assumed that living as well as possible is in an agent's self-interest. Unsurprisingly, "Within" will be used to name the defender of such a view. Without and Within are not often distinguished in modern moral philosophy, to its detriment. It is common for a philosopher to give his or her "theory of morality", unreflectively adopting one view over the other. As such, defenders of these theories beg central, normative questions against those who assume the other point of view. As a result, moral philosophers often end up talking past each other without realizing it.

The variety of theories emerging from Without is quite large. As noted, they may be cast in universalized or categorical terms, or in other terms giving no special consideration for the particular circumstances of the acting agent, including the agent's interests. These theories most often derive their authority either by an appeal to rationality or fear of punishment, but in either case the demands of morality take the interests of the agent to be (more or less) irrelevant. So, Without may give a theory that defines rightness in terms of universalizable maxims, or in terms of the greatest good for the greatest number, without regard for how this "right" action may affect the agent. Within will think that Without's view of morality is at best merely incomplete for it leaves individualized agents, and the quality of their lives, (more or less) out of the picture. At worst Within will see Without as immorally, unfairly preventing the agent from living as well as possible. On the other hand, if Within turns around and articulates a moral theory in which the prescriptions of morality are sensitive to the particular interests of the agent who is trying to live well by it, Without will not consider the resulting theory to be, to that extent, a moral theory at all; considering what is in one's own self-interest is not considering anything that counts as moral. Perhaps these are considerations of prudence, or expedience, but not morality.

Within may, for example, articulate a moral theory in which it is wrong to be an alcoholic or a glutton, even if the only harms of this are self-inflicted. Without may respond by saying, "People who harm only their own self-interest are not guilty of any moral offense. What makes a moral theory a moral theory is precisely the fact that it ignores an agent's interests in making its prescriptions. Moral theories are checks on people's naturally aggrandizing sense of self-interest. While what Within suggests may be part of a theory of prudence or practical rationality, it is not in the moral game". Within replies, "Nothing deserving to be called 'morality' demands anything less than a person live as well as possible, which will not happen unless, at the very least, individuals consider, to some significant degree, their own interests as such". And some versions of Within may add, "Without and I agree on the fact that morality must be other-regarding, but its content is not solely other-regarding and must take into account the interests of the agent trying to live a moral life".

It is worth noting that the distinction between Without and Within may not, in the end, be a sharp one, but vague instead. As we will see, there are more moderate versions of both theories. As briefly mentioned above, some versions of Without may allow for the demands of morality to be modulated to one degree or another by the interests or projects of the agent. And some moderate versions of Within may conceive of morality and self-interest as distinct normative principles that are in need of some sort of conceptual articulation. Given moderate versions of Without and Within, they may become difficult to distinguish from each other, though this of course does not alleviate us from the necessity of settling on a single conception of *morality* from which to begin our theorizing.[2] In the end, we will most likely find ourselves with a continuum of conceptions of morality with more rigorous forms of Without and Within at the extremes.

Unless we settle the dispute between Without and Within, prior to normative or metaethical theorizing, the resultant theories will not be responsive to the concerns of different theorists who will inevitably disagree with the starting points of the other.[3] As an example, consider the following situation. Suppose one could save the life of one's child by buying an organ obtained illicitly, perhaps from a prisoner on the other side of the world.[4] One could see how one might be tempted by the love of one's child to make the deal, while simultaneously being repulsed by the idea of such malfeasance. Those who have adopted Without's conception of morality will treat the tension in the situation as being between nonmoral (self-interested or selfish) considerations and moral considerations. They tend to think that there is something conceptually incoherent about the moral permissibility of favoring one's own interests over the interests of others; they typically say, "Morality demands that we sacrifice our own welfare or self-interest for the

---

2. I thank Samuel Scheffler for bringing this to my attention.

3. One might speculate on whether the present debate is part of normative ethics or metaethics. As mentioned in the acknowledgments, I think part of the difficulty involved in it is that it straddles the line, or blurs it. In one sense, it forces normative questions about conduct: how do moral considerations relate to self-interested or prudential considerations? In another, it forces metaethical questions regarding the proper conceptual analysis of *morality*, or the meaning of "morality." Not distinguishing clearly between the normative and the metaethical may be part of trouble. One possibility is that Without is working with a more normatively laden conception of morality, since as Frankena (ibid) notes, it builds substantial normative commitments into the meaning of "morality", while Within's conception is more normatively neutral and metaethically oriented toward living well, whatever that may turn out to be.

4. I thank Christopher Morris for the example.

good of others". On the other hand, those adopting Within's point of view will count all the considerations at play "moral considerations", and would see no incoherence in the bare idea of the moral permissibility of sacrificing the welfare or the good of another for one's own sake. So, Falk has his interlocutor "In" say, "It may also be that . . . someone ought to stand up for his own good even to the detriment of another. It could be sound advice to say to a woman in strife with herself and tied to a demanding parent, 'You ought to consider yourself, and so break away now, hard as it may be on the parent'" (see p. 240). Of course, Within may find it impermissible to buy illicit organs. But that need not imply that the self-interested, non-impartial considerations that lead one to look after one's child as best as possible are anything less moral.

Defenders of Without tend to believe that morality and self-interest constitute distinct normative perspectives or domains, such that morality is an external force that imposes itself on self-interest. Those who accept Without's conception of morality may differ over how frequently these two domains are incompatible due to their prescribing contradictory behavior. One may also be a moral skeptic while sharing Without's conception of morality by doubting the legitimacy or authority of the moral perspective. Within may believe that morality and self-interest can pull apart, but do not necessarily constitute distinct normative domains. Egoists who accept Within's conception of morality may think of it as almost always leading away from what is good for the agent, thereby rejecting morality whenever it is inconvenient. Because of Aristotle, it is most common for those accepting Within to see morality as necessary but insufficient for a well-lived life, and that other nonmoral goods are also necessary to self-interest. Such positions are challenged by situations in which there is tension in trying to preserve both morality and these nonmoral goods.[5] A more extreme version of Within takes the proper understanding of "morality" and "self-interest" to show that there can be no tension between them since, in fact, they amount to the same thing. So, the Stoics who think that living morally is sufficient for a well-lived life do not distinguish between what is moral and what is best for the agent. Unfortunately for these extreme positions, the "proper understanding" of morality and self-interest ends up being significantly different than common sense suggests. If one accepts the view of Socrates in *Gorgias*, the position that virtue is sufficient for happiness, then one is committed to the possibility of being "happy on the rack" (473c). Aristotle considers such views nonsense (*Nicomachean Ethics* VII, 13).

In arguing against moral skepticism, Without has a number of possible strategies to adopt. One tradition centers the issue on the relations between justice, typically conceived of as being wholly other-regarding, and self-interest, where Without then attempts to defend justice, or just acts, as rational or justified despite the fact that justice can demand "self-sacrifice" and, in general, ignores the interests of those who defend it (see Morris's contribution).[6] A more revisionary, Nietzschean conception of justice rejects much of its traditional other-regarding content, to make it more consistent with the interests of the self-chosen few who resist the other-regarding pressures of social convention or contract (Risse). Without's morality, understood without reference to self-interest, is definitive and supremely authoritative because it is of or from something better, grander,

---

5. See, for example, "Aristotle: An Unstable View," chapter 18 of Annas (1993).

6. Henceforth, I will merely parenthesize a philosopher's name when his or her contribution to the present volume is referenced.

or higher than any individual's self-interest. Morality, on this view, issues from a source that deserves our deference, respect, and perhaps even reverence. The source may be the good abstractly conceived, as nonnatural or supernatural; or it may be "naturalized" as the welfare, pleasure, or satisfaction of humanity as a whole; or it can be defined in terms of the dictates of rationality. On any version of Without, the self-interest of the (rationally) deliberating person plays no specially weighted role in the determination of what ought to be done; it may be permissible or even required that agents tend to their own interests, but this must not be at the expense of other-regarding moral duty or go beyond what can rationally be expected of anyone.

Perhaps most often, skeptics of morality take their real dialectical adversary to be Without, so that those very features of morality that identify it as such for Without are seen as erroneous, fallacious, incoherent, queer, or fictitious (Joyce). The "special status" of morality, the "peculiar institution" of it (to use Williams's (1985) ringing phrase) can be lamented as well as revered. For many others, the justified reason to be moral is fear of retribution and/or punishment for immorality. Strong authority, from political sovereignty up to omnipotence, may be required by Without for engendering moral motivation. Nevertheless, this very status of morality as requiring an external sanction puts it on the defensive.

On the other hand, Without can muster an offense by showing how its "supreme authority" is, in fact, rational and cogent from the first-person perspective, and does not require external sanction (Nagel, Schmidtz). On such views, belief in the authority of Without's morality is justified when it is taken on its own terms. Further still, Without may point out that despite the fact that moral prescriptions do not refer to any particular agent's self-interest, they need not be at odds with an individual's self-interest. On a hopeful interpretation of Without's morality, one may think that any decent moral theory must be livable, and if obeyed, it can allow for large amounts of mutual reward to accrue to those who are lucky enough to live in a moral society (Scheffler). If social institutions were made just, and children were taught to be just, then the sacrifice to self-interest any individual will be asked to make might be kept at a low minimum. A more negative program might find "live-ability" to be irrelevant to the formulation of moral demands, and any reconciliation between morality and self-interest would be mere wishful thinking. On such a view, if morality is regard for others and not for the self, then the two are defined incompatibly, and such is the case when the former is conceived as a check on the latter. As such they are more frequently than not, if not always, going to be at odds with each other. At least, perhaps, neither has dominion over the other, and any congruence between the two is accidental and likely to be rare (Finlay).

The situation that emerges from adopting Within's conception develops differently. With regard to replying to the egoist skeptical of morality, Within's general strategy is to show that one cannot both look out for one's self-interest and ignore the demands of morality. Morality is seen as at least part of a well-lived life. In a fashion similar to Without, one may accept the idea that morality and self-interest are two separate principles, and yet note that this, by itself, does not imply that the practical import of the moral principle can be understood in terms of considerations that do not overlap at all with those of self-interest. One might argue that the moral impulse is an internal principle directed toward something that the individual values at least as much (and possibly more) than the individual's self-interest if it were to be considered in isolation. This still leaves open the possibility of a situation arising in which one's principled dedication to morality requires what would otherwise appear to be a sacrifice of self-interest. And, as noted, this is consistent with thinking that respecting the moral principle is necessary for a well-maintained sense of self-interest. Or one might think that morality is merely the "best bet" for success in life (Hursthouse, 1999), or, more strongly, one might think that it is at least partly constitutive of a life in which one's self-interest is maintained as well as possible. Nevertheless, if one's position leaves open the possibility of a tension between these two internal principles, then a mechanism for their adjudication will be needed, if it is not assumed up front that one principle always trumps the other (Wedgwood).

These problems do not arise for a more radical version of Within that understands the moral life as the best life possible for a person. What is moral and what is in one's best self-interest, all things considered, will be the same when these are understood properly. On such a view, one may distinguish regard for others from self-regard but one must balance these considerations so that one's well-lived life, one's happiness, is not independent of one's self-respect and one's self-respect is not independent of how one treats others (Bloomfield). As such there may be times when one's own interests take moral precedence over the interests of others. Morality would then have supreme authority over one's life, because it is defined formally in terms of what leads to the best life possible for the individual; even in tragic dilemmas, behaving immorally will always be the greater of evils. Thus, Within's conception of morality must take seriously the Paradox of Happiness, that an overweening concern for one's self-interest prevents one from doing what is in one's self-interest.[7] Selfish concern for oneself leads one away from the best life possible for a person, but a selfless abnegation in favor of the concerns of others is also doomed to lead away from a well-lived life. Our responsibilities to ourselves are no less nor more "moral" than our responsibilities toward others. The traditional problem of such a view is that it typically requires a reevaluation of what is in a person's self-interest, as well as of the content of morality, such that a person's self-interest will always be in accord with what is morally right, and vice versa. So, for people living well, what others might commonly find harmful to their self-interest, such as being passed over for some honor, will not be given any import at all. From the first-person point of view, one's moral values will lead one through a life that is thought to be better than any possible other, given who one was when born in whichever particular circumstances.

For Within, it should be unsurprising that the topics of moral psychology and moral motivation loom large. For example, properly distinguishing moral motivation from egotistical motivation will require careful work (Annas). On one hand, morality seems to demand a certain purity of motive, while on the other, an agent need not be ignorant that performing the morally right act will be what is best for that agent, all things considered. The knowledge of how one's actions may benefit one ought not to provide motivation for a moral person, yet one cannot pretend not to know what one knows. Thus, Within will have to explain how moral people avoid being willfully ignorant of how their actions affect them personally while avoiding having such thoughts "pollute" their motivation to do the right thing (Irwin). For example, enjoying the rewards of being moral

---

7. What I am calling the "Paradox of Happiness" here has the same formal structure as Sidgwick's "Paradox of Hedonism." For the self-defeating nature of egoism in the face of such paradoxes, see Stocker (1976).

(perhaps merely by gaining the sort of gratification that comes from doing a good job) does not seem problematic after the right deed has been performed, but the motivational force provided by the expectation of these rewards before the deed is problematic. If, however, "virtue is its own reward", then one wonders why these rewards would be necessarily productive of a life in which self-interest is well maintained (Kupperman). Another possibility is that if Within is right, then morality and self-interest may become so intertwined it is then difficult to distinguish one from the other from a psychological point of view: our motivations, our emotional lives, and, in general, our characters will have to smoothly embody an amalgam of both other- and self-concern and the reactive emotions these engender (Stocker).

Given the number of conceptual possibilities in which a relation between morality and self-interest can be articulated, it is no wonder that progress on how these ought to be related has been so slow and difficult. We must somehow—or decide whether we wish to—distinguish between what "morality" commonly means and what it ought to mean, between what most people think and what we all ought to think. The same is true for "self-interest", since there is always a possible gap between what is truly good for a person, all things considered, and what that person wants most (or desires or prefers), even when given an optimal amount of time to reflect. (I take it for granted that no viable theory can hold that people are infallible regarding what is good for them, even given copious reflection.) The philosophical hope must be that at least some of these possible conceptions of morality are shown up front to be incoherent or misguided, for one reason or another, that modern or future data from the social sciences might shed light on the subject, and that from there, philosophical argumentation can take us from fact and reason to an improvement in both theory and (most optimistically) practice. There are few more difficult philosophical problems and probably even fewer more important to the quality of human life.

There is no pretense to claim that the conceptual framework laid out here is the only way to understand or approach the topic of morality and self-interest. One could do so by trying to sort out the confusing relations between morality and ethics. Or one might try to step forthrightly into normative theorizing by considering work that tries to answer directly the question "Why be moral?" There are historical approaches in which the development of the options is traced in the hope of learning something new about the issue by exploring its developmental history. A more theoretic approach might be collecting a series of articles on the relation of justice to the rest of morality, or by trying to contrast normative theories so that consequentialism and deontology are on one side of the debate, and virtue theories on the other. The editorial hope is that the fundamental conceptual distinctions drawn here, informed by Falk and Frankena as noted, represent the most incisive approach to the material, capable of shedding light on "Why be moral?", on history, as well as on the current shape of normative theorizing. The editorial claim is that a justified determination of the relation between morality and self-interest ought to precede normative and (more familiar) metaethical theorizing.

I

MORALITY WITHOUT SELF-INTEREST

A. Morality on the Defensive

1

The Trouble with Justice

CHRISTOPHER W. MORRIS

1. Justice Is Different

Must we always be just? Presumably. Do we always have reasons to be just? That is another question, and it is not obvious the answer is yes. Justice is different in some ways that make a difference.[1]

Contrast justice with some of the other central virtues—for instance, prudence, courage, temperance, or wisdom. Justice is different. Unlike these others, it is principally a social virtue; its interpersonal element is central. Other virtues, such as generosity, as well as benevolence or charity, are also interpersonal. But unlike justice, acts of generosity or benevolence are not owed to specific people. One ought to help others, but the choice of when and where to act benevolently is for the most part up to the individual. In modern terms their requirements are duties of imperfect obligation; those of justice are for the most part owed to specific individuals (duties of perfect obligation).[2]

The "cautious, jealous virtue of justice"[3] is different in other ways. It is cautious in that it would rarely have us aim for the best, seeming instead to settle for the stable and the secure. It is jealous, as Hume notes, demanding obedience even on occasions when its usefulness is not obvious.

1. Earlier versions of this essay were presented at the University of Amsterdam (on two occasions), the Graduate Center of the City University of New York, the University of Maryland, College Park, and the University of Virginia. I am grateful for comments offered on all of these occasions, as well as written comments from Paul Bloomfield, Peter Carruthers, William Galston, Verna Gehring, David Lefkowitz, and an anonymous reader for Oxford University Press. A shorter and earlier version of this essay was published in *Philosophy and Public Policy Quarterly* 24, no. 3 (Summer 2004): 14–20.

2. While there are several distinctions that are marked by these terms, this seems the most fundamental in contemporary philosophy. See Onora O'Neill, "Duty and Obligation," *Encyclopedia of Ethics*, 2nd ed., ed. L. Becker and C. Becker, 1:425 (New York and London: Routledge, 2001).

3. David Hume, *Enquiry Concerning the Principles of Morals*, 3rd ed., ed. P. H. Nidditch (Oxford: Clarendon, [1751] 1975), sec. 3, part I, 145.

My classical list of virtues may signal another contrast. Justice is an imperial virtue, and its partisans often seek to secure its dominance, sometimes even by banishing other virtues from the realm of ethics or morality. In modern moral philosophy there is a disposition to identify justice with most or sometimes all of morality. This kind of imperialism raises questions about the distinction between the moral and the nonmoral; we need not try to settle these questions now, for the difficulties they present pale besides our trouble with justice.

The trouble with justice can be stated simply: it seems that sometimes we do not have reason to be just, specifically reasons of the right kind. It's obvious that we sometimes are not motivated to act justly, but my concern in this essay is with (normative) reasons for action, not (nonnormative) motives. The problem is also not, as we shall see, what Hobbes's Foole said, that "there is no such thing as Justice".[4] The Foole is often interpreted as a moral skeptic, and the difficulty that concerns me is different from that posed by this textbook adversary of moral philosophers. The moral skeptic seems to deny that morality is what it is said to be; rather, it is "merely a chimerical [i]dea without truth…[a] mere phantom of the brain…".[5] The trouble with justice, however, is not that the virtue, like Harry, is dead. Rather, it is that *sometimes* we do not seem to have reasons to be just or, as we shall see, reasons of the right kind.

Fictional immoralists of the kind characteristically found in philosophical texts are a distraction from more realistic adversaries. Genuine immoralists seem to be psychopaths, humans who are clearly defective in particular ways, affective and cognitive. By contrast, most of the unjust or evil people we know seem to recognize most of the fundamental norms of justice, apply them to many people, and have recognizable human dispositions and sympathies, however limited they may be (it is said that "Goebbels loved children and dogs"). Real immoralists do not seem to be moral skeptics.

The trouble with justice is more of an everyday problem, one that is insufficiently appreciated. Hobbes's classical presentation of the Foole, read slightly differently than usual, is a first statement of the worry: the Foole "questioneth, whether Injustice…may not *sometimes* stand with that Reason, which dictateth to every man his own good" (italics added). The trouble with justice is that *sometimes*, on occasion, it seems we do not have reason to be just. As even thieves and ruffians recognize, we need justice. But sometimes it seems to pay not to be just. It appears that on occasion we do not have reason, or the right kinds of reasons, to be just. That is the trouble. How could this be?

My initial contrast of justice and other virtues suggests a classical approach to the trouble. We could try to show that even if justice is different from the other virtues, it is needed in the way that we need the other virtues. In the way that we cannot live well without courage or moderation, so we need justice. The worry about this approach has been clear since Plato's defense of justice in the *Republic*. Plato succeeds well enough in showing that "justice in the soul" (or individual justice) is a virtue:

4. Thomas Hobbes, *Leviathan*, ed. Richard Tuck (Cambridge: Cambridge University Press, [1651] 1991), chap. 15, 101.

5. Immanuel Kant, *Groundwork of the Metaphysics of Morals*, trans. H. J. Paton (New York: Harper, [1785] 1964), part II, 111.

It is left for us to enquire, it seems, if it is more profitable to act justly, to engage in fine pursuits and be just, whether one is known to be so or not, or to do wrong and be unjust, provided one does not pay the penalty and is not improved by punishment.

But Socrates, [Glaucon] said, this enquiry strikes me as becoming ridiculous now that justice and injustice have been shown to be such as we described. It is generally thought that life is not worth living when the body's nature is ruined, even if every kind of food and drink, every kind of wealth and power are available; yet we are to enquire whether life will be worth living when our soul, the very thing by which we live, is confused and ruined, if only one can do whatever one wishes, except that one cannot do what will free one from vice and injustice and make one acquire justice and virtue.[6]

What Plato is not able to show is that we have equal reason to do what we are required to do by "justice in the city" (social justice). The relation between the two, individual and social justice, is not as Plato hopes. It seems perfectly possible, indeed likely, that the demands of social justice will often not be beneficial to the just individual. Not surprisingly, Plato has the greatest difficulty showing that the rulers will be particularly pleased with their "spartan" lot.

Aristotle explicitly recognizes the other-directed nature of justice: "justice is the only virtue that seems to be another person's good, because it is related to another; for it does what benefits another, either the ruler or the fellow member of the community".[7] It is unclear from his account why we should always want to be just (according to the general, rather than the special virtue). In a good community the laws will aim at "the common benefit of all.... And so in one way what we call just is whatever produces and maintains happiness and its parts in a political community". Justice, he says, is a distinctive virtue: it is

complete virtue in relation to another. And that is why justice often seems to be supreme among the virtues.... Morever, justice is complete virtue to the highest degree because it is the complete exercise of complete virtue. And it is the complete exercise because the person who has justice is able to exercise virtue in relation to another, not only in what concerns himself; for many are able to exercise virtue in their own concerns, but unable in what relates to another....[8]

This type of justice [general as opposed to special justice], then, is the whole, not a part, of virtue.... For virtue is that same as justice, but what it is to be virtue is not the same as what it is to be justice. Rather, insofar as virtue is related to another, it is justice, and insofar as it is a certain sort of state without qualification, it is virtue.[9]

But it is far from obvious that virtuous people will always have reasons to be just in relations to others in the way they have reasons to be prudent or temperate.

In her early work Philippa Foot raised the question with startling explicitness.

6. Plato, *Republic*, trans. G. M. A. Grube (Indianapolis: Hackett, 1974), book IV, 444e4–445b2.

7. Aristotle, *Nicomachean Ethics*, 2nd ed., trans. T. Irwin (Indianapolis: Hackett, 1999), V, 1, 1130a3–5.

8. Ibid., V, 1, 1129b1–1130a6.

9. Ibid., V, 1, 1130a10–14.

But what, it will be asked, of justice? For while prudence, courage and temperance are qualities which benefit the man who has them, justice seems rather to benefit others, and to work to the disadvantage of the just man himself. Justice, as it is treated here, as one of the cardinal virtues, covers all those things owed to other people: it is under injustice that murder, theft and lying come, as well as the withholding of what is owed for instance by parents to children and by children to parents, as well as the dealings which would be called unjust in everyday speech. So the man who avoids injustice will find himself in need of things he has returned to their owner, unable to obtain an advantage by cheating and lying....We will be asked how, on our theory, justice can be a virtue and injustice a vice, since it will surely be difficult to show that any man whatsoever must need to be just as he needs the use of his hands and eyes, or needs prudence, courage or temperance?

Foot adds, infamously, "Before answering this question I shall argue that if it cannot be answered, then justice can no longer be recommended, as a virtue".[10]

Justice seems to be in trouble.

2.   Source of the Trouble

The question is whether one always has a reason to be just (and a reason of the right kind). It is not obvious that the answer is affirmative. Why is that? Justice has a number of features that may be the source of trouble. The first I have already mentioned: the interpersonal and other-regarding nature of justice. Just acts appear not to aim, at least directly, at the good of the actor. Why be just on those occasions when one does not care for the good of others?

It is easy to think that undue attention to the interests of the self—egoism—is the source of the trouble here, but that is a mistake. Selfishness and other vices of self-interestedness may not be uncommon. But they are not essential to the problem. Thinkers like Hobbes, who thought that humans are rather selfish, formulate the skeptical worry about justice in terms of the interests of the self. But self-interestedness is only an extreme form of partiality, and it is partiality that is the source of the problem. Whenever justice asks us to benefit another, someone with whose interests we are not sufficiently concerned, the question may arise as to why we should do as required. The interests of friends and countrymen may appeal to us more.

Aristotle's proposal that (general) justice is the whole of virtue may be relevant here as one may think that the other-directed nature of justice will not bother the virtuous. After all, "The worst person, therefore, is the one who exercises his vice toward himself and his friends as well [as toward others]. And the best person is not the one who exercises virtue [only] toward himself, but the one who [also] exercises it in relation to another, since this is a difficult task"[11] This move will not, however, solve the problem. Consider a virtuous man, one who is prudent, wise, temperate, generous, and so on. He has many friends and treats them as he should.

10. Philippa Foot, "Moral Beliefs" (1958–59), in *Virtues and Vices* (Oxford: Clarendon, [1978] 2002), 125.

11. *Nicomachean Ethics*, V, 1, 1130a7–9 (words in brackets are Irwin's).

He recognizes, as befits a wise soul, that men are social or "political" animals. And he even possesses Humean sympathy (so he is not cruel to animals). We tend to think that all humans or at least persons have moral standing and that we may not take their lives or restrict their liberties except under certain special conditions. Certainly, slavery is a grave injustice. Our hypothetical man, endowed with the usual virtues, will act rightly most of the time; he will admire the courage of his adversary; he will make sacrifices for his friends and family and polis; and he will refrain from tormenting his enemies. But, at least on occasion, he may not have reason to refrain from profiting from injustices to distant peoples. It may be that so doing enables him to contribute to the building of a great temple or orphanage. Enslaving barbarians will offend his sympathetic nature. However, investing in companies that employ prison laborers in fascist or Communist countries may not. "Fellow-feeling", to move from classical to early modern times, is sufficiently partial to pose a problem for justice. As Hume noted, "[O]ur natural uncultivated ideas of morality, instead of providing a remedy for the partiality of our affections, do rather conform themselves to that partiality, and give it an additional force and influence".[12]

I singled out the other-directed, interpersonal nature of justice as the first feature that seems to be a source of trouble. The second feature is somewhat different. Justice is not only cautious, but it is also jealous and very demanding. By this I do not necessarily mean that its requirements are onerous. That is a matter of considerable controversy. Some people think that justice demands only respect for a few, essentially negative conditions; others think that we must turn over the bulk of our possessions and advantages to the poor and illfavored. It is important to see that my claims are independent of these controversies about what we might think of as the demands of justice. Rather, what I am thinking of is the *constraining* nature of the virtue. Justice requires that we abide by certain norms or rules, that we respect the rights of others, and that we give them what they are due. We are not merely to strive to do this; we must not do less. These are minimal demands, compliance with which is no grounds for praise. But they are also *constraints* of a certain normative kind. It is this feature of justice that is the source of much recent controversy in moral philosophy, and it is the second attribute to which I draw our attention.

Suppose that we think of justice as aiming at an end, the common good or the general interests of people (or something else). Then the question will arise as to why one should abide by a particular requirement of justice on those occasions when one could, more efficiently, secure the common good or general welfare by other means. In contemporary terms, why act in constrained, nonconsequential ways in situations where alternative acts better secure the goal in question? Here the problem is not so much that the norms or rules of justice are crude, imperfect mechanisms, that they "seek their end in an oblique and indirect manner" as Hume says. Rather, it is that they appear to require us to act in nonconsequential ways, that they instruct us often to refrain from acting on the balance of reasons. The problem is one of the rationality of action.

---

12. David Hume, *A Treatise of Human Nature*, 2nd ed., ed. P. H. Nidditch (Oxford: Clarendon, [1739–40] 1978), book III, part II, sec. ii, 489.

It is this particular feature of justice—and of deontic notions in general—that is the cause of much contemporary concern and controversy in contemporary moral philosophy and the theory of rational choice. If one thinks of practical rationality as having a maximizing structure—or at least as requiring action in accordance with the balance of reasons—then it is puzzling how requirements that would have us eschew acting in a maximally effective way can be justified. It is, of course, this feature that is addressed by contemporary revisionist accounts of practical rationality that find special significance in the ways in which intentions or plans affect our rational deliberations and actions.[13]

Justice is, as we have noted, both cautious and jealous, and its cautious nature may be exaggerated by its lawful form. The third and last feature of justice that I wish to highlight is its normative nature in one particular sense of the term. Justice guides us principally through norms or rules or laws, in an archaic, nonspecialized sense of this last term.

Suppose that we follow Aristotle in thinking that justice should aim at "the common benefit of all.... And so in one way what we call just is whatever produces and maintains happiness and its parts in a political community". The laws will usually be imperfect means of securing these ends, something effective usually and for the most part. Given that the best city, whether that sketched by Plato or by another theorist, may be beyond the reach of humans, the best for us will be a community ruled by laws that will secure our well-being usually and for the most part. This means that sometimes particular just acts will be useless. Hume notes this in his account of the artificial nature of justice. He argues that the rules of justice "seek their end in an oblique and indirect manner". He notes that

> tho' the rules of justice are establish'd merely by interest, their connexion with interest is somewhat singular, and is different from what may be observ'd on other occasions. A single act of justice is frequently contrary to *public interest*; and were it to stand alone, without being follow'd by other acts, may, in itself, be very prejudicial to society. When a man of merit, of a beneficent disposition, restores a great fortune to a miser, or a seditious bigot, he has acted justly and laudably, but the public is a real sufferer. Nor is every single act of justice, consider'd apart, more conducive to private interest, than to public; and 'tis easily conceiv'd how a man may impoverish himself by a signal instance of integrity, and have reason to wish, that with regard to that single act, the laws of justice were for a moment suspended in the universe. But however single acts of justice may be contrary, either to public or private interest, 'tis certain, that the whole plan or scheme is highly conducive, or indeed absolutely requisite, both to the support of society, and the well-being of every individual. 'Tis impossible to separate the good from the ill.[14]

If we think that justice must require, at least on occasion, that we be guided by (nonideal) practices or conventions,[15] then we should expect to find single acts of justice that appear

---

13. A good, brief introduction to this literature is found in Edward F. McClennen, "The Rationality of Being Guided by Rules," in *The Oxford Handbook of Practical Rationality*, ed. A. R. Mele and P. Rawlings (Oxford: Oxford University Press, 2004), chap. 12. See also the references in the bibliography to the work of Michael Bratman, David Gauthier, Edward F. McClennen, Joseph Raz, and Scott Shapiro.

14. Hume, *A Treatise of Human Nature*, book III, part II, sec. ii, 297.

15. "One part of the politically just is natural, and the other part legal." *Nicomachean Ethics*, V, 7, 1134b19–20.

to be useless or even harmful. Hume's example of restoring a fortune to a miser or bigot makes the point, and other cases will come to mind.[16] Conventional norms, in general, will often be either under- or overinclusive, a common feature of legal norms.

The trouble with justice seems, then, to be connected to three features: the virtue's other-regarding or interpersonal nature, its constraining nature (in the sense explained), and the fact that its requirements usually take the form of norms or rules.[17] It might be helpful to step back and to ask why we need justice and what this tells us about the virtue.

3.   Why Justice?

We need justice in order to live well. But the particular kinds of situations that give rise to the need for justice also create the problems with justice. Not everyone will favor the story I am starting to tell. Contemporary American philosophy is dominated by neo-Kantian theory in ethics and is quite hostile to classical as well as to Humean accounts of the virtue. But such theorists should have sympathies to much I have said so far, even if their favored vocabulary is not mine.

Utilitarian and consequentialist theorists should also not be too displeased, but for very different reasons; they have long had difficulties with justice, and some have recommended that the virtue not be overpraised. J. S. Mill famously argues that "justice is a name for certain moral requirements, which, regarded collectively, stand higher in the scale of social utility, and are therefore of more paramount obligation, than any others; though particular cases may occur in which some other social duty is so important, as to overrule any one of the general maxims of justice".[18] Mill argues that we redescribe exceptions so as to avoid asserting that "there can be laudable injustice," but that is exactly what consequentialists are committed to.

The story I tend to favor is best told by Hume, though it is also Hobbes's, and earlier, briefer statements may be attributed to Plato's Glaucon and to Epicurus. In brief, Hume's story is that the human condition is generally one in which there is a certain amount of conflict. He and Hobbes differ as to the amount of conflict and quite possibly as to the cause of some of it.[19] But the account is roughly the same. Our partiality and the prevalence of scarcity among the objects of our wants mean that there will be conflict. Plato's hope that human interests, properly understood, do not conflict is

16. Additionally, if a right to act is a right to act wrongly (though not in ways seriously unjust), then particular acts of guaranteeing people their rights may result in wrongful or harmful behavior.

17. Norms and rules constrain in the sense in question here, but so do commands and other particular directives. So the problems generated by justice's connection to norms and rules (the third possible source of trouble) are of a different kind from justice's constraining nature (the second possible source).

18. John Stuart Mill, *Utilitarianism* (Oxford: Oxford University Press, 1998), chap. V, penultimate paragraph. Note that the "other social duty" above does not necessarily derive from some other part of justice. By contrast, John Rawls claims that "an injustice is tolerable only when it is necessary to avoid an even greater injustice". See Rawls, *A Theory of Justice* (Cambridge, Mass.: Harvard University Press, 1971), 3–4.

19. Hobbes thought that glory motivates much human action.

attractive but implausible. Even he did not seem to believe it; or perhaps he thought it possible only under certain unlikely conditions, one of which being that most people believe a falsehood, namely the "noble lie" that our souls are made of different metals. Interestingly, Marx's conjecture that the development of history will make it possible to live without justice under Communism, which appears to be of the same kind of story as Plato's, is consistent with Hume's. The latter, along with Hobbes and others, argues that in a condition of profuse abundance, where all our wants are satisfied, "in such a happy state, every other social virtue would flourish, and receive tenfold increase; but the cautious, jealous virtue of justice would never once have been dreamed of". Absent "the circumstances of justice" (Rawls's phrase), justice, "being totally useless, would be an idle ceremonial, and could never possibly have place in the catalogue of virtues".[20]

In small groups, especially of friends, it may be possible to think that one can do without justice. Aristotle's restriction of the number of people in a *polis* who count to the proper subset of (most) adult free males may have enabled him to think, in effect, that the other virtues, exercised "in relation to others", would suffice to secure the common good. That may be plausible in *poleis* of forty thousand citizens. But, as Hume notes, "[W]hen society has become numerous, and has encreas'd to a tribe or nation," the interests that bind us are less apparent.[21]

The conflicts that are to be found in "the circumstances of justice" and the possibility of mutually beneficial arrangements are what make justice *useful*. The norms or laws of justice seek to improve things, at least for all who strive to be just. They aim at the good of all, the common good, or the mutually advantageous. Different members of this tradition will offer alternative accounts of the conditions that the norms of justice are to satisfy. One important difference is between accounts that require that the norms be practice-based and others that understand justice solely in terms of (counterfactual) ideal agreements or standards.

An important element missing in classical accounts of this kind—I am thinking principally of Hobbes and Hume, but also Rousseau and, more contentiously, Aristotle — is an analysis of the way in which justice tends to the good of all. Rules or norms that secure our common good may well elicit our approval or endorsement, and that may be good enough much of the time; that is, that may suffice to ensure adequate compliance much of the time. But justice seems to entail more than can be delivered by approval, or at least more needs to be said. The norms of justice pretend to be reasons of a special kind. In terms introduced above, the norms of justice are said to be reasons that would have us act in ways that sometimes contravene the balance of reasons. We are to act as required, even if more good may be done by not so acting. The norms of justice are reasons that, we may say, *preempt* some of the other reasons we may have to act. Kant noted the absence of a plausible account of this feature of justice (or morality), and neo-Kantians think that one cannot be offered that which does not abandon the sort of story I have been recounting. But the kind of revisionist accounts of practical rationality mentioned earlier in passing offer exactly that, namely an account of preemptive reasons.[22]

---

20. *Enq. Concerning the Prin. of Morals*, sect. III, part I, 145.
21. Hume, *A Treatise of Human Nature*, book III, part II, sect. ii, 499.
22. See references in note 13.

We can see how a number of norms governing, for instance, what we may do regarding the lives and possessions of others (negative duties not to kill, assignment of liabilities for risky behavior, duties of rescue or of mutual aid), forms of interaction (norms governing truth-telling, fidelity, and the like), and status (norms governing respect for others) can be understood as addressing the problems we find in "the circumstances of justice". Hume's account is, I think, still one of the very best we have. He thinks of justice as an "artificial" virtue because it depends on conventions for its existence (and because the natural motives that move us to be benevolent or prudent are insufficient for justice). It may have a few features that make it difficult to generalize to a world such as ours, some of which may be due to its author's particularly benign and optimistic nature (e.g., conflicts of interest may be greater than Hume seems to think). And, most important, it does not seem plausible to think that all aspects of justice are practice-based (see, in part, my discussion below). We may find in David Gauthier's "morals by agreement" features of a more complete, plausible neo-Humean account of justice: the illuminating analysis of the problem in the terms of contemporary rational choice theory, a two-stage game-theoretical account of the norms of justice, and the revisionist account of constrained deliberation and action already mentioned.[23]

Accounts of this sort all make aspects of justice—specifically, the content of some norms—dependent on practices. Legal systems are an example of such practices, but much of justice is possible in the absence of (positive) law. Those constraints of justice that are reciprocal, that is, whose obligation is conditional on the constrained behavior of others, will also depend on practices. Practices, it should be noted, can often be improved. For one, they frequently may be indeterminate and need to be developed. In the best of worlds available to us, our practices and, consequently, our norms of justice will be imperfect in a number of ways. It is not clear how this could be avoided.[24] This means, however, that we should expect that

23. See, of course, David Gauthier, *Morals by Agreement* (Oxford: Clarendon, 1986), as well as the essays in Gauthier's *Moral Dealing: Contract, Ethics, and Reason* (Ithaca, N.Y.: Cornell University Press, 1990). Many parts of Gauthier's account are separable from the whole. For instance, the principle of distributive justice (MRC) may be detached from the moral theory or, as the author is now disposed to do, replaced by a Nash bargaining principle. The most neglected part of the theory may be the account of the ways in which preconventional rights and duties can emerge in anticipation of agreement (the two-stage account). In particular, Gauthier's so-called proviso is of considerable importance.

24. "We have to give up the hope...that we can actually arrive at moral norms shaped solely by moral reasons for action, in contrast to the norms shaped, in no small degree, by convention and arbitrary decision that we have now. Moral philosophy can provide grounds for criticizing our present norms. But when we have gone as far as criticism will, for the moment, carry us, we shall still not have eliminated all elements of convention and arbitrariness. Since life with these less than ideal norms is the only moral life we are ever going to have, we must get on with it" (James Griffin, "On the Winding Road from Good to Right," in *Value, Welfare, and Morality*, ed. R. G. Frey and C. W. Morris [Cambridge: Cambridge University Press, 1993], 176–77).

there will be situations where we find ourselves without reason, or reasons of the requisite sort, to be just. We are back where we started.[25]

4. What Should We Think? Three Responses

I noted three main sources of trouble with justice: the virtue's other-regarding or interpersonal nature, its constraining nature (in the sense explained), and the fact that its requirements usually take the form of norms or rules. These difficulties appear in many classical and contemporary discussions of justice (and morality). The first is a special concern of Plato, Hobbes, and Hume, as well as several contemporary thinkers. They may have exaggerated our self-concern, but there is no doubt that partiality is a problem for justice. However, if agents are capable of constraining their action and of following norms, the problems posed by partiality should be surmountable. They may not be intractable.

The second problem features centrally in many contemporary discussions. It is at the core of some contemporary debates about moral consequentialism. Many philosophers, along with economists and decision theorists, who adopt a maximizing conception of practical reason will also be concerned by the constraining nature of justice. Consequentialist (and maximizing) ways of reasoning cannot easily make sense of constraints. Solutions to the problem vary. I think that the revisionist accounts of practical rationality mentioned above (see n. 13) can provide the basis for an explanation of the constraining nature of norms of justice.[26] This conjecture is controversial and cannot be pursued here, and I propose to concentrate on the third problem. Even if the first two are resolvable, the third remains and seems most intractable. So it makes sense to examine it first.

Appearances, then, suggest that we sometimes lack reasons (or reasons of the right sort) to be just. And I have suggested different sources of the trouble. What to think? One reaction, of course, would be to deny the appearances. Given that I think that the best account of justice will most likely have this consequence—that we sometimes lack reasons (or reasons of the right kind) to be just—I shall not take up this suggestion. As we should expect, the main defenders of this response today are neo-Kantians.[27] I wish to consider three possible responses available to theorists drawn to the sort of account of justice I have sketched.

The first response is that suggested by Philippa Foot early in her career: justice is not a virtue. This is mistaken, and Foot herself did not defend it. Justice is simply too

25. In addition, there will be times when a norm is not yet established (i.e., a practice), when it will be indeterminate what reasons one has to comply with its demands. I do not discuss this situation in this essay.

26. David Gauthier's well-known account of "constrained maximization" specifically tries to understand how genuine constraint can be made compatible with maximization. But the problem arises with weaker, "balance of reasons" conceptions of rationality.

27. It would be misleading to think of consequentialists as denying the appearances in question, for they do not privilege justice; as I have said, they think of justice as an overrated virtue. In addition, many consequentialists recognize that we always have reason to be moral, not merely just.

important for *us*. But therein lies the problem: while prudence, courage, temperance, or wisdom are good for us, they are in the first instance good for *me* (each of us). Justice may be good for me, but indirectly; it is first of all good for us collectively. The difficulty is the familiar, even if rather oddly named, collective action problem.[28]

Let me move immediately to the second response. This is that of Hobbes, Hume, Gauthier, possibly Rousseau (and myself some years ago[29]). Essentially it consists in restricting the scope of norms of justice to the set of agents able and willing to abide by them. Justice on this view protects all and only those who find themselves in the circumstances of justice (e.g., who stand to benefit mutually from cooperation); the scope is less than universal. In the absence of the conditions required to stabilize norms of cooperation, Hobbes thinks that "nothing can be Unjust. The notions of Right and Wrong, Justice and Injustice have there no place. Where there is no common Power, there is no Law: where there is no Law, no Injustice.... It is consequent also to the same condition, that there is no Propriety, no Dominion, no *Mine* and *Thine* distinct...".[30]

It is not implausible to think that were someone "to fall into the society of ruffians, remote from the protection of laws and government..." that he may "make provision of all means of defense and security: And his particular regard to justice being no longer of use to his own safety or that of others, he must consult the dictates of self-preservation alone, without concern for those who no longer merit his care and attention".[31] But it is not only ruffians who are in danger of losing the protection of justice, it is also those unable to harm us:

> Were there a species of creatures intermingled with men, which, though rational, were possessed of such inferior strength, both of body and mind, that they were incapable of all resistance, and could never, upon the highest provocation, make us feel the effects of their resentment; the necessary consequence, I think, is that we should be bound by the laws of humanity to give gentle usage to these creatures, but should not, properly speaking, lie under any restraint of justice with regard to them, nor could they possess any right or property, exclusive of such arbitrary lords.

Creatures such as these will not be completely unprotected; but Hume thinks "[O]ur compassion and kindness the only check, by which they curb our lawless will...".[32]

---

28. For a good introduction of the collective action problem, see Michael Taylor, *The Possibility of Cooperation* (Cambridge: Cambridge University Press, 1987), chap. 1.

29. See, for instance, Christopher W. Morris, "A Contractarian Account of Moral Justification," in *Moral Knowledge? New Readings in Moral Epistemology*, ed. Walter Sinnott-Armstrong and Mark Timmons (New York: Oxford University Press, 1996), 215–42; and Christopher W. Morris, "Punishment and Loss of Moral Standing," *Canadian Journal of Philosophy* 21, no. 1 (March 1991): 53–79.

30. Hobbes, *Leviathan*, chap. XIII, penultimate paragraph. I should note that the passage and Hobbes's doctrine are more complex than these citations suggest.

31. *Enq. Concerning the Prin. of Morals*, sect. III, part I, 148. See also my "Punishment and Loss of Moral Standing."

32. *Enq. Concerning the Prin. of Morals*, sect III, part I, 152. Hume notes that "this is plainly the situation of men, in regard to animals", and that "in many nations, the female sex are reduced to like slavery...".

Unloved orphans, the infirm, and the unproductive, among others may also be left without the protection of justice, sheltered only by our compassion and kindness.

There is much more to be said about this possible implication of Humean justice. It is possible that the scope of the norms of justice can be extended in ways that will protect the infirm and nonautonomous.[33] But there are other sorts of cases where it seems that some people will be left out. Hume notes that "[T]he great superiority of civilized Europeans above barbarous Indians, tempted us to imagine ourselves on the same footing with regard to them [as with animals], and made us throw off all restraints of justice, and even of humanity, in our treatment of them". Hume thinks we were mistaken in so behaving. But consider a hypothetical but realistic case of caste slavery, where the enslaved are easily distinguished from the masters, where the practice is immensely profitable, and where sentiments of compassion and kindness are restricted to one's own kind. In such a condition while it would benefit the enslaved to act justly toward and to cooperate freely with others, it would be disadvantageous for the slave-owners to do so.[34] It seems implausible to think that slavery under such conditions would not be unjust. That would be unbelievable.[35]

In conditions of emergency it seems entirely plausible that many norms of justice could be overridden or would be suspended. But not all such norms: it would not be plausible to think that it would ever cease to be wrong intentionally to kill innocent, nonthreatening people—for instance, children, even those of our enemy. Further, it seems that killing the innocent in most of these circumstances would remain a wrong *to* them, something they have a right against us that we do not.

Suppose that the only effective means of defending ourselves against an adversary would be to harm, or to threaten to harm, the families and countrymen of our enemy. May we, for instance, retaliate against a nuclear attack by destroying enemy cities? Or may we torture and kill the families of terrorists who plant nuclear weapons in our cities? Presumably not. That is, it would be an injustice to do those things to innocent people.[36] It is simply not credible to say that such acts would not be unjust.[37] This is not to say that we would not, in the circumstances, have reason to act unjustly; that is the question under consideration.

---

33. See my "Moral Standing and Rational-Choice Contractarianism," in *Contractarianism and Rational Choice: Essays on David Gauthier's* Morals by Agreement, ed. Peter Vallentyne (Cambridge: Cambridge University Press, 1991), 76–95.

34. I discuss cases like these in my "Justice, Reasons, and Moral Standing," in *Rational Commitment and Social Justice: Essays for Gregory Kavka*, ed J. L. Coleman and C. W. Morris (Cambridge: Cambridge University Press, 1998), 186–207.

35. It will not do merely to say that the Humean account has the resources to extend the protections of justice to all humans or persons. What is important is whether under certain conditions, when the circumstances of justice are not fully satisfied, justice would *in fact* extend to all. ·

36. I take issue here with the author of "A Contractarian Defense of Nuclear Deterrence," *Ethics* 95, no. 3 (April 1985): 479–96.

37. The double negative is important as Hobbists or "realists" in the field of international relations would argue that such acts are beyond justice, neither right nor wrong.

The second response to the appearances—we do not always have reasons, or reasons of the right kind, to be just because some humans are not, in fact, protected by justice—is not to be taken up. Restricting the scope of the norms of justice is simply not credible.

I shall move right away to the third and only credible position that I can think of or understand. Many of the norms of justice seem to have universal scope in two respects: virtually all humans or persons are assumed to have moral standing, and all human agents have a number of obligations to anyone with moral standing. To possess moral standing is to be owed moral consideration; it is a status distinct from other kinds of value, such as that possessed by great works of art or valuable natural sites.[38] The scope of the norms of justice is not unlike that of law: the universal quantifiers are to be interpreted literally.

The scope of many norms of justice is universal in these two ways. In addition, the norms are intended as *authoritative*; that is, they are meant to be reasons (to act or to refrain from acting, to adopt certain attitudes, to assign responsibility, etc.) to all (to whom they apply) on all occasions (when they apply). A *reason for action* here is a consideration favoring an action that ought, in the absence of other considerations, to motivate an agent so to act. The authority justice claims over us is more than an additional consideration favoring action, to be added to the balance of reasons. For one, the reasons in question are meant not to be conditional on our interests or desires. The reasons justice claims to offer are not considerations that are just to be added to all the other factors that ought to determine one's deliberations, as I noted earlier. Rather, they are to settle the matter and to determine one's conduct (in the absence, presumably, of certain defeasibility conditions that would permit or even require acting otherwise). Even if the demands of justice do not override all other moral considerations, we can still agree that the reasons in question are meant to settle the question and to determine our conduct in the absence of other important considerations. We may think of these reasons as especially weighty, as it were. But I think that a mistaken analysis of reasons of this sort. They are not meant to be additional considerations that one is to *add* to the other factors that ought to be taken into account when deliberating about a choice. Rather, as I said, they are meant, in a sense, to settle the matter (subject to being defeated by certain other considerations). I think a better account can be had by understanding these reasons as *preemptive*. As Joseph Raz explains, "[A]uthoritative reasons are pre-emptive: the fact that an authority requires performance of an action is a reason for its performance which is not to be added to all other relevant reasons when assessing what to do, but should exclude and take the place of some of them".[39] So the norms of justice are *authoritative*; that is, they are *preemptive* reasons (to act or to refrain from acting, to adopt certain attitudes, to assign responsibility, etc.) to all (to whom they apply) on all occasions (when they apply).

38. I say that *virtually* all humans or persons have moral standing in order to sidestep difficult questions at the margins (e.g., abortion, advanced dementia). I also leave open the possibility that some rights may be lost, either by forfeit or alienation.

39. Joseph Raz, *The Morality of Freedom* (Oxford: Clarendon, 1986), 46 (emphasis deleted). Such reasons were earlier called "protected": Reasons to do the obligatory act and second-order reasons not to act on (otherwise valid) reasons to do something else (Joseph Raz, *The Authority of Law* [Oxford: Clarendon, 1979], 18).

Now the norms of justice that are, at least in part, "artificial" in Hume's sense are dependent for their force on the existence of certain conventions and practices. This is clear in the case of property: whether walking across someone's land or drawing from someone's well constitutes trespass or theft depends on the moral and legal conventions of the setting. In some cultures abandoned umbrellas or lost jewelry become the property of the finder, whereas in others finders have some obligation to find the owners. Norms of truth-telling and fidelity seem especially sensitive to the particularities of given practices.

We might, then, as with other systems of *conventional* norms, such as manners and the law, anticipate the existence of conflict between parts of justice as well as between justice and some of the other virtues. We might expect the (normative) laws of nature, whether established by an omniscient, benevolent deity or by nature itself, to form a consistent set.[40] But we should have no such expectation of any complex set or system of conventional norms. Just as we expect to find conflicts between different laws or different parts of the law, so we might expect to find conflicts between different norms of justice or between different virtues insofar as these have conventional aspects. The conflicts may not be deep or may only be apparent, but we have no reason to expect human-made conventions, developed over a long time, in varying settings, to be consistent. In an interesting and insightful essay cited earlier, James Griffin argues:

> Our norms are unlikely to have grown in a way that would make them a system; they have grown, by fits and starts, in response to pressing, heterogeneous practical needs. They have taken their shape partly from the kinds of circumstances we found ourselves in, from the sorts of problems that we faced. Since the problems were different— sometimes large-scale political, sometimes small-scale personal, sometimes about dispositions for facing moral life generally, sometimes about the way to decide out-of-the-way cases—it would not be surprising for different clusters of norms to have emerged[41]

If this is the case, we should not be surprised to find many instances of norms of justice that are not, in fact, always preemptive reasons.

Consider next a different kind of case, a particular and now familiar problem of conflicting norms. In many parts of the world today it is often said that resolving certain long-lasting conflicts and securing peace comes at the price of sacrificing justice.

Preemptive reasons, it should be stressed, need not be *conclusive*, that is, reasons that are not overridden by other reasons (or cancelled), or *absolute*, that is, reasons that cannot be overridden. For one way of drawing these distinctions, see Raz, *Practical Reason and Norms* (Oxford: Clarendon, [1975] 1999), 27.

40. Alan Donagan, "Consistency in Rationalist Moral Systems," *Journal of Philosophy* 81, no. 6 (June 1984): 291–309.

41. "I think we come to ethics with a false assumption. We expect the content of morality to derive from one kind of source—namely, from principles of one sort or another. We expect it to derive from the good, or from the right, or from fairly normative standards of rationality. The reality seems to me quite different. When we understand the forces shaping moral norms of property, say, we see how heterogeneous the forces are" (Griffin, "On the Winding Road from Good to Right," 171–72, 174).

Recently, in Argentina, South Africa, the Middle East, Northern Ireland, and several Central and Eastern European countries, many accommodations have been defended in the name of peace with the understanding, implicit or explicit, that justice is thereby sacrificed. Amnesties of different kinds have been defended as necessary for peace, even though they allow many crimes to go unpunished. Older and more familiar examples set justice against benevolence or liberty in opposition to equality. But the conflict between peace and justice is in some respects more interesting and harder to deal with. Justice is a virtue that would have us shun compromise and accommodation, at least in most contexts.[42] But in the contemporary cases, the conflict with the cause of peace seems so clear and pressing that it is not unreasonable to think that justice should lose; in nearly all of the cases alluded to above, it does lose. If so, the norms of justice are not always preemptive reasons. One might be tempted to respond by reinterpreting justice to be compatible with accommodation and compromise, but this maneuver is unlikely to succeed in all instances.

The failure of all norms of justice to be authoritative in all instances is a blow to the self-image of justice. This seems plausible with regard to some moral norms, for instance, those governing truth-telling or fidelity or property. Critics will respond by trying to show that apparent violations of these norms, where it appears we lack preemptive reasons to tell the truth or to be faithful to engagements, are in fact instances of the rules being defeated or our disregard of them excused. It is not plausible that *all* the cases where we have sufficient reason to tell a lie will be covered by the complex defeasibility or excusing conditions governing this norm. Consider cases where someone has told a falsehood with the intention to deceive, where it seems a violation of our norms of truth-telling to do so; are *all* the cases ones where the exceptions are handled by the norm or by some other moral consideration? Consider lying when pleading in a criminal trial. We might say that wrongdoers may lie and plead not guilty when accused of a crime because such pleas are part of a system designed to secure justice through adversarial proceedings. But what about the criminal who pleads innocence solely in the hope of acquittal, where there is no danger that a guilty (or *nolo contendere*) plea would risk increasing the penalty? The plea of innocence here is wrong even if legally permissible. But note that we do not for a moment think that the criminal has preemptive reasons to concede guilt.

Consider cases of theft. The poor who steal a loaf of bread to feed their hungry children are perhaps excused given their plight. But others who help themselves to some neglected cash found in an office drawer presumably are doing wrong or committing an injustice. Are there *never* any cases of this sort where we so act wrongly without disregarding any preemptive reasons against stealing? The cash we take, perhaps knowing that it will not be missed, might be used for our children's education or to take a long trip abroad with a friend. It seems somewhat far-fetched to think that *all* such cases of theft are instances of acting against preemptive reasons. Similarly, a physician may be tempted to favor a relative or friend in decisions on the allocation of spare organs, or an admissions officer may be tempted to favor someone in school

---

42. "Justice is the first virtue of social institutions, as truth is of systems of thought…an injustice is tolerable only when it is necessary to avoid an even greater injustice. Being first virtues of human activities, truth and justice are uncompromising". John Rawls, *A Theory of Justice*, 3–4.

or college admissions. Are there *no* such cases where the person would be acting wrongly but without acting against preemptive reasons?

The thesis that the norms of justice are not *always* preemptive reasons may appear much less plausible regarding certain central norms of justice, for instance, the principle prohibiting the intentional killing of nonthreatening innocent persons. The same may be true with the prohibition of cruelty. Do we not *always* have preemptive reasons to abide by these norms? If not, are *all* cases where it seems reasonable to disregard these norms ones where one is so *justified* or *excused*? Justice undoubtedly is understood to forbid such things; what is doubtful is that every agent in every situation in fact has preemptive reasons to comply. Consider particular cases of intentional killings of the innocent in wartime, for instance, the targeting of German cities at the beginning of the Second World War (when the survival of Great Britain was at stake) or the bombing of the Japanese cities at the war's end. It is hard to see how many of these bombings could have been just. But it is certainly possible that some of the bombings were wrong, though the statesmen who ordered them did not, in fact, have preemptive reasons to desist. They were not justified in bombing, and the situation did not excuse their acts; they acted wrongly but not against reason.

Suppose you have in your possession the family of the leader of a group of homicide bombers known to be planning to detonate several small nuclear weapons throughout your country. Would it not be unjust to coerce or torture them so as to deter the bombers, even if that were an effective means of defending your country? I should have thought so. But the injustice of this act would not necessarily be a reason, much less a preemptive reason for action.

I think it is quite clear what *justice* requires in each of these examples. Some details may have to be changed in order to achieve consensus. Consequentialist moralists may think that "morality" would have us override the concerns of justice. But I am not interested in battling these foes here. I take justice more seriously. However, it is not clear to me that we, in fact, have reasons of the requisite sort to be just in all of these cases. And there has to be more than a handful such cases.[43]

Now we should still expect justice to be *practical* even if its norms fail to be authoritative in all circumstances in which they apply. For one, there are many reasons to do what is right, even if one lacks the preemptive reasons that justice is said to give us. One might fear being caught or merely be squeamish or worry what others might think. Most of the time, just behavior seems overdetermined. So the trouble with justice may not, in practice, be all that troublesome. But it is troubling for moralists and theorists. I am not certain I am right, but there seems be trouble with justice.

---

43. Consequentialists will find these remarks inadequate. Kantians have even more reason to be annoyed, as I do not face up to the challenge their positions pose to my story. One can think of Kantianism in ethics as consisting in part as the hypothesis that rules or norms can always be specified so that the right values are captured and compliance is always required. I have not said enough to allow us to dismiss this possibility. That is a topic for another time.

2

Nietzsche on Selfishness, Justice, and the Duties of the Higher Men

MATHIAS RISSE

1. This study explores Nietzsche's views on selfishness and its role within his envisaged "revaluation of values" (TI, *Preface*; EH, *Clever*, 9).[1] I defend the following theses: Nietzsche advocates selfishness only for the "higher men," those characters who embody human excellence and whom he hopes will replace the person of guilt and *ressentiment*. Yet in spite of his praise for these characters' selfishness, Nietzsche nevertheless thinks that their selfishness is constrained by considerations of justice. What is most striking about Nietzsche's approach to morality is not so much that he is a champion of selfishness, but that he nevertheless endorses an account of justice, albeit one that provides for rights and duties that only hold among a relatively small set of alleged peers.

More specifically, I will proceed as follows. I will begin by discussing the evolution of Nietzsche's views on selfishness, which to some extent reflect the evolution of his views on morality through the 1880s, beginning with *Human, All Too Human* and *Dawn* and ending with the works of 1888. The *Twilight of Idols* contains a good statement of Nietzsche's mature view on selfishness. However, while this mature view does praise selfishness for the higher men, Nietzsche insists that even they are

1. Works of Nietzsche are from the *Kritische Studienausgabe*, 2nd ed., ed. Giorgio Colli and Mazzino Montinari (Berlin: Gruyter, 1988). I use the usual abbreviations for the works in English translation, that is, GM for *On the Genealogy of Morality*, TI of *Twilight of Idols*, D for *Dawn*, HAH for *Human All Too Human*, WS for *The Wanderer and His Shadow* (part of *Human, All Too Human* 2), UM for *Untimely Meditation*, GS for *Gay Science*, A for *Antichrist*, EH for *Ecce Homo*, Z for *Zarathustra*, BT for *Birth of Tragedy*, and BGE for *Beyond Good and Evil*. I use general translations by Walter Kaufmann and R. J. Hollingdale; however, I have modified the translations at various points, sometimes significantly, and do not document precisely where. I am grateful to Paul Bloomfield, Brian Leiter, and Kranti Saran for very helpful comments. Thanks also to Thomas Hurka for a helpful discussion of Nietzsche's account of rights and duties.

subject to duties.[2] I will then argue that these duties are plausibly seen as deriving from Nietzsche's strong belief in justice. Despite his self-declared immoralism, Nietzsche's praise for justice is a fixed point throughout his works. The standpoint of justice is one from which all valuations are assessed, and the higher men are not exempt from the demands this standpoint generates. At the same time, according to Nietzsche, this standpoint does not generate (and in fact rejects) a requirement of equal consideration for all persons.[3] When reflecting on Nietzsche's views of justice I will draw attention to certain similarities between Nietzsche's account of duties, on the one hand, and Rousseau and Kant's, on the other. Moreover, I will also address the metaethical status of these views and offer some critical observations on Leiter's (2002) way of reading Nietzsche as an antirealist about value.

Important parts of Nietzsche's mature work can be read as offering approaches to traditional philosophical problems in the spirit of the emerging biological sciences of his day, in particular physiology and evolutionary biology. Particularly striking in this context is his effort to offer explanations in the spirit of these sciences for the emergence of norms of conduct commonly seen as moral. I have argued elsewhere that he offers an account of that sort for the emergence of both guilt and *ressentiment* (cf. Risse [2001] and [2003]) and thus for the development of Christian morality and views he takes to be derivate of it (especially Kantian ethics and utilitarianism). Our next task in this study, then, is to explore whether Nietzsche can actually account for his claim that higher men abide by duties in a way that is in line with the accounts he gives for the emergence of guilt and *ressentiment*. While those accounts do have a high degree of internal plausibility, I will argue that Nietzsche fails to offer a successful account in that same scientific spirit for his view that the higher men abide by duties. This is not a disaster for Nietzsche because there is no reason (internal to his work or not) that would keep him from endorsing the view that the higher men have duties to one another; nevertheless, the existence of such an account in the same scientific spirit in which I think he tried to explain *ressentiment* and guilt would have created more unity in his views.

2. The term *higher men* is explicitly used, for instance, in BGE 26, 30, 228. Nietzsche uses different terms to denote the kind of character whom he admires for his embodiment of human excellence and its potential for replacing the person of guilt and *ressentiment*, such as "free spirit" in *Beyond Good and Evil* and "overman," *Übermensch*, in *Zarathustra*. Elsewhere, I have offered an account of this type of character within Nietzsche's generally physiology-oriented framework (see Mathias Risse, "Origins of *Ressentiment* and Sources of Normativity," *Nietzsche Studien* 32 [2003], sect. 6); see also Brian Leiter, *Nietzsche on Morality* (London: Routledge, 2002), 115–25.

3. My claim about Nietzsche's praise for justice may come as a surprise, particularly for readers who are aware of Philippa Foot's view that Nietzsche's immoralism consists in his rejection of *justice*; compare Foot, "Nietzsche's Immoralism," in *Nietzsche, Genealogy, Morality—Essays on Nietzsche's "Genealogy of Morals,"* ed. R. Schacht (Berkeley and Los Angeles: University of California Press, 1994). However, since Nietzsche's account of justice is accompanied by a spirited rejection of moral equality—which would make it almost unrecognizable to, say, John Rawls—it must be considered a highly revisionist account according to the contemporary understanding of justice.

This study touches on some of the elements of Nietzsche's thinking that are most alien to us today, in particular his unabashed insistence that societies should be arranged around the flourishing of the higher men and that justice does not require of those characters to pay any attention to those who to do not embody human excellence. Nietzsche's views, once properly in sight, will be alien especially to those who understand the task of moral philosophy in terms of developing the idea of moral equality of all human beings, a notion that Nietzsche despises. In this study, however, I will not be concerned with exploring what intellectual resources one might muster against Nietzsche's dismissal of moral equality. Suffice it to say that Nietzsche's writings, driven as they are by the desire to champion the cause of the "higher men" and by revealing how much human excellence is harmed by the insistence on moral equality, offer an ongoing challenge to all those of us who endorse such a notion of equality.

2. One of the books Nietzsche wrote in 1888, his frantically productive last year of sanity, was his idiosyncratic intellectual autobiography, *Ecce Homo*. In the chapter "Why I Write Such Good Books", he looks back at his works since the *Birth of Tragedy*. As Nietzsche exclaims in the section on *Human, All Too Human* (first published in 1878), "Where you see ideals I only see—the human, oh, the all-too-human". Indeed, Nietzsche's first book after the *Birth of Tragedy* aims to explain a broad range of human interactions in terms of selfishness. In book 1 of *Human, All Too Human* (entitled "Of the First and the Last Things"), Nietzsche explains that "[t]here is no longer an 'ought'; morality, insofar as it has been an ought, has been destroyed by our way of looking at things, just as much as religion has. Knowledge can let stand as motives only pleasure and pain, utility and injury" (HAH 34). Conventional morality, then, is squarely in the domain of Nietzsche's efforts to explain human activities in terms of self-interested endeavors. To confirm this point, he writes later that "[n]ever has a human done anything that was done solely for others and without any personal motive; how indeed *could* he have done anything that is without reference to him, and thus without inner necessity (which would have its basis in a personal need)? How could the ego act without the ego?" (HAH 133). Clark and Leiter (1997) argue that Nietzsche's view on the role of selfishness in the explanation of human action changes between *Human All Too Human* and *Dawn*, his next book, and that it is this change that makes room for the kind of attack on morality that would take center stage in his later writings. It will be useful for our investigation of Nietzsche's views on selfishness to discuss that claim. Whereas HAH 133 shows that his concern there is to demonstrate that allegedly moral motivation is selfishness in disguise, in *Dawn* Nietzsche appears to allow for genuinely moral and hence seemingly unselfish motivation. Crucially, to develop Clark and Leiter's view, it is his acknowledgment of such motivation that redirects his interest in morality, away from reinterpreting allegedly moral motivations for actions toward an exploration of the mechanisms that led to the presence of such motivations (an endeavor that, of course, presupposes that there is more to be said about moral motivation than that it can be reinterpreted in a manner that makes it look selfish in some way). Eventually, this approach leads Nietzsche to the investigations in the *Genealogy*, which look at the development of Christian morality in terms of three mechanisms that have shaped it: the emergence and impact of *ressentiment*, guilt, and the ascetic ideal, respectively.

As far as *Dawn* is concerned, this view of the development of Nietzsche's views on morality that puts a lot of emphasis on the change of his views about the possibility of nonselfish motivation between *Human, All Too Human* and *Dawn* draws on D 103, entitled "There Are Two Kinds of Deniers of Morality":

> "Denying morality"—that can mean *for one thing*: denying that moral motives, which men *claim* to have, have really driven them to their actions,—it is hence a claim that morality consists in words and belongs to the coarse and subtle cheating (in particular cheating on oneself) of humanity, and perhaps especially as far as those are concerned who are famous for virtue. *Moreover*, it can mean: denying that moral judgments rest on truths. Here it is admitted that they really are motives for actions, but that in this way it is *errors*, as basis for all moral judging, that drive humans to their moral actions. This is *my* viewpoint: however, I do not wish to deny in the least that in very many cases a subtle distrust according to the first viewpoint, and thus in the spirit of Larochefoucauld, would also be right and at any rate would be of greatest general utility.

As Clark and Leiter (1997) say on the strength of this passage, *Human, All Too Human* "labels as 'lie' and 'error' not morality, but the belief that human beings act from moral motives. It directs the polemic against this belief—and, ultimately, against a world it perceived as 'human, alas too-too-human.' Only when [*Dawn*] admits the existence of moral motivation can Nietzsche begin his actual campaign against morality. Rather than denying that morally motivated actions exist, he now claims that the presuppositions of such actions are erroneous" (xxvi). One reason to look for such a demarcation between *Human, All Too Human* and *Dawn* is Nietzsche's announcement in *Ecce Homo*, at the beginning of the discussion about *Dawn*, that with that book "begins my campaign against morality". However, D 148 (entitled "Views into the Distance") poses a difficulty for this reading of the evolution of Nietzsche's views. There Nietzsche says:

> If only those actions are moral, as I suppose one has defined, that are done for the sake of the other and only for his sake, then there are no moral actions! If only actions are moral—as another definition has it—that are done out of freedom of will, then there are no moral actions either! (…) In virtue of these errors we have so far assigned some actions a higher value, than they have: we separated them from the "egoistic" and the "unfree" actions. If now we reassign them to those [i.e., the moral actions to the egoistic and unfree actions, MR], as we must, we will certainly *diminish* their value (their feeling of value), below the appropriate measure, because the "egoistic" and "unfree" actions have so far been underestimated, based on this alleged profound and innermost difference. (…) And since those actions [the egoistic ones, MR] have so far been the most common, and will be so in the future, we are depriving the whole picture of actions and life of its *evil appearance*! That is a significant result! If man does not think of himself as evil, he ceases to be evil!

So D 103 and D 148, taken together, offer three claims about motivation: (1) D 103 states that moral motives at least sometimes motivate actions; (2) at the beginning of D 148 we find the claim that actions are never done exclusively for the sake of others; (3) and at the end of D 148, we read that *most* actions have been egoistic—which seems to suggest that *some* have not been. If we understand "egoistic" and "moral" such that an action must be either the one or the other but cannot be both, and if we equate "moral" with "done exclusively for the sake of others", (2) conflicts with both (1) and (3).

A straightforward resolution of this apparent inconsistency is to understand "moral" in terms of "done at least partially for the sake of others", where this would mean that the concerns of others played some role in the decision process (e.g., if the agent has a choice among various actions that more or less favor his concerns and those of others, then having *some* consideration for others would mean that the agent does not choose the one that best satisfies his own concerns, even though he may well not choose the one that best addresses the concerns of others). Then (1) asserts that sometimes actions are at least partially done for the sake of others; (2) asserts that actions are never done exclusively for the sake of others; and (3) asserts that most actions are done exclusively for one's own benefit. To explain (2), actions might not ever be done exclusively for the sake of others because there will always be at least the comforting feeling the agent has about "having done the right thing"; or this might be so because even those actions that are seen as moral turn out to be based on selfish grounds since the basis for having such moral motivation is itself based on selfish motives, such as the desire to go to heaven.

Yet while this reading of D 103 and D 148 renders Nietzsche's thought in book 2 of *Dawn* consistent, it weakens the contrast with *Human, All Too Human* that Clark and Leiter draw in terms of the role of selfishness in human motivation.[4] For what HAH 133 denies is not that anything is *ever* done for the sake of others, but that nothing is ever done *exclusively* for the sake of others. On the reading just presented, that claim is still present in *Dawn*. Still, Clark and Leiter are mostly right, if perhaps not about the starkness of the contrast between *Human, All Too Human* and *Dawn* in terms of the possibility of nonselfish motivation, then at any rate about the claim that Nietzsche's project changes, or evolves, in between these two books. Whereas indeed in *Human, All Too Human* the focus is on arguing that much human interaction that seems to call for other explanations can be explained in terms of selfishness, the focus in *Dawn* becomes explaining how moral motivation could arise—and that project seems to intrigue Nietzsche *regardless* of whether there is also some sense (that in HAH he would have been eager to identify) in which moral motives can be seen as being motivated on selfish grounds (as they can if they are adopted because of, say, fear of eternal damnation). And, again, it is this focus that ultimately leads to his views on how the presuppositions of morality were created that he expounds especially in *Beyond Good and Evil*, the *Genealogy*, the *Twilight*, and the *Antichrist*.

3. But once Nietzsche departs from *Human, All Too Human*'s concern with tracing human interaction to selfish motives, another question becomes prominent

---

4. To be sure, Clark and Leiter do make a reference do D 148, but not by way of discussing a difficulty that arises with regard to their claims about the relationship between HAH and D.

and preoccupies Nietzsche greatly—the question of the *value* of selfishness, which, of course, is just one question that arises within a larger set of questions about the value of morality. As long as the concern is to argue for the centrality of self-interest in explanations of human behavior, Nietzsche not only (and for obvious reasons) fails to ask about the origins of moral motivation but also fails to ask about the value of selfishness; yet in the period beginning with *Dawn* he raises both of these questions.[5] (*Human, All Too Human* is often classified as belonging to Nietzsche's positivist period, and his not asking these two kinds of questions at least partly explains why that is so.)

Nietzsche praises selfishness to the same extent to which he praises the characters whose self-interest is under consideration. In BGE 265, for instance, Nietzsche tells us that "egoism belongs to the essence of a noble soul". BGE 265 comes just a few sections after the introduction of the distinction between master and slave morality (in BGE 260), and no such affirmative remarks are made about the place of egoism in the soul of the "slaves". Confirming this differentiated praise of selfishness, the clearest statement of Nietzsche's evaluation of egoism in his mature writings appears in the *Twilight of Idols*, in a paragraph whose clarity speaks for itself:

> *The natural value of egoism.*—Self-interest is worth as much as the person who has it: it can be worth a great deal, and it can be unworthy and contemptible. Every individual may be scrutinized to see whether he represents the ascending or the descending line of life. Having made that decision, one has a canon for the worth of his self-interest. If he represents the ascending line, then his worth is indeed extraordinary—and for the sake of life as a whole, which takes a step *farther* through him, the care for his preservation and for the creation of the best conditions for him may even be extreme. The single one, the "individual," as hitherto understood by the people and the philosophers alike, is an error after all: he is nothing by himself, no atom, no "link in the chain," nothing merely inherited from former times; he is the whole *single* line of humanity up to himself. If he represents the descending development, decay, chronic degeneration, and sickness (...), then he has small worth, and the minimum of decency requires that he *take away* as little as possible from those who have turned out well. He is merely their parasite. (TI, *Skirmishes*, 33)

This differentiated assessment of selfishness is followed almost immediately by an assessment of altruistic morality:

> *Critique of the morality of decadence.*—An "altruistic" morality—a morality in which self-interest *withers away*—remains a bad sign under all circumstances. This is true of individuals; it is particularly true of nations. The best is lacking when self-interest begins to be lacking. Instinctively to choose what is harmful for *oneself*, to feel *attracted* by "disinterested" motives, that is virtually the formula of decadence. "Not to seek *one's own* advantage"—that is merely the moral fig leaf for quite a different, namely, a physiological, state of affairs: "I no longer know how to *find* my own advantage." Disintegration of the instincts! Man is finished when he be-

---

5. In the *Genealogy* Nietzsche emphasizes the importance of asking about the value of morality and then adds that the "most specific issue" to ask about in that context is what he refers to as "the value of the 'un-egoistic'" (cf. *Preface*, 5).

comes altruistic. Instead of saying naively, "*I* am no longer worth anything," the moral lie in the mouth of the decadent says, "Nothing is worth anything, *life* is not worth anything." Such a judgment always remains very dangerous, it is contagious: throughout the morbid soil of society it soon proliferates into a tropical vegetation of concepts—now as a religion (Christianity), now as a philosophy (Schopenhauerism). Sometimes the poisonous vegetation which has grown out of such decomposition poisons *life* itself for millennia with its fumes. (TI, *Skirmishes*, 35)

Needless to say, selfishness and altruism (as well as the related subject of Nietzsche's contempt for pity) are treated elsewhere in Nietzsche's work as well, especially since altruism is so intimately tied up with Nietzsche's critique of Christianity, but there is no need for us to follow the details.[6] What has been said suffices to show that Nietzsche is no unqualified champion of selfishness. For those characters who are not of the right kind to embody human excellence and to overcome the morality shaped by *ressentiment*, guilt, and the ascetic ideal, Nietzsche does not praise selfishness. On the contrary: neither does Nietzsche place any value on such characters being selfish, nor does he even think it would be good for them to stop "obeying into one direction" (BGE 188). As he tells us in the *Genealogy*, slave morality actually is the "prudence of the lowest order" (GM I, 13), and many people are well advised to adhere to it since "[f]or the mediocre it is a happiness to be mediocre" (A 57)—in which case, however, Nietzsche would not see much point in encouraging them to be selfish.[7]

   4. Yet while Nietzsche praises the selfishness of the higher men, he also thinks that their selfishness is constrained by duties, or, at any rate, that they take themselves to be constrained by duties.[8] "Immoralists", so Nietzsche says, "are not just persons of duty, but do not escape from their duties" (BGE 226; cf. also BGE 214 and

---

   6. Kelly Rogers, "Beyond Self and Other," *Social Philosophy and Policy* 14, no. 1 (1997) contains a compilation of the relevant passages (as well as excerpts from other philosophers on the subject of self-interest).

   7. The following protesting exclamation from EH, *Fate*, 7, is also telling about Nietzsche's regard for *selfishness* (where, however, we should continue to keep in mind TI's point that the value of selfishness depends on the value of the person who possesses it):

> That one taught men to despise the very first instincts of life; that one *mendaciously invented* a "soul," a "spirit" to ruin the body; that one taught men to experience the presupposition of life, sexuality, as something unclean; that one looks for the evil principle in what is most profoundly necessary for growth, in *strict* selfishness (—this very word constitutes slander!—); that, conversely, one regards the typical signs of decline and contradiction of the instincts, the "selfless," the loss of a center of gravity, "depersonalization" and "neighbor love" (—*addiction* to the neighbor!) as the *higher* value, what am I saying! the *absolute value*!

Equally telling about Nietzsche's disregard for selflessness is this passage from GS 345: "'Selflessness' has no value either in heaven or on earth; all great problems demand *great love*, and of that only strong, round, secure spirits who have a firm grip on themselves are capable".

   8. These two formulations distinguish a realist from an antirealist reading of the relevant passages. I will discuss this issue explicitly in section 6 below.

227). The masters mentioned in *Beyond Good and Evil* also acknowledge duties, but only toward one another while despising universal duties and while feeling entitled to treating all those who are not their equal as they please (BGE 26off.; esp. BGE 265). In BGE 265, after Nietzsche points out that egoism belongs to the essence of the noble soul and explains that that soul itself unhesitatingly accepts this as a fact, he continues in rather poetic language to praise the ways in which the duties that the noble soul acknowledges to its peers are part and parcel of its egoism:[9]

> [The noble soul] acknowledges—under circumstances that initially make it hesitate—that there are those of equal standing [*Gleichberechtigte*]; as soon as [the noble soul] is clear on the question of rank, it moves among those who are equal and of equal standing with the same certainty of shame and gentle awe that it has in its interaction with itself—following an inborn celestial mechanic of which all stars have a good sense. It is one *more* part of its egoism, this subtlety and self-restraint in interaction with its equals—every star is such an egoist—it holds itself in awe in them and in those rights that it delegates to them, it does not doubt that the exchange of honors and rights as the essence of all interaction is part of the natural state of things. (BGE 265)

To the extent that they help the less fortunate, these characters do so out of strength (as BGE 260 says), not out of duty (as we can infer from BGE 265) or out of pity (as BGE 260 says explicitly).[10] In BGE 272 Nietzsche says that it is a sign of nobility to count one's privileges among one's duties, but also not to devalue one's duties to duties toward everybody. So while it is characteristic of the duties of the higher men that those do not hold with regard to just anybody, but only with regard to those of the same "rank", it should also be clear that, whatever else those characters are who Nietzsche hopes will overcome the morality of guilt and *ressentiment*, they are not simply creatures who see themselves as not being subject to codes of conduct that are recognizably moral—provided, of course, we do not take the term *moral*, by definition, to entail a commitment to substantive equality of sorts (as

---

9. I am assuming throughout that it is the higher men who are meant by this talk about "noble souls".

10. Note, however, the following statement in A 57: "If the exceptional man handles the mediocre man with more delicate fingers than he applies to himself or to his peers, this is not merely kindness of heart—it is simply his *duty*". This statement conflicts with the account in chapter 9 of BGE, on which most of the material in the text draws. It is peculiar that, of all texts, it is in the *Antichrist*, which in general offers a very harsh treatment of some of Nietzsche's favorite topics, that he would acknowledge that the higher men have a duty to the mediocre types. Perhaps we should think of this as a glitch—after all, it is in BGE that Nietzsche discusses the duties of the higher men at greatest length and with most focus. Another possibility is that, in the *Antichrist*, Nietzsche means to say that the higher men feel such a strong overflow of power that they *perceive* it to be their duty to aid the mediocre types (in the spirit in which Nietzsche says that Zarathustra "handles even his adversaries, the priests" in a gentle manner [EH, *Books*, on Zarathustra]), whereas their duties to their peers really are their duties since they can be demanded from the standpoint of justice (on which more below), whereas the perceived duties to the mediocre types cannot be thus demanded. Yet neither of these explanations is entirely satisfactory.

opposed to a formal sort of equality expressed, e.g., in the idea of treating everybody in accordance with her or his rank).[11]

Nietzsche's insistence that the "higher men" acknowledge duties, and if only to one another, may at first seem puzzling, since he is, after all, a self-declared "immoralist" (EH, *Destiny*, 2–4; BT, *Preface*, 5). However, it is by now well understood that Nietzsche's "immoralism" does not amount to a rejection of just any set of norms of conduct, nor even to a rejection of all norms of conduct that cannot straightforwardly be reduced to coordination among selfish actors. Instead, Nietzsche rejects morality as a bundle of normative and empirical claims whose endorsement creates a situation that is detrimental to the achievement of human excellence.[12] So there is nothing inconsistent per se in the combination of Nietzsche's predilection for declaring himself an immoralist and his poetic praise of the duty-bound nature of the higher men. Yet not only does Nietzsche's critique of morality focus on a specific (if widespread) form of morality but his writings also abound with praise for *justice*. I submit that his insistence that the higher men are men of duty can be understood as being derived from the high regard in which Nietzsche holds justice.

5. A look at some of Nietzsche's discussions of and references to justice will confirm that he did indeed hold justice in the highest esteem throughout his writings; it will also enable us to give at least a rough account of how Nietzsche thought about justice. In the *Birth of Tragedy* Nietzsche praises Aeschylus for his "deep impulse for justice" and the "astonishing daring with which [he, in his poem on Prometheus] places the Olympian world on his scales of justice" (BT, 9). In the *Second Untimely Mediation*, we read that

> [n]o one has a higher claim on our admiration than the man who possesses the drive and the power for justice. (…) The hand of the just man authorized to sit in judgment no longer trembles when it holds the scales. Unsparingly he puts on weight after weight against himself. His eye does not become dim if he sees the pan in the scales rise and fall, and his voice rings out neither hard nor broken when he

---

11. For other passages indicating that Nietzsche does not abandon all codes of conduct that are recognizably moral, compare EH, *Skirmishes*, 38; the preface to *Dawn*; and the 1886 preface to HAH. Consider, in this context, also Nietzsche's insistence that he is the first *decent* person resisting the falseness and hypocrisy of centuries (EH, *Destiny*, 1; see also TI, *Skirmishes*, 37). These considerations may also explain the curious remark in TI, *Maxims*, 36: "Whether we immoralists are *harming* virtue? Just as little as anarchists harm princes. Only since the latter are shot at do they again sit securely on their thrones. Moral: *morality must be shot* at". This seems to say that Nietzsche understands his own criticism as a way of strengthening the Christian *sittliche Weltordnung*. However, this hardly makes sense in the larger context of TI. Instead, what it might mean is that the proper kind of moral codes can be identified thorough critique, that is, moral codes that are not only consistent with but restore *Anstand*, decency, just as attacks on princes make it possible for them to restore "true" power that they had begun to share in a constitutional manner.

12. Compare BGE 62 and 21; GM III, 14; and A 5 and 24 for that focus on the detrimental effects of morality on human excellence. Leiter (*Nietzsche on Morality*) calls ethical systems that Nietzsche rejects "morality in the pejorative sense".

delivers the verdict. (...) For he wills truth, not as cold knowledge without consequences, but as the ordering and punishing judge, truth not as a selfish possession of the individual but as the sacred entitlement to shift all the boundary stones of egotistical possessions, in a word, truth as the Last Judgment and not at all something like the captured trophy desired by the individual hunter. (UM II, 6)

In the *Wanderer and is Shadow*, Nietzsche tells us that virtues such as moderation, justice, and peace of mind would be regained by every free and conscious mind independently of morality (WS 212). Elsewhere in that book, Nietzsche emphasizes that one of the flaws of Christianity is that it destroyed all worldly justice (WS 81). For spelling out what is meant by justice will involve talk about "proportion" and "measure"—which, as Nietzsche tells us in HAH 114, is precisely what Christianity lacks. And in the *Twilight*, we find Nietzsche scoffing at Rousseau and the French Revolution for mistakenly thinking that equality is a demand of justice: "There is no more poisonous poison anywhere: for it seems to be preached by justice itself, whereas it really is the termination of justice. 'Equal to the equal, unequal to the unequal'—that would be the true slogan of justice; and also its corollary: 'Never make equal what is unequal'" (*Skirmishes*, 48). On the face of it, such statements may resemble ideas of fairness that insist on treating "like cases alike" (and different cases differently), but Nietzsche's point is to deny an underlying moral equality of persons.[13]

Another important discussion of justice occurs in the second treatise of the *Genealogy*. As Nietzsche points out in GM II, 4, there is an old idea that originates in the debtor-creditor relationship, namely, that every damage has its equivalent and can be paid off in some way. A debtor unable to pay off his debt must give the creditor something else he owns. This may amount to letting the creditor inflict torture on the debtor because people enjoy watching torture or inflicting pain themselves (GM II, 6). An individual's relationship with his community is a debtor-creditor relationship. The community protects him, requiring that he pay back his debts by respecting its rules. For these debtor-creditor relationships there is a background assumption that the individuals involved are roughly equally powerful (GM II, 8). These ideas (which come as part of a general "habit of comparing power with power, of measuring, of calculating", GM II, 8) give rise to a simple idea of *justice*: "Everything can be paid off, and everything must be paid off" (GM II, 8). Justice, as Nietzsche then argues in GM, 11, the single longest section in the *Genealogy's* second treatise, does not depend on *ressentiment*-driven moralities. *Ressentiment* and justice are psychologically entirely different phenomena. As Nietzsche explains, justice achieves "in the long run the opposite of what all revenge wants, which sees only the viewpoint of the injured one, allows only it to count—from now on, the eye is trained for an ever *more impersonal* appraisal of deeds, even the eye of the injured one himself" (GM II, 11).[14] Let me quote one final passage on justice, from Nietzsche's 1886 preface to HAH:

13. This view that justice insists on inequality among people also appears in *Zarathustra*, part II, in the Tarantulas section. For dismissals of equality, cf. also BGE 219; GS 377; TI, *Skirmishes* 48; A 43; A 57; and EH, *Books*, 5.

14. HAH 92 offers a brief discussion of justice that is quite similar to the later and longer one in GM.

You shall get control over your For and Against and learn how to display first one and then the other in accordance with your higher goal. You shall learn to grasp the sense of perspective in every value judgment—the shifting, distortion, and apparent teleology of the horizons and everything that belongs to perspective; also the amount of stupidity which opposite values involve, and all the intellectual loss with which every For and Against has to be paid for. You shall learn to grasp the *necessary* injustice in every For and Against, injustice as inseparable from life, life itself as *conditioned* by the sense of perspective and its injustice. You shall above all see with your own eyes where injustice is always at its greatest: where life has developed at its smallest, narrowest, neediest, most incipient and yet cannot avoid taking *itself* as the goal and measure of things and for the sake of its own preservation secretly and meanly and ceaselessly crumbling away and calling into question the higher, greater, richer— you shall see with your own eyes the problem of *order of rank*, and how power and right and spaciousness of perspective grow into the heights together.

Justice is a standpoint of impartial assessment. But this passage from HAH makes clear that Nietzsche thinks this standpoint is a mere conceptual possibility. Justice can never be fully obtained, since eventually some stance will have to be taken, and that stance will inevitably neglect some perspective and thus fall short of genuine impartiality (cf. also GM III, 12, the famous "perspectivism" passage).

What emerges from these various passages is an account of justice that endorses the following claims:

1. Justice is concerned with pondering questions from an impartial standpoint.
2. The standpoint of genuine impartiality cannot actually be obtained since any view that is eventually taken will neglect certain aspects; however, the impossibility of reaching this standpoint is consistent with some judgments being more impartial than others, and Nietzsche has the highest admiration for individuals who are capable in this regard.
3. Judgments that must be made impartially include judgments about what counts as equivalent in exchanges of objects or services, or in restoration of or retribution for harm, where impartiality is needed to ensure that such transactions are not being bound up tightly with the interests of specific sides. What is required is a proportionate assessment of the different aspects of the question.
4. Demands of equality without reference to rank are inconsistent with justice. Individuals are of different value, and impartiality will therefore not give them equal weight. Instead, Nietzsche favors the language of "rank" over the language of equality. It is in virtue of this rejection of equality that Nietzsche's views on justice are highly revisionist vis-à-vis most post-Enlightenment thought on this subject.[15]
5. Impartiality requires that individuals of the same rank treat one another in certain ways. That is, such individuals have duties to one another,

15. For the language of "rank" see also BGE 257, 263; and A 57. BGE 219 explicitly links justice and the maintenance of order of rank. In the following passage from BGE 265, Nietzsche makes explicit the connection between comparisons of rank, egoism, and justice:

and this includes the duties the higher men have to each other, as we saw in the previous section.

6. Let me add a few remarks to this account of justice. First, Nietzsche never bothers to explain systematically what counts as "equivalent" either for goods or for (the rank of) persons. However, there could be no general answer to that question, because Nietzsche also acknowledges that "across different peoples, moral estimations are necessarily different" (GS 345). So the kind of comparisons that lies behind the idea that everything can be paid off and everything must be paid off will differ across peoples, and this must hold true also for comparisons of rank. Yet it is not up to the society to adopt values as they please, but they adopt those that fit them best (cf. TI, *Anti-Nature*, 6; GM, *Preface*, 2).[16] Moreover, Nietzsche does believe that certain structural similarities hold across "all healthy societies", especially that they are composed of certain physiologically distinguishable types who attend to different tasks (A 57), and thus that all such societies are composed of individuals of different ranks.

Second, note that Nietzsche's insistence on the fact that higher men have duties shares important features with Rousseau and Kant, two philosophers whom Nietzsche attacks so fiercely. Like Nietzsche in BGE 265, both of them argue that if individuals only understood themselves properly, they would acknowledge constraints on their selfishness and abide by them. Rousseau's general will is the collective will of the community, and one reason why it can be said to be that is because it is also identifiable with the will of any individual member's true self. So if individuals were only to discover their true self and let their actions be guided by it, they would ipso facto act in accordance with the general will. Similarly, following Kant, individuals would act in accordance with the Categorical Imperative if only they acted not out of the whims of some desire, but respected the demands of their will (which for Kant is an organ of rationality), which asks of them to act for reasons that are impartial across all individuals. Rousseau, Kant, and Nietzsche all take duties as *expressions* of the self, properly understood, rather than *constraints* on it. Those actions that the individual has a duty not to do are precisely those actions that do not fit with his or her nature, properly understood. Whereas Nietzsche insists in the discussion of *Beyond Good and Evil* in *Ecce Homo* that the former book is a critique of modernity, he maintains one important feature of what is characteristic of moral approaches in modern times, namely, the idea that duties are expressions of the self, properly understood.[17]

At the risk of annoying innocent ears, I propose the following: egoism belongs to the nature of the noble soul—I mean that unshakeable faith that to a being such as "we are" other beings must be subordinate by nature and have to sacrifice themselves. The noble soul takes this fact of its egoism without any question mark and without the feeling that there is harsh compulsion or arbitrary power in it, much more as something that may be established in the fundamental law of things. If he sought out a name for this, he would say "It is justice itself."

16. To make this view consistent with Nietzsche's praise for the impartial standpoint of justice one would have to assume that such impartiality accommodates societal peculiarities in the assessment of rank.

17. What I say about Kant in this paragraph should be uncontroversial. As far as Rousseau's general will is concerned, I follow Gopal Sreenivasan, "What Is the General Will?" *Philosophical Review* 109 (2000).

Of course, there are considerable differences as well: First of all, both Kant and Rousseau offer an account of the normative force of their respective constructs. The Categorical Imperative is considered binding because otherwise the mind would allegedly fall into a certain kind of contradiction with itself. The general will is supposed to be binding on the individuals in virtue of being the will of their true selves. Nietzsche's account, as opposed to that, is too sketchy and metaphorical to offer an account for how the relevant duties are binding, or at least be perceived to be binding by the agents themselves. This is a point to which we will return in section 7. Moreover, Kant is concerned with constraints on actions that involve all rational creatures, Rousseau with constraints that involve at least all citizens of a politically independent city (such as Geneva, which seems envisaged for the *Social Contract*), whereas Nietzsche claims that the higher men will recognize their kind, honoring them for what they are, and again, his insistence on justice is accompanied by scorn for the value of moral equality, a value whose centrality is also characteristic of moral approaches of modern times.

Nevertheless, the approach of finding the source of duties within the individual distinguishes Nietzsche alongside Kant and Rousseau from two other ways of grounding duties. First, their approach differs from a theistic one that finds the source of duties in a divine figure. And second, it differs from a model of cooperation among rational egoists in which self-interested characters learn to constrain their short-term activities for the sake of long-term benefits (which on many accounts would only yield a nonmoral and rather limited sense of duty, but would explain acceptance of norms, and would do so in a way different from what Nietzsche thinks grounds the duties of the higher men).[18]

A third question that arises now is about the metaethical status of the comparisons Nietzsche endorses.[19] While Nietzsche does call the idea of "everything can be paid off" (GM II, 8) "naïve" and thus presumably subject to elaboration, his comments about justice and rank, on the face of it, sound like factual claims. After all,

18. John Richardson (*Nietzsche's New Darwinism* [Oxford: Oxford University Press, 2004]) expresses a related thought. He says that Nietzsche's views have affinities with theories that recent metaethics has called "practical reasoning theories", according to which (a kind of) objectivity in ethics is indeed feasible, but depends not on theory's matching independently real goods, but on the proper exercise of practical reason (cf. 124). To exercise reason properly can be understood in a Kantian or Hobbesian manner, depending on whether reason is guided by categorical reasons or self-interest. Richardson suggests that Nietzsche enacts "a new discipline of practical reasoning", which guides individuals in their search for their own "personal makeup" (125) in a manner that is informed by facts about our species' and culture's evolution provided by science.

19. I discuss the metaethical status of Nietzsche's views on justice partly because this subject arises naturally at this stage and partly because there has been a lot of interest in Nietzsche's metaethical commitments, fueled, in particular, by the publication of Leiter (*Nietzsche on Morality*), who, in turn, offers one particular bit of textual support for his view that is concerned with justice (among other bits of evidence). However, since the nature of discussions in this area is rather sophisticated, I will have to pursue a few points in some detail over the next pages. A reader not much interested in these metaethical issues could proceed to section 7 right away.

Nietzsche does not only state there what he thinks justice is but he also observes that people naturally start making exchanges in ways that reflect certain equivalences of value. This suggests that people's behavior naturally falls into a pattern that corresponds to judgments about justice. Or recall UM II, 6, where Nietzsche characterizes the man of justice as one who "wills truth," and the truth that he wills presumably consists in judgment of justice. Such claims bring traces of moral realism into Nietzsche's corpus, that view, that is, that finds evaluative facts in the fabric of the world. However, such a reading conflicts with the strong presence of antirealist language in his writings. One of the clearest examples of such language is his statement in GS 301 that "[w]hatever has *value* in our world does not have value in itself, according to its nature—nature is always valueless, but has been *given* value at some time as a present—and it is *we* who gave and bestowed it."[20] Leiter (2002) argues that the presence of such passages in Nietzsche's text should, on balance, make us read him as an antirealist about value: Nietzsche, that is, denies that "there is any objective vindication for his evaluative position" (146). On a thoroughly antirealist reading, Nietzsche would make no claim that the higher men in fact "have" duties, but merely that they feel disposed to act in certain ways; furthermore, Nietzsche would not argue that his notion of justice is reflected in moral facts in the world, but that, instead, it is an expression of his own attitudes. Leiter does not think, however, that Nietzsche's antirealism extends to what he calls prudential, "good-for", judgments, such as the judgment that "herd morality is good for the herd": "Rather, his anti-realism applies to the 'revaluative' judgment that follows upon these judgments of welfare: that is, the judgment that *because* herd morality is *good for* the herd but *bad for* higher men, herd morality (or the universal reign of herd morality) is bad or disvaluable" (147).

The topic of Nietzsche's metaethical commitments is too large to discuss here with the required care, but we must address it briefly within the context of our discussion of justice. Leiter's recent discussion offers a good context to do so. Let me begin with two observations on Leiter's discussion that bear on our assessment of Nietzsche's view of justice. The first observation concerns one piece of textual evidence Leiter quotes in support of his antirealism thesis and that is worth considering here because he reads it as being directly concerned with the metaethical status of *justice*. (Let me hasten to add, though, that this is of course not the only bit of textual evidence Leiter offers.) Leiter (2002, 147) quotes GS 184 as saying "justice…is by all means a matter of taste, nothing more", which seems like a direct application of the statement from GS 301 (which I just quoted) to justice. If this were indeed what GS 184 says, it would offer strong support for Leiter's antirealist reading. However, GS 184 does *not* link the term *justice* to the predicate "is by all means a matter of taste, nothing more" as suggested by Leiter's rendering of the passage. The term used in German is *Justiz*, which literally denotes the judiciary branch, but a philologist like Nietzsche might possibly also use it to denote "justice". However, *Justiz* is the word that functions as the title of GS 184, and it is about Nietzsche's preference for accepting thefts over having scarecrows posted around him that this aphorism says that it is "a matter of taste, nothing more". This is altogether too cryptic and inconclusive to serve as (even merely supportive) evidence for Nietzsche's antirealism about justice.

20. Compare also D 3 and TI, *Improvers*, 1.

The second observation, more central for the view that Nietzsche should be read as an antirealist about nonprudential value but that is not specifically about justice, concerns another claim of Leiter's, namely, that "the language of truth and falsity, real and unreal" is conspicuously absent from how Nietzsche writes about value (154). However, such language is not absent from Nietzsche's discussions of value. In EH, Nietzsche complains that "one has deprived reality of its value, its meaning, its truthfulness, to precisely the extent to which one has mendaciously invented an ideal world. (...) The *lie* of the ideal has so far been the curse on reality" (*Preface* 2), and similar formulations in which Nietzsche attaches value to the real apparently because it is real can be found in TI, *Skirmishes*, 32 ("How much greater is the worth of the real man, compared with any merely desired, dreamed-up, foully fabricated man? with any ideal man? And it is only the ideal man who offends the philosopher's taste."); A 15 (where Nietzsche complains that Christianity "de-values" the real world); as well as A 9 and EH, *Fate*, 7. All these passages suggest that Nietzsche, in spite of his insistence that "we" bring value into the world, at least takes *his* evaluations (and especially when those are made from the standpoint of justice) to be informed by facts, and, what is more in this context, he feels entitled to dismiss other evaluations if they are too detached from what he takes to be real. Put differently, Nietzsche seems to think that evaluative stances can be judged as better or worse depending on the extent to which they are responsive to facts.

The presence of such passages does indeed seem to make it difficult to deny that Nietzsche thinks there is such an importance of facts for evaluations. In particular, as far as justice is concerned, the kind of impartiality required by justice must at least take facts for what they are, and the bindingness of demands that are being made from the standpoint of justice depends on whether they take the facts into consideration. To be sure: as long as we take moral realism to be defined as a view that finds evaluative facts in the fabric of the world, passages such as those just quoted can be accommodated. For then one could say that, sure enough, Nietzsche himself values reality higher than imaginary realms, but that does not mean that that value judgment *itself* is meant to be factual. However, the presence of such passages sits uneasily with ascribing a kind of antirealism about nonprudential value to Nietzsche according to which he *not only* fails to deny the existence of moral facts but *also* denies that some valuations (presumably his own) stand in some privileged relationship to facts (in the sense that he thinks they are more plausible for incorporating facts, or better supported by the facts, as opposed to other views that fail short on this score) and make a claim on others in virtue of standing in such a relationship. Leiter's antirealism indeed seems to be of that latter sort; for, again, Leiter thinks Nietzsche "must ultimately deny that there is any objective vindication for his evaluative position" (146). That view underestimates the insistence on fact-responsiveness that seems to characterize Nietzsche's metaethical stance.[21]

To be sure, these passages do not deliver the conclusion that Nietzsche was a realist about value, but they do suggest that Nietzsche acknowledges a notion of *objectivity* of values that could be developed either within a realist or antirealist framework (one in which moral objectivity would be understood without ontological

21. Richardson (*Nietzsche's New Darwinism*) makes the same point (cf. 114).

commitments). For Leiter, antirealism and the unavailability of a notion of objectivity are tied by definition, and this sort of view (i.e., one that does not even grant that Nietzsche acknowledges a notion of objectivity) is hard to square with what Nietzsche says.[22]

Leiter (2002) has an interesting response to such worries about regarding Nietzsche as an antirealist in his sense. Leiter (cf. 159–61) points out that there is yet another set of passages that needs to be integrated into a discussion of Nietzsche's metaethics, namely, his denial of the importance of truth. (For instance: "The falseness of a judgment is for us not necessarily an objection to a judgment", BGE 4). Most people, however, as Nietzsche is keenly aware, will not share this view on the unimportance of truth (with Nietzsche himself thinking that what matters is not whether a claim is true, but whether believing it supports a given form of life). According to Leiter, when Nietzsche writes as if he uses factual statements to bear on value judgments, he speaks to such readers, imitating, for the sake of the argument, *their* presumed metaethical stance without thereby committing himself to that stance. That is, Nietzsche at least sometimes writes for an audience that thinks factual statements bear on value judgments and tries to refute their value judgments by reference to facts and hence in terms of inferences that those readers (but not Nietzsche himself) would accept.

Yet this move is problematic for two reasons. First, it offers a recipe for denying the importance of passages that go against Leiter's preferred reading of Nietzsche: whenever passages do not fit that reading, they can be classified as being directed to readers who do not share some of Nietzsche's views but whom he would like to persuade of something regardless of that disagreement. This by itself is not conclusive because, in spite of having the feature just emphasized, this may of course be exactly what Nietzsche is doing. However, the second concern is that that the passages at issue here would be directed at readers whom Nietzsche does not seem to be keen on reaching in the first place. For instance, the very first statement of the *Antichrist* points out that this book belongs "to the most rare of men". That is, one of the books from which some of those critical passages above stem is directed precisely not at those for whom, according to Leiter, those passages seem to be written. In BGE 30 we read that "[o]ur highest insights must—and should—sound like follies and sometimes like crimes when they are heard without permission by those who are not predisposed and not predestined for them", which again renders it hard to believe that

---

22. Maudemarie Clark and David Dudrick ("Nietzsche and Moral Objectivity," in *Nietzsche and Morality*, ed. Brian Leiter and Neal Sinhababu [Oxford: Oxford University Press, forthcoming]) develop the view that Nietzsche was an antirealist who nevertheless acknowledges a notion of objectivity. This is not an uncommon view in the contemporary metaethical debate: both Allan Gibbard (*Wise Choices, Apt Feelings: A Theory of Normative Judgment* [Cambridge, Mass.: Harvard University Press, 1990]) and Simon Blackburn (*Ruling Passions: A Theory of Practical Reasoning* [Oxford: Clarendon, 1998]) offer views that are not realist but nevertheless go to great lengths to establish a notion of objectivity in ethics without an ontological posit that would serve as a reference point for such a notion; for an attempt to accommodate the "objective pretensions" of moral discourse, see also Mark Timmons (*Morality without Foundations* (New York: Oxford University Press, 1999]).

Nietzsche would write for an audience other than those selected few who can understand him. And in GS 381, Nietzsche points out that "one does not only wish to be understood when one writes; one wishes just as surely *not* to be understood", depending, so it is plausible to add, on the reader. Difficulties in understanding a book, so Nietzsche goes on to say, do not speak against the book, because the author may not have tried to make himself understood by just "anybody", again suggesting that Nietzsche does not write for just "anybody".

Leiter (cf. 147/148) is aware of these passages and refers to them in support of this view that Nietzsche is an antirealist about nonprudential value. However, the presence of these passages about Nietzsche's intended audience makes it hard to explain the existence of those passages that connect factual statements and value statements in terms of Nietzsche's interest to reach an audience that does *not* belong to the selected few in whose grasp his thoughts are. This move, then, does not help dissolve worries about Leiter's specific version of reading Nietzsche as an antirealist about value.

7. Above I pointed out that Nietzsche's account of duties in BGE 265 does not offer an account parallel to Rousseau's or Kant's that would explain why the duties he postulates are binding, or at least would be perceived to be binding by the agent. Now we will press this point further. Let me explain what we may reasonably hope to find in Nietzsche's works. Nietzsche is intrigued by the emerging biological sciences of his day, in particular evolutionary biology and physiology. One of his goals in his writings of the 1880s is to propose mechanisms of the sort that could occur in explanations in such disciplines to account for the emergence of the kind of moral psychology he rejects, especially the moral psychology underlying Christianity.

Elsewhere I have proposed readings of Nietzsche's accounts of guilt and *ressentiment* along these lines (cf. Risse [2001] and [2003]). Nietzsche does not simply announce to his readers that he holds an evaluative standard according to which a character shaped by guilt and *ressentiment* is dismissed whereas other types are praised; he also offers a scientifically minded explanation for how it happened that the "herd-man" could make believe that he was "the only type of man allowed" (BGE 199). A natural question to ask at this stage is whether Nietzsche offers an explanation of that sort for how it could be the case that the higher men would act in accordance with duties and rights—something that would put scientifically minded substance to that metaphorical talk about the "inborn celestial mechanic" in BGE 265. So what we are asking is whether Nietzsche has a story to tell that applies his naturalistic program of "translating men back into nature" (BGE 230) to the question of the development of rights and duties, and thus to justice, in much the same way in which he also applies that program to the questions just mentioned. Put differently, does Nietzsche have a story to tell as to why the higher men take themselves to be subject to duties? (It should be clear that this question arises regardless of whether or not we take Nietzsche to be a metaethical realist or antirealist.)

Nietzsche does offer what we can take to be such an account in *Dawn*, where he provides us with a "natural history of rights and duties":

> Our duties—are the rights of others over us. How have they acquired such rights?
> By taking us to be capable of contracting and of requiting, by positing us as similar

and equal to them, and as a consequence entrusting us with something, educating, reproving, supporting us. We fulfill our duty—that is to say: we justify the idea of our power on the basis of which all these things were bestowed upon us, we give back in the measure in which we have been given to. It is thus our pride [*Selbstherrlichkeit*] that bids us do our duty—when we do something for others in return for something they have done for us, what we are doing is restoring our self-regard—for in doing something for us, these others have impinged upon our sphere of power, and would have continued to have a hand in it if we did not with the performance of our "duty" practice a requital, that is to say, impinge on their power.—My rights—that are part of my power which others have not merely conceded me, but which they wish me to preserve. How do these others arrive at that? First: through their prudence and fear and caution: whether in that they expect something similar from us in return (…); or in that they consider that a struggle with us would be perilous or to no purpose. Or in that they see in any diminution of our force a disadvantage to themselves, since we would then be unsuited to forming an alliance with them in opposition to a hostile third power. Then: by donation and cession. In this case, others have enough and more than enough power to be able to dispose of some of it, and to guarantee to him they have given it to the portion of it they have given: in doing so they presuppose a feeble sense of power in him who lets himself be thus donated to. That is how rights originate: recognized and guaranteed degrees of power. (D 112)

The concern here is not specifically with higher men, but this account would presumably have to apply to them as well (and right and duties could, of course, also exist among different groups of peers, as is clear from GM II, 8). This passage comes soon after D 103, where Nietzsche explains that his goal is to explore mechanisms that account for the emergence of moral motivation. This is one example of that project.

Let us see what to make of this account of rights and duties—more specifically, in the spirit of Nietzsche's naturalistic outlook, what to make of this account of *behavior* in accordance with what we commonly understand rights and duties to be. (At any rate, for Nietzsche, moralities are "sign languages of affects" [BGE 187].) I will merely discuss the notion of duty. Parallel considerations apply to rights. According to D 112, individual interaction involves interference in one another's "spheres of power": whenever somebody does something for us, gives something to us, or helps us out, she expands her range of activities in a manner that intimately affects and constrains ours. The only way of undoing this interference and thus to make us whole again is by expanding our own range of activities in a manner that intimately affects and constrains hers and thereby undoes the imbalance thus achieved. We must return what we have received, or something of equivalent value. To give to each what she is owed amounts to restoring one's sphere of power. An individual's motivation for fulfilling the duty is her pride affected by the interference with her sphere of power. And this is the mechanism that might account for the "celestial mechanic".

To make sense of this talk about duties, let us first elucidate Nietzsche's talk about "spheres of power". To this end, it is useful to appeal to what Leiter (2002) calls Nietzsche's "Doctrine of Types" (cf. 8–10), according to which each individual has a fixed psychophysical constitution defining him as a type of person. Facts about one's type explain one's beliefs and values. In particular it is the case that "our thoughts, values, every 'yes', 'no', 'if' and 'but' grow from us with the same necessity with which a tree bears its fruits—all related, and each with an affinity to each, and testimony to one will, one health, one earth, one sun" (GM, *Preface*, 2). With this doctrine in place, we can approach the notion of power. An individual's power is his ability to create optimal circumstances for his psychophysical constitution (or his growth in activity, as Richardson [1996, 21] puts it, where the relevant activity is what is characteristic of an individual's type). As Nietzsche tells us in GM III, 7, "[e]very animal (..) instinctively strives for an optimum of favorable conditions in which fully to release his power and achieve his maximum feeling of power; every animal abhors equally instinctively, with an acute sense of smell 'higher than all reason,' any kind of disturbance and hindrance which blocks or could block his path to the optimum". This, in turn, delivers two explications of "spheres of power" and thus of duties. A sphere of power is either a person's range of activities under optimal conditions of the sort mentioned in this quote, or, alternatively, a person's range of activities under constraints ("normal conditions"). Nothing depends on which explication we choose. A person's pride is offended, or at least challenged, when her sphere of power is affected, if only by somebody's doing her a favor. Again, what his account of duties sets out to explain is the *behavior* we associate with the execution of duties, doing so in terms of an urge and thus in physiological terms.

8. But how successful is this as an account of dutiful behavior? Note first that this account only works for the case of those who are roughly equals. For otherwise, pride and the infringement of spheres of power may not match up. For instance, if I am a mathematician and receive lots of help from Carl Friedrich Gauss or David Hilbert, the infringement on my sphere of power is considerable since their help is presumably extraordinary. However, since they are such outstanding mathematicians, my pride need not be affected much, as surely it would be if a college sophomore would attempt to solve my math problem. At the same time, in the case of the sophomore, my sphere of power may not be much affected if his help turns out to be insubstantial. This point does not raise a problem for Nietzsche, since he only envisages this account as being successful for the case of equals. However, it is at least worth noting that this constraint is also internal to the functioning of the account itself.

There are, however, at least two serious concerns about Nietzsche's account. First of all, it is puzzling why my doing you a favor would actually restore my sphere of power, which was originally violated when you did me a favor. The question that arises here is similar to the one that occurs about retributivist accounts of punishment, namely, why doing X to an offender who committed X himself would "restore" a previously existing state of affairs, or whether instead the resulting state of affairs would be one in which X has been committed twice. Similarly, my doing you a favor after you did me one might just not restore anything but might produce a state of affairs in which two spheres of powers have been violated. Note also that the German word in D 112 that I translated as "pride" is *Selbstherrlichkeit*—which literally denotes the property of having dominion over oneself. To the extent that it seems dubious that a second infringement would restore a state of affairs in which no sphere of power is violated, it also seems dubious whether agents themselves will regard such new infringement as a restoration of one's having dominion over oneself.

The second worry about Nietzsche's account is that it can only accommodate a specific kind of duty, that in which individuals have to do something for others because those have done something for them first. That is, the account can accommodate only so-called positive duties, and not even all of those, but only positive duties that respond to beneficial actions of others. Negative duties (that is, duties to refrain from certain actions) cannot be accommodated by this account. To many philosophers, an account of rights and duties that cannot accommodate negative rights and duties is deficient because it omits the cases we care about most. However, perhaps Nietzsche has no need for such duties and intentionally means to propose a revisionist account of rights and duties that does not include negative rights and duties. In particular, the higher men only owe one another for infringements of spheres of power, and there are no other rights or duties. But if this is Nietzsche's view at the time of *Dawn*, he has changed it when he writes *Beyond Good and Evil*, and so this account cannot count among Nietzsche's mature views. For in BGE 259, we read:

> Mutually refraining from wounding each other, from violence, and from exploita-
> tion, setting one's will on the same level as that of another: this can in a certain crude
> sense become a good custom among individuals, if conditions are given for that
> (namely, a real similarity in the quantity of their power and their estimates of value,
> as well as their belonging together within a single body). However, as soon as one
> tried to extend this principle, possibly even to the basic principle of society, it would
> immediately reveal itself for what it is, as the will to a denial of life, as principle of
> disintegration and decay. Here we must think through to the basics and fend off all
> sentimental weakness: life itself is essentially appropriation from and violating and
> overpowering strangers and weaker men, oppression, hardness, imposing one's own
> forms, annexing, and at the very least, at its mildest, exploitation. (…) Even that body
> in which, as previously assumed, individuals treat each other as equals—and that
> happens in every healthy aristocracy—must itself, if it is a living body and not dying
> out, do to all those things to other bodies that the individuals in it refrain from doing
> to each other: it will have to be the embodied will to power (…).

In this chilling passage, Nietzsche makes clear that he thinks the higher men do endorse negative duties and corresponding rights: they refrain from hurting one another. But this cannot be accommodated by the account of rights and duties in D 112. Therefore, the behavioral accounts of rights and duties we find in D 112 cannot elucidate Nietzsche's "celestial mechanic" of BGE 265. I am not aware of any other passages in Nietzsche's works that would fill this gap. This does not mean such an account could not be provided, but Nietzsche does not do so himself and thus leaves it mysterious just why higher men should abide by duties. What is available, of course, is an account of cooperation among self-interested agents, where agents abide by rules that require short-term sacrifices for the sake of mutual long-term benefits. Perhaps this is the best path to pursue for somebody interested in offering a scientifically minded account of behavior in accordance with rights and duties, but it seems that Nietzsche was interested in a different sort of account. The absence of the sort of account that Nietzsche seemed to be interested in does not undermine his commitment to the view that the higher men are subject to rights and duties. Yet such an account would have added more unity to Nietzsche's views, and without it, he leaves an important claim unsubstantiated.

3

Morality, Schmorality

RICHARD JOYCE

In his contribution to this volume, Paul Bloomfield analyzes and attempts to answer the question "Why is it bad to be bad?" I too will use this question as my point of departure; in particular I want to approach the matter from the perspective of a moral error theorist. This discussion will preface one of the principal topics of this paper: the relationship between morality and self-interest. Again, my main goal is to clarify what the moral error theorist might say on this subject. Against this background, the final portion of this paper will be a discussion of moral fictionalism, defending it from some objections.

Bloomfield is correct to claim that the best way of removing the appearance of tautology or poor formation from the question "Why is it bad to be bad?" is to gloss it as elliptical for something along the lines of "Why does being morally bad have a deleterious effect on my self-interest?" The two "bad"s are intensionally nonidentical: one (I will assume) refers to a nonmoral notion of prudential badness (whatever is, all things considered, harmful to one's welfare[1]), while the other refers to a kind of ostensibly distinct *moral* badness. Though both notions have enough intuitive meat to them for discussion to proceed, neither is unproblematic. (I will return to these problems later.) On this interpretation, the question "Is it bad to be bad?" can be seen as an inquiry concerning whether two intensionally nonequivalent concepts are such that in fact (or even, perhaps, necessarily) the extension of one includes the extension of the other.[2] To

---

1. Contra W. D. Falk (this volume), in this paper I am not using the term "prudence" to denote to a policy of risk-avoidance, but rather am identifying prudence with acting in whatever way advances one's interests, all things considered. (And the relevant notion of "interests" I am leaving unspecified.) I am happy also to use the term "expediency" as a synonym for the same. Despite Falk's insistence that "expediency" must implicate some notion of *convenience*, my dictionary tells me that it also means simply "self-serving."

2. I take it that nobody will claim that the two concepts are coextensive; that every act of imprudence is a moral wrong. My having a cup of coffee before going to bed may be prudentially foolish, but surely doesn't count as even a mild moral crime.

ask the question "*Why* is it bad to be bad?" is to presuppose that this *is* the case, and to inquire in virtue of what this is so.

The moral error theorist thinks (1) that the predicate "…is morally bad" is a logical predicate (in contrast to the semantic noncognitivist, who thinks that it is a predicate only in a grammatical sense), (2) that sentences of the form "φ is morally bad" are generally uttered with assertoric force (in contrast to the pragmatic noncognitivist, who thinks that such sentences are used to perform some other linguistic function), and (3) that the predicate "…is morally bad" has an empty extension (in contrast to, e.g., the moral realist, who thinks that the property of moral badness is instantiated).[3] The third contention is the most controversial, and there are various reasons that might lead one to endorse it; it is not my intention in this paper to attempt to make any of these reasons compelling. Perhaps the error theorist thinks that for something to be morally bad would imply or presuppose that human actions enjoy a kind of unrestricted *autonomy*, while thinking that in fact the universe supplies no such autonomy (Haji 1998, 2003). Perhaps she thinks that for something to be morally bad would imply or presuppose a kind of inescapable, authoritative imperative against pursuing that thing, while thinking that in fact the universe supplies no such imperatives (Mackie 1977; Joyce 2001). Perhaps she thinks that for something to be morally bad would imply or presuppose that human moral attitudes manifest a kind of uniformity, while thinking that in fact attitudes do not converge (Burgess [1978] 2007). Perhaps she thinks that there exists no phenomenon whose explanation requires that the property of moral badness be instantiated, while thinking that explanatory redundancy is good ground for disbelief (Hinckfuss 1987). Perhaps she thinks that tracing the history of the concept *moral badness* back to its origins reveals a basis in supernatural forces and magical bonds—a defective metaphysical framework outside which the concept makes no sense (Hägerström 1953). Perhaps she thinks all of these things and more besides.[4] The details are not important here; the point is that the error theorist accuses morality of being fatally flawed, such that any value system with the flawed element(s) extirpated simply wouldn't deserve the name "morality". The only detail that need be noted here about the moral error theoretic position is that it is usually restricted to the moral realm. Of course, in principle one could endorse a radical *global* error theory, in which case one would by implication be an error theorist about morality (along with modality, colors, other minds, cats and dogs, etc.), or one could be an error theorist about all normative phenomena, which, again, would include an error theory for morality. But typically the moral error theorist thinks that there is something *especially* problematic about morality, and does not harbor the same doubts about normativity in general. The moral error theorist usually allows that we can still deliberate about how to act, she thinks that we can still make sense of actions harming or

---

3. The options mentioned in this sentence are not intended to be exhaustive.

4. For the sake of brevity I will talk as if the error theorist thinks there is only one thing problematic about morality. But of course an error theorist may be impressed by a number of considerations against morality. Perhaps morality has a lot of little or medium-sized problems—none of which by itself would ground an error theory, but all of which together constitute A Big Problem.

advancing our own welfare (and others' welfare), and thus she thinks that we can continue to make sense of prudential "oughts."[5] She allows that prudential badness is instantiated but insists that moral badness is not. Thus, on the assumption that the question "Is it bad to be bad?" amounts to an inquiry about the truth value of a universal conditional ("Is it the case that: For any x, if x is morally bad, then x is prudentially bad?"), the moral error theorist will think that the answer to the question is vacuously "Yes" because the conditional has a false antecedent irrespective of how the variable is instantiated.[6] (Note that she will also, for the same reason, answer "Is it good to be bad?" in the positive.) Thus, she will object to the presupposition behind the question "Why is it bad to be bad?" In this respect the question is, for her, not unlike "Why is it bad to annoy a witch?" Her answer is "But you *can't* annoy a witch—there aren't any!"

But there is another way of understanding the elliptical element of the question that allows the possibility of the error theorist giving a substantive and interesting "Yes." If she treats the reference to moral badness as denoting the extension *that it is widely assumed to have*, the extension is not empty at all (though see below). After all, the error theorist is well aware that there is a broad range of actions—both types and tokens—that are widely thought to be morally bad: breaking promises, stealing, unprovoked violence, Hitler's Final Solution, gluttony, sloth, envy, and so on and so forth.[7] She can understand the question "Is it bad to be bad?" as "Will performing *these* actions [gesturing to those actions that are widely considered to be morally bad] have a deleterious effect on the interests of the perpetrator?" For token actions that have already been performed—for example, Ernie's lying to Bert last week—the question must be either "Did this action have a deleterious effect on Ernie's interests?" or "Would performing an action of the same type have a deleterious effect on the interests of the perpetrator?" These are all questions that the error theorist might answer positively, thus allowing that the question "*Why* is it bad for me to pursue such things?" must have an answer.

(By comparison, suppose an anthropologist were studying a culture in which certain persons are considered to be witches. The anthropologist might recognize that it's a good thing—good for his research, that is—if he stays on friendly terms with these persons, even though he doesn't believe that they possess the supernatural powers necessary for actually being witches at all. He might say "It is good to be friendly

---

5. In this paper I assume that prudence naturally takes the form of a normative system, that it involves "ought" claims, reasons for action, etc. In fact, one could deny this. All that is minimally necessary for believing in prudence is to accept that individuals can be harmed. Thus even if one thought that all "ought" claims are false—even all nonmoral ones—one could still uphold that "…is prudentially bad" has a nonempty extension.

6. There are some complications here concerning (A) whether the domain of the variable is restricted to actual entities, and (B) whether the error theorist holds that moral predicates are necessarily empty or just actually empty. Addressing these complications is unnecessary.

7. Although for the sake of simplicity I tend to speak just of actions being morally bad, I don't mean to exclude morally bad character traits, states of affairs, intentions, policies, properties, objects, and so forth.

to those persons that are hereabouts considered to be witches," but there would be nothing impermissible, or, in general, misleading, if he were, for convenience, to express this elliptically as "It is good to be friendly to the witches hereabouts.")

One problem with this interpretation is that there may be significant disagreement among the people "hereabouts" as to what counts as morally bad, such that even the predicate "…is widely assumed to be morally bad" threatens to turn up empty. After all, moral discourse, it is often observed, is characterized by a high degree of intractable disagreement. Perhaps, though, there are at least *some* things for which there is sufficient concurrence that we can speak of "what is widely assumed to be bad" (strangling babies?), and perhaps the error theorist confines her question merely to these actions. Or perhaps the error theorist just passes the buck to her interlocutor, and says: "Tell me what things you consider to be morally bad, and I will tell you whether (and, if so, in virtue of what) their pursuit is imprudent".

Another feature of the question to which attention should be drawn is the fact that it may receive different answers for different people, or for the same person at different times, or for the same person (or counterparts, if you prefer) at different possible worlds. Perhaps it will frustrate Ernie's interests to lie, but it won't frustrate Bert's interests to lie. Perhaps it will frustrate Ernie's interests to lie today, but he'll be okay if he waits till next Friday. Or perhaps it will frustrate both Ernie's and Bert's interests to lie, but it will do so for very different reasons: for example, Ernie would have to live with crippling guilt, whereas Bert would be sent to bed without any dinner. Or perhaps as a matter of fact everyone has a prudential reason to avoid badness (and perhaps they all have the same reason), but there are possible circumstances where the pursuit of the bad would become prudentially good (for at least some persons).

It has been a long-standing aspiration of a certain school of moral philosophy—upon whose roll appears the name "Bloomfield, P."—that all such contingent messiness could be swept aside by the provision of a universal, permanent, monolithic and (perhaps) necessary positive answer to the question. Bloomfield's solution is that all bad human agents undermine their self-respect and thus frustrate their own interests. As far as go the principal theses of this paper, Bloomfield may be entirely right. But I happen to doubt that he is, and I find my sense of courtesy to the good editor of this volume prevailed over by an intellectual urge to join the fray; hence I cannot forego making a couple of critical comments.

First, it should be noted that at best his argument shows that there is something self-damaging about a certain kind of radical, ubiquitous, all-encompassing, self-conscious attitude toward what is (widely assumed to be) bad: pleonexia. But whether there even *are* any such awful characters around is a moot question. The agents who perform those actions widely thought of as bad—breaking promises, stealing, and so on—are rarely inclined to appeal to Thrasymachean or Machiavellian iconoclasm to attempt to justify themselves. Most everyday wrongdoers,[8] I submit, believe that what they are doing *isn't* really bad (and that if others disagree it's because they're not

---

8. Here I am using the term "wrongdoers" in a purely descriptive manner: to pick out those people who are widely considered to be wrongdoers. Not wanting to beg the question against the error theorist, I should really keep the term in scare quotes throughout, but I refrain from doing so for stylistic reasons.

properly acquainted with the details of the case). Wrongdoing is born of negligence as often as it is born of arrogance. Many wrongdoers castigate themselves for their actions, and even perform them regretfully. Wrongdoers are not always selfishly motivated by gewgaws: Consider a mafia hit man acting out of obligation and loyalty (perhaps even love) for the paterfamilias. Few wrongdoers fail to distinguish between the out-group (a domain of potential victims) and the in-group (a domain of friends, family, loved ones, those with whom one has binding obligations, etc.). In short, the pleonectic may be a fascinating philosophical case study, but he hardly represents the typical or paradigmatic instance of badness.

Bloomfield seems to think that the pleonectic represents the toughest case, and thus that if even Thrasymachus and his ilk can be shown to be harming themselves, then surely all those more mundane wrongdoers must proportionally follow suit. But this expectation is, in my opinion, ill-founded. Though the pleonectic does in some sense occupy an extreme wing of villainy, it doesn't follow that any injury he does himself must by implication be suffered to a lesser degree by less radical wrong-doers. Consider, for example, the claim that the pleonectic lives a life without "true love" and lacking "real friendship". We can all accept that any human who chooses such an existence is very probably damaging himself. But what about a lesser wrong-doer who, say, is creative with the truth when filing his taxes, or is needlessly curt to a taxi driver? It might be claimed that this person has harmed himself to a lesser degree by missing an opportunity for *some* true love and *some* real friends (i.e., the love and friendship of the victims, perhaps). But there is surely nothing wrong with this kind of loss per se, for *everyone*—even the thoroughly virtuous—must eschew *some* potential friendships. (I don't recall that Mother Teresa ever sent me a Christmas card.) I see no grounds for assuming that a mundane wrongdoer cannot enjoy the full complement of genuine friends, or that the occasional bit of everyday misconduct (directed at nonfriends) must, to some small degree, undermine those friendships. Consider instead the claim that certain pleonectics must be guilty of psychological compartmentalization. We can all agree that extreme compartmentalization of one's thoughts and desires is a harmful state. But what about *a little* compartmentalization? There is presumably nothing wrong with "a bit" of compartmentalization, since, again, it is an attribute that *every* human exhibits; it's the nature of human psychology. It might be complained that in this context the term "compartmentalization" is intended to denote only the pernicious, pathological variety. But then we are free to deny that the mild transgressor must manifest *any* such attribute, and any insistence that he does so simply begs the question.

If I am correct that the harm that the pleonectic (allegedly) does himself derives from aspects of the very extremism of his attitude, then there are no grounds for thinking that a lesser degree of the same kind of self-harm is in store for the everyday moral transgressor. And thus we have not been shown how moral badness per se is self-injurious, but rather only how a proper subset of moral badness is bad—and a very small (and perhaps actually empty) proper subset of moral badness at that.

The second critical comment I will make against Bloomfield's argument is that it at best shows that there is some kind of *fault* with the pleonectic, but it not clear how this fault translates into an injury. The pleonectic, according to Bloomfield, has but a simulacrum of self-respect; what she takes to be self-respect is "faulty in its foundations". Because the pleonectic accords others no respect, she cannot coherently respect herself, for to do so would be based on the (allegedly) impermissible distinction that "I deserve more because I am me". Though the pleonectic may be quite convinced that he does have self-respect, he is, in fact, self-deceived. To grant Bloomfield this case (something that I am, in fact, very far from doing) would be to acknowledge that a milestone in philosophy has been achieved. An argument demonstrating the irrationality of wrongdoers is something that Simon Blackburn has described as the "holy grail of moral philosophy" (1984, 222). Nevertheless, even if Bloomfield's argument delivered the grail into our hands, this would not achieve the goal he set himself, for it is simply not clear how being irrational or self-deceived entails doing oneself harm. "I am special because I am me" may be a misguided or irrational thought (though even this I am highly doubtful of), but why *self-harmful*?

If someone is habitually irrational in all her deliberations then it is not unreasonable to suppose that this will land her in various kinds of trouble; and it is not hard to see that self-deception will often be self-injurious. But to show that irrationality and self-deception are on very many occasions harmful is insufficient to establish that there is anything harmful about these phenomena per se. This is especially evident when the charge of irrationality/self-deception is so unobvious that it takes a philosopher to establish it—against a background of more than 2,000 years of like endeavors meeting with a body of staunch academic opposition. When the accusation concerns so inconspicuous and subtle a phenomenon, any assumption that the typical harms that issue from canonical and obvious irrationality/self-deception must also issue from the inconspicuous instances must be suspended. In other words, if Bloomfield were to succeed in demonstrating that every moral wrongdoer is to some extent self-deceived, then he would have shown us that the domain of self-deception is very different than it is widely assumed to be, and thus any previous assumptions about the general harmfulness of self-deception (based, as they are, on a different class of prototypes) would stand in need of reexamination.

Just as space allowed Bloomfield to make his case but briefly, so too I will not attempt to respond to his final "five things that could be said to Thrasymachus" in any detail. My main suspicion is that they are indeed things that could be said *to Thrasymachus* (i.e., to the pleonectic), but have considerably less force against a more everyday wrongdoer. That someone who cheats slightly on his taxes, or is needlessly discourteous to the taxi driver, is suffering from schizophrenia, that he must endure the anxieties of dissimulation, that he is missing the "the joy of seeing things as they actually are"—that he is leaning toward any of these wretched states *even slightly*—is, at best, an optimistic claim in need of empirical support. Of course there is a kind of satisfaction that comes from a job done with moral integrity; but there is also a satisfaction that comes from getting away with something. Of the people who have experienced both, of course there are some who prefer the first kind of pleasure; but there are also, I'll wager, those who prefer the second kind. (Many of us are not insensitive to both kinds.) The latter people may very well be self-deceived—it is not my intention here to deny it—but what needs to be asked is whether they are *harming themselves*. To appeal to a "joy" that comes from having true beliefs may sound appealing—especially to a philosopher—but I don't think it stands up to scrutiny. Do true beliefs *always* bring this joy? I don't recall the last time

I felt even a hint of ecstasy when contemplating that $1 + 1 = 2$. Perhaps Bloomfield means to restrict his comment just to a certain domain of epistemic success: a joy that comes from having true beliefs about our own value in comparison to that of other humans. Again, Bloomfield's opponent need not deny the very possibility of such a joy, nor even deny that it might be quite widespread. All she need deny is the universal claim that Bloomfield's argument requires if it is to succeed: that such joy is available to *anyone* in *any* circumstance, and that it can never be outweighed by a countervailing joy that flows from gaining benefits (and not necessarily mere gewgaws) secured through an act of moral transgression.

It is not my intention to criticize Bloomfield's argument beyond these gestures, because the main point to which I want to draw attention is that as far as the moral error theorist is concerned Bloomfield could be 100 percent correct. Chances are, what the moral error theorist is likely to say in response to the question "Is it bad to be morally bad?" (understood as outlined above) is "Sometimes it is, sometimes it isn't". But were she instead to answer "Yes: always, for everyone, necessarily"—and then go on to justify this answer by appeal to Bloomfield's argument—she would in no sense undermine her commitment to a moral error theory. Embracing a moral error theory rationally eliminates from one's serious practical deliberations certain kinds of justification: One can no longer, for example, refrain from doing something because one believes that it is morally forbidden. But it implies nothing about what actions one should actually perform (or refrain from performing). Contrary to popular belief, the moral error theorist is not a scheming villain, acting pleasantly solely in order to avoid punishment or to lull her victims into complacency. (As Richard Garner puts it: "The amoralist need not be an immoral, heartless, selfish jerk who denies the obvious" [1994, 279].) The moral error theorist may have as much compassion, love, and generosity as anyone else; she will just not believe these characteristics, or their attendant actions, to be *morally* desirable.[9] Nor does the embrace of a moral error theory obviously exclude any particular *nonmoral* forms of justification from figuring in one's deliberations. The moral error theorist may be motivated largely by compassion, or by self-interest, or by a sense of loyalty to her friends and family, or (more likely) a mixture of these things (and others besides) depending on the situation.[10] There is simply no reason to assume that having such a (nonmoral) basis to one's deliberations is going to end up prescribing sneaky nastiness. On the contrary, for most people, in most ordinary situations, it is fair to assume that a proper sensitivity to such nonmoral considerations is likely to favor acting in accordance with (what most people think of as) moral requirements. So the moral error

---

9. We mustn't be distracted by the fact that such emotions as love and generosity are often called *"moral* emotions". If they warrant this label it is in virtue of the fact that they are considered morally praiseworthy, but it is clear that one can have these emotions without making any moral judgment. The moral error theorist does not have her position undermined if *others* choose to judge her character, actions, and emotions in moral terms.

10. There is, of course, a kind of loyalty that is based on judgments of moral obligation. I submit, however, that one can also have *feelings* of loyalty—feelings of attachment and affection that involve desires to protect the welfare of another person—that need not be "moralized" by the subject in the least.

theorist is as willing and able as anyone else to endorse claims such as "I ought not break promises", "I ought not steal", and so on—it is just that for her the "ought" is a nonmoral one. And, as I say, perhaps the moral error theorist will read Bloomfield's paper and believe it, thus arming herself with a foundation for thinking that self-interest will *always and for everyone* come out on the side of morality. None of this jars her commitment to a moral error theory in the least.

If any of this feels uncomfortable, then it may be useful to consider an analogy. Picture a theistic error theorist—better known as an "atheist". Suppose there were a kind of prescription that could be marked as "…according to God": "You ought not kill, according to God", "You ought not testify as a false witness against your neighbor, according to God", and so on. The atheist is unmoved by these prescriptions qua divine commands; he doesn't believe in God, so doesn't believe that there are any commands issuing from God, so doesn't believe that one ought not kill, according to God. It hardly follows, however, that the atheist is inclined to go around killing, or, indeed, that his reluctance to kill is in any flimsier than that of the Pope. The atheist may be as determined to refrain from killing as anyone else, for any number of reasons. Perhaps he thinks that it is morally wrong, perhaps he has so much sympathy for his fellow human that the thought sickens him, perhaps he recognizes certain forms of self-harm that would ensue from killing, perhaps all of the above. The atheist is still inclined to enthusiastically assert "I ought not kill"—and perhaps takes himself to have grounds for holding that this is true always and for everyone—but he will remain clear in his own mind that he is not employing the "ought…according to God" locution. And this, clearly, doesn't undermine his atheism in the least.

The comparison between atheism and moral error theory is useful to bear in mind when it comes to responding to a possible objection to what has been argued. The objection runs as follows: You error theorists argue that morality is flawed, yet you still think that we ought to refrain from stealing, keep promises, not initiate violence, and so on. But if the foundational moral question is "How ought one to live?" and you have answered this, by reference to self-interest, in such a way that the answer is "Keep promises, refrain from stealing, don't initiate violence, and so on" then you *have* endorsed a morality. You have allowed that moral normativity can be identified with prudence (or at least with a proper subset of prudence). So your moral error theory collapses.

In order to understand the moral error theorist's response to this objection, some distinctions must first be drawn. We must note, to begin with, the sense in which even the moral error theorist "believes in morality": She believes that *moralities* exist, in the same way that the atheist recognizes that religions exist.[11] What the error theorist does not do is epistemically endorse any morality. I say "*epistemically endorse*" so as to exclude certain pragmatic ways in which a morality might be endorsed, such as approving of its practical output (agreeing that one ought not break promises, ought not steal, etc.), or acknowledging that the institutions of morality are instrumentally beneficial.

---

11. I'll assume without argument that endorsing a religion entails endorsing theism. Some might object to this (raising the case of Buddhism, e.g.), but the niceties of that debate do not interest me.

Note also that the error theorist need not have granted that there *is* a systematic answer to the question "How ought one to live?" Perhaps Ernie should live one way, given his circumstances and upbringing, and Bert should live another, given his. (Indeed, it may be precisely in virtue of thinking that there is no answer to the question "How ought *one* to live?" that someone is a moral error theorist.) But let us suppose that we are dealing with a kind of error theorist who, for whatever reason (perhaps having been convinced by Bloomfield's argument), accepts that the question can receive some kind of universal, systematic answer—that there is a way that "one" ought to live.

The above objection in fact suggests two challenges for this type of moral error theorist. The first is that acknowledging that the question "How ought one to live?" can receive any positive answer in itself constitutes or implies the epistemic endorsement of a morality. The second is that answering this question *in a way that underwrites a particular content* (keeping promises, not stealing, etc.) constitutes the epistemic endorsement of a morality. In both cases the moral error theorist will offer much the same answer: she will disagree because she believes that there is something special about moral normativity (something that, she thinks, is deeply flawed) such that merely to answer how one ought to live, or even to answer it in a way that underwrites keeping promises, and so forth, is insufficient to amount to the epistemic endorsement of a morality. Imagine, by analogy, the atheist facing the objection that insofar as he thinks that there is a way we ought to live then he is, despite himself, really a theist, *because that's all there is to theism*. He will, quite rightly, object that that's *not* all there is to theism, that to epistemically endorse a theistic framework requires subscribing to some substantive metaphysical theses about the existence of a divine being who enjoys such properties as omnipotence, omniscience, and so forth. It is in virtue of disbelieving these theism-constituting theses that the atheist is an atheist. Similarly, the moral error theorist also thinks that to endorse any moral system requires subscribing to some substantive (and, presumably, "metaphysical", in some broad sense of the word) theses, and it is in virtue of her disbelief in these theses that she is a moral error theorist. (The kind of theses in question were pointed to in the third paragraph of this paper.)

In fact, the idea that giving *any* positive answer to the question "How ought one to live?" constitutes the epistemic endorsement of a morality seems highly implausible. Suppose the answer comes back: "Do whatever the hell you feel like". There would seem to be something terribly misleading in the insistence that living according to this rule constitutes endorsing a *morality*. (If one really wanted to stretch the word "morality" to this extent, the moral error theorist can always just disambiguate: "Well, okay, in that unnaturally strained sense of 'moral,' of course I endorse morality—but nevertheless there is a far more familiar customary usage regarding which I remain a disbeliever". We can imagine the atheist saying something comparable if faced with the serious assertion that *God is love*.) The objection, as it is stated above, contains an element that implies that not just *any* positive answer to this question will constitute the endorsement of a morality; rather, there appears to be a contentful constraint on what can count: prudence (or a proper subset thereof[12])

---

12. See note 2. For the sake of brevity I will drop this qualification about proper subsets.

becomes a candidate for constituting a morality only to the extent that it endorses keeping promises, refraining from stealing, not initiating violence, and so on. But even with the addition of this constraint on content, the moral error theorist will — for the same reason as before — remain unimpressed with the proposal that she has, despite herself, endorsed a morality. Whatever argument or arguments have led her to embrace moral skepticism will almost certainly constitute grounds for resisting this objection. To repeat: The moral error theorist believes that for something to be morally bad (say) would require the instantiation of some property that (1) is not supplied by the universe (as a matter of fact or necessarily), and (2) is *essential* to moral badness, such that anything lacking this feature just won't count as moral badness. (For ease of reference, let us call this property the "special feature" that the error theorist attributes to morality.) Assuming that we are dealing with an error theorist who allows that there is nothing particularly fishy about prudence, then we are *ex hypothesi* dealing with someone who thinks that prudential normativity lacks the special feature that dooms moral normativity. Thus the moral error theorist will not think that prudence is a good contender for being identified with moral normativity: Someone whose deliberations are guided solely by prudential considerations — even if these considerations speak in favor of all the things that morality is typically assumed to prescribe — is not thereby epistemically endorsing a morality.

It might be objected — by a moral noncognitivist, for example — that morality is not the kind of thing that requires *epistemic* endorsement at all. It might be objected that the only kind of endorsement needed is practical, and that so long as a person is generally behaving himself then he is endorsing morality in the only sense that matters. However, the dialectical point that I am making is that whatever argument(s) have led a person to defend a moral error theory will include grounds for thinking that moral judgment is a matter of *belief*, that *epistemic* endorsement is coherent and called for. The objection under consideration is that the moral error theorist somehow undermines her own position if she accepts prudential normativity and accepts that it speaks in favor of general niceness. This objection cannot be founded on an insistence that noncognitivism is true, for the error theorist *ex hypothesi* won't agree to this.

For all that, noncognitivism could be true; nothing I say in this paper is designed to convince anyone otherwise. At no point is my intention to establish that the moral error theorist is *correct*. Perhaps the special feature that the error theorist attributes to morality is instantiated by the universe after all. Or perhaps the error theorist is mistaken in thinking that this feature is an *essential* characteristic of moral normativity; perhaps a kind of normativity lacking this feature would nevertheless satisfy enough of our other desiderata to count as the real thing. A moral philosopher advocating an error theory must be prepared to defend herself on both fronts. This job is made difficult by the fact that it is often extremely difficult to articulate precisely what it is that is so troubling about morality. And this failure need not be due to a lack of clear thinking or imagination on the error theorist's part, for the thing that is troubling her may be that there is something deeply mysterious about morality. The moral error theorist may, for example, perceive that moral imperatives are imbued with a kind of mystical practical authority — a quality that, being mysterious, of course *cannot* be articulated in terms satisfactory to an analytic philosopher. Such an error theorist is forced to fall back on vague metaphors in presenting her case: Moral properties have a "to-be-pursuedness" to them (Mackie 1977, 40), moral facts would require that "the universe takes sides" (Burgess [1978] 2007), moral believers are committed to "demands as real as trees and as authoritative as orders from headquarters" (Garner 1994, 61), the phenomenology of believing oneself morally required to act is to think "Well, I just *have* to" (Joyce 2001, 141), and so on. Indeed, it may be the very perniciously vague, equivocal, quasi-mystical, and/or ineliminably metaphorical imponderabilia of moral discourse that troubles the error theorist.[13] (For useful discussion of this point, see Hussain 2004.)

As I have indicated earlier in this paper, it is not my intention on this occasion to present any particular error theoretic argument regarding morality. For a start, doing so would take too long, and, moreover, it is more useful here to keep things broad so as to give consideration to the moral error theorist in a generic sense (hence these unsatisfying references to a "special feature" that the error theorist attributes to morality). It might be thought that without presenting any particular argument it will be impossible to assess whether the error theorist is reasonable in claiming that prudential normativity cannot be identical to moral normativity. It might be thought that we really need to have the error theorist spell out what she takes the essential and problematic feature of morality to be, so we can judge whether she is correct in claiming that prudence lacks it. But in fact I think that we can get a pretty good taste of how that argument will go without committing our (usefully generic) error theorist to any particular line of reasoning. Indeed, it seems to me that anybody—whether error theorist or not—should be extremely uncomfortable about any proposal to identify moral imperatives and values with prudential imperatives and values.

Let us begin by thinking about how prudential normativity works. Suppose it is claimed "Ernie ought not eat cookies in bed", using a plain and simple prudential "ought". The sentence is true (with the prudential "ought") only if eating cookies in bed will harm Ernie in some way. Perhaps doing so will lead to crumbs in his pajamas, leading to sleeplessness. But it is possible that there is harm to other parties involved too. Perhaps what is under consideration is Ernie's decision to eat cookies in *Bert's* bed, thereby annoying (harming) Bert, which will lead to Bert retaliating against (harming) Ernie in some way. (Or perhaps God punishes Ernie, or perhaps Ernie pollutes his own soul, or perhaps Ernie fails to respect himself, etc.—the details don't matter.) The important thing to notice about a prudential "ought" that involves harm to more than one party is the counterfactual asymmetry between the harms: If in eating cookies in Bert's bed Ernie will harm himself but somehow (magically, perhaps) Bert will escape harm, then the prudential claim would remain true; but if in eating cookies in Bert's bed Ernie will harm Bert but will somehow manage

---

13. Compare Wittgenstein, who concluded that moral language is "nonsense" on the basis of his observation that moral discourse consists largely of similes, yet "a simile must be a simile for something…[but] as soon as we try to drop the simile and simply state the facts which stand behind it, we find there are no such facts" ("Lecture on Ethics," *Philosophical Review* 74 [1965]: 10). Interestingly (in light of what I will discuss later in this paper), although he concludes that nonsense is "the very essence" of moral expressions (11), Wittgenstein adds that engaging in moral thinking is a tendency of the human mind that "I personally cannot help respecting deeply and I would not for my life ridicule it" (12).

to avoid the self-harm, then the prudential claim would have to be retracted. (In the latter case, of course, it may remain true that Ernie ought not to eat cookies in Bert's bed, *using some other kind of "ought"*.) Reflecting this, let us say that in prudential normativity the self-harm is *primary*—it is what *makes* the action imprudent.

Now let us contemplate the proposal that moral normativity might be identified with prudential normativity. (Note that I am not targeting the view that acting in morally bad ways is imprudent—Bloomfield's position—but rather the stronger identification claim that moral badness *is* imprudence.) Consider the Nazis, whose actions were so horrendous that even trotting them out endlessly as a philosophical example shouldn't dampen our horror at what they perpetrated. The error theorist may despise the Nazis as much as anyone, but nevertheless withholds assent from the claim that what they did was *morally* wrong. (Obviously, the error theorist needs to be careful in voicing this claim, for it is likely to be misconstrued as indicating some kind of tolerance for the Nazis, whereas in fact she simply thinks that all moral language is bankrupt: that the Nazis' actions were not morally wrong, not morally right, not morally permissible, not morally anything.) Let us focus our attention on a particular SS guard, who herded frightened Jewish children into the gas chambers with full knowledge of what he was doing. Let us stipulate that no possible defense could be mounted for his deeds; if any action is a moral crime, it is his.[14] Now let us adopt the proposal that the wrongness of his actions is nothing more than their imprudence (i.e., that moral badness is imprudence). This means accepting that what primarily makes the guard's action wrong is that he harmed *himself*. The fact that he harmed others contributes to the wrongness, but only derivatively (in that in harming others he harmed himself), and it is the harm to himself that really determines his wrongness. It also means accepting that what determines the *magnitude* of his crime is the magnitude of the injury he does himself (i.e., in harming so many innocent victims he damaged himself severely). Furthermore, it means accepting a counterfactual: that if the guard had killed all those innocent people *but had managed somehow (magically, perhaps) to avoid the consequential self-harm*, then there would have been nothing wrong (i.e., morally/prudentially wrong) with his actions.

This, I hope, sounds appalling. It might not be unreasonable for us to agree that the guard *did* harm himself in various ways, but the idea that the wrongness of his actions derives ultimately from that self-harm is a monstrous thought—almost as monstrous as the thoughts the guard uses to justify his actions to himself. The example illustrates the enormous difference between prudential and moral norms, and does so at an intuitive level, without pretending to articulate what a moral norm is. (We are supposed to think "Whatever exactly a moral norm is, it's not like *that*".) There are many ways to demonstrate the difference between these two types of normativity. To perform an action that harms oneself (e.g., to drink strong coffee before going to bed) may amount to doing something that one ought not to do, but it's not the right

14. The moral error theorist who thinks that moral predicates have empty extensions across all possible worlds will struggle to take this last conditional phrase literally as a counterfactual truth. I submit, however, that even she can understand the spirit of the claim, and treat it as an acceptable rhetorical pronouncement that stands in for some true complex proposition.

kind of "ought-not-ness" to count as a *transgression*—and the notion of transgressing is surely fundamental to moral thinking. The "emotional profiles" of prudence and morality appear intuitively to be very different. Our basic emotional response to someone's self-harm is *pity*. The emotion of *retributive anger* makes little sense within the framework of prudential normativity, for what sense is there in the idea that someone who has harmed himself *deserves* the infliction of further harm (or, moreover, that the severity of the harm we inflict should be proportional to the degree of self-harm)?[15] Harming oneself per se doesn't (and shouldn't) provoke the emotion of *guilt*; it provokes the phenomenologically very different form of self-castigation of thinking "I'm so stupid" (and is *that* what we think the SS guard should be feeling?). Without underwriting guilt, it is implausible that prudential considerations could form the lifeblood of a moral *conscience* in the way that moral considerations do. Consider also the reparations that on many occasions we would insist that the moral criminal make to his victims. On the morality-qua-prudence view, the primary victim of any crime is always the criminal himself. Perhaps compensating the other victims (or simply apologizing to them) will be a means for the criminal to benefit himself, to undo the self-injury that he has inflicted, but there is no reason to assume that this is the only or the best way for him to accomplish this end, and thus if he finds some other way of compensating for the harm he did himself (taking a relaxing holiday? treating himself to a special gift? forgiving himself?) then this act of direct self-profit may well be the preferable course for him.

It may help to clarify my central claim—that moral badness and imprudence are nonidentical—if it is observed that it is consistent with maintaining any or all of the following:

1. Performing actions of the types that are typically thought of as morally bad will cause self-harm.
2. (1) is true always, necessarily, and for everyone.
3. Moreover, the degree of self-harm is proportional to the magnitude of the (assumed) moral badness.
4. Some actions are considered both morally bad *and* imprudent, making it sometimes difficult to tease the two apart.
5. When we try to dissuade someone from performing a morally bad action, the negative consequences that will befall him are likely to be among the first things we mention. (We may even have a deeply entrenched and institutionalized cultural tradition of appealing to the punishments of an all-powerful divine entity in order to back up our moral judgments, thus ensuring that we think of moral transgressions as imprudent.)
6. Sometimes normative frameworks are "nested", such that one is obliged, according to framework A, to follow the prescriptions of framework B.

15. This is not to deny that there may be other grounds for punitive response for which the idea of *desert* plays no role. In punishing the SS guard we may hope to discourage him from harming himself in this manner again, or hope by example to discourage others from such heinous acts of self-harm.

Thus, in some circumstances a person may think it morally required to be prudent. This, again, makes it hard to tease the two apart, but does not indicate the absence of a distinction. (By analogy, a parental authority may decree to a child "Do what the teacher tells you to". If the teacher then orders "No talking", then we may say that not talking has been prescribed both directly by teacherly authority and indirectly by parental authority. But the two normative frameworks are nevertheless distinct, and their respective values and rules may have very different characteristics.)

7. Moral norms need not be exclusively other-regarding.[16] The sentence "You ought not neglect your health" may be used to express a piece of prudential advice, or could be used to state a self-regarding moral imperative. These respective usages would display different characteristics. (If used morally, for example, the "ought" claim will make legitimate certain kinds of criticism for noncompliance that a prudential usage would not.)

8. To observe the distinction between moral normativity and prudence is not to disparage prudence or suggest that it must take a backseat to morality.

The form of argument pursued above—examining the characteristics of a normative system that is being offered as a candidate for vindicating morality, and declaring that it displays insufficient mesh with our pretheoretical desiderata concerning what moral normativity is like—is a regular task for the moral error theorist; she will find herself doing it again and again. Defeating the candidacy of *prudence* is fairly undemanding, I think, and can be successfully accomplished while keeping the discussion at a rough, intuitive level. But the error theorist's task may not always be so easy, and for other claimants it may be necessary for her to spell out in as much detail as possible what she takes to be distinctive (and problematic) about morality, analyze carefully the characteristics of the candidate, and compare the two. The error theorist may accept that some candidates fare better than others—some may have a much better claim than prudence—but she believes that ultimately none comes close enough to deserve the name "morality". The closest satisfiable satisfier of all our moral desiderata still counts at best as "schmorality".

Let me be clear what is meant by "schmorality" in this context. Picture a continuum comprised of what can be thought of (in a benignly vague manner) as "normative frameworks." At one end we have value systems that clearly count as *moralities*: Christian ethics, deontological systems, Moorean intuitionism, Platonic theories about the Form of the *Good*, and so on. The error theorist doesn't doubt that these moralities exist, but she thinks that none of them deserves to be epistemically endorsed. At the other end we have things that clearly don't count as moralities: the rules of chess, etiquette, doing whatever the hell you feel like, and so on. The moral error theorist is free to epistemically endorse the claims of such systems (e.g., she thinks that "You must not move your knight in a straight line" is true). Somewhere on this continuum will lie normative frameworks for which it is not immediately apparent whether they count as moralities: Some people will think

16. Compare Falk (this volume).

they do; others will think they don't. Call these items "contenders", of which one example is prudence. The error theorist, as we have seen, thinks that prudence is a poor contender for being a moral system. (Indeed, even those with no sympathies with moral skepticism should assent to this.) Note that calling prudence a poor contender for being a moral system is not to call it a poor moral system (which would imply that it is a moral system), any more than a hopeless contender for being elected president is thereby a hopeless president.[17] It is not that the error theorist fails to epistemically endorse prudence (she may agree that Ernie ought not eat cookies in bed); but rather she thinks—for the kinds of reasons outlined above—that there is simply insufficient mesh between prudential normativity and moral normativity for prudence to count literally as *a morality*. And the moral error theorist thinks this about *every* contender: either it may be epistemically endorsed but is too far from the "morality" end of the spectrum to count literally as a morality, or it is close enough to count as a morality but (for various reasons) cannot be epistemically endorsed. Indeed, holding this combination of views is constitutive of being a moral error theorist. Every contender is thought to be either unsuccessful–that is, there is nothing in the world answering to its claims, there is nothing that renders these claims true–or a schmorality: something bearing a resemblance to a morality—enough, perhaps, to be mistaken for the real thing by the inattentive—but which falls short of really being so.

What determines whether something is a morality or a schmorality? In my opinion, the answer turns on how the concept *morality* is *used*. If concept A is used in a certain manner, but turns out to be problematic for various reasons (i.e., it is uninstantiated by the world), and concept B is an instantiated contender for replacing A, then B can be an adequate successor only if it too can be used in the same manner. For example, even when we realized that nothing is absolutely simultaneous with anything else, the relativistic notion of simultaneity was able to take over seamlessly, since it works just as well in everyday contexts for creatures whose movements don't approach a significant fraction of the speed of light. We can *use* the concept of relative simultaneity in the same way as we can use absolute simultaneity, which suggests that the change didn't amount to replacing one concept with a different concept at all, but rather we just made a revision internal to a single concept. Thus we are not forced to the radical position that every pre-Einsteinian assertion of two events occurring simultaneously is false. By comparison, when we discovered that there are no diabolical supernatural forces in the universe, we had no further use for the concept *witch*. Perhaps we could have carried on applying the word "witch" to women who play a certain kind of local cultural role on the margins of formal society—perhaps we might even have located a cluster of naturalistic properties that all and only these women have—but carrying on in this way would not have allowed us to *use* the word "witch" for the purposes to which we had previously put it: to condemn these women for their evil magical influence and justify their being killed. Thus, there was little point in persisting in using the word "witch" to stand

---

17. Someone once claimed to me, in all seriousness, that golf was his religion. The correct response is not that golf is a very poor religion, but that it doesn't count literally as a religion at all.

for certain instantiated naturalistic properties; we dropped it and concluded that all historical assertions that certain women were witches—even the loosely spoken ones—were false; we became error theorists about witches.[18]

The question, then, in the moral case, is "What do we use morality for?" The answer will almost certainly be extremely complex, and is, moreover, largely an empirical business. It is extraordinary how rarely this matter has been squarely faced, and deplorable that on those occasions that are exceptions, vague intuitions from the armchair have, more often than not, been thought to suffice. And yet on this question, as we have seen, depends the issue of whether all our moral utterances are true or false. If a contender for satisfying our pretheoretical desiderata for *morality* turns out to be something that we couldn't even use for the purposes that we have customarily put moral discourse—if, for example, we couldn't use it to justify deserved punishment, if it couldn't undergird the emotion of guilt, if it couldn't act as a bulwark against a range of motivational infirmities—then we have good reason for thinking that we have in our hands but a *schmorality*. And if this is so of the *best* satisfiable candidate(s), then we should all be moral error theorists. Obviously, no deliberation of this kind can proceed until we know just what it is that we *do* use moral discourse and moral thinking for. Thus, until the jury delivers its verdict on this empirical matter, the fundamental metaethical disagreement between the moral error theorist and the moral success theorist (i.e., the cognitivist who believes that moral assertions are often true) remains at a stalemate.

Let me give one brief example of this kind of exchange, more for the sake of clarity than argumentative success. David Lewis offers a candidate for satisfying the noun "value": that "something of the appropriate category is a value if and only if we would be disposed, under ideal conditions, to value it" ([1989] 2000, 68). The interesting details need not detain us here; the important point is that one of the discomforting implications of Lewis's offering is that, since human psychology is contingent, we might have valued different things (even under ideal conditions), thus there could have existed values different from those that actually do exist. Lewis's gentle example is that we might have valued seasickness and petty sleaze, but obviously far nastier things could have turned out to be good, according to his theory. Lewis admits that this rampant relativism is a disturbing implication, yet still thinks that his offering may be "as near right as we can get" to satisfying our problematic moral notions, supporting the conclusion that although "strictly speaking" the moral error theorist wins the day, "loosely speaking" values exist (92–93). Lewis may be correct. But how can we tell? How do we know when "Close enough is good enough"? According to my thinking, we must ask whether Lewis's "values" can play the same practical roles in our lives as moral values hitherto have done. What is interesting about Lewis's discussion is that he himself suggests a use to which we put values—one that turns out to undermine the candidacy of his favored claimant. The telling moment comes when he suggests why it is that relativism "feels wrong": He says that perhaps it is because "a large and memorable part of our discussion of values consists

18. This paragraph is taken from my *The Evolution of Morality* (Cambridge, Mass.: MIT Press, 2006), chap. 6.

of browbeating and being browbeaten.[19]…The rhetoric would fall flat if we kept in mind, all the while, that it is contingent how we are disposed to value" (92). Lewis's intention is to diagnose the source of our uneasiness about relativism, but if we take seriously the thought that such rhetorical impact is an important part of the use to which we put moral considerations (both interpersonally and, perhaps, intrapersonally), then he has provided us with evidence *against* the adequacy of his theory of value, since he has identified an important practical purpose that would be lost if we adopted his replacement concept. (It is perhaps a depressing thought that this might be a central function of moral discourse, but, as I declared above, this is something for which hopeful or romantic guesses won't stand in for evidence.[20]) Thus there is at least one consideration—by Lewis's own lights—in favor of thinking that his "values" are not the real McCoy, in favor of thinking that he has provided us with a schmorality rather than a morality.

Suppose the error theorist is correct in holding that the closest satisfiable claimants for our moral concepts are all schmoral concepts. The question arises as to what she then does with moral concepts. The natural assumption is that the error theorist will also be an eliminativist: that she will recommend the abolition of moral language in all unembedded positive contexts. (These last qualifications are supposed to indicate that nobody thinks that we should eliminate moral language *altogether*; the error theorist will still assert things like "There exists nothing that is morally bad" and "St. Augustine believed that stealing pears was morally wrong".) The popular assumption is that if we catch a professed moral error theorist employing moral talk then we can triumphantly cry "Aha!" and accuse her of committing the intellectual vice that Quine (in a tone of disgust) characterized as engaging in "philosophical double talk which would repudiate an ontology while simultaneously enjoying its benefits" (1960, 242). Any such accusation is an argument not against the moral error theory but against the theorist—showing her to be a hypocrite, disingenuous, in bad faith, or vacillating between belief and disbelief. (Perhaps, on the latter charge, the error theorist is like Hume's Pyrrhonian, who, it will be recalled, cannot live his skepticism because "nature [is] too strong for it" [(1740) 1978, 657].)

But eliminativism does not follow logically from the error theory. The question of what one *ought to do* with one's moral discourse need not be a moral inquiry but may be construed as a practical question: Perhaps it involves a prudential "ought", or perhaps a hypothetical "ought" concerning how the agent's (idealized and fully informed?) desires may be optimally satisfied.[21] I don't intend to adjudicate on this

19. Lewis here footnotes Ian Hinckfuss ("The Moral Society: Its Structure and Effects," *Discussion Papers in Environmental Philosophy* 16 [1987]. Canberra: Philosophy Program (RSSS), Australian National University).

20. Of the uses to which we put morality, to ignore some, in this calculation, on the grounds that they are considered "immoral" would, obviously, be to beg the question against the moral error theorist.

21. These disjuncts are distinct on the assumption that psychological egoism is false (an assumption that I feel confident in making). The falsity of psychological egoism means that a person—even a moral skeptic—may have genuinely nonderivative desires for others' welfare. Any "ought" claim that constitutes advice on how such an altruistic desire will be best satisfied need not correspond to a prudential "ought".

matter; all that is of concern here is that it is a kind of practical question that (we have allowed) the moral error theorist has the resources to address. Let us just say that the error theorist will opt to eliminate moral discourse only if that conclusion is supported by some kind of cost-benefit analysis in comparison with other options. Yet what are the other possible options figuring in this calculation? The option of carrying on as if nothing has changed—of continuing to assert moral propositions and to hold moral beliefs *even while maintaining moral error theoretic commitments*— is surely a nonstarter, for the kind of doxastic schizophrenia involved in such a life not only violates epistemic norms but can also be expected to lead to various kinds of pragmatic handicap. But there is a third option: The error theorist may consider taking a fictionalist attitude toward morality. The fictionalist's point of departure is summed up nicely by Hans Vaihinger: "An ideal whose theoretical untruth or incorrectness, and therefore its falsity, is admitted, is not for that reason practically value-less and useless; for such an idea, in spite of its theoretical nullity, may have great practical importance" (1935, viii).

To adopt a fictionalist stance toward morality is to continue to make moral *utterances* and have moral *thoughts*, but withhold assertoric force from the utterances and withhold doxastic assent from the thoughts. The fictionalist can be seen as an error theorist who attends to both epistemic and pragmatic norms.[22] His respect for epistemic norms means that he steadfastly refuses to *believe* any moral claim; his sensitivity to pragmatic norms means that he seeks and embraces the expedient option.[23] On the assumption that morality is in various respects useful when it is asserted and believed, eliminativism will (*ceteris paribus*) constitute a practical cost; and if morality is *very* useful then eliminativism will constitute a *big* cost. The fictionalist option, therefore, becomes attractive if (and only if) it promises to recoup some of these costs. The advocate of fictionalism holds that some of these losses may be recovered by adopting a policy of employing moral language, engaging in moral deliberation, and being moved by moral emotions, but throughout it all remaining disposed to deny the truth of any moral proposition if pressed in an appropriately serious manner (e.g., when in the philosophy classroom), thus not really believing any of it (thus not violating any epistemic norms), and thus deflating a host of well-thumbed philosophical problems concerning the ontology of moral facts and our access to them. Regarding actual moral discourse, the fictionalist remains an error

22. Sometimes the label "fictionalist" refers to a philosopher advocating that we adopt a fictive stance; sometimes it refers to someone who has adopted that stance. (If certain critics of fictionalism are correct, there are no fictionalists in the latter sense.) Though potentially confusing, this equivocation seems benign in most contexts.

23. I should like to draw attention again to the distinction observed in note 21. An error theorist may have reason to adopt the fictive attitude because doing so promises to satisfy certain of her (idealized and fully informed?) desires—and I see no grounds for denying that (some of) these desires may be genuinely altruistic in content. Thus, in fact, it need not be self-interest that recommends the adoption of the fictive stance. Nevertheless, counsel that appeals to self-interest is more likely to have a broader general influence, and thus (giving consideration also to the demands of concision) I will continue to fudge over this subtlety, and speak as if self-interest were the only relevant consideration motivating the fictionalist.

theorist: He thinks that this discourse does aim at the truth but systematically fails to secure it. On the grounds of expediency he advocates a revolution in our attitudes toward morality, and regarding the (imaginary) postrevolution moral discourse, the fictionalist is no error theorist, for, come the revolution, moral discourse will no longer aim at the truth.[24] The tricky part of expounding fictionalism is to make out a kind of attitudinal acceptance *other than belief* that can play a central role in serious intellectual inquiry and serious practical deliberation.

There are many objections to fictionalism in general, and some to moral fictionalism in particular. (For discussion, see Hussain 2004; Kalderon 2005a, 2005b; Nolan, Restall, and West, 2005.) In what remains I will discuss three objections that are similar in that each holds that moral fictionalism somehow undermines the error theory on whose shoulders it stands, thus rendering itself redundant (in the sense that if the error theoretic account of Xs becomes implausible, then although taking a fictive attitude toward Xs remains an intelligible option, there is no need to do so). The first two objections can be interpreted as maintaining that anyone attempting to fictively accept morality must be epistemically endorsing a morality after all. The third objection doesn't quite amount to this, but is related in that it holds that embracing (a particular kind of) fictionalism will destabilize a particular kind of argument in favor of the moral error theory.

First, one might complain that if the policy of uttering and thinking moral propositions can be recommended on prudential grounds, then moral discourse has been vindicated after all. Indeed (the complaint might continue), the fictionalist has supplied evidence against his own error theory, since he has provided grounds for equating moral norms with prudential norms. This is somewhat different from the objection to moral error theories that we encountered earlier. Then the claim was that if the error theorist agrees that *acting* in accordance with assumed moral norms is justified on prudential grounds, then he has provided morality with all the justification that it needs. Now the claim is that if the error theorist agrees that *talking and thinking* in moral terms is justified on prudential grounds, then he has provided morality with all the justification that it needs.[25] But the response is much the same. We should start by bearing in mind the distinction between epistemic justification and instrumental justification. If someone holds a gun to your head and says "Utter the sentence '1 + 1 = 3' or I'll shoot!" then the act of utterance will be prudentially wise (instrumentally justified), but the content of the utterance will be no less false—and any act of believing it no less illegitimate (no more epistemically justified)—for that. Recall that the error theorist has been impressed by the thought

---

24. The kind of fictionalism being described here is the "revolutionary" branch. In contrast, a "hermeneutic" fictionalist argues that we have been taking a fictive attitude toward the target discourse all along (and thus the hermeneutic fictionalist is not an error theorist). Hermeneutic moral fictionalism is advocated by Mark Kalderon (*Moral Fictionalism* [Oxford: Oxford University Press, 2005b]) and criticized by Jason Stanley ("Hermeneutic Fictionalism," *Midwest Studies in Philosophy* 25 [2001]).

25. Crispin Wright may be interpreted as presenting an argument along these lines. See Wright, *Truth and Objectivity* (Cambridge, Mass.: Harvard University Press, 1992), 10; Wright, "Truth in Ethics," in *Truth in Ethics*, ed. B. Hooker (Oxford: Blackwell, 1996), 3.

that moral propositions have substantive metaphysical (and problematic) implications or presuppositions that prudential propositions lack. The fact that the act of uttering one of these flawed sentences may be instrumentally justified hardly shows that the sentence must be true, or that believing the sentence is epistemically justified. Nor does the fact that uttering a normative sentence is prudentially justified mean that the sentence really expresses nothing other than a prudential norm. On this last point it might be useful to consider a comparison. A person might choose to cultivate the personality trait (assuming that it deserves to be so-called) of having altruistic emotions toward his friends and family.[26] Quite how one goes about such an act of "cultivation" need not bother us now; the point is that some act of deliberate choice is involved, which, if successful, results (at some time in the future) in having interests in the welfare of certain others—interests that do not depend on the contribution that the others' welfare makes to one's own interests. The important thing to notice is that at the time of original deliberation the person may be calculating entirely in selfish terms; she may realize that having altruistic emotions will, in various ways, contribute to her own welfare. This observation, however, in no way undermines the possibility that the love and sympathy that this person eventually comes to feel are genuinely altruistic in nature. One can be selfishly motivated to become a less selfish person, and may succeed. Similarly, one can be motivated on grounds of self-interest to adopt a policy of accepting a certain class of normative claims—which are distinct from prudential claims—and may succeed.[27]

The objection just discussed was that moral fictionalism undercuts its own error theoretic basis—that adopting a fictive attitude toward morality amounts to an epistemic endorsement of it—and thus if one wants to maintain a moral error theory one had better eschew fictionalism, which more or less amounts to advocating that the error theorist be an eliminativist. The second objection is that the fictionalist stance is incoherent because the distinction between belief and "acceptance" cannot be maintained (see Putnam 1971, 68–69; Newman 1981). On this view, if someone acts, talks, thinks, and feels in accordance with having moral beliefs, then he actually *does* have moral beliefs. Thus, this objection also amounts to the allegation that attempting to adopt a fictive attitude (about anything this time, not just morality) will amount to an epistemic endorsement, and that if one wants to be an error theorist one had thus better steer clear of fictionalism.

Since *belief* is a contested notion, the suspicion arises that some accounts of belief will allow for a separate category of *acceptance* while others—for example, neobehaviorism—will not. And so it may seem that the only means of responding to this objection is to provide a convincing argument for one of the former accounts. But in fact there is good reason for thinking that *all* parties have cause to allow this distinction, even the neobehaviorist. Consider the crudest kind of behaviorism that

26. Note that here I am considering altruistic emotions in a nonmoral sense. To *like* someone—to have a nonderivative concern for his welfare, to be motivated to act to further his interests, to feel affection toward him—is a capacity that might be enjoyed by a creature entirely lacking the cognitive sophistication to make any moral judgments at all. (See notes 9 and 10.)

27. Compare David Schmidtz, "Choosing Ends," *Ethics* 104 (1994), on "maieutic ends".

says that all it is to believe that p is to act as if one takes p to be the case. Even so boorishly extreme a behaviorism will want to allow that on occasions a person may act as if she takes p to be the case without believing that p. Actors, for example. This observation alone forces the acknowledgment of some category of acceptance distinct from belief: It is the attitude actors take toward elements of the fiction into which they enter. The thing about actors, of course, is that they are disposed to "step out" of the fiction; they don't act *all the time* as if they take p to be the case. But the crucial detail to notice about the fictionalist is that he too remains disposed to step out. There are contexts where he does *not* speak as if he takes p to be the case: namely, when he is in the critical context of declaring his endorsement of the moral error theory.

But the person pressing this objection may persist. Even though acknowledging some kind of attitude—distinct from belief—deserving the name "acceptance", she may doubt that one can be in this state with respect to some subject matter *nearly all the time*. Our crude behaviorist may revise slightly: All it is to believe that p is to act *at least nearly all the time* as if one takes p to be the case. The idea that the matter might depend on the *amount of time* one spends "immersed" in the fiction compared to the amount of time one spends "outside" it, strikes me as terribly improbable. What constitutes "nearly" here? Even acknowledging that the answer may be vague ("Around 90 percent"), it seems crazy to think that if I spend 95 percent of my time acting as if p were the case then I believe that p, but if I spend only 85 percent of my time acting in this way—all else remaining the same—then I do not believe that p. (I'm sure there's a better objection to this than "Horrible theory!" but I'm happy on this occasion to rest matters there and trust in the reader's agreement.)

Far preferable would be the provision of some account of the *nature* of the two kinds of context, such that we can see that in one context utterances match what one really believes, even if it is a context entered into very rarely in comparison with the other context. Above I called the context of expressing disbelief (e.g., when doing metaethics) the more "critical" context, and this is the term I have used on other occasions (Joyce 2001, 2005). It is, perhaps, an ill-chosen word, since it suggests that there is something "uncritical" about the fictionalist's engagement with moral matters in everyday life. It is important to see that "critical" here is a term of art, indicating an asymmetrical relationship between the two kinds of context (or, rather, naming a pole at one end of a continuum of contexts). Context n is more critical than context m if and only if n is characterized by a tendency to scrutinize and challenge the presuppositions of m, but not vice versa. This is consistent with m being the more "critical" in a vernacular sense of the word. For example, working out the plot of a complex novel may involve a great deal of careful thinking, whereas the thought "It's all just a fiction" is a simple matter. Nevertheless, in the sense intended, the latter is the more "critical" context since it questions the world of the novel. Similarly, when immersed in morality the fictionalizing error theorist may deliberate extremely carefully about consequences, weigh outcomes thoroughly, deploy acute powers of imagination and reflection, and so on, and yet still not inhabit his "most critical context" where he denies moral truth across the board. Though this amounts to not much more than a gesture—most prominently leaving us wondering just what is meant by "scrutinize and challenge"—I believe it is a promising way of addressing the problem, which, if successful, will make the *amount of time* one spends in the critical context irrelevant to the question of what one believes.

Those who doubt the viability of the belief/acceptance distinction may have their skepticism alleviated if they reflect on the seeming ubiquity of the phenomenon—or, at least, of closely related phenomena. The human proclivity for engaging with fiction (novels, movies, etc.) is the most conspicuous example, but arguably there are many less obvious instances of similar mechanisms operating in everyday life. Michael Bratman (1992) has argued persuasively that all practical reasoning involves accepting (but not believing) certain propositions as a background to effective deliberation. On the assumption that psychological simulation involves a kind of acceptance-without-belief, acceptance may be implicated in hypothetico-deductive reasoning, ascribing mental states to others, and predicting others' behavior (see discussion in Davies and Stone 1995a, 1995b). Simulation probably plays a central role in empathy (Goldman 1992) and visual imagination (Currie 1995). Vaihinger (1935) supplies numerous mundane examples of our treating something "as if" it were true while knowing that it is not. (While Vaihinger almost certainly errs on the side of overenthusiasm, his catalog of examples of the fictional stance is nonetheless instructive.)[28]

The fictionalist's strategy here is unashamedly one of finding partners in innocence. Although it is unlikely that there is a single belief/acceptance distinction that all the aforementioned phenomena exhibit, there is enough family resemblance here that it is not unreasonable for the fictionalist to think that by cozying up *his* kind of belief/acceptance distinction to these other commonplace examples he can dispel some knee-jerk doubts. Is someone who reads a novel disingenuous or self-deceived? Is someone who engages in role-play suffering from anything deserving the name "schizophrenia"? Is someone who accepts a proposition as a background assumption when deliberating manifesting bad faith? Does feeling empathy make one a hypocrite? And does engaging any or all of these practices have deleterious effects on one's interests? I take it that the answer to all is "No". Now, as admitted, the kind of belief/acceptance distinction at the heart of the moral fictionalist's case may not be quite the same as these other instances, but its similarity to these "innocent" examples is sufficient at least to show that such accusations (that the practicing fictionalist is in bad faith, suffers from self-deception, etc.) cannot be pronounced lightly. The onus, of course, is first on the fictionalist to articulate with precision what the distinction he has in mind amounts to; accusations of bad faith, schizophrenia, and so forth must be suspended until then. Then, of course, the burden falls to the opponent of fictionalism to replace the vague rhetorical sense of terms like "bad faith" and "schizophrenia" with something literal (and obviously undesirable).

28. There are other "belief versus acceptance" distinctions in the philosophical literature that probably have little to do with the phenomenon (or family of phenomena) that is relevant here. Bayesian decision theorists often distinguish between partial belief and full acceptance (see M. Swain, ed., *Induction, Acceptance, and Rational Belief* [Dordrecht, Holland: D. Reidel, 1970]). There is debate about whether collectives of individuals can have belief or merely acceptance (see K. B. Wray, "Collective Belief and Acceptance," *Synthese* 129 [2001]). See also L. J. Cohen, *An Essay on Belief and Acceptance* (Oxford: Clarendon, 1992); K. Frankish, "A Matter of Opinion," *Philosophical Psychology* 11 (1998).

The third objection to fictionalism that I will briefly comment on targets a particular brand of moral fictionalism—but since it is a kind that I have on occasion defended (Joyce 2001, 2005), I feel moved to respond. The fictionalism in question is one that hypothesizes that engaging in moral discourse is useful in a particular way: namely, that this engagement stimulates *motivation* in a pragmatically desirable manner. (Any fictionalist theory that assigns a different sort of usefulness to morality will not be affected by this objection.) It may be hypothesized, for example, that the expediency of moral discourse derives from its capacity to act as a bulwark against various kinds of practical infirmity—for example, weakness of will, discounting future gains, and so on—better than clearheaded instrumental deliberation. Thinking of an action as something that "just *must* be done" may encourage performance of that action more reliably than explicitly conceiving of the action as one that serves one's long-term best interests; imagining the omission of that action to be something that will not merely frustrate one's desires but make one *reprehensible* and *deserving of punishment* may be more likely to result in resolve to perform the action. This, it seems to me, is an intuitively attractive idea, especially when it is made clear that the moral judgment may come "embedded" in an emotion, such as guilt or punitive anger. There is plenty of empirical evidence that self-directed moral emotions have motivational efficacy (see Carlsmith and Gross 1969; Freedman 1970; Tangney and Dearing 2002; Ketelaar and Au 2003; Zhong and Liljenquist 2006; Tangney et al. 2007).

So what problem does this hypothesis pose for fictionalism? There is of course the burning question of how taking a *fictive* attitude toward a set of norms and values could possibly engage motivation in this way. But that is an empirical question that I don't propose to discuss here (see Joyce 2001, 2005, 2006); rather, I am interested in the theoretical question of whether supporting this hypothesis makes trouble for the error theoretic basis of fictionalism. There are two reasons for thinking that it might. The first is that if a moral judgment engages motivation in this manner, then doubt is cast on the claim that moral judgments are a cognitive affair. But if moral judgments are in fact a *noncognitive* affair, then the moral error theory collapses, for one of the distinguishing features of this metaethical theory is its commitment to cognitivism.

This objection is confused. Noncognitivism is a thesis about what kind of mental state(s) moral judgments express; it denies that the state expressed is *belief* (i.e., it denies that moral judgments are assertions). One popular form of noncognitivism— emotivism—claims that what is expressed is some (specifiable) conative or emotional state. To advocate cognitivism, however, is not to make the wild claim that moral judgments have nothing to do with emotions. Cognitivism is compatible with the view that moral judgments reliably prompt emotional activity. It is compatible with the view that moral judgments generally, or even always, flow from seething emotional activity in the brain. It is compatible with the view that what goes on when one makes a moral judgment is that one "projects" one's emotional life onto the events of the world. It is compatible with the view that the human capacity for moral judgment is a discrete biological adaptation that evolved precisely by virtue of its tendency to affect human emotions in a fitness-enhancing manner. None of these possibilities—nor, indeed, all of them jointly—entails the denial of the claim that moral judgments are assertions. Cognitivism is compatible even with the claim that the connection between moral judgments and emotional activity is a *necessary* one (though I should add that this is not a claim I endorse). Consider, by analogy, the act of promising. The criteria for a promise to have occurred involve a range of linguistic conventions in which both promiser and promisee need be versed; for example, the addressee must hear and understand the words uttered, and the speaker must take it that this is the case. If the addressee doesn't hear the "I promise…" claim, or doesn't understand what the utterance signifies, then the act of promising misfires, and no promise has occurred (see Austin 1962). The satisfaction of these criteria will require both speaker and addressee to have certain *beliefs*—for example, the speaker must believe that his addressee hears and understands. This connection is a necessary one: It is not possible that any person could succeed in making a promise to another person without having such a belief. And yet we would hardly say that the act of promising *functions to express the belief that one's audience hears and understands* (rather, a promise expresses an intention). Therefore, since a kind of speech act and a mental state may be necessarily linked without the former *functioning to express* the latter, then even if it were the case that moral judgments necessarily engage motivational states, noncognitivism is not the automatic conclusion (see Joyce 2002).

The second potentially problematic implication of assuming that the usefulness of moral thinking lies in its impact on motivation is even more limited in scope: It is a problem only for the error theorist who has employed a particular kind of argument to establish her error theory. Several philosophers who harbor skeptical misgivings about morality derive their doubts (in part) from a commitment to a Humean psychology, according to which beliefs and desires are distinct and but contingently linked states (see Williams 1981; Mackie 1977; Joyce 2001). John Mackie, for example, thinks that moral imperatives imply external reasons claims[29] (to import Bernard Williams's terminology), but, like Williams, he thinks that all non-institutional reasons claims are internal. (An internal reason is one that suitably connects with a person's "subjective motivational set"; an external reason is one that does not.) The basis of this latter opinion (for Williams at least) is the thought that any reason must potentially motivate a person, but only internal reasons can do so—and his ground for thinking this is that believing oneself to have an external reason cannot (alone) prompt motivation, because no belief can do that.

It should be stressed again that one might be a moral error theorist on grounds having nothing to do with any of these considerations. But if one *is* moved by this argumentative thread to adopt a moral error theory, and if, in addition, one is moved to become a fictionalist by the thought that morality is useful *because of its influence on motivation*, then, it may be supposed, one has some explaining to do. (It may sound like a fairly specialized position that is being defended—and indeed it is so—but it is not an uninhabited position, and the objection has been raised on more than one occasion.[30]) How could a moral *belief* (understood in Humean terms)

29. See J. L. Mackie, *The Miracle of Theism* (Oxford: Clarendon, 1982), 115.

30. Yes, I'm afraid I've been reading the reviews of my own book (*The Myth of Morality* [Cambridge: Cambridge University Press, 2001]); see S. McKeever, review of *The Myth of Morality*, by Richard Joyce. *Ethics* 114 (2003); and R. J. Wallace, review of *The Myth of Morality*, by Richard Joyce, *Notre Dame Philosophical Reviews* (2003). See also N. J. Z. Hussain, "The Return of Moral Fictionalism," *Philosophical Perspectives* 18 (2004).

function to influence motivation? In fact, the explaining is fairly easy. The hypothesis that moral judgments are useful because they influence motivation need involve only the claim that moral judgments *often* or *reliably* or *defeasibly* or *contingently* engage motivational structures. (Indeed, even "sometimes" will suffice.) It is perfectly possible that moral beliefs are just that—beliefs—and that beliefs alone never prompt motivation; but it may also be claimed that such beliefs, when they figure in an ordinary person's psychological economy—an economy that includes typical desires and emotions—will generally have an impact on motivation.

Having deflected these criticisms (and finding no other compelling), I feel confident in claiming that the fictionalist position is at least *coherent*. Whether the fictionalist stance is psychologically feasible, and whether it will supply the promised pragmatic gains, remain serious empirical uncertainties. Though on other occasions I have advocated the case for fictionalism (Joyce 2001, 2005), it must be underscored—as I did at the time—that while there is certainly a place for plausible speculation when it comes to directing people's attention, nothing confident can be claimed in advance of the *a posteriori* footwork. Perhaps in the end the data will not favor the fictionalist option. Perhaps eliminativism will be the better course for the moral error theorist, in which case she may use the term "schmorality" in its customary pejorative sense: to scoff "*Morality, schmorality!*" But it is important to remind ourselves that even the eliminativist error theorist will still have plenty of good and strong reasons—many of them self-interested reasons—for being nice to her fellows.

B. Morality on the Offensive

4

Because It's Right

DAVID SCHMIDTZ

Morality teaches us that, if we look on her only as good for
something else, we never in that case have seen her at all.
She says that she is an end to be desired for her own sake,
and not as a means to something beyond. Degrade her,
and she disappears.

—F. H. Bradley ([1876] 1927, 58)

I. Does Moral Philosophy Rest on a Mistake?

Morality can be painfully demanding, so much so that we sometimes question the wisdom of complying with it. Yet, arguments that we have good reason to be moral are as old as Plato's *Republic*. Indeed, according to H. A. Prichard, making this argument work is the central preoccupation of moral philosophy. But Prichard also believes that to the extent this is true, the whole subject of moral philosophy rests on a mistake (1968, 1).[1]

---

1. At one time, Philippa Foot (*Virtues and Vices* [Berkeley and Los Angeles: University of California Press 1978], 126) agreed with Plato that "if justice is not a good to the just man, moralists who recommend it as virtue are perpetrating a fraud". Likewise, David Gauthier (*Morals by Agreement* [Oxford: Oxford University Press, 1986], 2) says "the acceptance of duty is truly advantageous". Kurt Baier ("Moral Reasons and Reasons to Be Moral," in *Values and Morals*, ed. A. I. Goldman and J. Kim [Dordrecht: D. Reidel, 1978]) and Kai Nielsen (*Why Be Moral?* [Buffalo: Prometheus, 1989]) agree that "Why be moral?" is a legitimate question, although Nielsen's answer is pessimistic. On the other side, Prichard's view that the question itself is illegitimate is endorsed by J. C. Thornton ("Can the Moral Point of View Be Justified?" in *Readings in Contemporary Ethical Theory*, ed. K. Pahel and M. Schiller [Englewood Cliffs, N.J.: Prentice Hall, 1970]), Dan Brock ("The Justification of Morality," *American Philosophical Quarterly* 14 [1977]), and John McDowell ("Are Moral Requirements Hypothetical Imperatives?" *Proceedings of the Aristotelian Society* 52 supp. [1978]), among others. Prichard was not the first to take such a view, either. For example, see essay II of F. H. Bradley's *Ethical Studies* (Oxford: Oxford University Press, [1876] 1927) or Henry Sidgwick's introduction to *The Methods of Ethics*, 7th ed. (Chicago: University of Chicago Press, [1907] 1962).

Prichard is neither the first nor the last person to dismiss an entire discipline as a mistake, but Prichard has an argument that poses a real challenge to moral philosophy, an argument that repays sympathetic analysis. Prichard's article emerges from a particular and peculiar philosophical tradition known as British intuitionism, yet the challenge it poses to moral philosophy is anything but parochial. On the contrary, the article has had and continues to have an influence independent of, even in spite of, the intuitionist tradition from which it emerges. For example, it anticipates and to some extent undoubtedly inspires the current antitheory movement in ethics.[2] Nevertheless, although dozens of articles cite Prichard's famous essay, often with approval, it has seldom met with sustained criticism.[3] This paper reconstructs and criticizes Prichard's argument, then uses that critique to lay foundations for the larger project of constructing a plausible moral philosophy.

Prichard says we begin to question whether we really ought to do our alleged duty—to keep a promise, for example—when we recognize that doing our duty will not give us what we desire. We then question things we usually accept as duties. We ask if there is any proof that we truly have a duty to act in ways usually called moral.[4] Prichard sees two ways of interpreting this request. We could be asking whether being moral is prudent. Alternatively, we could be asking whether being moral is good in some nonprudential sense—good for others, for example, or intrinsically good quite apart from its consequences (2).[5] Prichard thinks both versions of the question are mistakes, and I will look at each in turn.

How can we determine what is moral in the first place? We cannot simply check what is moral. At least, we cannot do so in the same way we can check who is prime minister. Nevertheless, like the term "prime minister", the word "moral" is a word we

2. Antitheorists characterize (and consequently reject) moral theorizing as an attempt to mechanically deduce all particular moral conclusions from a single universal principle. Robert Louden (*Morality and Moral Theory* (New York: Oxford University Press, 1992), chaps. 5 and 6) agrees that any theory fitting that description ought to be rejected, but argues that the best and historically most prominent moral theories (i.e., those of Aristotle and Kant) do not fit the description.

3. W. D. Falk ("'Ought' and Motivation," reprinted in *Ought, Reasons, and Morality* [Ithaca, N.Y.: Cornell University Press, 1986]) accuses Prichard of equivocating between internalist and externalist senses of moral "oughts". The only other substantial critique of Prichard, to my knowledge, is Kurt Baier ("Moral Reasons and Reasons to Be Moral," in *Values and Morals*, ed. A. I. Goldman and J. Kim (Dordrecht: D. Reidel, 1978), 231–38). For an especially acute critique of intuitionism more generally, see Stephen Darwall "Ethical Intuitionism and the Motivation Problem," in P. Stratton-Lake, ed., *Ethical Intuitionism: Re-evaluations* (Oxford: Clarendon), 2002.

4. Actually, I suppose today we frame the question in terms of right action rather than moral action. My main reason for moving between these terms is stylistic, speaking of doing what is moral when I am trying to follow Prichard and of doing what is right otherwise. When speaking of persons rather than of actions (*being* moral as opposed to being prudent), or of separating the subject of morality from other subjects such as prudence, I find "being moral" and "morality" more natural than "being right" and "rightness", but again, my reasons for choosing one word rather than another are in most cases stylistic rather than deeply philosophical.

5. Except where otherwise noted, page references in this chapter are to H. A. Prichard, *Moral Obligation* (Oxford: Oxford University Press, 1968).

inherit from an existing language. It comes to us laden with meaning. We can stipulate what we will be referring to when we say "brillig", for that is not a term of ordinary language, but there are only so many things we could correctly refer to as "eggplant". Like the word "eggplant", the word "moral" is more than a made-up sound. We cannot simply stipulate that it refers to, say, the property of maximizing utility, any more than we could stipulate that the word "eggplant" refers to rutabagas.

A term's *extension* consists of the set of things to which the term refers. The term "prime minister" may, under certain circumstances, have Jean Chrétien as its extension. Even so, we would not want to say Jean Chrétien is the *meaning* of the term "prime minister". One implication is that we might not know who is prime minister, despite knowing exactly what the term means. Similarly, even if we settle what the word "moral" means, we can still be uncertain about what is in fact moral.

As it actually happens, though, we tend to be surer of the word's extension than of its meaning. We have a shared understanding that being moral involves being honest, kind, peaceful, and so on. (I will refer to this consensus as commonsense morality.) It may not be part of the meaning of "moral" that honesty is moral, but honesty may be and commonly is understood to be part of the term's extension.

Moreover, the consensus is not only that we should call these things moral but also that we should *be* these things, which gives us a clue to the word's meaning. When a person refers to an act by saying, "That's immoral" listeners normally understand the speaker to be saying there is reason not to do the act.[6] Further, listeners will interpret the speaker as saying something other than that the act will not satisfy an agent's desires. When a person says lying is immoral, listeners normally will understand the speaker to mean there is a *special* reason not to lie—special because it is grounded in something other than an appeal to the agent's desires.

This way of understanding the term's use may not fully capture the term's meaning, any more than a set of injunctions to be kind, honest, and peaceful fully covers morality's extension. The conclusion (so far) is only that moral reasons are understood to appeal to something other than the agent's desires. Moral reasons are *categorical*, which means they have a claim on us independent of how they appeal to our interests and desires.[7]

When people argue about what is right, they may disagree about what constitutes this special kind of reason. Or they may agree that the property of maximizing pleasure constitutes a special reason for endorsement, but quarrel over which actions (or character traits or institutions, etc.) have this property. Even so, when people argue about

---

6. It seems easier here to speak of wrongness rather than rightness as being associated with special reasons for action. That one course of action involves telling the truth does not imply that one should take that course, but that another course of action involves telling a lie has clear implications. Roderick Wiltshire ("The Wrong and the Good," unpublished) argues that wrongness is a natural kind and rightness is not. Rightness is simply the logical complement of wrongness, in the way "nondog" is the logical complement of "dog".

7. I use the terms *categorical* and *deontological* almost interchangeably. An imperative is categorical if it makes no appeal to the agent's interests and desires, and deontological if it makes no appeal to consequences of any kind. Thus, as I use the terms, a categorical imperative is a kind of deontological imperative.

whether something like affirmative action is right, they have a shared understanding that it *matters* whether affirmative action is right. People who argue about what is moral share an understanding that in order for an act to be morally required there must be a special reason to do it. That is why people care about what conclusion they reach regarding whether something like affirmative action is morally required (or forbidden). As they see it, whether they have special reasons to support (or resist) the practice goes hand in hand with whether the practice is morally required (or forbidden).

But do we need to prove we have such special reasons? As Prichard sees it, moral philosophy rests on the mistaken assumption that we do — a mistaken assumption that without proof that we have special reasons, we have no basis for saying we *ought* to conform to commonsense morality. Why is this assumption a mistake? Prichard asks us to consider how we would prove that conforming to commonsense morality (which I will refer to as being CS-moral) is moral. According to Prichard, there are two ways to try to prove that being CS-moral is moral, and both of them inevitably fail. The first way is to prove that being CS-moral will give us something we want (3). The second way is to prove there is something good (not necessarily for us) either in right action's result or in right action itself. Prichard's objections to these two approaches are as follows.

The first way fails because proving that being CS-moral will give us what we want is beside the point. The demonstration may show that being CS-moral is prudent, but not that being CS-moral is moral. As Prichard puts it, the exercise might convince us that we want to be CS-moral but cannot convince us that we ought to be (3).[8] To show that being CS-moral is moral, we have to show that we have characteristically moral reasons to be CS-moral, that is, reasons that at a minimum do something more than appeal to our desires.

The second way, according to Prichard, boils down to saying happiness or working for happiness is good and therefore we should work for happiness in general (or if not for happiness, then for whatever the fundamental good happens to be). This answer has an advantage over the first approach, for at least it clearly does more than appeal to our desires. (Even if the act is for our own good only, this goes somewhat beyond mere appeal to desires.) But this second way also fails, Prichard says, for it presupposes the view that the rightness of acts has to do with what they accomplish. The "fatal objection" to any teleological theory "is that it resolves the moral 'ought' into the nonmoral 'ought', representing our being morally bound to do some action as if it were the same thing as the action's being one which we must do if our purpose is to become realized (p.117)".[9]

8. And, as Stephen Toulmin ("The Logic of Moral Reasoning, and Reason and Faith," in *Readings in Contemporary Ethical Theory*, ed. K. Pahel and M. Schiller [Englewood Cliffs, N.J.: Prentice Hall, 1970], 417) adds, making us want to do what we ought to do is not the philosopher's task.

9. Prichard's point applies to theories grounding rightness in collective prudence as well. So Prichard's objection not only challenges the Platonic project but also most contractarian theories as well. For example, the objection cuts against the view expressed by Kurt Baier ("Why Should We Be Moral?" *Readings in Contemporary Ethical Theory*, ed. K. Pahel and M. Schiller [Englewood Cliffs, N.J.: Prentice Hall, 1970]) that we should be moral because being moral makes us all better off.

So goes my reconstruction of Prichard's argument.[10] In summary, the rightness of keeping a promise, say, does not depend on whether keeping it will have good results at all, let alone on whether keeping it is in the promisor's interest. Because attempts to prove we ought to do what we believe is right inevitably appeal in one way or another to the goodness of doing what we believe is right (2), Prichard concludes that the only place to look for an answer to the question of why we should do what is right is manifestly the wrong place to look. The reductionist urge to ground rightness in something more fundamental is misguided, for rightness neither can be nor needs to be grounded in anything else. The sense of an action's rightness is, in fact, absolutely immediate (7). We see that being CS-moral is moral by direct apprehension, if we see it at all. Trying to *prove* that being CS-moral is moral is a mistake not unlike the epistemological mistake of trying to prove we are awake when we know we are awake by direct apprehension (16). It is an instance of the mistake of seeking a grounding for that which is itself bedrock.

The next two sections respond to Prichard's argument. I argue that there is no mistake in asking whether being moral is prudent. Then I argue that there is no mistake in asking whether it truly is moral to do things like keep promises.

II.   Morality versus Prudence

Prichard concedes that it can be perfectly legitimate to ask why we should perform a certain act when the act is incompletely described in relevant ways. The question becomes illegitimate, in Prichard's view, when the act is described well enough that special reasons to perform the act are, in effect, built into the act's description. For example, it may not be obvious that Kate has reason to give her neighbor a hundred dollars, but it is perfectly obvious that she has reason to *repay a debt* by giving him a hundred dollars (8). Described in this more complete way, the act carries its reason on its sleeve. When an act is described in such a way that asking why we should do it becomes tantamount to asking why we should do what is required, the answer becomes obvious: we should do it because it is required.[11]

Still, an act that is well described in moral terms may remain incompletely described in prudential terms. The question "What's in it for me?" may remain unanswered. We could dismiss the latter question as morally irrelevant, but this would be to ignore the question rather than answer it. Even if Prichard is correct that it is impossible to give an argument why we *morally* ought to do the right thing, this does not foreclose the possibility that philosophers might yet show that it is prudent to do the right thing. Nothing in Prichard's argument counts against undertaking the Platonic project of showing that being moral is profitable.

---

10. Prichard also rejects the idea that an action's rightness lies not in its actual result but rather in its intended result, but present purposes do not require us to address this further argument.

11. To call an act right is ambiguous. One might be saying the act is required or that it is permitted. The former sense is more relevant here. I use *right* and *required* interchangeably in what follows.

Prichard goes on, however, to engage the Platonic project more directly. Prichard says proving that we have a prudential motive to do the right thing would be beside the point. If we are talking about being moral, we are not talking about doing the right thing for prudential reasons. Rather, to be genuinely moral is to do the right thing precisely because it is right. In Prichard's words, "a morally good action is morally good not simply because it is a right action but because it is a right action done because it is right, i.e., from a sense of obligation" (10).[12]

It may seem, as evidently it seemed to Prichard, that the project of reconciling prudence and morality cannot proceed unless this Kantian line of argument is rebutted. This is not so. Even if we grant that being moral involves following a categorical imperative, we remain free to ask whether we are better off following a categorical imperative. And one way or another, the question has an answer. Whether or not moral imperatives are categorical, there remains a fact of the matter concerning whether following moral imperatives is to our advantage. To try to show that being moral turns out to be prudent is not to assume that moral imperatives are prudential imperatives. On the contrary, we can try to prove a conditional of the form "If I want X, then I should be moral" without in any way presuming that moral imperatives have this same conditional form.

If we were asking whether prudence can be a proximate *motive* for being moral and if we took "being moral" to entail "being motivated by a sense of rightness rather than by prudence", then Prichard's objection would be decisive. The question would be a mistake. The actual question, however, is whether there is an extensional overlap between being moral (and thus being motivated by a sense of rightness) and being prudent, in which case Prichard's objection is off topic.[13] Asking whether doing the right thing is prudent does not presume only prudential answers could motivate our being moral. It does not presume prudence is even *among* the things that could motivate our being moral.

Demonstrating the existence of an extensional overlap need not motivate people to be moral. But really, that was never the point. The point is that even agents committed to doing what is right *because it's right* might nevertheless wonder whether they would have done anything differently had they been more self-consciously prudent. Moral agents might care about this issue not because they seek a motivation for being moral but rather because they, like Glaucon, sometimes wonder whether they have prudential reasons to *regret* being moral.

In summary, Prichard thinks it is a mistake to try to prove that being moral is for our own good, for the attempt presupposes that whether we ought to be moral

---

12. Perhaps this is why Prichard thought the connection between the sense of rightness and one's reason to be moral has to be "absolutely immediate". If anything intrudes between the two, one will no longer be doing the right thing for the right reason.

13. Prudence involves acting in one's best interest simpliciter rather than acting in one's best interest *because* it is in one's best interest. Otherwise, if we interpret prudence in the latter sense, prudence and morality exhibit a particularly uninteresting kind of incompatibility; the real issue about the overlap between moral and prudent behavior will inevitably resurface, cast in other terms.

depends on whether being moral is prudent.[14] But we need presuppose no such thing. Asking about these things does not commit us to reducing morality or moral motivation to mere prudence. This version of the question is no mistake.

III. What Do We Do When We Do the Right Thing?

The previous section conceded that we should do what is right because it is right, but showed that this concession is hardly a conversation stopper. Whether it is prudent to be moral remains an issue. Further, even from the moral point of view, it is not enough to say we should do what is right because it is right. As Prichard would agree, the question we face as moral agents is not about philosophical generalizations, but rather about what to do when we get face-to-face with particular situations. And saying we should do what is right would be to miss the point of our asking what we should do. The point is, we need to have concluded that a course of action *is* right before the incantation "because it's right" can express a reason to undertake that particular course of action. Naturally, we should do what is right, and we should do so because it is right. But why should we keep promises? Why, in some rare cases, should we break them? Why should we tell the truth? Why, in some rare cases, should we lie instead? What should we think keeping promises and telling the truth have anything to do with rightness?

"Why should I do what is morally required?" is the sort of question that wears its moral answer on its sleeve, even if it does not wear its prudential answer on its sleeve. But that is not the same kind of question as "Why should I tell the truth?" Rightness may wear moral motivation on its sleeve, but what rightness patently does not wear on its sleeve is its extension. Indeed, the question of which particular actions are right remains wide open. So Prichard has not only left undone the legitimate task of

14. One could see Prichard as rejecting rationalism in ethics in the same way Michael Oakeshott rejects rationalism in politics. That is, we understand and appreciate ethical traditions only from the inside, by living within them and by knowing their history. It is hubris to criticize traditions on the grounds that they fail to serve purposes we think ought to be served, or that they do not serve their purposes as well as imaginable alternatives. Such criticism is from the outside in, which is not a legitimate critical perspective. Instead, one must get inside the institution and experience the duties it imposes face-to-face and case-by-case. See the title essay in Oakeshott (*Rationalism in Politics* [Indianapolis: Liberty, 1991]). This theme also runs through the work of Alasdair MacIntyre. (The thesis that modern moral concepts are holdovers from earlier traditions, in which they had a significance that has since been lost, finds one of its earliest and most concise expressions in G. E. M. Anscombe ["Modern Moral Philosophy," *Philosophy* 33 (1958): 1, 5–8].)

Now, there is merit in the Anscombe-MacIntyre-Oakeshott line of argument. Nevertheless, moral philosophy is itself a body of traditions and practices. Distancing oneself from the practice of criticizing ethical traditions and viewing that practice with a critical eye amounts to taking an outside-in approach to a central tradition of moral philosophy. Thus, to indulge in such criticism is also to tacitly endorse outside-in criticism. In effect, it involves criticizing philosophy from outside in by pointing out that philosophy too partakes of outside-in criticism. A telling critique will say something interesting about how to distinguish between the use and misuse of outside-in criticism.

identifying prudential reasons not to regret being moral; he has also left us the more fundamental task of identifying what morality requires.

The latter was no accident, of course, for Prichard was, after all, an intuitionist. He says we intuit what is right. Be this as it may, the question in which we are actually interested is logically prior to this epistemological question. That is, even if we grant that there are occasions on which we intuit that some act X is right, we still want to know what it is about X that triggers our intuitions.[15] Consider this: if we had no idea what triggers our intuitions, what grounds would we have for taking our intuitions seriously?[16]

One might insist that intuitionism is not only an epistemological thesis but also a thesis about what rightness is; a right action simply is an action that directly and immediately strikes us as something we have reason to do. I do not believe Prichard held this ontological thesis, but in any event, this ontological variant of intuitionism amounts to a rather sinister reductionism. It reduces rightness to the sphere of that which directly and immediately strikes us as required. Consider what it implies about things we do not directly and immediately apprehend as required—things whose rightness (or wrongness) we do not come to fully appreciate merely by getting face-to-face with them. If we cannot directly apprehend that keeping a certain promise is required, may we rule out *on those grounds* the possibility that keeping the promise is required? Surely not.

If we take intuitionism to be addressing the question of what rightness is, we are taking it to be an alternative *kind* of reductionism rather than an alternative *to* reductionism. It is more charitable to accept that Prichard's intuitionist epistemology leaves open the ontological question about what properties occasion our intuitions.

Perhaps we learn general principles by generalizing from particular instances. We get face-to-face with particular instances, as Prichard says, and then learn general principles by induction.[17] Even so, the order in which we learn particulars and gen-

15. Although Prichard's article does not say what triggers our intuitions, those who worked within the intuitionist tradition had a great deal to say about it. The point, though, is not that nothing can be said, but rather that something needs to be said. And when we begin to say what warrants us in intuiting that X is wrong, we begin to leave Prichard's brand of intuitionism behind.

16. With more ordinary intuitions, the answer might be experience. That is, we may have learned from experience to trust that sort of intuition. ("No, I do not want to get into that person's car. I see no reason not to, but *something* is telling me not to.") Still, the lesson of experience will not be simply that we should trust intuition, but that we have *reason* to trust intuition—doing so is for our own good, and we have a history of regretting the consequences of failing to do so. (So, I am not intending this as a concession to Prichard.) I owe the thought to Paul Bloomfield.

17. This is one of intuitionism's core insights. Another is that, in forming moral judgments, we draw upon tacit knowledge, some of which we are not capable of fully articulating. Similarly, a wine taster may have an astonishing ability to discern when and where the grapes came from, yet the information he or she finds in the wine's taste may be too subtle to put into words. These two ideas—that our knowledge is fundamentally of particulars rather than universals and that much of what we know is incorrigibly inarticulate—are also central tenets of the moral antitheory movement (cf. note 2). A reading of Prichard thus is a useful introduction to the antitheory literature.

eral principles is not the issue here. Even if we learn particulars first, there must be something about particular requirements that makes them requirements. Whether or not we learn the particulars first, a question inevitably remains regarding what we are seeing in a particular act when we see it as required. What makes promise keeping rather than promise breaking required? And why do we think promise keeping in some exceptional cases is not required after all, and may even be forbidden? What makes those cases different? That we see them differently is not what makes them different. We need to identify what is being seen when some cases of promise keeping are seen as required and others as forbidden or at least not required.

The list of required acts has to be more than a mere list. If membership in the category were determined arbitrarily, then Prichard would be wrong, for in that case membership in the category of required acts would not imply any special reason to do the act. Prichard wants to say that an act being correctly labeled "required" is itself a good reason to do it—so good that we need no other reason. I would not disagree. My point is only that if our intuitions are picking out some things as right and others as wrong, and doing so in a nonarbitrary way, this implies that acts we intuitively identify as right differ in some nonarbitrary way from acts we intuitively identify as wrong. What then is the difference?

One might think this misses the real point, which is that to call an act required is to *state* a special reason to do it. But suppose we *mistakenly* call an act required. In that case, we *think* we have stated a special reason to do it, whereas in fact there is no such reason to do it. We could say that to *correctly* call an act required is to state a special reason to do it, but then we still need to know what it is in an act that makes it true that the label "required" is correctly attached. If Prichard is correct in saying special reasons for action are entailed by an act's being required, then we cannot label an action "required" (or more precisely, we cannot know we have labeled the action correctly) until we know we have the requisite reasons for attaching the label, that is, that there really are special reasons for doing the act in question. We do not create the special reason merely by (perhaps mistakenly) applying the label.

For an act to be right, there must be a reason why it is right. Prichard's concern—that deriving a sense of rightness from something else would run contrary to our actual moral convictions (4)—is baseless. Indeed, if there were nothing in the keeping of a promise to ground our judgment that it is right, then the judgment itself would be baseless, which is contrary to our convictions if anything is.

Prichard is correct to say we already have a reason to perform an action when we see that it is required. We do not need to know what makes actions required in order to know we ought to do what is required. Still, one can ask what makes required actions required; in which case, we had better have something to say about when there is good reason to see an action as required. To answer questions of that sort, we need a rule of recognition for morals.

IV.   A Rule of Recognition for Morals

I argued against Prichard on two fronts. First, we can have something to say about whether being moral is prudent. Second, we need to say something about what makes right actions right in particular cases. It is time to consider what these critical points tell us about the more positive task of constructing a moral theory. My approach is unlike Prichard's, to be sure, but it is still in part a response to Prichard's challenge to modern moral philosophy. His challenge has stood the test of time even if his own way of responding to it has not.

My approach to moral theory begins by borrowing from H. L. A. Hart. Hart's legal theory distinguishes between primary and secondary legal rules (1961, 89–93). Primary rules comprise what we normally think of as the law. They define our legal rights and obligations. We use secondary rules, especially rules of recognition, to determine what the law is.[18] For example, among the primary rules in my neighborhood is a law saying the speed limit is thirty miles per hour. The secondary rule by which we recognize the speed limit is: read the signs. Exceeding speed limits is illegal, but there is no further law obliging us to read signs that post the speed limit. So long as I stay within the speed limit, the police do not worry about whether I read the signs. In reading the signs, we follow a secondary rule, not a primary rule.

We can think of moral theories in a similar way. For example, utilitarianism's recognition rule is the principle of utility: X is moral if and only if X maximizes utility. As it stands, the principle defines a family of moral theories rather than any particular member thereof. The different flavors of utilitarianism are produced by replacing X with a specific subject matter. Act-utilitarianism applies the principle of utility to actions themselves. Act-utilitarianism's fully specified recognition rule—an act is right if and only if it maximizes utility—then translates directly into act-utilitarianism's single rule of conduct: maximize utility. Rule-utilitarianism applies the principle of utility to sets of action-guiding rules. The resulting recognition rule states that an action guide is moral if and only if following it has more utility than would following any alternative action guide. Of course, the utility-maximizing set of primary rules might boil down to a single rule of conduct saying "maximize utility". Then again, it might not.[19]

Deontological theories are harder to characterize. We could begin with a generic recognition rule saying X is moral if X is universalizable.[20] Applying the rule

18. We speak here primarily of determining law in an epistemic sense, but in Hart's theory, secondary rules also determine the law in an ontological sense. For a discussion of the different senses in which secondary rules determine the law, see "Negative and Positive Positivism," in Jules Coleman (*Markets, Morals, and the Law* [Cambridge: Cambridge University Press, 1988]).

19. I see no reason to think it would. Recognition rules are not ultimate rules of conduct; primary rules are not mere rules of thumb. Primary rules do not defer to the "ultimate" rules in cases of conflict. Again, consider the legal analogy. In a situation where obeying the speed limit somehow interferes with reading the signs, the primary rule is still binding. The speed limit does not give way to a "higher" law bidding us to read the signs. Likewise, in ethics, if we recognize that, in the world we actually live in, following the rule "keep promises no matter what" has better consequences than following alternative rules like "keep promises if and only if doing so maximizes utility", then the principle of utility (qua recognition rule) picks out "keep promises no matter what" as being among morality's rules of conduct.

20. I acknowledge that there are broader conceptions of deontology than this, revolving around a more general idea that being moral is a matter of having reverence for the moral law.

to maxims yields a more specific recognition rule (something like "a maxim is moral if acting on it is universalizable"), which in turn yields a set of imperatives, reverence toward which is grounded in considerations of universalizability. Perhaps the idea of universalizability does not have enough content to yield determinate imperatives on its own. Deontology may need a second recognition rule formulated in terms of respect for persons as ends in themselves, so that the two rules can converge on a set of concrete imperatives. But that is another story.

A moral *theory* consists of a recognition rule applied to a particular subject matter. Given a subject matter, a rule of recognition for morals specifies grounds for regarding items of that kind as moral. By "grounds" I do not mean necessary and sufficient conditions. In act-utilitarianism, the principle of utility presents itself as necessary and sufficient for an act's morality, but trying to contrive necessary and sufficient conditions is not the only way (and I think not the best way) to do moral theory. To have a recognition rule, all we need is what I call a *supporting* condition.

A *supporting condition* is a qualified sufficient condition, qualified in the sense of being a sufficient basis for endorsement in the absence of countervailing conditions. Formulating recognition rules in terms of supporting conditions rather than attempting to specify necessary and sufficient conditions is one way of acknowledging intuitionist claims that we could never fully articulate all of the considerations relevant to moral judgment. We can allow for that possibility (without letting it stop us from doing moral theory) by formulating recognition rules in terms of supporting conditions—conditions that suffice to shift the burden of proof without claiming to rule out the possibility of the burden being shifted back again, perhaps by considerations we have yet to articulate.

As an example of a supporting condition, we might say, along the lines of act-utilitarianism, that an act is right if it maximizes utility, barring countervailing conditions. In two ways, act-utilitarianism, properly so-called, goes beyond merely offering a supporting condition. First, it denies there are countervailing conditions, thereby representing the principle of utility as a proper sufficient condition, not just a supporting condition. Second, act-utilitarianism says an act is right only if the act maximizes utility, thereby representing the principle of utility not only as sufficient but also as necessary for an act's morality.[21]

I do not think we will ever have a complete analysis of morality, any more than we will ever have a complete analysis of knowledge. We use such terms in a variety of related ways, and there is no single principle nor any biconditional analysis to which the varying uses can all be reduced. That is not an admission of defeat, though, for the important thing is not to find the one true principle but rather to look for principles that can form a backbone for a useful rule of recognition. Three points are worth highlighting.

---

21. Samuel Scheffler (*The Rejection of Consequentialism* [New York: Oxford University Press, 1982]) defends a "hybrid" theory, which departs from act-utilitarianism by holding that maximizing utility is sufficient but not necessary for an act's morality.

1.   A Moral Theory Can Range Over More Than One Subject Matter

We devise moral theories to help us answer questions raised by the subject of individual choice and action, of course. Yet, we might also want to assess individual character.[22] Or we might want to assess the morality of the institutional frameworks within which individuals choose and act and develop their characters. These are distinct subject matters. So, moral theories range over a variety of subject matters. Any given theory *may* be monistic, ranging over only one, while ignoring or trying to reduce others, but pluralistic theories (pluralistic in the sense of ranging over more than one subject matter) are a real option.

2.   A Moral Theory Can Incorporate More Than One Recognition Rule

There is nothing in the nature of morality to indicate that we should aim to answer all questions with a single recognition rule, because there is nothing in the nature of recognition rules to suggest there cannot be more than one. Modern ethical inquiry is often interpreted (maybe less often today than a few years ago) as a search for a single-stranded theory—a single rule of recognition applied to a single subject matter, usually the subject of what moral agents ought to do. Maybe Kant and Mill intended to promulgate single-stranded theories; friends and foes alike often take them to have done so. In any case, when interpreted in that way, their theories can capture no more than a fragment of the truth.

The truth is: morality is more than one thing. A theory will not give us an accurate picture of morality unless it reflects the fact that morality has more than one strand. Accordingly, I would not try to derive all of morality from a single recognition rule.

I once began a paper by noting that utilitarianism (which says rightness is determined by consequences) and deontology (which says it isn't) both express powerful insights into the nature of morality. "On the one hand, doing as much good as one can is surely right. On the other hand, it is also right to keep promises, sometimes even in cases where breaking them has better consequences" (1990, 622). The paper concluded on a grim note. "We have intuitions about morality that seem essentially embedded in theories that contradict each other. Something has to give" (627). At the time, I was stumped by this dilemma, but it has become clear that what can and should give is the assumption that morality is single-stranded. When we come to despair of finding the single property shared by all things moral, we can stop looking for essence and start looking for family resemblance. By abandoning the search for a single-stranded moral theory, we put ourselves in a position to notice that whether rightness is determined solely by consequences might depend on the subject matter.

3.   A Moral Theory Can Be Structurally Open-Ended

Utilitarianism and deontology, or single-stranded interpretations thereof, try to capture the whole truth about morality with a single recognition rule. By the lights of

---

22. As Michael Stocker says, "Good people appreciate the moral world in ways which go beyond simply seeing what is to be done" (*Plural and Conflicting Values* [New York: Oxford University Press, 1990], 114).

either theory, the other theory is a rival competing for the same turf. The theories are closed systems in the sense that, having incorporated one recognition rule, and claiming to capture the whole of morality with it, they have no room for others.

By contrast, I see morality as an open-ended series of structurally parallel strands, each with its own recognition rule, each contributing different threads of morality's action guide. Any particular recognition rule has a naturally limited range, applying only to its own subject matter. No particular recognition rule pretends to capture the whole of morality, and so verifying that they do not do so will not refute the theory.

One might think we ought to be looking for the single recognition rule underlying all of morality, since a theory with more than one recognition rule would violate the principle of parsimony. But such an objection oversimplifies the principle of parsimony. The question is not whether a theory is simpler in the beginning, but whether it is simpler in the end. Gracefully admitting the real complexity of morality at the outset can make for a simpler theory in the end. Analogously, when astronomers abandoned the assumption that planetary orbits were circular, having only one focal point, and accepted the reality of elliptical orbits, which have two focal points, their theories became simpler, more elegant, and more powerful.

V. The Normative Status of Morality's Recognition Rules

H. L. A. Hart, himself a legal positivist, argued that rules of recognition for law may or may not pick out what is moral when they pick out law. Herein lies a crucial disanalogy between rules of recognition for morals and for laws. Questions about legality are sometimes answered by simply "looking it up". Arguably, we do not need to know we have moral reason to obey a law in order to recognize it as law. Legal positivism is, roughly speaking, the thesis that a recognition rule can correctly pick out a rule of conduct as legal even though the rule is immoral. But there can be no such a thing as moral positivism, since it is not possible for a rule of recognition to *correctly* pick out rule of conduct X as right when X is *not* right. It may not be essential to *laws* that they have an inner morality, but we can entertain no such agnosticism about morality itself. It is in the nature of Prichard's conception of morality (unlike law) that a recognition rule can correctly identify actions as morally required only if there is decisive reason (absent countervailing conditions) to perform them. Only such a recognition rule lets us stop the conversation—as Prichard would want to stop it—upon concluding that our recognition rule identifies an action as morally required.

We need to say more about what it means to regard X as right. I will approach this issue by starting with a different question; namely, what is being questioned when a person asks "Why be moral?"

First, when asked in earnest, "Why be moral?" is a question about something that matters. "Why stand on one foot?" is, on its face, an idle question, but "Why be moral?" is not. Second, the "Why be moral?" question matters despite the fact that it patently does not presume that being moral matters to people from their first-person singular perspectives. Whether people have first-person singular reasons to be moral is pointedly left open. Thus, the implicit urgency comes from another source.

It stems, I would say, from the fact that morality essentially is something that matters to us from a first-person plural perspective. My endorsement begins to look like characteristically moral endorsement when grounded in the thought, not that *I* have reason for endorsement, but that *we* have reason for endorsement. While endorsement as rational need not go beyond the first-person singular, endorsement as moral at a minimum goes beyond first-person singular to first-person plural.[23]

The second thing to say is that the transcendence of the singular perspective involved in moral endorsement cannot go much farther than this. If moral endorsement involves taking a plural perspective, then we can imagine how being moral could be disadvantageous for you or me and yet we could still have clear reason to endorse being moral. For example, many theorists now think of cooperating in a Prisoner's Dilemma as a paradigm case of being moral.[24] While disadvantageous from an I-perspective, it remains rational in the sense of being to our advantage from a we-perspective. It is from a plural perspective that, in a Prisoner's Dilemma, we find something irrational about individual rationality. When you and I each decide not to cooperate, I am doing the best I can given your noncooperation, and you are

---

23. There is truth in Thomas Nagel's thesis (see Nagel, *The View from Nowhere* [New York: Oxford University Press, 1986]; or 1991) that individuals inhabit both personal and impersonal points of view. The distinction between first-person singular and first-person plural perspectives, though, borrowed from Gerald Postema ("Conflict, Conversation, and Convention: Reflections on Hume's Account of the Emergence of Norms of Justice"), captures that truth in terms that seem a bit more concrete and more firmly rooted in everyday experience. We can, though, imagine cases where the personal/impersonal distinction arguably would be more natural. For example, we might ask whether Robinson Crusoe can inhabit a plural perspective (and if not, would he be incapable of moral endorsement?). Presumably, the answer is yes, at least in a subjunctive sense. (That is, Crusoe can ask himself whether he would want his eventual rescuers to understand what he did to survive, whether he expects they would approve.) But this distinction is not far from being what we might instead capture in the terminology of personal and impersonal.

Finally, the idea that to endorse something as moral is to endorse it from a plural perspective does not beg the question against egoist or otherwise individualist moral theories. It is within the realm of possibility that I might endorse a sufficiently refined sort of egoism not only for me but for you too, and not only because it is best for me but because it is best for you too. In short, I can from a plural perspective endorse that we each tend our own gardens. Again, to belabor a distinction that I know from experience to be not at all obvious, recognition rules are not rules of conduct. Rules of conduct are what we look at. Recognition rules are what we look with.

24. See especially David Gauthier (*Morals by Agreement* [Oxford: Oxford University Press, 1986]). A Prisoner's Dilemma is a game in which individuals make separate decisions about whether to contribute to cooperative venture. In essence, the problem is, if an individual contributes, the benefits will be dispersed in such a way that the marginal benefit per unit of contribution is less than one unit to the contributor but more than one unit to the group. See David Schmidtz (*The Limits of Government: An Essay on the Public Goods Argument* [Boulder, Colo.: Westview, 1991], 105). In an obvious way, people are better off as a group if they contribute, but in an equally obvious way they are better off as individuals if they do not.

doing the best you can given mine, and yet *we* are not doing the best we can. However, if being moral were pointless not only from a singular perspective but also from a plural perspective as well, then it would be pointless, period. Being moral would be something we would have reason to avoid in ourselves and condemn in others. Being moral, though, is not like that. Being moral need not be prudent from a singular perspective, but part of the essence of being moral is that we have reason to endorse it from a plural perspective.

One thing that makes moral reasoning different from legal reasoning is that questions about how we recognize morality are hard to separate from questions about whether we have reason to endorse it. Morality's recognition rules pick out the extension of "moral" just as the law's recognition rules pick out the extension of "legal". Morality's recognition rules, however, pick out X as moral by homing in on properties that, from a plural perspective, give us reason to endorse X. We sometimes can discern the rules of the road by reading the signs. We sometimes can discern the applicable law simply by looking it up. Analogously, we might sometimes be able to discern what is moral simply by consulting what we (correctly) take to be a moral authority. But in formulating a theory about what makes something moral, we are seeking to identify truth-*makers*. So, although recognition rules essentially serve an epistemological role, they serve that role by tracking moral ontology. Moreover, to constitute the sort of theory that could play a recognition rule's epistemological role in a moral agent's life, we have to be talking about *usable* truth-makers. A theory's recognition rules, then, have to direct us to look for a kind of truth; moreover, they have to direct us to look for a kind of truth that we are capable of finding. (What else could morality be?)[25]

It is because morality is bound up with what we have reason to endorse from a plural perspective that "Why be moral?" is a pressing question. The "Why be moral?" question we inherited from Plato is a question about the relation between two kinds of *telos*—between what matters to us as individuals and what matters to us as a society. Because morality, as we conceive of it and as Plato conceived of it, matters to us from a first-person plural perspective, we have reason to hope it matters to us (or can be made to matter to us) from our first-person singular perspectives as well.

If, *per impossible*, morality did not matter from our plural perspectives, then neither would it matter whether morality could be reconciled with our singular perspectives. In different words, both Socrates and Glaucon care from a plural perspective about Glaucon's being moral. They are treating the question of whether morality can be reconciled with Glaucon's singular perspective as up in the air, yet there is some perspective, some other perspective, from which it is not up in the air. They *want* the answer to be that being moral is mandated by Glaucon's singular perspective. Analogously, we care about whether people cooperate in a Prisoner's Dilemma. It is in the interest of both players to decline to cooperate, so from their singular perspectives it makes no sense to be trying to convince them to cooperate. What makes sense in caring whether they cooperate is that there is a different perspective, a plural perspective, from which cooperating will make them better off.

---

25. I especially want to thank Philip Pettit for pressing me on this point.

Who Are We?

This takes us to one of the points at which satisfactory moral theorizing becomes really, really difficult. Unfortunately, while the scope of a person's I-perspective is more or less fixed (encompassing the person's own interests and preferences), the we-perspective does not have fixed borders, making it hard to characterize the we-perspective with any precision. It should go without saying, though, that the plural perspective is no mere fiction. (It is not for nothing that natural languages have words like *we* and *us* for plural self-reference.) When I speak of the we-perspective, what I have in mind is not the sort of group perspective you and I might take when we identify ourselves as fellow Mets fans, but rather the particular perspective we take when we worry about the "Why be moral?" question.

That perspective usually does not encompass the whole world.[26] If I see that my mowing the lawn will hamper your efforts to write your book, then my taking a we-perspective involves identifying with you as a member of the group of people who will be affected by my mowing the lawn. If I see that mowing the lawn will adversely affect people in a faraway country (because they are waiting anxiously for your book), then my taking a we-perspective involves identifying with them as well. The scope of my we-perspective expands and contracts along with my awareness of whose interests are at stake.[27] This does not mean I should not mow the lawn. We could not live together if we did not allow ourselves the latitude to impinge on one another in various ways. Your latitude may not serve my ends, and mine may not serve yours, but what is relevant from the plural perspective is that *our* latitude serves our ends. We are better off in virtue of members of our group having that kind of latitude.

VI. The Descriptive Boundaries of Moral Inquiry

This, then, is the normative status of morality's recognition rules. Being recognized as moral has normative force because, when morality's recognition rules pick out X

26. Geoffrey Sayre-McCord ("On Why Hume's 'General Point of View' Isn't Ideal—and Shouldn't Be," *Social Philosophy and Policy* 11 [1994]) directly addresses this issue. The original version of this essay went to press before Geoff's article appeared, but the ideas in this paragraph are similar enough to Geoff's to make me wonder whether I got them from him. In any case, I thank Geoff for wonderfully illuminating conversations on such topics over a period of years.

27. The scope of my plural perspective will not always coincide with the scope of yours, which is one reason why we sometimes disagree about what is moral. Discussing our differences often helps us extend our perspectives in ways that bring them into alignment, though, so disagreement that can be traced to differences in perspectival scope need not be intractable. If you convince Kate that her we-perspective until now has failed to encompass the interests of members of other races, for example, she will broaden her perspective accordingly. Or if she willfully refuses to do so, her kind of we-perspective reveals itself to be quite unlike the perspective that I am attributing to people who earnestly ask the "Why be moral?" question.

as moral, they do so by recognizing that X has properties we have reason to endorse from a plural perspective.[28]

Consider the following objection. Kate has reason from a plural perspective to endorse Disneyland. "We'll have a lot of fun there. Nearly everyone does", she says to her friends. Yet, though Kate endorses Disneyland from a we-perspective, she is endorsing it not as moral, but as amusing, or something like that. To endorse something as moral is to endorse it from a plural perspective, but not everything endorsed from a plural perspective is thereby endorsed *as moral*.

I agree with the objection. Certainly, we should not equate endorsing Disneyland from a plural perspective with endorsing Disneyland as moral. How then should we think of the plural perspective's role in moral theory? From a plural perspective, we do not pick out maxims (e.g.) as moral. Still less do we pick out Disneyland as moral. Instead, we pick out a criterion for assessing maxims, given that maxims are subject to moral assessment.

Now, if something is a lot of fun for almost everyone, why is that not a property that we have reason to endorse from a plural perspective? Or if being a lot of fun is such a property, then what distinguishes endorsing something as fun from endorsing it as moral? Section IV noted that it is not the task of recognition rules to circumscribe their own subject matter. On the contrary, any theory pretty much takes a subject matter as given. There has to be a subject that gives rise to moral questions before we can have occasion to devise theories to answer those questions. We begin with an intuitive understanding that subjects giving rise to moral questions include (roughly speaking) things that bear on human flourishing in communities, regarding which human action can make a difference. (Let me stress that I am not offering my intuitions as recognition rules for morals. Intuition enters the picture as a source of questions, not as a tool for answering them.) The subject matters of moral inquiry are pretheoretically given, that is, given in the sense of raising moral questions prior to our devising moral theories to answer them.

Accordingly, "X is moral if X is a lot of fun" is not a recognition rule for morals because, when applied to any of the specific subject matters over which moral theories range, the property of being a lot of fun is not a reason for endorsement from a plural perspective. We do not in fact recognize it as reason to endorse capital punishment or promise keeping or any of the subjects that normally raise moral questions.[29] We do recognize it as a reason for endorsement when the subject is amusement parks, but that would make it a basis for moral endorsement only if amusement parks as such were among the pretheoretically given subject matters of moral inquiry,

---

28. Note that this is a characterization of the perspective from which we formulate recognition rules. Whether *being* moral necessarily involves taking a plural perspective is a separate question. (Do morality's rules of conduct include an injunction to take a plural perspective? No, they do not, any more than the rules of the road include an injunction to read the signs.)

29. I suppose that if all we knew was that X is a lot of fun and does no harm whatsoever, then we might consider that grounds for endorsing X as morally permissible. If given the additional information that X = Disneyland, we might not retract our endorsement. We would not have judged X to be morally required, though, even before learning that X = Disneyland.

and they are not. A moral perspective is more specific than a plural perspective not because it is a more narrowly defined perspective, but rather because it consists of taking a plural perspective only with respect to issues already defined, intuitively and pretheoretically, as moral issues.

To summarize, a recognition rule like the principle of utility could embody a genuine reason for endorsement from a plural perspective and still fail to exclude Disneyland as a subject for moral assessment. However, it is not incumbent on recognition rules to have the internal resources to limit their subject matters. We test a purported recognition rule not in abstraction, but rather as applied to a pretheoretically given subject matter. We test it by asking whether it homes in on a property that, given the subject matter, grounds endorsement from a plural perspective. For example, if we apply the principle of utility to Disneyland, and then afterward decide that Disneyland, per se, is not a subject of moral inquiry, it would be a mistake to blame the principle of utility for the misapplication.

We considered how recognition rules distinguish what is right from what is not, given a subject matter with respect to which such questions arise. I have no theory to tell me what the subject matters of moral assessment are; on my theory, that is a *pre*theoretical question. I have only a sense that morality and moral assessment concern what makes it possible for human beings to flourish together. Given this pretheoretical understanding of the general character of the subject matters of moral assessment, amusement parks are not among morality's subject matters, but *institutions* are. Thus, Disneyland is subject to moral assessment not as an amusement park, but rather as an institution that has a bearing on whether people flourish within their communities. (Similarly, Michael Jackson is subject to moral assessment not as an entertainer but rather as a person whose choices have an impact both on himself and on many other people.) Likewise, acts, rules of conduct, and character traits are subjects of moral assessment because they affect whether people flourish within communities.

No doubt our intuitive conception of the proper subjects of moral assessment is more complicated than this, and I am not proposing to shed much light on our intuitive and pretheoretical understanding of the descriptive boundaries of moral assessment. It remains that, given an understanding of the subject matters of moral inquiry—of the kinds of things concerning which moral questions arise—we have something about which we can theorize. We can devise a theory about how those questions should be answered and why.

The descriptive boundaries of the subject matters of moral inquiry are given prior to our doing moral theory. They define what we want to have a theory about. Given a predefined subject matter, my proposal is that we capture the normative bite of morality's recognition rules when we say they home in on properties that, with respect to that particular subject, we have reason to endorse from a plural perspective. If amusement parks are not among the subject matters of morality, then morality's recognition rules do not range over amusement parks in the first place, which is why morality's recognition rules cannot pick out Disneyland, per se, as moral.

As with other intellectual endeavors, we need some sense of a subject matter and of questions to which it gives rise before we can have any reason to devise theories about it. Long before we begin to formulate moral theories, we already classify certain issues as moral issues. Roughly speaking, when an issue is crucial to human flourishing in communities, and when human beings can make a difference regarding that issue, we tend to see it as raising moral questions, and thus as a subject calling for moral theory. In this sense, the subject matters of moral inquiry are (at least provisionally) a pretheoretical given.[30]

VII.   Is the Right Prior to the Good?

One might worry that if we analyze the rightness of acts in terms of the goodness of states of affairs, the concept of rightness loses its turf, so to speak. The concept becomes superfluous, and we may as well dispense with it entirely. But this worry is not well founded. To explain our grounds for identifying an act as right is not to explain rightness away. The explanandum does not disappear merely in virtue of having been explained. In different words, giving an account of an action guide's normative force does not eliminate the need for an action guide. We cannot dispense with talk about what is right because we cannot dispense with talk about what we should do. We can still speak of keeping promises because it is right (or because breaking promises would violate rights).

Only when we ask how we *recognize* that keeping promises is right (or that breaking promises would violate rights) do we move from morality proper to moral epistemology: that is, from questions addressed at the action-guiding level to questions addressed by recognition rules. This is crucial. If we thought of recognition rules as part of morality's action guide, we would be missing the distinction between recognition rules and rules of conduct. To properly address Prichard's objections to teleology, a theory must isolate its teleology at the level of recognition rules, so that the concept of rightness can take on a life of its own at the action-guiding level. When a theory's teleology is embedded in recognition rules, it specifies terms by which we recognize what is required, in the process leaving moral agents with an action guide that tells them what is required and which they follow because doing so is required.

In short, recognition rules, which have a teleological spirit, support action guides, parts of which may not support action guides. In turn, action guides support particular actions or choices. For the sake of example, suppose the principle of utility is morality's recognition rule and that this principle recognizes a set of ten commandments against lying, stealing, and so forth, as morality's rules of conduct. If we thought of the principle of utility as something like morality's ultimate rule of

---

30. Partly for this reason, I think a method of seeking "reflective equilibrium" is practically unavoidable in moral theorizing. I do not think of seeking reflective equilibrium as a meta-principle or a moral theory or even a formal philosophical method, really. I think of it simply as a matter of remaining responsive to that which is pretheoretical. In the context of a given subject matter, we assess candidate action-guides (e.g.) by the light of our recognition rules. In turn, though, we assess our recognition rules by asking whether the action-guides they yield are plausibly responsive to what, pretheoretically, seems important about that particular subject matter. I thank Thomas Pogge for discussions of this point.

conduct, then we naturally would interpret the ten commandments as rules of thumb—rules that give way to the principle of utility when it is obvious that following them will not maximize utility. A recognition rule, however, is *not* an ultimate rule of conduct. Rather, it identifies morality's rules of conduct, a set of ten commandments in this case, and the ten commandments are thereby certified as the ultimate rules of conduct. Conduct is judged not according to whether it maximizes utility, but rather in accordance with whether it follows the ten commandments.

a.   Reading the Signs

Consider a legal analogy. "Read the signs" may be the rule by which we recognize rules of the road, but if we found ourselves in a situation where obeying a speed limit would somehow prevent us from reading a traffic sign, that would not be enough to make the speed limit give way. It would not even begin to make the speed limit give way. The highway patrol judges our conduct by the rules of the road, and would be properly unimpressed if we said we violated the rules of the road out of commitment to a "higher law" bidding us to read the signs.

Given that recognition rules are not rules of conduct, ultimate or otherwise, it is entirely possible that some of morality's rules of conduct are deontological (that is, they make no appeal to consequences) even if morality's rule of recognition is teleological.[31] A rule by which we *recognize* deontological imperatives can be teleological without in any way affecting the deontological force of the imperatives thus identified. An imperative may dictate an action without appealing to the action's role in serving the agent's purposes; indeed, it may dictate action without appealing to *anyone's* purposes. This leaves open whether the imperative has teleological support. It may serve a purpose to be committed to keeping promises come what may, even though it sometimes happens that keeping a promise serves no purpose. It serves a purpose to keep regular office hours even though some of those hours predictably will be spent waiting in vain for students to drop by.

A teleological recognition rule, applied to imperatives, is analogous to a rule of recognition in law; we need it only when pondering whether a particular imperative is moral. Upon recognizing an imperative as moral, we thereby know what we need to know to see that we have a moral reason to follow it. Having settled that the imperative is morally imperative, the rule of recognition has no further role to play. It drops out, leaving us with action-guiding imperatives that may well present them-

---

31. At best, Prichard says, the element of truth in the view that rightness is tied to goodness is that unless we recognize that an act will give rise to some good, we would not recognize that we ought to do it. But, he adds, this does not mean pain's badness is the reason not to inflict it (5). This looks like a massive concession, but Prichard mentions it in passing as if it were unimportant. In a footnote, Prichard claims that if pain's badness grounded the wrongness of inflicting it, then inflicting pain on oneself would be as wrong as inflicting it on others. But this does not follow. Suppose two rules of conduct (Do not inflict pain on others; do not inflict pain on yourself) are grounded in the same principle (Pain is bad). Contra Prichard, the common grounding implies nothing about whether the two rules of conduct are equally stringent.

selves to us in deontological form. In any event, the action-guiding imperative, not the rule of recognition, is what guides action.

A "soft" deontological prohibition is insensitive to consequences in normal cases but makes exceptions in extraordinary cases. We saw how there could be a teleological grounding for imperatives that are normally insensitive to consequences. In contrast, *absolute* imperatives are insensitive to consequences even when the universe is at stake. It is conceivable, though just barely, that we could have teleological grounds for recognizing an absolute imperative as moral. It might have good consequences to internalize the rule "I will not lie—not even to save the universe", so long as it never actually happens that we need to lie to save the universe. I doubt that there are any teleologically well-grounded absolute rules of conduct, but the idea is perfectly coherent. The idea that morality is teleological at the level of recognition rules does not preclude the possibility of there being absolutely exceptionless rules of conduct.

b.   When Good Reasons Are Redundant

There is, of course, a controversy in moral philosophy over whether the right is prior to the good. Some theorists dismiss the idea that morality's recognition rules are teleological; they assume it contradicts their belief that the right is prior to the good. It would be a mistake to dismiss my theory on that basis, though. My theory is entirely compatible with the view that the right is prior to the good at the *action-guiding* level. We should keep promises because it is right, and at the action-guiding level this is all that needs to be said. But that does not tell us what makes promise keeping right, or even (in cases of doubt) whether promise keeping is right. When it comes to recognizing what is right, the good is prior to the right, and must be so. We judge acts in terms of right, but when we need to explain what makes an act right, or whether it is right in a doubtful case, we can do so only in terms of good. So, regarding the controversy over the relative priority of the right and the good, the truth is, (1) the right is prior at the action-guiding level, and (2) the good is prior at the level of recognition rules.[32]

Teleological considerations need not enter a moral agent's deliberations about what to do. If we cannot act without breaking a promise, then under the circumstances that may be all we need to know in order to know we categorically should not act. Sometimes, though, we do not know what morality requires of us. Some promises should not be kept, and we do not always know which promises are which.

---

32. Although John Rawls's official position is that in justice as fairness the right is prior to the good (*A Theory of Justice* [Cambridge: Harvard University Press, 1971], 31), his theory's recognition rule is paradigmatically teleological. We're to recognize a principle as just by asking whether people behind a veil of ignorance would perceive a basic structure informed by the principle as being to their advantage. "The evaluation of principles must proceed in terms of the general consequences of their public recognition and universal application" (138). This is not the sort of statement one expects to find at the core of a theory in which the right is supposed to be prior to the good. Perhaps what Rawls really wants to say is that the right is prior to the good at the action-guiding level.

When we do not know, we need to fall back on recognition rules, which identify the point of being categorically required (that is, required on grounds that do not appeal to the agent's interests and desires) to act in one way rather than another.

Prichard thinks that if one understands that keeping a particular promise is required, one thereby recognizes reason to keep it. In that case, pointing out that keeping promises has good consequences would be irrelevant. Prichard is right, and now we can see why. When we already recognize that we are required to keep a promise, pointing out good reasons to keep it is *redundant*. The redundancy of pointing out good reasons to keep a promise, when we already see that keeping it is required, is what makes the good reasons irrelevant.[33] But what if we have not yet recognized that keeping a particular promise is required? In that case, coming to see that breaking the promise would have bad consequences is not redundant at all. In that case it is Prichard's point that is irrelevant, for in that case we are not asking why we should do what is required. Rather, we are asking whether keeping *this* promise is required in the first place.

c.   It's Not Just a Good Idea. It's the Law.

One might be troubled by the idea of keeping a promise simply "because it's right". "Because it's right" may seem oddly abrupt as a reason for action. However, it certainly is not peculiar to morality. For example, when a motorist's impatient passenger asks her why she is driving at twenty miles per hour, it would not be peculiar for the motorist to reply by saying "because it's the law". Her passenger now knows why she is driving at twenty miles per hour and might go on to ask how she knows that it is the law. She might answer that she read the speed limit sign. In a more philosophical if still somewhat impatient frame of mind, the passenger might then ask what the *telos* is of the twenty miles per hour speed limit. What justifies it? The driver may not know. But she still knows the law. Further, if she knows that there is a school in the neighborhood, then she can add that the school's presence justifies the law (and she can say this even though she has no idea whether the school's presence is what actually motivated authorities to impose the speed limit). A conversation about morality might unfold in the same way. Asked why she keeps promises, a person might say, "Because it's right". She might be asked how she knows keeping promises is right or she might be asked about the *telos* of promise keeping, but those will be different questions.

In summary, Prichard denies that the good plays a role in determining the right. He infers this from the premise that we keep promises because doing so is right, not because doing so is good. I accept the premise, but the inference is invalid. Of course we should keep promises because it is right, and at the action-guiding level this is all that needs to be said. But this is different from asking why promise keeping

---

33. Even so, we should not concede to Prichard that pointing out good reasons to keep promises is *always* irrelevant to someone who believes promise keeping is required. Even someone who believes promise keeping is required might be unable to articulate good reasons to keep promises and might learn something from discussion.

is right, or (in cases of doubt) whether promise keeping is right. To answer the latter questions, we need to formulate good reasons to keep promises. And pointing out that promise keeping is right is to *imply* there are good reasons rather than to *identify* them. Explaining why we ought to do what is right and identifying what is right in the first place are different tasks.

VIII.   Conclusion

We examined H. A. Prichard's argument that the question "Why be moral?" is fundamentally confused. It turns out, however, that there is no confusion involved in asking the question from a prudential point of view. It turned out that asking the question from the prudential point of view does not presuppose any reduction of morality to a system of prudential imperatives. On the contrary, we can intelligibly ask whether following categorical imperatives is to our advantage. One way or another, the question has an answer.

A recognition rule cannot be constituted in such a way that the action guide it picks out is as likely to lead us to do bad as to do good. Morality's recognition rules cannot be arbitrary with respect to goodness. Otherwise, arbitrarily identifying an act as right will not give us a reason to do it. And the idea that we could identify an act as morally imperative without in the process coming to have a reason to perform it is contrary to the supposition shared by Prichard that we should do what is right because it is right. A recognition rule for right action essentially picks out, as right, actions for which there are good reasons, which is precisely what allows us to conclude, as Prichard wants us to conclude, that to recognize their rightness is to recognize good reason to do them.

We have not explored any particular theory about the content of morality's recognition rules beyond saying they recognize a thing as moral by recognizing reason to endorse it from a plural perspective. *Rational Choice and Moral Agency* offers a theory (I call it moral dualism) about the content of morality recognition rules, and about the respective subject matters over which they range. This essay's burden has been to show why we can safely reject H. A. Prichard's conclusion that undertaking to identify such rules is a mistake. Further, we can reject his conclusion while allowing that his premises (as I understand them) are not without merit.[34]

34. This is a revision of chapter 6 of David Schmidtz, *Rational Choice and Moral Agency* (Princeton, N.J.: Princeton University Press, 1995). Copyright by the author.

5

The Value of Inviolability

THOMAS NAGEL

One of the most difficult and widely discussed questions in recent moral theory is that of the status of human rights—the rights of individuals not to be violated, sacrificed, or used in certain ways, even in the service of valuable ends, either by other individuals or by governments and intermediate institutions. The protection of rights can extend to many different things:

Inviolability of the physical person;

Freedom of association, expression, and religion;

Personal privacy and security in one's personal possessions;

Freedom from coercive external control with regard to sexual conduct, style of life, and choice of work or profession.

These are all examples of negative rights—rights not to be interfered with, used, or coerced. I will not be concerned here with the common extension of the concept of rights to cover certain positive benefits that everyone is thought to be entitled to. Thus claims of right, in the moral sense, are now frequently made about such things as minimum standards of health care, shelter, subsistence, and education, as well as to political representation. Groups are also sometimes asserted to have rights to political recognition and self-determination. The reason for claiming such things as rights—apart from the natural tendency for rhetoric to escalate—is that they have some claim to be given priority over other values, a claim to be taken care of first, for everyone, even if this cannot be justified by balancing their utility against other components of the general good or general welfare. There is probably no harm in attaching the term "right" to the minima that ought thus to be guaranteed to everyone—provided it does not produce confusion with negative rights, which are likewise equally to be accorded to everyone, and provided it does not beg any questions about the relative priorities between positive and negative rights, should they conflict. But I shall say no more about these matters here. My concern is with rights to be free from various kinds of direct maltreatment.

There is substantial difference of opinion, of course, over what rights in these different domains people have, or, to put it differently, what rights should be accorded to them and protected against violation. But when I speak of the *status* of human rights, I am referring to something else, namely the question of the correct moral explanation and understanding of such rights as there may be: what they are and why we have them. The answer we give to this question will influence our view about what specific rights there are, but the two questions can be considered to some extent independently. Those who are in broad agreement about what rights people have can disagree profoundly over their status or source, and vice versa. On the other hand, it is possible to frame the issues over the status of rights without assuming a very precise account of what rights people have. It is enough to point to some typical examples, and to the sort of role played in moral argument, criticism, and justification by the appeal to human rights.

The idea is that certain ways of treating people are to be excluded in advance from consideration as possible means for the achievement of any social or political end—ruled out as impermissible, without inquiring whether they might be useful. The fact that human rights are supposed to set limits to the means that can be used to further any end has given them their current prominence in the discourse of international criticism, since if there are such things as human rights, an appeal to them can circumvent disagreements about the relative value of different disputed ends and the likelihood of their achievement by different means. Rights, if they exist, set limits in advance to what may be considered in that instrumental light. Of course, usually those who protest against a particular violation of human rights have other objections to the policy of the violator as well: They may believe that the ends being pursued are bad, or that the means are not likely to achieve them, or at least that they will do more harm than good—so that the violations would be wrong even if there were no such thing as human rights. But the appeal nevertheless has a point, because it purports to offer an independent ground of objection, which does not depend on challenging the general aims or policies of the government or institution under attack: It purports to find something whose wrongness can be universally acknowledged by those whose aims and empirical beliefs differ widely.

Human rights are often protected by law, in which case they become legal rights; but the two concepts are not the same. Not only are many legal rights not general human rights, but many governments fail to recognize or legally protect certain fundamental human rights, which the subjects of those governments are nevertheless widely thought to possess, so that their violation is a moral offense. The concept of human rights is a moral concept, and it implies that the existence of the rights that all people have, which ought to be protected and respected whether they actually are or not, is to be explained not by the action of any government but by something more universal—something about human beings and their situation in general.

But what is the explanation? There are two types of answer to this question.

One is that the recognition and protection of rights is an essential instrument for the promotion of human happiness and human interests: that the result of failing to accord to all individuals this special type of inviolability is bad in ways that can be recognized and identified without referring to the concept of rights at all. On this account, rights are morally derivative from other, more fundamental values: the goods of happiness, self-realization, knowledge, and freedom, and the evils of misery, ignorance, oppression, and cruelty. Rights are of vital importance as means of fostering those goods and preventing those evils, but they are not themselves fundamental either in the structure of moral theory or in the order of moral explanation. Rather, they must be institutionally or conventionally guaranteed in order to provide individuals with the security and discretion over the conduct of their own lives necessary for them to flourish, and in order to protect against the abuse of governmental and collective power.

This instrumental position is represented by Mill and Sidgwick, in development of the method of rule-utilitarian analysis created by Hume,[1] and it has had many distinguished adherents since then.[2] The idea is that in order to promote the best results in the long run, we must develop strict inhibitions against treating any individual in certain ways, not only when the consequences in the particular case would be clearly bad but also sometimes even when we believe that doing so would in this case produce the best results in the long run. For a number of reasons, the argument runs, the alternative policy of deciding each case by reference to the general good serves the general good much less effectively than a policy that puts certain types of choice beyond the reach of such an optimizing calculation: the policy of optimizing in each case is not always the optimific policy. The arguments for this position are familiar, and I shall not rehearse them here.

The other type of answer is that rights are a nonderivative and fundamental element of morality. They embody a form of recognition of the value of each individual that supplements and differs in kind from that which leads us to value the overall increase of human happiness and the eradication of misery—and this form of recognition of human value is no less important than the other. The trouble with this answer is that it has proven extremely difficult to account for such a basic, individualized value in a way that makes it morally intelligible. The theory that rights are justified instrumentally, by contrast, is perfectly clear and based on uncontroversial values. In these remarks I want to see what can be done to develop the conception of rights as nonderivative and noninstrumental—the alternative to the first conception, that they are important instruments to the achievement of valuable ends that can be identified independently. To this extent my discussion is aligned with John Rawls's claim that the right is prior to the good.[3] However, partly because I am talk-

1. John Stuart Mill, *Utilitarianism* (Oxford: Oxford University Press, 1998), chap. 4; John Stuart Mill, *"On Liberty" and Other Writings* (Cambridge: Cambridge University Press, 1989); Henry Sidgwick, *The Methods of Ethics*, 7th ed. (Chicago: University of Chicago Press, [1907] 1962); David Hume, *A Treatise of Human Nature*, ed. L. A. Selby-Bigge (Oxford: Clarendon, [1740] 1978), book 3; David Hume, *Enquiry Concerning the Principles of Morals*, ed. L. A. Selby-Bigge, rev. P. H. Nidditch (Oxford: Clarendon, [1751] 1975).

2. For example, R. M. Hare, *Moral Thinking* (Oxford: Oxford University Press, 1981). T. M. Scanlon's "Rights, Goals, and Fairness," in *Public and Private Morality*, ed. S. Hampshire (Cambridge: Cambridge University Press, 1978), has some connection with this tradition, but it also has affinities with the alternative analysis I wish to discuss.

3. John Rawls, *A Theory of Justice* (Cambridge, Mass.: Harvard University Press, 1971).

ing about general moral theory rather than about social justice, what I have to say will be rather different. The general moral concept to which I shall appeal is not fairness but inviolability. It is a version of Kant's idea that persons should not be treated merely as means.

I shall concentrate on trying to develop the second type of answer because, although it is far more obscure than the first, it seems to me to be part of the truth. But let me emphasize the value and interest of the first type of answer, which contains a great deal of truth even if rights can also be given a noninstrumental interpretation. Clearly, the violation of individual rights has been one of the greatest causes of human misery, ignorance, and oppression, and their protection brings great benefits to those societies that recognize them. What is more, most of the egregious violations of human rights with which the world is filled cannot be given even the semblance of a justification on any moral theory; they are usually naked exercises of power designed to protect or advance the interests of one individual or group at the expense of others. After all, no more efficient methods have yet been devised to discourage political opposition than torture and murder. So to some extent, the defense of human rights does not depend on the resolution of this theoretical issue; there are many grounds on which to condemn their violation. Yet as I have said, the appeal to a universal standard of individual treatment has its uses. In any case, the question bears on the understanding of our moral judgments; and the answer may influence our ideas of the substantive content of rights as well.

I begin with a familiar point from recent moral philosophy. The feature of rights that makes them morally and theoretically puzzling is a logical one. If they are taken as basic, it is impossible to interpret them in terms of a straightforward positive or negative evaluation of certain things happening to people, or certain things being done to them. The reason is that rights essentially set limits to what any individual may do to any other, even in the service of good ends—and those good ends include even the prevention of transgressions of those same limits by others. If there is a general right not to be murdered, for example, then it is impermissible to murder one person even to prevent the murders of two others. It is difficult to see how such a prohibition could be morally basic; in fact, it seems paradoxical, if it cannot be justified by its utility in the long run.

There is a technical distinction that can be used to describe this logical property of rights—the distinction between *agent-neutral* and *agent-relative* principles. Agent-neutral values are the values of certain occurrences or states of affairs, which give everyone a reason to promote or prevent them. If murder is bad in an agent-neutral sense, for example, it means that everyone has a reason to try to minimize the overall number of murders, independent of who commits them—and this might in some circumstances mean murdering a few to prevent the murder of a larger number. But if, on the other hand, murder is wrong in an *agent-relative* sense, this means that each agent is required not to commit murder *himself*, and nothing is directly implied about what he must do to prevent murders by others. The agent-relative prohibition against murder of course applies to those others—in this sense the agent-relative principle is just as *universal* as the agent-neutral one—but it governs each agent's conduct only with respect to the murders that *he* might commit. The same applies to torture, enslavement, and various other violations. If the prohibitions against them are agent-relative, then I may not torture someone even to prevent two others from being tortured by someone else, and so forth.

The logical peculiarity of noninstrumental rights can be described by saying that they cannot be given an interpretation in terms of agent-neutral values—not even in terms of the agent-neutral value of what they protect. Rights have a different logical character: They prohibit us from *doing* certain things to *anyone* but do not require that we count it equally a reason for action that it will prevent those same sorts of things *being done* to someone, but not by oneself.

If murder were merely an agent-neutrally bad type of *occurrence* and nothing more, then the badness of one murder would be outweighed by the badness of two or three others, and one could be justified in murdering one innocent person to prevent three others from being murdered. But if there is a right against murder, it does not give way when murdering one innocent person is the only means of preventing the murder of two or three others. A right is an agent-relative, not an agent-neutral value. Rights tell us in the first instance what not to *do* to other people, rather than what *to prevent from happening to them.*

It is compatible with this conception of rights that they are not absolute, and that there may be some threshold, defined in consequential, agent-neutral terms, at which they give way. For example, even if there is a general right not to be tortured or murdered, perhaps there are evils great enough so that one would be justified in murdering or torturing an innocent person to prevent them. But this would not change the basic character of the right, since the threshold will be high enough so that the impermissibility of torture or murder to prevent evils below it cannot be explained in terms of the agent-neutral badness of torture or murder alone. Even if it is permissible to torture one person to save a thousand others from being tortured, this leaves unexplained why one may not torture one to save two.

It is this qualified independence of the best overall results, calculated in agent-neutral terms, that gives rights their distinctive character. Of course if rights are instrumental—derivative from the agent-neutral value or disvalue of certain sorts of outcomes—then there is no problem, because their agent-relative character is not something morally basic. But if they are not merely instrumental, then they can, as I have said, seem paradoxical; for how could it be wrong to harm one person to prevent greater harm to others? How are we to understand the value that rights assign to certain kinds of human inviolability, which makes this consequence morally intelligible?

This peculiar feature of rights has been the subject of extensive discussion by Robert Nozick, Judith Jarvis Thomson, and Samuel Scheffler, among others.[4] I want to explore an answer to the question that has been proposed by Frances Kamm. The answer focuses on the *status* conferred on all human beings by a morality that includes agent-relative constraints of this kind—a status conferred by the *design* of the morality. The status is precisely that of a certain kind of *inviolability*, which we identify with the possession of rights, and Kamm's proposal is that we explain the

---

4. Robert Nozick, *Anarchy, State, and Utopia* (New York: Basic, 1974); Judith Jarvis Thomson, *The Realm of Rights* (Cambridge, Mass.: Harvard University Press, 1990); Samuel Scheffler, *The Rejection of Consequentialism* (New York: Oxford University Press, 1982).

agent-relative constraint against certain types of violations in terms of the agent-neutral value of inviolability itself. This is a way of narrowing the gap between deontological and consequentialist ethics without reducing the former to the latter.[5]

Being inviolable is not a *condition*, like being happy, or free—just as being violable is not a condition, like being unhappy or oppressed. To be inviolable does not mean that one *will not be violated*. It is a moral *status*: It means that one *may not* be violated in certain ways—such treatment is inadmissible, and if it occurs, the person has been wronged. So someone's having or lacking this status is not equivalent to anything's happening or not happening to him. If he has this status, he does not lose it when his rights are violated—rather, such treatment counts as a violation of his rights precisely because he has it.

This yields a kind of answer to the "paradox" of rights. It is true that a right may sometimes forbid us to do something that would minimize its violation—as when we are forbidden to kill one innocent person even to prevent two other innocents from being killed. But the alternative possibility differs from this one not just in the numbers of innocents killed. If there is no such right, and it is permissible to kill the one to save the two, that implies a profound change in the status of everyone—not only of the one who is killed. For in the absence of such a right, no one is inviolable: anyone may be killed if that would serve to minimize the number of killings. This difference of status holds for everyone, whether or not the situation will ever arise for him.

So even if we suppose, for the sake of argument, that in a world in which such rights were recognized and respected by most people, the chances of being killed would be higher than in a world in which they were not (perhaps because the means available to control violators would be weaker than they would be if utilitarian methods were employed)—still, this would not be the only difference between the two worlds. In the world with no rights and fewer killings, *no one* would be inviolable in the way that, in the world with more rights and more killings, *everyone* would be inviolable—including the victims.

We may actually have an example of this sort of choice in the criminal enforcement practices of modern liberal societies. I would not be surprised if the rate of violent crime in the United States, for example, could be substantially reduced if the police and courts were free to use methods that carried a greater risk of violating people's rights than the methods now legally permitted in order to control, arrest, and imprison criminal suspects. Violent crimes are also violations of people's rights so the balance might be quite favorable: The average person's chance of being mugged or murdered might decrease much more than his chance of being beaten up by the police or falsely imprisoned would increase. Yet a believer in individual rights will reject what appears to be the lesser evil in this case, preferring to maintain

---

5. See Frances Myrna Kamm, "Harming Some to Save Others," *Philosophical Studies* 57 (1989): 251–56; Frances Myrna Kamm, review of *The Limits of Morality*, by Shelly Kagan, in *Philosophy and Phenomenological Research* 51 (1991): 904–5; and Frances Myrna Kamm, *Morality, Mortality, vol. 2* (New York: Oxford University Press, 1996). A similar idea is suggested briefly by Warren S. Quinn in "Actions, Intentions and Consequences: The Doctrine of Doing and Allowing," *Philosophical Review* 98 (1989): 312.

strict protections against maltreatment and strict standards of evidence and procedural safeguards for suspected offenders, even at the cost of a higher crime rate and
a higher total rate of rights violations. I believe that such a policy is difficult to justify
on rule-utilitarian grounds, and that it expresses instead a recognition of the value of
inviolability for everyone, quite apart from the value of not being violated.

This may strike you as a pretty abstract difference to hang a moral argument on.
But I think it is not without weight. What actually happens to us is not the only thing
we care about: What *may* be done to us is also important, quite apart from whether
or not it *is* done to us—and the same is true of what we *may do* as opposed to what
we actually do.

I have now introduced two rather abstract distinctions: (a) the distinction between
the agent-neutral value of human freedom from various kinds of violation and the
agent-relative restriction against *interfering* with people's freedom in those ways, and
(b) the distinction between the value of what actually *happens* to people or is done
to them and the (noninstrumental) value of their being or not being *liable* to such
treatment—its being or not being allowable. And we are trying to explain the moral
significance of agent-relative rights by saying that not only is it an evil for a person to
be harmed in certain ways, but for it to be *permissible* to harm the person in those
ways is an additional and independent evil.

Is such an explanation possible? It is not supposed to be merely an argument for
creating or *instituting* rights, through laws or conventions. In a sense the argument is
supposed to show that the morality that includes rights is *already true*—that this is the
morality we ought to follow independently of what the law is. The argument is that
the most plausible alternative morality, which is based solely on the agent-neutral
value or disvalue of the actual enjoyment or infringement of certain freedoms, and so
forth, fails to give any place to another very important value—the intrinsic value of
inviolability itself. The argument is that we would all be worse off if there were no
rights—even if we did not suffer the transgressions that in the case of there being no
rights would not count as violations of our rights—ergo, there are rights.

This is a curious type of argument, for it has the form that P is true because it
would be better if it were true. That is not in general a cogent form of argument; one
cannot use it to prove that there is an afterlife, for example. However it may have a
place in ethical theory, where its conclusion is not factual but moral. It may be suit-
able to argue that one morality is more likely to be true than another, because the
former makes for a better world than the latter—not instrumentally, but intrinsically. This would require that we be able to conceive and compare alternative moral
worlds, to determine which of them is actual.

I will not attempt a full defense of the idea here. Let me just observe that one
might interpret Bernard Williams's very different criticism of utilitarianism, on the
ground that it would undermine individual integrity, as relying on an argument of
this type.[6] He imagines a world in which people are subject to the strong conditions
of negative responsibility (responsibility for every evil they can prevent) that play an
essential part in utilitarianism, and claims that this would be a bad thing in itself, in

6. Bernard Williams, "A Critique of Utilitarianism," in *Utilitarianism: For and Against*,
ed. J. J. C. Smart and Bernard Williams (Cambridge: Cambridge University Press, 1973).

a way that utilitarianism cannot take account of, since it is not something bad that happens to people, but something bad that simply would follow if utilitarianism were the true morality; namely, that people would have to choose between personal integrity and moral decency. Whether or not the argument has merit, this is one way to understand it—and the interpretation is also consonant with the Nietzschean flavor of Williams's critique of morality.

Let me return to rights. One problem with any argument of this type is that it seems in danger of being circular. For what is the value that a morality without rights would fail to recognize and realize? It seems to be nothing more nor less than the existence of rights, for which "inviolability" is just another name. I do not think this is too great a cause for worry, however. Any attempt to render more intelligible a fundamental moral idea will inevitably consist in looking at the same thing in a different way, rather than in deriving it from another idea that seems at the outset completely independent. In this case the system of agent-relative constraints embodied in rights is seen as the expression of a status whose value for individuals cannot be reduced to the value of what actually happens to them, and that is not as trivial as saying that people have rights because they have rights.

Another problem is that this explanation of rights in terms of the value of the status they confer might be thought instrumental or consequentialist after all, if not actually rule-utilitarian.[7] For what is the value of this status, if not the value for the people who have it of being *recognized* as not subject to certain kinds of treatment, which gives them a sense of their own worth? It seems difficult to distinguish this argument from an instrumental argument for the institutional establishment of rights as a means to improving people's well-being.

The answer to this objection is that we cannot understand the well-being in question apart from the value of inviolability itself. What is good about the public recognition of such a status is that it gives people the sense that their inviolability is appropriately recognized. Naturally, they are gratified by this, but the gratification is due to recognition of the value of the status, rather than the opposite—that is, the status does not get its value from the gratification it produces. (This is analogous to the question of whether guilt is the reason to avoid wrongdoing, or whether, on the contrary, an independent recognition of the reasons not to do wrong is the explanation of guilt.) It may be that we get the full value of inviolability only if we are aware of it and it is recognized by others, but the awareness and the recognition must be of something real.

Further, this understanding of rights enables us to place them in the same framework of Kantian universalizability, which helps us to understand agent-neutral values and their moral consequences. This may provide a way of thinking about the relation between deontological and consequentialist aspects of morality which, without obliterating the distinction, goes some way toward reducing the stark moral dilemmas that they can generate—though I do not suggest that it eliminates them.

Let me say something about my understanding of the source of universalizability as a moral criterion. Morality is possible only for beings capable of seeing themselves as one individual among others more or less similar in general respects—capable,

---

7. I am indebted to Joseph Raz for discussion of this point.

in other words, of seeing themselves as others see them. When we recognize that although we occupy only our own point of view and not that of anyone else—there is nothing cosmically unique about it—we are faced with a choice. This choice has to do with the relation between the value we naturally accord to ourselves and our fates from our own point of view, and the attitude we take toward these same things when viewed from the impersonal standpoint that assigns to us no unique status apart from anyone else.

One alternative would be not to "transfer" to the impersonal standpoint in any form those values that concern us from the personal standpoint. That would mean that the impersonal standpoint would remain purely descriptive, and our lives and what matters to us as we live them (including the lives of other people we care about) would not be regarded as mattering at all if considered apart from the fact that they are ours, or personally related to us. Each of us, then, would have a system of values centering on his own perspective, and would recognize that others were in exactly the same situation.

The other alternative would be to assign to one's life and what goes on in it some form of impersonal as well as purely perspectival value, not dependent on its being one's own. This would then imply that everyone else was also the subject of impersonal value of a similar kind; the result would be some version of universal morality.[8]

It may seem excessively self-absorbed, but I believe that the choice between these two alternatives depends on the attitude one decides to take toward oneself in making it. Admittedly, the second alternative makes one subject to claims deriving from the lives of others in a way the first does not. But the first alternative, by refusing to admit the impersonal value even of one's own life, amounts to a decision to regard oneself as in a sense less valuable, *impersonally worthless*. I believe, as did Kant, that what drives us in the direction of universalizability is the difficulty each person has in regarding himself as having value only *for himself*, but not *in himself*. If people are not ends in themselves—that is, impersonally valuable—they have a much lower order of worth. Egoism amounts to a devaluation of oneself, along with everyone else.

Given this characterization of the choice, it is easier to understand the pressure toward universalizability and the morality it generates. But the content of that morality depends on the kind of valuation of oneself that is carried over to the impersonal standpoint. It is at this point that we can better understand rights in relation to agent-neutral values.

The agent-neutral value of happiness, freedom, and so forth is simply the direct impersonal transformation of the personal value that each of us accords to those things in his own life. But there is not in the same way a purely personal analogue of the universal value expressed by agent-relative constraints, or rights. Rights protect certain kinds of autonomy and independence of the individual, which are, in fact, personally valued by each of us. But the direct impersonal analogue of those values would be an agent-neutral value, which would not be equivalent to a general principle of inviolability. So a different type of account is needed.

8. I have tried arguments of this kind in several places, including *The Possibility of Altruism* (Oxford: Oxford University Press, 1970) and *The View from Nowhere* (New York: Oxford University Press, 1986).

The admission of agent-neutral impersonal values is an advance over pure egoism in the evaluation of oneself, for it makes what happens to one a matter of impersonal concern to anyone. But it remains deficient in one way that is analogous to one of the deficiencies of egoism. Egoism permits others not merely to disregard my interests, but to use me in any way that will serve their aims. But just as egoism implies that anyone may legitimately sacrifice me or use me in the service of his personal ends, so a morality based solely on agent-neutral values, such as utilitarianism, implies that anyone may sacrifice me or use me in the service of *those* values, that is, in the service of the general welfare. (Indeed, according to utilitarianism, I am required so to treat myself, as well as others.) The question is whether the fact that my own welfare is one component of those agent-neutral values to which I may be sacrificed is enough to compensate for this new kind of "sacrificeability" or "violability".

The preference for a morality that includes rights depends on a negative answer to that question. It depends on the judgment that, while an agent-neutral morality constitutes an advance over egoism in the evaluation of ourselves, it is still defective by comparison with a further possible advance, to a morality that counts us not only as impersonal ends for others but also as beings whose autonomy, apart from being something that others have reason to promote, sets a limit to what others may do. Without this, there would remain a significant type of impersonal value that we would fail to accord to ourselves.

But what is the true value of this value? How much weight should it carry in the design of a morality?

The only way I can think of to address this question is to ask what it is reasonable for any individual to want for himself, and to derive a universalizable result from that. I realize that this is not only a strange form of moral argument—regarding rights as a kind of generally disseminated intrinsic good[9]—but also very unclear in its results: I don't suggest that we can assign any straightforward measure of utility to the status of being inviolable. Yet I believe there is something in Kamm's approach. As she says, we can regard inviolability as having an *agent-neutral* value for *everyone*, which would be defeated by a moral system that endorsed the violation of *anyone* for the greater good. We can distinguish the desirability of not being tortured from the desirability of its being impermissible to torture us; we can distinguish the desirability of not being murdered from the desirability of our murder's being impermissible; we can distinguish the desirability of not being coerced from the desirability of its being impermissible to coerce us. These are distinct subjects, and they have distinct values. To be tortured would be terrible; but to be tortured and also to be someone whom it was not wrong to torture would be even worse.

Care is needed here in stating the position. For clearly it is worse to be killed unjustly than, say, accidentally. And it may even be right to say that if it were *not* wrong to torture us to prevent a greater evil, being tortured would be less bad than if it *were* wrong. But I am talking here about the separable evil of *being someone it is not wrong to torture*—which would apply, in the absence of rights, to everyone, whether he is tortured or not.

⌐ A bit like a public good, complete with its own version of a free-rider problem: even peopl who don't recognize the rights of others have them.

There is certainly something strange about this, for I am claiming that it is a compensation for liability to the added evil of being wronged rather than merely suffering harm that one is *capable* of being wronged in this way—that this status of heightened (logical) susceptibility to injury is, in a sense, a good thing to have, quite apart from any consequences for the likelihood of such injury. But this is just an instance of the fact that those who have more can lose more, and that it can be worth it.

Obviously that cannot be true in general, of every imaginable form of inviolability and its correlative susceptibility to injury. It would not be a good thing to be someone it was wrong to touch, or to address by his first name, for example, even though we could interpret this as a kind of protection against untoward intimacy. In other words, it is not the enhanced possibility of injury *per se* that makes the possession of rights valuable, but the specific content of the right and the consequent significance of the correlated susceptibility to injury. Someone whom it is not wrong to kill as a means to a good end simply *has less*, in some important sense, than someone with a right to life. He does not possess a certain type of value, and this is a significant lack.

The defense of noninstrumental rights depends on the judgment that the possession of certain sorts of inviolability, as a matter of moral status, is valuable enough to outweigh the logically correlated possibility of actually suffering the corresponding violation. It also depends on the judgment that this can outweigh some increase in the empirical probability of suffering the corresponding type of harm, considered apart from whether it is a moral injury or not.

Thus the right not to be killed so that one's organs can be used to save the lives of others may be valuable enough to outweigh a reduction in the chances of one's life being saved by an organ transplant. An instrumental justification of a right not to be killed for such purposes would have to depend, by contrast, on the likely results of the recognition of such a right for what actually happens to people—most notably but not exclusively the results for their likelihood of living or dying.

If we factor this peculiar "status" value into the standard method of assessment by universalizability, the result is as follows. If there is a right to life, one person may not be killed to save five. For simplicity let us compare this with a consequentialist principle whereby one person may be killed to save five—ignoring for the moment the obvious difficulties of implementing such a policy. If the only evil to be weighed is death, then clearly the second principle comes out ahead by the universalizability test, for each person, putting himself simultaneously in the place of all the potentially affected parties, must regard a 1/6 chance of death in such circumstances as preferable to a 5/6 chance—or perhaps more accurately, must regard dying in one life as preferable to dying in five.

If we add in the value of inviolability, the assessment will be different. Each of us has to compare (a) the situation of the one person's being killed and *all* of us being morally liable to such treatment, with (b) the situation of the five dying and *none* of us being liable to being killed for such reasons. But does this really change anything? If I were one of the five victims whose life could be saved by killing someone else, would it be any compensation to think that, although I am going to die, I am at least someone it would be impermissible to kill to save the lives of five others? "Compensation" probably isn't the right word, but the moral situation does seem to me to have this form, and there is some very large value in the status of inviolability conferred by such a right—perhaps nearly as great as the value of survival itself.

Applying the universalizability test here is rather harder than adding apples and oranges, but I believe that is what has to be done to determine the thresholds, defined in consequentialist terms, at which even noninstrumental rights must give way. I believe there are such thresholds, and that even if rights are not instrumental they are not absolute. Their extent depends in part on other values besides the noninstrumental value of inviolability. But I believe that if we include that value in their justification, it renders them less puzzling.[10]

I have said practically nothing about what sorts of inviolability are important. My general view is that the true domain of this value is the personal: one's life, one's body, one's mind, freedom of action and personal association or attachment, sexual freedom, freedom of expression, and freedom of inquiry. These are the regions in which a noninstrumental defense of rights is most promising. There are familiar controversies about other kinds of freedom of choice and association, and also about rights to harm oneself—with addictive drugs, for example. Libertarians defend strong rights of economic liberty, but I believe general economic inviolability does not have this kind of value. The only credible defense of economic rights that goes beyond the domain of the purely personal is an instrumental one—based on the usefulness of free enterprise and private capital accumulation in promoting the general welfare. With regard to the other question, freedom to harm oneself, I feel very unsure, partly because it is difficult to know how to weigh in the usual moral framework the competing claims of an earlier self who does the harm and a later self who suffers the consequences. Perhaps if the consequences are sufficiently separated in time, there are forms of self-destruction that are violations of one's own rights, rather than merely manifestations of eccentric preferences.

Most rights will not be absolute, and determining plausible thresholds can be difficult. I believe such questions can be addressed only by factoring the value of inviolability into a broader framework of universalizability, along with other, more familiar values. I haven't tried to explain how the conflicts between these different types of values would be resolved by a universalizability test, and it would not be easy to do so. I have merely described in outline a new way of looking at the issue. Even if it is viable, it may make rights only slightly less mysterious, but at least it would permit us to see them as part of a larger moral system without reducing them entirely to instruments for the promotion of other ends. If it accomplishes nothing else, Kamm's explanation of the significance of noninstrumental rights should at least clarify the choice of whether or not to believe in them.[11]

---

10. A fuller account would have to distinguish the value of different degrees of inviolability, as determined by the level of the threshold at which it gives out. Presumably, if there are thresholds, this value does not increase in direct proportion to the consequences one may not violate the right in order to avoid. A degree of inviolability will, in general, have the following form: persons may not be subjected to treatment T unless the net advantage of doing so, including the treatment itself, is greater than A.

Act-utilitarianism is equivalent to setting A equal to zero. An absolute right would set A at infinity. Rights with finite positive thresholds still represent significantly valuable degrees of inviolability, capable of outweighing other advantages in the justification of a morality.

11. This essay is the English version of "La valeur de l'inviolabilité" from *Revue de Métaphysique et de Morale* (1994): pp. 149–166.

C. Potential Congruence and Irreconcilability

6

Potential Congruence

SAMUEL SCHEFFLER

Can morality conflict with self-interest? That is, can circumstances arise in which doing the wrong thing will advance the agent's interests, while doing the right thing will set those interests back? To many people it seems obvious that the answer is "yes". The whole point of morality, it may be said, is to serve as a check on individual self-interest. Morality can hardly perform that function unless it offers directives that not only can but frequently do differ from those of self-interest itself. Yet some philosophers have argued that, appearances to the contrary notwithstanding, the answer is actually "no". Once we have a proper understanding of morality and of the nature of individual interests, we will see that morality and self-interest can never in fact conflict.

Both answers have something to be said for them. On the one hand, it is true that those who insist on the ubiquity of conflict sometimes rely, implicitly if not explicitly, on unduly restrictive conceptions of morality or individual interests or both. Often, for example, they try to demonstrate the frequency of conflict by describing what is said to be a common sort of case. In cases of this kind, someone faces a choice between two options, and there is some explicitly or paradigmatically moral consideration—about the duty to keep one's promises, say, or to assist those who are in need—that supports one of the options. Choosing that option, however, would compromise some personal project or relationship that the agent cherishes. So there is said to be a dilemma: the agent must choose between morality and self-interest. But this characterization is appropriate only if one assumes that morality itself attaches no weight to the agent's ability to cultivate projects and relationships, or that judgments about what is right or wrong can only be supported by explicitly or paradigmatically moral considerations. Upon reflection, these assumptions seem implausible, and once one recognizes this, it becomes surprisingly difficult to identify clear cases of conflict between morality and self-interest.[1]

1. For argument to this effect, see my *Human Morality* (New York: Oxford University Press, 1992), 30–33, 56–60, 111–14.

On the other hand, it seems correct to say that the standpoints of morality and self-interest represent distinct normative perspectives, which play different roles in our reflections about how to live and in our practices of interpersonal criticism. Although identifying clear cases of conflict between them may not be a straightforward matter, it would nevertheless be very surprising if they were guaranteed always to coincide.

There is another pertinent consideration whose bearing on this issue is sometimes overlooked. Some of the clearest instances of apparent conflict between morality and self-interest involve situations of oppression or grave injustice. In such situations, it seems that morality may require an individual who is the beneficiary of injustice to take a stand against it, even if doing so means incurring significant costs in self-interested terms. Yet if morality and self-interest do conflict in such cases, these are conflicts that human practices and institutions helped to create and which they might well have avoided. If this is correct, then it would be a mistake to address questions about the relation between morality and self-interest without considering how the social and political context structures the choices that individuals face.

In *Human Morality* I developed an account of the relation between morality and the standpoint of the individual agent that was meant to be sensitive to all of these considerations. According to that account, the relation between morality and self-interest is best described as one of *potential congruence*. This notion involves three constituent ideas. The first is that, although moral requirements do not always coincide with the individual agent's interests, moral norms serve to regulate the conduct of human beings, and their content is constrained by their regulative role, in the sense that they must be capable of being integrated in a coherent and attractive way into an individual human life. The second idea is that, despite the undeniable strength of self-interested motives, powerful motivations that are responsive to moral considerations can also emerge during the course of an individual's development, motivations that are deeply rooted in the structure of the individual's personality. These motivations help to shape the interests of those who possess them, and while their presence does not guarantee that conflicts between moral demands and the agent's interests will never arise, it does reduce the frequency of such conflicts, and moral motivations do not normally work to the long-term disadvantage of their possessors. The third idea is that it is, to a large extent, a practical social task—and a practicable social goal—to achieve a degree of fit between what morality demands and what people's motivational resources can supply. This is because what morality demands depend on the state of the world in morally relevant respects, and what a person is motivated to do depends on how the person has been educated and socialized. These factors in turn are dependent, in obvious ways, on the institutional structure and broader practices of the society in which one lives.

Although I continue to accept the essentials of this account, I want in this essay to think through some doubts about it, in the hope of refining the account and reassessing its force. For the most part, the doubts I will discuss challenge the significance and even the reality of the problem to which the account is addressed. If there is no genuine problem to begin with, then the account may seem misguided or unnecessary. It may seem to rest on a mistake. Before addressing these doubts, I will expand a bit on each of the three constituent ideas that I have mentioned, borrowing freely from what I said in the book.

I interpret the first idea as meaning that, within generous limits, morality makes room for personal projects and relationships. In ordinary circumstances, it is permissible for agents to develop and pursue a wide range of personal projects and to cultivate personal relationships of many different kinds. This is not because a feasible morality must compromise with the depressing realities of human nature and human motivation. It is not because, given what imperfect creatures humans are, we must settle for a morality of the second best. It is, rather, because morality at its best is a system for regulating human action and interaction, and it would not be a plausible system of that kind if it were not sensitive to the most fundamental aims and interests of those to whom it applies—to the goods and purposes that they hope to achieve through their actions and interactions. A putative moral system that did not make room for people to cultivate personal projects and relationships would not be a better or purer morality; it would be no morality at all.

The second idea asserts that the psychological bases of effective moral motivation have sources deep within the self. Partly for this reason, mature moral motivation does not function as a self-contained component of the person's motivational repertoire. Instead, it has diverse and widespread effects on the individual's deliberations, emotions, and interactions with others. This does not mean that morally motivated people go in for a great deal of explicit moral reflection or deliberation. Most do not. But moral concerns influence our perceptions of salience and the content of our deliberations even when we are not thinking in explicitly moral terms. Moral beliefs are implicated in our emotional lives, inasmuch as the possibility of experiencing "reactive attitudes" like guilt, resentment, indignation, and a sense of indebtedness depends on such beliefs. And morality helps to structure social relations, not only in the sense that some level of compliance with moral norms is required if social relations are to flourish but also in the sense that the liability of others to experience reactive attitudes is a condition of the possibility and desirability of entering into certain sorts of relationships with them.

For morally motivated individuals, then, moral concerns are woven throughout the fabric of their personalities and their interpersonal relations, and this by itself casts doubt on the starkness of the contrast between morality and self-interest. But there is also a further consideration that reinforces these doubts. As a person acquires moral motives, one thing that happens is that the person increasingly attempts to shape his or her projects, insofar as it is possible to do so, to avoid conflicts with moral requirements. And since one's projects and commitments help to determine what is in one's interests, this means that the individual in effect shapes his or her own interests in such a way as to avoid perceived conflicts with morality. The upshot is that, in addition to structuring our perceptions and our deliberations, our emotions and our relations to others, moral beliefs also help to shape our projects, our commitments, and our interests themselves.

Taken together, the first two components of the notion of "potential congruence" imply that the relation of morality and self-interest is characterized by a high degree of mutual accommodation. On the one hand, morality makes significant room for individuals to pursue the personal projects and relationships that help to define their interests. On the other hand, morally motivated individuals shape their own interests in such a way as to minimize conflicts with morality. The phenomenon of mutual accommodation does not guarantee that conflicts between morality and self-interest will never arise, but it does explain why it can be tempting to think that this is so, and why it can be difficult in practice to identify clear cases of conflict.

The third and final element of the notion of potential congruence is the idea that the degree of conflict between morality and self-interest is not fixed or invariant, but depends instead on the nature of the prevailing social and political institutions and practices. These institutions and practices can influence the frequency and severity of such conflicts in a number of ways. For one thing, a society's institutions—for example, its schools, family institutions, child-care arrangements, and criminal justice and mental health systems—can do either more or less to nurture the psychological bases of effective moral motivation, and thus, indirectly, to encourage people to shape their interests in ways that avoid conflict with morality. In addition, the justice or injustice of social and political institutions can directly influence the frequency with which conflicts between morality and self-interest actually arise. In severely unjust societies, morality is likely to demand more of people than it does in just societies, and the range of morally acceptable pursuits open to people is likely to be narrower, thus making it more difficult for individuals to shape their interests so as to avoid conflicts with morality. Taken together, these points imply that human institutions and practices help to determine the prevalence, both of the motives that lead people to try to shape their interests in such a way as to satisfy moral norms, and of some of the primary factors that can frustrate such attempts. This means that the degree of conflict between morality and self-interest is in some respects a social and political issue.

To summarize: the idea of potential congruence asserts that the relation between morality and the interests of the individual agent is characterized by a high degree of mutual accommodation, so that the frequency and severity of conflict between these two perspectives is significantly reduced. Conflicts are nevertheless possible in principle, but the extent to which they arise in practice is not fixed or immutable. Instead, the frequency of conflict depends to a considerable degree on the character of the prevailing social and political institutions. Achieving convergence between morality and self-interest is in part a social and political task.

Ruth Chang has pointed out[2] that the account of the "priority" of morality developed by Thomas Scanlon in his book *What We Owe to Each Other*[3] (and elsewhere) is similar in a number of respects to my account of potential congruence. Scanlon too suggests that there is a form of mutual accommodation that serves to reduce the degree of conflict between morality and an individual's projects and relationships. On the one hand, he says that "contractualist morality makes room for projects and commitments".[4] Or, as he puts the point elsewhere, moral require-

---

2. Ruth Chang, "Putting Together Morality and Well-Being," in *Practical Conflicts: New Philosophical Essays*, ed. P. Baumann and M. Betzler (Cambridge: Cambridge University Press, 2004), 118–58, at 152. Chang herself offers a novel proposal for "putting together" morality and well-being. I find her proposal interesting but obscure.

3. T. M. Scanlon, *What We Owe to Each Other* (Cambridge, Mass.: Harvard University Press, 1998).

4. T. M. Scanlon, "Reasons, Responsibility, and Reliance: Replies to Wallace, Dworkin, and Deigh," *Ethics* 112 (2002): 507–28, at 514.

ments "leave room for other values".[5] On the other hand, he says that these "other values have a built-in sensitivity to moral requirements".[6] "Properly understood," he writes, they "have a built-in sensitivity to the demands of right and wrong".[7] Scanlon also maintains, although for slightly different reasons than the ones I have mentioned, that "the degree to which there is a conflict between the morality of right and wrong and the goods of personal relations depends greatly on the society in which one lives".[8] Thus, all three elements of the idea of potential congruence have clear parallels in Scanlon's account.

Chang cites Jay Wallace as expressing doubts about whether what she calls "the Scheffler-Scanlon strategy" can eliminate all conflicts between moral and prudential considerations.[9] But the idea of potential congruence explicitly allows for continuing conflicts, maintaining only that such conflicts are less extensive than they are sometimes taken to be, and that their frequency depends in part on the prevailing social and political institutions. Nor do I believe that Scanlon sees his position as eliminating all conflict between moral and prudential considerations.[10] And while Wallace does express doubts about certain aspects of Scanlon's position, he goes on to offer a "reconstructed"[11] version of that position which retains much of its basic content. Elsewhere, moreover, Wallace himself invokes the idea of "congruence" in discussing the relation between morality and considerations of individual well-being.[12] He rejects Sidgwick's bleak conviction that the contrast between morality and self-interest reflects the ineliminable "dualism of practical reason",[13] and argues

5. Scanlon, *What We Owe to Each Other*, 161.

6. Scanlon, "Reasons, Responsibility and Reliance," 514.

7. Scanlon, *What We Owe to Each Other*, 166.

8. Ibid.

9. Chang, "Putting Together Morality and Well-Being," 152. She is referring to the discussion in R. Jay Wallace, "Scanlon's Contractualism," *Ethics* 112 (2002): 429–70, at 451–59.

10. However, Scanlon does wish to argue that, when conflicts arise, then "we have good reason to give priority to the demands of right and wrong" (*What We Owe to Each Other*, 166). Wallace's doubts about Scanlon's position are focused primarily on this aspect of his view, and perhaps this is true of Chang's doubts as well. By contrast, the idea of potential congruence is neutral on the question of what we have most reason to do when conflicts between morality and self-interest arise. It is compatible with the claim that, in such cases, we always have most reason to do what morality requires, but it is also compatible with the denial of that claim. In *Human Morality* I expressed doubts about the claim but argued that, given the phenomenon of potential congruence, its falsity would pose less of a threat to the authority of morality than is sometimes supposed.

11. Wallace, "Scanlon's Contractualism," 457.

12. R. Jay Wallace, "The Rightness of Acts and the Goodness of Lives," in *Reason and Value: Themes from the Moral Philosophy of Joseph Raz*, ed. R. J. Wallace, P. Pettit, S. Scheffler, and M. Smith (Oxford: Clarendon, 2004), 385–411, at 403ff.

13. Henry Sidgwick, *The Methods of Ethics*, 7th ed. (London: Macmillan, 1907), xii–xiii, 404n, 496–509. Sidgwick traces the idea to Bishop Butler. For a contemporary defense of a version of this kind of dualism, see Roger Crisp, "The Dualism of Practical Reason," *Proceedings of the Aristotelian Society* 96 (1996): 53–73. Crisp says that I develop a dualistic view in *The Rejection of Consequentialism* (Oxford: Clarendon, 1982; rev. ed. 1994), but I regard this as a misinterpretation.

instead that "the differing standpoints can be brought into substantive alignment",[14] so that a "congruence in practical reason" can be attained.[15] He does not claim that this suffices to eliminate all conflicts between the two standpoints. Instead, he acknowledges that, as a practical matter, the two perspectives can "continue to diverge from each other", and that bringing about convergence is a "social and psychological problem, not a philosophical one".[16] Thus, in the end, Wallace's position also has a number of elements in common with the idea of "potential congruence" as I have described it.

As I have been emphasizing, the appeal to potential congruence is not meant to establish complete convergence between morality and self-interest. Nor does it claim that, whenever they diverge, a rational agent must always give priority to morality. So potential congruence is not offered as a demonstration that a "rational egoist" must always comply with moral requirements. Nor is it offered as a reply to the "amoralist", that stock figure of philosophical discussion who is supposed to deny that he or she has any reason to care about morality. Still less does it provide the basis for an argument that is meant to sway actual flesh-and-blood villains, thugs, or moral monsters, whose relations to the philosophical stereotypes of the rational egoist and the amoralist are unclear—certainly their problem is not that they suffer from an excess of *prudence*—and who are presumably uninterested in philosophical argument in any case.

Insofar as the rational egoist, the amoralist, and the villain are thought to present challenges to morality or grounds for skepticism about it, the idea of potential congruence provides no direct response to those challenges. One form of skepticism to which it does provide a response is the view that morality is always an alien, external force that is imposed on the individual from outside and is systematically at odds with his or her good. Against this sort of skepticism, the idea of potential congruence asserts that moral concerns can be integrated in a coherent and attractive way into an individual life. This is possible, moreover, because morality itself facilitates an important form of personal integration; it provides a way of integrating an ideal of equal respect for others with one's natural interest in pursuing one's own projects and commitments. This emphasis on the possibility of integrating moral concerns into an attractive human life and on the integrative role of morality itself provides a contrast to the dichotomous picture of a "dualism of practical reason". Morality and self-interest can indeed come into conflict, but conflict between them is neither systematic nor pervasive, and it should not be treated as a fundamental structural feature of human reason itself.

I will therefore set aside the objection that the potential congruence of morality and self-interest would not eliminate all conflicts between them nor provide a basis for responding to all forms of moral skepticism. This observation is perfectly correct and is not anything I would want to deny, but it is not an objection to the idea of potential congruence as I have explained it. There are, however, three other objections that I want to consider.

14. Wallace, "The Rightness of Acts and the Goodness of Lives," 403.
15. Ibid., 408.
16. Ibid., 406.

First, it may be claimed that self-interest is too narrow a notion for the contrast between it and morality to be interesting or philosophically significant; to the extent that the idea of potential congruence is a response to that contrast, it therefore rests on a misconception. The claim, in other words, is that while the contrast between morality and self-interest is indeed a sharp one, this is only because self-interest is a narrowly prudential or welfarist notion. Given the narrowness of self-interest, it enjoys no special authority in rational deliberation, and the fact that it can conflict with morality poses no special problem. Our narrow self-interest can conflict with many of our nonmoral aims as well, just as those aims can conflict with one another. While conflicts among our various moral and nonmoral aims raise many questions for the theory of practical reason, it is misleading to focus on the contrast between morality and self-interest in particular, or to suggest that the conflict between these two perspectives poses an especially vexing philosophical problem.

I am sympathetic to much of the spirit of this objection, but I do not think that it casts doubt on the idea of potential congruence or deflates the philosophical significance of the underlying issue to which that idea is a response. Although I have so far been content to frame the underlying issue in terms of a contrast between morality and self-interest, I agree that, if we understand self-interest narrowly, as it is perhaps natural to do, then questions about the relation of morality to self-interest in particular lose much of their force. However, I do not believe that the underlying problem disappears if self-interest is thought of as a narrow notion. Without appealing to narrow self-interest, we can still raise the question of whether compliance with moral norms always contributes to a good or meaningful life for the agent. Recast in this way, the question loses none of its interest or significance. We might perhaps construe it as a question about the relation between morality and a broad notion of self-interest.[17] However, I accept—for reasons I will spell out more fully later—that it may be preferable to abandon the terminology of "self-interest" altogether, and to frame the underlying question in some other way. We might formulate it instead as a question about the relation between morality and the agent's good or between morality and individual well-being. Or, alternatively, we might speak of the relation between morality and what Wallace calls the "standpoint of eudaimonistic reflection," by which he means the deliberative perspective "from which we are concerned with the question of the contribution of our activities to the goodness of our own lives".[18] The important point is that, whichever piece of terminology we use, the appearance that conflict is possible will persist, and the urgency of investigating that possibility will only be enhanced if narrow self-interest is replaced by a broader notion whose claims on our attention are more compelling.

A second objection concerns the deliberative role and, in consequence, the normative significance of notions like "self-interest" and "well-being", however they are understood. Scanlon and Joseph Raz have argued forcefully that such notions have at best a very limited role to play in individuals' deliberations about what to do.

17. As I noted at the outset, some people think that, given a suitably broad understanding of individual interests, the possibility of conflict between morality and self-interest is eliminated.

18. Wallace, "The Rightness of Acts and the Goodness of Lives," 399.

Scanlon, for instance, says that the concept of well-being has "surprisingly little role to play in the thinking of the rational individual whose life it is".[19] Although the successful pursuit of valuable ends normally contributes to one's well-being, this fact does not explain why these ends are valuable or why we pursue them. Instead, we pursue ends that we perceive as valuable because of their perceived value and not because of their contribution to our well-being. Or as Scanlon puts it: "[F]rom an individual's own point of view many of the things that contribute to his or her well-being are valued for quite other reasons. From this point of view the idea of one's own well-being is transparent. When we focus on it, it largely disappears, leaving only the values that make it up".[20]

In developing this argument, Scanlon's immediate target is not the contrast between morality and self-interest, or between morality and individual well-being. He is instead concerned to demonstrate that well-being is not a "master value" that dominates practical reasoning, is best understood in teleological terms, and is therefore congenial to consequentialist moral thought. Nevertheless, his argument might be thought to imply that the supposed contrast is misconceived and that there is no significant question to be asked about the relation between morality and self-interest, or between morality and well-being. If this is correct, we might again be tempted to conclude that the appeal to potential congruence rests on a mistake. I do not think that Scanlon's argument has this implication, however. Even if we accept that, from the deliberative perspective of the agent, well-being "largely disappears, leaving only the values that make it up", we can still ask about the relation between morality and those values that "make up" well-being. The question loses none of its interest when framed in this way, and the appeal to potential congruence seems just as relevant. This is, in effect, the lesson that Scanlon himself seems to draw. As we have seen, he does not address the relation between morality and well-being in those terms, but he does consider the relation between contractualist morality and personal "projects and commitments"—or between morality and "other values"—and his account of that relation has much in common with the appeal to potential congruence.

It is also worth remembering that the transparency of well-being, as Scanlon describes it, is exclusively a first-person deliberative phenomenon. So even if we limit our attention to the relation between morality and well-being—as opposed to the relation between morality and the values that make up well-being—more would need to be said before concluding that the phenomenon of deliberative transparency deprives questions about that relation of all of their significance. After all, Scanlon points out that, despite its deliberative transparency and the fact that it is not a "master value", the notion of well-being does have an important role to play from the third-person perspective of a benefactor. With respect to the normative significance of well-being, then, there is an asymmetry between the first- and third-person perspectives, and this raises a number of important questions that I cannot pursue here. In the context of this discussion, the pertinent point is simply that one cannot assume,

---

19. Scanlon, *What We Owe to Each Other*, 109. Similarly, Raz says that "normally our own well-being is not an independent factor in our deliberations". See Raz, "The Central Conflict: Morality and Self-Interest," in *Engaging Reason: On the Theory of Value and Action* (Oxford: Oxford University Press, 1999), 303–32, at 317.

20. Scanlon, ibid., 133.

absent additional argument, that the deliberative transparency of well-being would undercut the contrast between morality and well-being altogether. This would be true only if the putative significance of that contrast were exhausted by its relevance for first-person deliberation.

In any case, however, the deliberative transparency of well-being and related notions is not complete, for there are some contexts in which people *do* deliberate about the effects of different choices on their interests. Moreover, as Wallace argues, it is possible to reflect on the course of one's life and to ask questions about its good-ness or meaningfulness that have obvious deliberative relevance. Even if this kind of "eudaimonistic" reflection is not best characterized as being concerned with one's "well-being" or one's "interests", the relation between the eudaimonistic and moral perspectives raises questions that are most naturally understood as variants of the ones that have often been framed in terms of morality and self-interest.

For these reasons, I do not think that the phenomenon of deliberative trans-parency, important though it is, shows that questions about the relation between morality and the perspective of the individual agent are misplaced. Despite the (considerable) deliberative transparency of well-being, it is possible to ask about the relation between morality and the values that constitute individual well-being, and it is also possible to ask whether and to what extent compliance with moral norms con-tributes to the goodness or meaningfulness of individual lives. In addressing these questions, the idea of potential congruence seems to me to retain its interest and relevance. Or, at any rate, the phenomenon of deliberative transparency does not by itself suggest otherwise.

Nevertheless, there is room for serious doubt about whether either morality or "self-interest" (as I will continue, for the time being, to call it) retains sufficient unity for there to be a clear or interesting question about the relation between these two "standpoints" or "perspectives". This is the third objection that I want to consider. It is likely to seem pressing if we reject the dualism of practical reason, accept the deliberative transparency of well-being, and agree that there are diverse values and aims whose pursuit can contribute to good or meaningful lives. If we endorse a form of value pluralism and do not suppose that individual well-being or self-interest plays a privileged or even a very significant role in practical deliberation, then the putative contrast between morality and self-interest may seem to crumble or dissipate: to become just one more untenable dualism.

This line of thought has been developed with particular force by Raz.[21] Raz advo-cates a strong form of value pluralism, and he denies that "morality forms a distinct body of considerations which differs from that involved in other areas of practical

---

21. Many of Raz's writings are relevant, but see especially the three essays included as chapters 11–13 of *Engaging Reason*: "On the Moral Point of View" (247–72), "The Amoralist" (273–302), and "The Central Conflict: Morality and Self-Interest" (303–32). In his review of *Human Morality*, Raz appeals to the disunity of morality in criticizing my views. See Raz, "A Morality Fit for Humans," *Michigan Law Review* 91 (1993): 1297–1314. His discussion in that review foreshadows a number of the arguments developed in the three essays in *Engaging Reason*. Amélie Rorty also appeals to the disunity of morality in criticizing *Human Morality*. See her "Moral Complexity, Conflicted Resonance and Virtue," *Philosophy and Phenomeno-logical Research* 55 (1995): 949–56.

thought"[22]. There is, he suggests, no "philosophically deep way of dividing consider-ations into moral and non-moral".[23] Different distinctions of this kind may legitimately be drawn in different specific contexts and for different specific purposes. But there is no unified or canonical understanding of the moral domain that underlies them all, and to which the various context-dependent distinctions are ultimately answerable. Instead, Raz argues, "[W]hen we deliberate we consider which reasons are most press-ing in a way which transcends and defies the common division of practical thought into moral and self-interested (and other) considerations".[24]

In mounting his arguments, Raz tends to assume that there would be a philo-sophically interesting contrast between morality and self-interest only if there were some "ontic, metaphysical, or epistemic significance to the distinction between moral and non-moral considerations".[25] More specifically, he thinks that those who believe in such a contrast imagine that "moral values form either epistemically or metaphysically a separate range of considerations which can be validated or estab-lished only by special arguments".[26] For example, they may think that prudential values are "relational" in character: that is, such values pertain to what is *good for* particular individuals. By contrast, moral values are "nonrelational" in character: that is, they pertain to what is good *simpliciter*. Moral values are dependent on pru-dential values in the sense that the well-being of individuals or the satisfaction of their interests is good *simpliciter* only because it is good for those individuals. This implies that a person could pursue prudential values without recognizing moral val-ues, and it supports the thesis that morality and self-interest are distinct domains.

Against this line of argument, Raz maintains that there is a reciprocal relation-ship between relational and nonrelational goods. Although it is true that nothing can be a good unless it is possible for it to be good for someone, it is also true that relational values presuppose nonrelational values, in the sense that nothing can be good for a person unless it is also good *simpliciter*. Indeed, Raz maintains that there is nothing more to something's being good for a person than its being a good *sim-pliciter* with which the person has the opportunity to engage in appropriate ways. He takes this to suggest "that self-interest does not constitute a distinct point of view in any 'deep' sense"[27] and, correlatively, that the distinctiveness of moral values is only a superficial phenomenon. The recognition of such values is on a par with the recognition of other goods and is "no more difficult than recognizing the value of good wine".[28] This does not imply that no distinction of any kind can be drawn between morality and self-interest, but it does imply that the distinction between them is not metaphysically or epistemologically fundamental. Or, as he says else-where, "[M]oral values and moral requirements may differ in content from other values and requirements, but they do not differ fundamentally in the source of their

22. Raz, *Engaging Reason*, 274.
23. Ibid., 247.
24. Ibid., 306.
25. Ibid., 250.
26. Ibid., 259.
27. Ibid., 265.
28. Ibid., 281.

normativity".[29] The upshot, Raz thinks, is that "though a person's self-interest can conflict with moral considerations, there is no fundamental conflict between the two".[30] Moreover, "while cases in which self-interest is at odds with morality provide one context in which reason sometimes requires agents to act in ways detrimental to their self-interest this is not the only context in which this can happen".[31] In other words, although it is possible for morality and self-interest to conflict, there is no ontological gulf separating moral and self-interested considerations, and many things other than morality can conflict with self-interest as well.

Raz's arguments present a significant challenge to conventional ways of understanding the relation between morality and self-interest. The basic question those arguments raise is whether either morality or self-interest is a sufficiently unified concept for there to be any interesting question about the relation between them, or for questions about the rational authority of either to make good sense.

In thinking about Raz's challenge, perhaps the first issue that arises concerns the relation between two different ideas. The first idea is that neither morality nor self-interest is a sufficiently unified domain for questions about their relation to be of any great philosophical interest. The second is that the difference between morality and self-interest is not philosophically or metaphysically "deep". One response to Raz would be to deny that the first idea follows from the second. One might argue that morality and self-interest are sufficiently unified domains that questions about their relations to each other remain significant, even if the distinction between them does not correspond to any fundamental distinction in the metaphysics or epistemology of value, and even if one accepts both value pluralism and the deliberative transparency of well-being. According to this view, the unity of each of these domains is compatible with value pluralism, and it may be metaphysically "shallow" without being humanly or philosophically insignificant.

In a way, this response is suggested by Raz's own writings, for those writings exhibit a certain internal tension. At times, his appeals to value-pluralism, deliberative transparency, and the essential context-dependence of the distinction between moral and nonmoral considerations seem meant to destabilize the very concepts of morality and self-interest. If, for example, there is no deep or context-independent way of distinguishing moral from nonmoral considerations, and if the values commonly thought of as "moral" display the same diversity and heterogeneity as other values, then the question of morality's relation to self-interest may be thought too indeterminate to admit of any answer at all. As Wallace puts it, in summarizing Raz's view: "If morality does not constitute a unified normative domain…, then the general question about the normative force of 'moral' considerations will fail to get a grip—it will be basically unclear what we are even asking about".[32] Here the tendency of Raz's arguments is to suggest that "global" questions about the relation

29. Ibid., 305.
30. Ibid., 265.
31. Ibid., 321.
32. Wallace, "The Rightness of Acts and the Goodness of Lives," 385. In this spirit, Raz expresses support in "A Morality Fit for Humans" for the idea "that there is no such thing as a moral point of view" (1309).

between morality and self-interest should be seen as giving way "to an indefinite succession of first-order deliberative questions that confront individual agents as they make their way through life, questions that can be resolved only by reflection on the nature and significance of the concrete values that are at stake".[33]

Other passages, however, suggest that the aim of Raz's arguments is not to destabilize the concepts of morality and self-interest, but rather to normalize—or to deflate the significance of—conflicts between them. In these passages, his point is not that morality and self-interest are too indeterminate for us even to understand what would count as a conflict between them. It is, rather, that such conflicts are not rooted in any basic metaphysical or epistemological dichotomy and that, instead of being assigned unique importance, they should simply be assimilated to other forms of practical conflict. For example, this seems to be the spirit of the various passages I have quoted in which Raz affirms that conflicts between morality and self-interest are possible but says that they are neither fundamental nor unique. It is also suggested by his remark to the effect that moral values and requirements may differ from other values and requirements in their content but not in the source of their normativity. These comments presuppose that morality and self-interest are sufficiently unified domains that it is possible to talk sensibly and truthfully about them and their relations, even if those relations do not correspond to any fundamental metaphysical distinction. Indeed, what Raz says about their relations in such passages has something in common with the idea of potential congruence, at least insofar as that idea too affirms the possibility of conflict between morality and self-interest but denies that such conflicts are ubiquitous or built into the structure of practical reason.

It is this strand in Raz's argument that may encourage the sort of response to his challenge that I have mentioned. In other words, it may encourage the thought that morality and self-interest are sufficiently unified domains that their relations to each other remain philosophically and humanly significant, even if the distinction between them is "metaphysically shallow". The residual disagreement between Raz and the interlocutor who offers this response would presumably be a disagreement about how significant, given the shallowness of the distinction, the relation between morality and self-interest really is. From the premise that the distinction is shallow, Raz concludes that the relation is of diminished significance. The interlocutor concludes instead that the significance of the relation does not depend on the depth of the distinction.

In effect, the two different strands in Raz's argument leave us with two different questions to address. First, there is the question of whether it makes sense to think of morality and self-interest as unified domains at all, given the assumptions of value pluralism, deliberative transparency, and lack of metaphysical depth. Second, if it does make sense to think of the two domains as unified, but only in a metaphysically shallow way, then there is also the question of whether the relation between them retains any philosophical significance. Is the contrast between these two "standpoints" or "perspectives" of continuing interest, if it is not grounded in any basic metaphysical distinction?

33. Wallace, ibid., 386.

One way to approach these questions is by reflecting on the range of perspectival evaluative judgments with which we are familiar. By "perspectival evaluative judgments" I mean evaluative judgments that are explicitly or implicitly relativized to a particular "perspective" or "standpoint" or "point of view". I mean to include within this category purely evaluative judgments, such as judgments about what is good or bad, or better or worse, from a particular standpoint or perspective, and also normative judgments, such as judgments about what, from a given perspective, is the right or wrong thing to do. Perspectival evaluative judgments are a commonplace feature of our thought and discourse, and they come in many different kinds. Let me mention some examples.

First, there are judgments about what would be good or bad for a particular person or for a subject of some other kind. Some development may be said to be good for John or bad for Mary, good for the philosophy department or bad for the country. Second, there are judgments that specify how particular individuals evaluate a given action or event. From John's perspective, the U.S. invasion of Iraq was a noble undertaking, while from Mary's perspective it was a crime. Here the point is not that the invasion was good for John and bad for Mary, but rather that he evaluated it in one way and she in another. The statement that some development was a good thing from John's standpoint is ambiguous, for it may express a judgment of either of the first two kinds. It may mean either that it was good for John or that John evaluated it as a good thing. This ambiguity is made possible by the fact that, in both of these types of judgment, the relevant standpoint is defined by a *person* (e.g., John).

Third, perspectival evaluative judgments sometimes have the character of action-guiding instrumental claims or hypothetical imperatives. From the standpoint of termite eradication, it would be much better to use the toxic spray than the nontoxic one. Here the "standpoint" is defined by a particular *goal* (termite eradication), and a certain course of action (using the toxic spray) is singled out as the better way to achieve that goal. Fourth, perspectival judgments are sometimes used to indicate the bearing of a particular value on an action, policy, or other item. From an efficiency standpoint the administration's economic policy is ideal, but from the point of view of fairness it leaves much to be desired. Here each "standpoint" is defined by a particular *value* (efficiency, fairness), and a certain item (the administration's economic policy) is assessed in relation to each of those values, respectively. Fifth, some perspectival judgments represent assessments along a particular dimension of the excellence of an action or performance. The skater's performance was crowd pleasing but from an athletic standpoint it was unexceptional. In this case the standpoint is defined by a certain kind of *activity* (athletic activity) and the standards of excellence that apply to it.

Finally, perspectival judgments are sometimes used to express all-things-considered conclusions about the acceptability or unacceptability of a specified course of action relative to a given system of norms. From the standpoint of etiquette what he did was intolerable. From a legal standpoint there is no doubt that what she did was wrong. From a constitutional perspective this piece of legislation ("act of Congress") fails to pass muster. From the standpoint of religious doctrine what he did was impermissible. In these cases the relevant standpoint is defined by a *system of norms*. One familiar context in which such all-things-considered perspectival judgments are made is when two systems of norms give conflicting directives. From a legal standpoint what she did was perfectly acceptable but from a religious standpoint it was a sin. And so on.

Although these various kinds of judgments differ from one another in important respects, several general observations are possible. First, the perspectival language in all of these judgments is metaphysically superficial. The talk of "standpoints" or "points of view" or "perspectives" is meant to specify the nature of the concern that lies behind a given judgment, and not to stake an ontological claim. Of course, the ontological status of a particular underlying concern (fairness, the legal system) may be contested or require interpretation, but our ordinary talk of standpoints is not by itself meant to address such issues, nor is its point to reify standpoints themselves as additional items to be included in one's ontology.

Second, all of these judgments leave room for questions about the authority of the specified standpoint or perspective, and the answers need not be the same in every case. Why should we care what is good for John, or from his point of view? What kinds of claims do the value of efficiency, the legal system, or the norms of etiquette have on us? In general, perspectival language serves to bracket these questions and not to foreclose them.

Third, perspectival judgments of most of these kinds have obvious deliberative relevance. Yet neither the mere truth nor the mere assertion of such a judgment normally implies that the judgment itself either does or should enter explicitly into anyone's deliberations. In particular, it does not imply that the judgment should enter into the deliberations of the agent who "occupies" the standpoint, in cases where the standpoint is occupied by an agent, nor into the deliberations of the agent whose actions are being assessed, in cases where the judgment is a judgment about someone's actions. The judgment that something would be good for John does not entail that that very judgment either does or should enter explicitly into John's deliberations. Nor does the judgment that a certain action is acceptable from a legal standpoint entail that that judgment itself either does or should enter explicitly into the deliberations of the agent. The deliberative relevance of perspectival judgments can vary from case to case and requires nuanced characterization.[34]

---

34. For additional discussion of the deliberative relevance of moral judgments in particular, see *Human Morality*, 29–38. As I argue there: "[M]ost morally acceptable conduct is prompted by thoughts with no overtly moral content. Nor is this true only, as one might initially suspect, of morally permissible, as opposed to morally required, conduct. The thought with which one does the right thing need not be 'this is the right thing to do'; it can just as easily be 'he's hungry' or 'she didn't mean to' or 'that would hurt his feelings' or 'I said I'd be there'. This means that a morally successful agent will need to be sensitive, not only to overtly moral considerations (moral considerations narrowly understood), but also to considerations like those just mentioned, which lack overtly moral content, but which nevertheless have an important bearing on the moral assessment of what one does (moral considerations broadly understood). What a morally successful agent will certainly not need to do is to engage at all times in the explicit moral assessment of his or her own conduct" (33).

Compare Scanlon: "'Being moral' in the sense described by the morality of right and wrong involves not just being moved to avoid certain actions 'because they would be wrong,'

We should also note that, with respect to at least some of the types of judgments I have mentioned, questions can be raised about how such judgments relate to more specific evaluative judgments. Questions of this sort often arise with respect to all-things-considered judgments made from the perspective of a system of norms. What is the relation, for example, between the judgment that an action is legally prohibited and the judgment that it is a crime or a felony, or that it is an instance of murder or manslaughter? What is the relation between the judgment that an action is contrary to the rules of etiquette and the judgment that it is rude or boorish or impolite? Similar questions sometimes arise with respect to other types of perspectival judgments as well. What is the relation between the judgment that a given performance exhibited a high degree of athletic excellence and the judgment that it involved a display of unusual strength or agility or speed? In all of these cases the relations between the general and specific evaluative judgments require interpretation. What accounts for the fact that each of a number of diverse specific judgments may be related to a single general judgment? Are the specific judgments grounds for the more general judgments? Do they reflect the fact that one general evaluative property may be instantiated in different specific ways? Do the general judgments identify properties or reasons that are independent of the properties or reasons picked out by the more specific judgments, or do judgments of the first kind merely alert us to the presence of properties or reasons picked out by judgments of the second kind? These questions and others like them are of evident philosophical interest and the answers to them may not be at all obvious. But, outside of philosophical contexts, the mere fact that such questions can be raised does not deter us from making the more general judgments or shake our confidence in our ability to attach meaning to them.

The overall tendency of this line of thought is to "normalize" questions about the relations between morality and self-interest, by setting them in the broader context of perspectival evaluative judgments as a class. In so doing, it suggests that the distinction between the two perspectives need not be understood as metaphysically deep in order to play a role in our thought, and that the unity of each perspective can be maintained in the face of value pluralism. To this extent, it supports the less radical of the two strands in Raz's argument.[35] But it also suggests, on behalf of Raz's interlocutor, that the significance to us of questions about the relation between morality and self-interest need not depend on the "depth" of the distinction between

---

but also being moved by more concrete considerations such as 'she's counting on me' or 'he needs my help' or 'doing that would put them in danger.' A morally good person is sometimes moved by 'the sense of duty' but more often will be moved directly by these more concrete considerations, without the need to think that 'it would be wrong' to do otherwise" (*What We Owe to Each Other*, 155–56).

35. It is also generally in the spirit of the following passage from Raz: "[W]e are used to carving up the domain of value into smaller domains. We often assess events in terms of their significance to the subdomains. We recognize that some may care about some subdomain more than about others. None of this requires attributing independent sources of normativity to the subdomains" (*Engaging Reason*, 315). See also Raz's remarks about points of view on page 249 of *Engaging Reason*.

them. The significance of the questions may instead derive, for example, simply from the perception that the two perspectives can conflict sharply, that each plays an important role in human affairs, and that the power of self-interest has the potential to undermine compliance with moral norms and so to threaten the stability of social life.

It may seem tempting to extend this line of thought by saying that morality and self-interest constitute two different normative systems. Judgments about what one ought to do from the standpoint of morality and judgments about what one ought to do from the standpoint of self-interest both belong to the category of all-things-considered judgments made from the perspective of a system of norms. As such, these judgments do not by themselves imply that the unity of either system, or the distinction between the two systems, is anchored in metaphysical facts. Questions about the unity and authority of each system and about their relations to each other are on a par with questions about other systems of norms. Some philosophers draw distinctions in the metaphysics or epistemology of value by way of answering these questions, but the interest and importance of the questions is independent of those answers.

One problem with this way of extending the earlier line of thought is that it is unclear what is meant in saying that self-interest consists in a system of norms or principles. This terminology may seem natural when we are talking about legal, moral, or religious codes of conduct, but the case of self-interest does not seem relevantly analogous. To be sure, there are facts about what is in a person's interest, and sometimes these facts provide people with reasons for action. However, although I can think of many moral principles, and although it is not uncommon for people to cite such principles in explaining and justifying their conduct, I find it difficult to think of comparable "principles of self-interest", unless perhaps one counts the idea that one should take one's future interests into consideration in deciding what to do now. But if that is a principle of self-interest, it is not what most people have in mind when they worry about conflicts between morality and self-interest. So I think that it is a distortion to represent morality and self-interest as competing systems of principles. It is, moreover, a distortion that is characteristic of dualistic accounts of practical reason. In those accounts it is sometimes combined with a utilitarian understanding of morality, so that practical reason is seen as fundamentally divided between two conflicting norms, one of which (self-interest or "prudence") says that one should always pursue one's own good and one of which (morality) says that one should always pursue the good of all. This formulation represents morality and self-interest as rival but structurally parallel practical principles. In this way, it treats them as competing "systems" of norms, although each system consists ultimately in but a single principle.

These reflections lead me to conclude that, even if the distinction between morality and self-interest is not taken to be metaphysically "deep", the use of those particular terms to characterize the relevant distinction may import a certain bias in favor of dualism about practical reason. When combined with the reservations expressed previously about the narrowness of self-interest, this fact provides reason to frame the relevant contrast in some other way. As earlier suggested, it should perhaps be described as a contrast between morality and the good life, or between morality and the standpoint of eudaimonistic reflection, rather than as a conflict between morality and self-interest.

The important thing, of course, is not the terminology itself, but rather that the underlying issue should be clear and that the terminology should not serve to obscure it. The basic question concerns the extent to which compliance with moral norms is compatible with the ability of individual agents to lead good and fulfilling lives. Leading such a life normally involves the successful development and pursuit of choiceworthy projects and aims, and the development and maintenance over time of valuable and rewarding interpersonal relationships. The question is whether compliance with moral norms may at times deprive people of the resources or opportunities necessary to develop and sustain valuable projects and relationships, or in other ways hinder their ability to do so. Since it seems unobjectionable (though an understatement) to say that individuals have an interest in leading good and ful-filling lives, and so in developing and sustaining valuable projects and relationships, it would be possible to frame this as a question about whether compliance with moral norms can hinder the ability of individuals to satisfy these interests. Such a formulation need not deny the deliberative transparency of the concept of one's own interests; individuals normally deliberate about their projects and relationships, and not about the interests they define. Nor need it deny value pluralism; individuals may make good lives for themselves through their engagement with a wide and diverse range of valuable activities and relationships. Nor, again, need it presume the dualism of practical reason; the standpoint of the individual's interests, as here understood, is for obvious reasons an evaluative standpoint that is very important to us, but its importance need not be accounted for in metaphysical terms and is com-patible with the acknowledgment of a variety of evaluative standpoints.

Still, as I have already suggested, formulating the central question as a question about the relation between morality and self-interest is apt to be misleading, for sev-eral reasons. Despite what I have just said, it may easily be taken to involve a denial of deliberative transparency or value pluralism, or a commitment to the dualism of practical reason. In addition, the notion of self-interest, even when it is understood relatively broadly, may appear to suggest a narrower concern than the kind of con-cern about the goodness of individual lives that I have described. Finally, the formu-lation in terms of self-interest may seem to grant unwarranted authority to a form of "rational egoism" whose philosophical and human credentials are weak, and whose claims are not the source of the underlying worry that needs to be addressed. For all of these reasons, I believe that an alternative formulation would be preferable although, as I have said, what is important is not the terminology itself, but rather that the basic question should be clear.

The idea of potential congruence provides one answer to that question. As we have seen, it asserts that morality itself leaves significant room for individuals to develop and pursue the personal projects and relationships that help to define their interests and their good; that morally motivated individuals craft their projects and structure their commitments—and in so doing shape their own interests—in such a way as to minimize conflict with morality; that, in consequence of these two factors, compliance with moral norms will not normally hinder the ability of morally moti-vated individuals to lead good and fulfilling lives; and that although conflicts between moral requirements and the good of the individual agent can nevertheless arise on occasion, the frequency and severity of such conflicts are not fixed or immutable, but depend in part on social and political arrangements that are subject to human control.

Some may challenge this answer, as the third objection I have been considering does, by denying that morality is sufficiently unified for the idea of potential congruence to make sense. Yet I have argued that—insofar as I understand what the metaphor of depth is meant to convey in this context[36]—the unity of morality need not be secured at a philosophically or metaphysically "deep" level in order for the idea of potential congruence to make sense. Although many philosophers do understand the unity of the moral domain as underwritten by significant metaphysical or epistemological distinctions, potential congruence by itself demands little in the way of metaphysical or epistemological depth.[37] It demands only that "morality" be a sufficiently clear and coherent concept as to admit of determinate application, at least in central cases, and to allow the question of morality's relation to the good life to arise. For this reason among others, I doubt whether any thesis of the disunity of morality

36. This is a significant qualification. I have so far proceeded as if it were clear what is meant in saying (or denying) that a distinction is philosophically or metaphysically deep. But the metaphor of depth is just that—a metaphor—and what it is meant to include (or exclude) is not always clear. Different passages from Raz's writing suggest a variety of different things that he means to be denying when he denies that the unity of morality, or the distinction between morality and self-interest, is deep. For example, at various times he seems to be denying (a) that there is "ontic, metaphysical, or epistemic significance to the distinction between moral and non-moral considerations" (*Engaging Reason*, 250), (b) that "morality forms a distinct body of considerations which differs from that involved in other areas of practical thought" (*Engaging Reason*, 274), (c) that "moral values form either epistemically or metaphysically a separate range of considerations which can be validated or established only by special arguments" (*Engaging Reason*, 259), (d) that moral values "differ fundamentally in the source of their normativity" (*Engaging Reason*, 305), (e) that there is something "very special about…moral arguments, which sets them apart from…others" (*Engaging Reason*, 305), (f) that moral considerations are "a class apart" (*Engaging Reason*, 305), (g) that "moral values and reasons for action are established as values and reasons by specifically moral procedures or forms of reasoning" ("A Morality Fit for Humans," 1304), (h) that "moral values and reasons are distinct from other values and reasons so that their recognition requires a capacity, or modes of thought, reasoning, or experiencing things which are not involved in the recognition or pursuit of nonmoral goals or values" ("A Morality Fit for Humans," 1304), and (i) that "moral values and reasons constitute a special point of view" ("A Morality Fit for Humans," 1308). These claims differ from one another and some of them are vague. Accordingly, although I have argued that the unity of morality need not be secured at a metaphysically deep level in order for questions about the relation between morality and the individual good to be significant, this may of course depend on which of the passages quoted above is taken to fix the meaning of "depth."

37. In "The Central Conflict: Morality and Self-Interest," Raz writes: "The best exploration known to me of the relations between morality and other reasons which assumes that morality is a separate domain is S. Scheffler's *Human Morality*" (*Engaging Reason*, 312n). Although I appreciate the compliment, I must dissent from Raz's characterization of my view if it is meant to suggest that I regard the separateness of morality as a metaphysically deep fact.

that is radical enough to jeopardize the idea of potential congruence is likely to prove true. But if it did, and if what we call "morality" were to be understood instead as a shapeless assortment of heterogeneous values and norms, then I see no reason offhand why potential congruence should not be recast as a thesis about the relation between the heterogeneous values in question and the good of the individual agent. So long as we recognize those values as values, questions about their role in facilitating or hindering the achievement of a good or meaningful life will continue to arise, and the idea of potential congruence—with its emphasis on mutual accommodation and on the contingency of conflict—will continue to provide one approach to answering such questions.[38]

38. I am indebted to Niko Kolodny for comments on an earlier draft of this paper.

7

Too Much Morality

STEPHEN FINLAY

It is widely believed that morality conflicts to a significant degree with self-interest. I shall defend this ordinary wisdom, but advance a view on which the conflict is much more radical than is ordinarily thought. More precisely, I shall argue that what we morally ought to do seldom coincides with what is best or even what is good for us, on the basis of an exceptionally stringent view of our moral requirements and an unexceptional view of self-interest. I shall also suggest that while there is no simple answer to the question of which, out of morality and self-interest, ought to take priority in our lives, virtually all of us will find the requirements of morality—but those of self-interest too—excessive.

The question of the relation between morality and self-interest is for many nonphilosophers one of the most interesting and pressing questions addressed by philosophical ethics, but they are likely to find the philosophical treatment frustrating: whereas nonphilosophers intend to inquire into the relation between two largely determinate things, philosophical disagreement is largely conceptual; philosophers use "morality" and (to a lesser extent) "self-interest" in widely divergent ways. Most of these philosophers disclaim interest in arguing over what the words mean: you're free to use "morality" however you like, so long as you stipulate that use clearly. But you have to get the meaning of the word *right* if you intend your treatment to address the question that others mean to ask, and to minimize the risk of misleading people. I shall therefore be arguing for particular accounts of what "morality" and "self-interest" ordinarily mean.

"What they ordinarily mean *for whom?*" some may ask. I concede that "morality" has had and still has many meanings and uses. The meaning I am after is that, first and foremost, which it has for me. This may seem to belie the claim to be seeking the "ordinary" meaning of the word; however, I believe that I inherit the meaning as a member of a language community, and that the meaning that "morality" has to my ears is also the meaning it has to others in that community, even to some who have conflicting *theories* about its meaning. How far that community extends I am not sure, although it seems clear that we live in the midst of rival communities; for some it really seems that "morality" has essentially to do with what some deity commands (e.g., Anscombe [1958] argues that the moral "ought" has no meaning otherwise), and this sounds to my ears like a foreign usage. My account does, however, possess the resources to explain this divergence.

What then do we mean by "morality"? As I understand it, "morality" has both a formal and a substantive sense. In the formal sense it has close ties to social convention, hence the etymological link to "mores". A morality is a fundamentally social phenomenon: a normative code qualifies as a morality in this formal sense just in case it is a code that some society or social group *expects* (demands) people either within the group or more universally to conform to as fundamental and overriding.[1] We speak of "moralities" in this conventional sense without presupposing anything about content. But this formal characterization falls short of Morality, or what we consider to be (substantively) morally right and wrong. The fact that fundamentalist Islamic morality sanctions stoning women for adultery, for example, doesn't dispose us to judge that it is morally permissible for fundamentalist Muslims to stone adulteresses to death; substantive morality (or ours, at least) is not relativistic. Rather, what we judge to be morally right or wrong is fixed by the normative code that occupies this privileged status in our *own* moral community.

Being a member of a particular moral community doesn't require actual subscription to or fundamental concern with your community's moral code, but merely that your communicative context presupposes these social expectations[2]—the extreme example is the amoralist who declares, "I know it's wrong, but I don't care", but even for most of us (as I shall argue) moral considerations are only one kind among many, lip service to their overriding status notwithstanding. This account might still seem objectionably conventionalist. First, it may seem to disallow fundamental moral breaks from one's community.[3] But by a "moral community" I merely mean a group of people whose discourse presupposes a normative code as fundamental for communicative and rhetorical purposes. This might be only a subset of the actual community (at the limit it might consist of a single person, a moral revolutionary), and it is no condition on a morality that its subscribers demand it only from others in their moral community—indeed, this is not true of our own morality. Second, this account might be taken to construe the normative authority of morality as being essentially conventional; that we ought to comply *because* it is socially demanded of us. But this is a mistake; I haven't yet made any claims about the source of morality's authority for us. Social pressures to be moral are not intrinsically moral motivations, which spring rather from the incorporation of morality into our personal values.

1. Traffic and etiquette codes are socially demanded, but are not supposed to be fundamental and overriding; in certain circumstances violations are socially permitted, even expected. A similar view of the nature of a morality is offered in Kurt Baier, "The Point of View of Morality," *Australasian Journal of Philosophy* 32, no. 2 (1954).

2. See my "The Conversational Practicality of Value Judgement," *Journal of Ethics* 8, no. 3 (2004). By failing to relativize terms like *wrong* explicitly to a particular normative code, a speaker pragmatically expresses the social expectation that a certain code is shared and fundamental.

3. G. E. M. Anscombe, "Modern Moral Philosophy," *Philosophy* 33 (1958).

When I ask, therefore, what we mean by "morality", I mean Morality: the normative code with which my own moral community demands conformity as overriding. People in a divine-command-oriented moral community might mean something different, but this essay does not address them or their usage.

There is close isomorphism between morality and self-interest. For one thing, each is a normative domain: there is a moral "ought" and an "ought" of self-interest (and many more besides).[4] The concepts of morality and self-interest have both a subjective aspect, to do with motivation, and an objective aspect, involving action or behavior. Being morally motivated to perform an action is neither necessary nor sufficient for one's action being morally right—we can do morally wrong things with the best intentions, and we can do the right thing with the worst intentions—and similarly an act's being self-interestedly motivated is neither necessary nor sufficient for its being in one's self-interest. My claim, that morality and self-interest conflict, is therefore ambiguous. I am interested here in objective conflict; I claim that the actions we morally ought to perform are seldom the actions that are in our self-interest to perform. It will also turn out on my account that moral and self-interested motivation are mutually exclusive;[5] insofar as motivation is moral, it cannot be self-interested.[6] Importantly, neither are they mutually exhaustive; most motivation is neither moral nor self-interested. It does not follow and is not the case that moral motivation is incompatible with objective self-interest, or that self-interested motivation is incompatible with morally right action. We *can* do the morally right thing while pursuing our own personal good (e.g., stopping a terrorist from detonating a bomb on one's flight). And some level of morally good motivation (falling short of motivation to act as we morally *ought*—i.e., as is morally *best*) is plausibly an indispensable component of our own good for at least most of us; it enriches our lives, and a life without it is likely to be petty and impoverished.[7] But acting as we morally ought is only seldom in our own interest.

There are superficial similarities here with the thesis of Susan Wolf's seminal essay "Moral Saints", which also "call[s] into question the assumption that it is always better to be morally better".[8] However, my thesis is significantly different.

---

4. Many philosophers claim the normative "ought" is univocal, e.g., Judith Jarvis Thomson, "Normativity," in *Oxford Studies in Metaethics* 2, ed. R. Shafer-Landau (Oxford: Oxford University Press, 2007).

5. For an opposing view, see Neera Kapur Badhwar, "Altruism Versus Self-Interest: Sometimes a False Dichotomy," *Social Philosophy and Policy* 10, no. 1 (1993).

6. This is not to say that an action cannot be *jointly* morally and self-interestedly motivated.

7. Peter Singer, *How Are We to Live? Ethics in an Age of Self-Interest* (Amherst, N.Y.: Prometheus, 1995), 230–33; David Schmidtz, "Reasons for Altruism," *Social Philosophy and Policy* 10, no. 1 (1993). While there is an intrinsic human disposition to have concerns that extend both geopolitically and temporally beyond the self, one's own life is a small, short-lasting affair that typically spends its last few decades, if not cut short, in decline. A purely self-interested life is therefore a life of small and diminishing rewards in comparison to the rewards of a life of interest in broader and more enduring matters (pure self-interest has no "legacy"). Our objective self-interest itself therefore counsels us not to live an overly (subjectively) self-interested life.

8. Susan Wolf, "Moral Saints," *Journal of Philosophy* 79, no. 8 (1982): 438.

First, Wolf is concerned in large part with quasi-aesthetic or third-party criticisms of moral perfection (she argues that "there seems to be a limit to how much morality we can stand"[9] *in other people*), rather than with the conflict between one's own morality and one's own self-interest, which is my concern here. Although Wolf characterizes the perspective from which she finds moral perfection wanting (the "point of view of individual perfection") as concerning the good of the "individual himself", she is explicit that this is not concerned with a person's self-interest, but rather "with what kind of interests it would be good for a person to have", and even allows that moral sainthood may be in the self-interest of certain kinds of people. Even then, she urges that "we have reason not to aspire to this ideal, and that some of us would have reason to be sorry if our children aspired to and achieved it".[10] The view put forward in this essay is thus similar but not the same.[11]

An attractively simple and intuitive approach to defining and individuating normative domains is to do so teleologically, as determined by particular ends or goals;[12] the self-interested *ought* is determined by the end of attaining one's own good, the *ought* of etiquette by the end of meeting social expectations, the epistemic *ought* by the end of having beliefs that accurately represent reality, and so on. On my teleological view of normative language, "good" and "ought" are to be understood as relativized to particular ends; φ-ing is *good* relative to some end E if and only if (and to the degree that) φ-ing promotes E, and one *ought* (in order that E) to φ if and only if φ-ing is, out of all available alternatives, *best* (i.e., most good) relative to E.[13] The "oughts" of morality and self-interest are thus to be individuated by reference to particular ends. We must look to the content of morality and self-interest.

The Content of Morality Is Purely and Radically Other-Regarding

The realm of morality is commonly characterized in two distinct ways: first, by a particular kind of *content*. Morality is commonly seen as purely *other*-regarding, as

9. Ibid., 423.

10. Ibid., 436.

11. For other contrasts see notes 17, 28, 43, 49, and 52.

12. See also Paul Ziff, *Semantic Analysis* (Ithaca, N.Y.: Cornell University Press, 1960), chap. 6; J. L. Mackie, *Ethics: Inventing Right and Wrong* (New York: Penguin, 1977); Gilbert Harman, *The Nature of Morality* (New York: Oxford University Press, 1977). A popular rival approach appeals to "norms" or rules (e.g., the work of Allan Gibbard, Stephen Darwall, and David Copp). But rules, unless they can be justified by appeal to something beyond themselves, are merely conventional and arbitrary. While there are rules of etiquette, chess, and inference, the reason why one *ought* to comply with them is not simply that they are rules, but in order (respectively) to meet social expectations, play chess, and preserve truth. A morality of rules accordingly lacks normative authority unless those rules have a deeper justification—that is, serve some important end.

13. This begs no questions against proponents of a "categorical" ought, because an end-relational "ought" will be inescapable for us if the end in question is inescapable: Kant's categorical ought is therefore accommodated, as "ought (in order that one acts only on maxims one can will as universal law)", where this end is inescapable for us insofar as we are rational beings. It is plausible that this is Kant's own view.

having its basic function in placing constraints on the pursuit of one's own ends and interests for the sake of the interests of others. Second, morality is distinguished by a particular kind of *force*. It is presented as "categorical" (demanding things of us regardless of our ends and interests) and as "overriding" (trumping other sorts of considerations). Both of these elements are in need of interpretation, however: what does the other-regardingness and categoricity of morality amount to? Here I will address first the content of morality, arguing that it is indeed *purely and essentially* other-regarding, concerned only with the interests of others, and then consider an objection to this view based on morality's force. I then argue that morality is *radically* other-regarding, championing others' interests without mercy for the self.

Practically everybody agrees that other-regarding considerations have a central place in morality—paradigms of morally right behavior are acts that directly benefit others (e.g., the story of the good Samaritan) while the paradigms of immorality are acts that directly harm others (e.g., genocide, torture)—but opinions divide as to whether these exhaust its area of concern.[14] Here I'll briefly offer some considerations that weigh in favor of a view of morality as purely and essentially other-regarding. Morality may be thought to heed the interests of the self in two ways: (1) positively (there may be actions that we have a moral duty or morally ought to perform *for our own sakes*, that is, duties to ourselves) and (2) negatively (moral demands may be limited/constrained in certain ways that protect our interests [e.g., we morally ought to help the poor, but are not obliged to do so to the extent of making ourselves destitute]). In addressing whether morality is *purely and essentially* other-regarding I am concerned only with positive consideration of the self; negative consideration is relevant rather to the question of how far our other-regarding obligations extend.

Moral duties to oneself are sometimes invoked in order to protect us from the extreme self-abnegating demands of others' interests. On this view I'm not morally obligated to expend all my resources of time, money, assets, and energy in helping all those in desperate need of help, because I am morally obligated to myself to preserve my life, pursue my own projects, and so forth.[15] But if this were the case, then self-sacrifice beyond this limit, wherever it lies, would be *morally wrong*. To my ear it is absurd to condemn a person as *immoral* because he sacrificed too much for the sake of others—unless some others were somehow harmed by that sacrifice.[16] Some might think it irrational or foolish, for example, should one be trapped in a burning and overcrowded building, to refrain from fighting toward the exit in order that oth-

14. For example, the discussions of William K. Frankena, "Recent Conceptions of Morality," in *Morality and the Language of Conduct*, ed. H. Castaneda and G. Nakhnikian (Detroit: Wayne State University Press, 1963); W. D. Falk, "Morality, Self, and Others" reprinted within.

15. For example, Jean Hampton, "Selflessness and the Loss of Self", *Social Philosophy and Policy* 10, no. 1 (1993); 1997, Kelly Rogers, "Beyond Self and Others," *Social Philosophy and Policy* 14, no. 1 (1997): 1–20, Ayn Rand, *The Virtue of Selfishness* (New York: New American Library, 1964).

16. Criticism of the philanthropist Zell Kravinsky (see below) centers on the charge that his sacrifices are harming his family and friends.

ers might escape, but it is contrary to our ordinary grasp of the meaning of "moral" to suggest that such behavior is immoral or morally wrong. It seems rather a classic case of supererogation: going (commendably, from a moral point of view) "beyond the call of duty". Morality is not properly conceived, for example, as directing us to balance our interests against those of others, because of this basic asymmetry: supposing there is a morally correct balance to strike, deviations to the benefit of the self are appropriately deemed immoral, while deviations to the benefit of others are not. (Standard utilitarianism, which bids us count ourselves as morally worth no more but *no less* than anyone else, falls afoul of this point,[17] although it largely concurs with me about the radicalness of morality's other-regarding demands.) It is quite compatible with this view that we may be subject to some moral obligations to take care of ourselves, because we may need to do so in order to be better able to promote the interests of others. Suicide is generally morally wrong, for example, for reasons that are as other-regarding as any.[18]

The usual objection to the claim that morality is purely other-regarding is that this is absurdly, perversely self-abnegating.[19] This is motivated by consideration of morality's characteristic categorical force. Indeed, the combination of morality's content and force is at first glance troubling, suggesting an extreme devaluation of the self according to which ultimately only others matter, and others' needs must always be placed above one's own. This has led commonsense morality to be condemned as perverse by a number of thinkers. As I observed, however, the nature of this categorical force is in need of interpretation; the objection construes this force in a particular *rationalist* way. The moral perspective is thereby construed as either (1) simply constitutive of the overall perspective of deliberation/practical reason as such (so that the moral "ought" is simply the all-things-considered "ought" or ought-simpliciter), or (2) a privileged normative perspective that uniquely enjoys rational priority over all others. In either case no considerations can trump or override moral considerations. While a few philosophers champion the radical position that some extreme sort of self-abnegation is rationally required of us,[20] it is widely believed that reason also enjoins us to a healthy concern for our own interests; some even claim that this exhausts the dictate of reason. Many philosophers therefore offer theories sweetening the content of morality by including duties to self and self-regarding constraints on duties to others, and others try to reconcile other-regarding morality and self-interest by interpreting other-regarding morality as nothing but the counsel of enlightened self-interest.

On the view I am advancing, self-regarding considerations do not belong in what is ordinarily meant by "morality". Is this view then perversely self-abnegating?

17. Contrast Susan Wolf, "Moral Saints".

18. Some have argued on similar grounds that the morally best course of conduct is a quite extensive pursuit of one's narrowly conceived personal advantage (e.g., Adam Smith, Bernard Mandeville, Ayn Rand), but this is implausible.

19. For example, Rand, *The Virtue of Selfishness*; Falk, "Morality, Self, and Others"; Rogers, "Beyond Self and Other"; Hampton, "Selflessness and the Loss of Self."

20. Shelly Kagan, *The Limits of Morality* (New York: Oxford University Press, 1989); Peter Singer, *How Are We to Live? Ethics in an Age of Self-Interest*, 1995.

It is so only if it accepts the rationalist interpretation of morality's categorical force — which I do not.[21] Morality is only one kind of practical consideration, one normative point of view among many, without any special rational authority. It is purely other-regarding simply because this is its essential character, and its relation to other normative domains is complex, not that of simple supremacy. The categorical force of morality is a social and pragmatic or rhetorical phenomenon rather than a rational one; we can understand it by looking to the *formal* characterization of morality above. Moral demands are "inescapable" (not contingent on a person's intentions or desires) just because they arise from ends that the moral community demands people respect as fundamental and overriding — in other words it is moral criticism, not the authority of moral reasons, that is inescapable.[22] There is no need to suppose, therefore, that it is a conceptual truth that morality is rationally overriding.

It is a widespread view among philosophers, however, that morality is rationally overriding and trumps all other considerations. Many think this overridingness is what we should take as focal in the concept of morality;[23] the role of other-regarding considerations would then be a contingent detail of content. But this fails to capture the ordinary concept of morality. It does not seem incoherent to ask yourself seriously, "Why should I be moral/do the morally right thing?" to judge yourself to lack sufficient reason for being moral, or to find the pinnacle of moral virtue to be unworthy of your aspirations and encouragement.[24] This does not prove that morality lacks overriding normative authority, but it does mean that it would be a substantive rather than a conceptual truth that morality is overriding were it in fact the case. On the other hand, the idea that (e.g.) gratuitous cruelty could turn out to be morally right seems (absent some story about how it would actually be beneficial to others) quite incoherent.[25] Nothing deters people from the theory that morality is defined by the command of God, for example, more effectively than the implication that had God commanded cruelty then cruelty would be morally right. (Some, of course, are not deterred.)

We can therefore conclude from the authority of ordinary usage that it is a conceptual truth that morality addresses to each of us only considerations arising from

---

21. Samuel Scheffler, *Human Morality* (New York: Oxford University Press, 1992), 25–27) provides an excellent overview of the options here.

22. These two senses of categoricity are famously distinguished in Philippa Foot, "Morality as a System of Hypothetical Imperatives," *Philosophical Review* 81, no. 3 (1972). See also David Brink, "A Puzzle about the Rational Authority of Morality," *Philosophical Perspectives* 6 (1992).

23. For example, Thomas E. Hill Jr, "Reasonable Self-Interest," *Social Philosophy and Policy* 14, no. 1 (1997); see also William K. Frankena's survey in "Recent Conceptions of Morality."

24. Susan Wolf, "Moral Saints."

25. Falk ("Morality, Self, and Others," 249–50) claims that "usage here leans uneasily either way," (although, he admits, it "favors the non-formalist more than the formalist" — see similar admissions in Hampton 1993. But the expressions he cites in favor of the formalist strike me as largely obsolete today: "moral agent", "moral freedom", "moral strength", "moral powers" (227).

the interests of others, and turn now to address the extent of these demands. But here I will be arguing against ordinary opinion, which considers morality to be most of the time an indulgent mistress. She permits us to live our lives in peace, provided we tithe modestly to charitable causes and don't try to advance ourselves by directly injuring the interests of others, and only on rare occasions commands us to do something difficult, costly, or uncomfortable—and even then she permits us to put our own and our loved ones' safety and basic needs first.

On the contrary, I shall argue, morality requires us to do the utmost we can in promoting moral ends. Morality is based on the ends of altruism, but it is not merely altruism. Altruism is subjective motivation toward some others' good for their sakes, but any "others" will qualify—one's "fellow Americans", convicted serial killers, one's spouse. Any such motivation is intrinsically morally good, although it may occur in a motivational mix that is itself morally bad or wrong.[26] Morality, however, corresponds to a more universalistic concern: it is dictated by something like a *general benevolence*, which desires for everyone their good.[27] In my view, morality is defined in terms of such an end: what we morally ought to do is approximately what we ought to do *in order that others not lack their good*. Objectively, morality concerns what we do, not our motivations for doing it; morality requires us to act in conformity with what promotes the ends of general benevolence.

This account is significantly indeterminate, reflecting my own uncertainty about the content of morality. Do morality's concerns encompass the interests of members of other animal species, as I believe, and if so what are the minimal conditions for moral status? Does it exclude the interests of those guilty of serious moral violations? How does it enjoin us to weigh the interests of different individuals against one another? Does it require us to pursue the happiness of others, or merely the alleviation of their sufferings and deprivations? Fortunately, my case does not require a ruling on any of these difficulties. There are sufficient millions of people in good moral standing who are suffering and dying at every moment of our lives (victims of poverty, war, famine, disease, homelessness, sex slavery, genocide, oppression, etc.) that our moral debts to others are radically, insistently, unflaggingly demanding on us. According to the latest mailing I received from UNICEF, for example, 3.6 million people are threatened with malnutrition in the country of Niger alone. You, the reader, are failing to act as you morally ought simply in virtue of the fact that you are presently wasting your time (from a moral point of view) reading philosophy when there are so many people desperately needing your help.

Common sense classifies the kinds of self-sacrifice I am talking about as "beyond the call of duty": the *supererogatory*. Such acts are said to be morally admirable in the extreme, and the agents who perform them—people like Mother Teresa, Oskar

---

26. Kelly Rogers ("Beyond Self and Other," 9) offers the case of a woman who selflessly tries to help her husband escape from prison as an example of morally worthless altruism. In my view the altruism itself is morally good, but the woman's overall motivational state is not because she fails to be motivated by relevant considerations of third parties' conflicting interests.

27. The similarities with Jesus' ethical teaching to love others as you love yourself (where I assume self-love is assumed rather than exhorted) are, I am sure, quite nonaccidental.

Schindler and others who rescued Jews from the Nazis, and Zell Kravinsky (the Philadelphia resident who has given away millions of dollars, and one kidney, to strangers)—are said to be moral "saints" or "heroes". But it is denied that these acts are obligatory or that we morally *ought* to perform them.[28] I shall now argue that appeals to the supererogatory fail to establish any such limits on what we morally ought to do for others.

When coastal communities around the Indian Ocean were devastated in 2004 by a tsunami, each of us faced a moral choice: how would we personally respond? Most people (I hope) believed that they morally ought to do something, and likely will have felt righteous about giving a few hundred dollars. Obviously, there is more that any one of us could have done: for example, sell our house or run up our credit card debt, in order to help alleviate suffering. It will be generally agreed, I think, that if giving hundreds of dollars is morally good, then selling one's house and giving hundreds of *thousands* of dollars is morally *better*; the notion of supererogation presupposes that the supererogatory act is morally superior to the obligatory act. But as a rule, "best" seems to imply "ought":[29] if the I–94 is the best route to drive to Chicago, then it's the route you ought to take; if medicine X is the best child's pain reliever, then it's the pain reliever you ought to give your child for her pain; if the best move is pawn to Q5, then that's the move you ought to make. It sounds very odd to say, "A is the best, but you ought to choose B". Similarly, therefore, if giving hundreds of thousands of dollars to tsunami victims is the morally best action I can perform, it is the action I morally *ought* to perform.[30]

It will be objected that rejection of the supererogatory flies in the face of common sense and is absurd. But the authority of common sense is not so univocal: this demanding view of morality is not merely a perverse creation of philosophers, but is also the view reached by many serious, sober, reflective nonacademic members of our moral community. Moral saints themselves act as they do because they come to judge that they *ought* so to act, that the situation demands action of them. In reaching that judgment they do not take themselves to be somehow specially distinguished people; their judgments are not, in general, to be explained in terms of a perceived special responsibility to the people they help. To declare this treatment of supererogation absurd on the grounds of common opinion is thus to beg the question against a significant group of people. Perhaps the case will be pressed by appeal to methodological democracy: moral saints are in the minority, so their view can safely be deemed deviant. It is an uncomfortable even if not an absurd thought that our orientation toward moral saints is to esteem them for their morally admirable acts while

---

28. For example, J. Urmson, "Saints and Heroes," in *Essays in Moral Philosophy*, ed. A. Melden (Seattle: University of Washington Press, 1958); Wolf, "Moral Saints."

29. There is a lengthy literature on this "paradox of supererogation", which is considerably more sophisticated than my brief treatment here. See, for example, Jonathan Dancy, "Supererogation and Moral Realism," in *Human Agency*, ed. J. Dancy (Stanford, Calif.: Stanford University Press, 1988); see also Raz 1975, Zimmerman 1993, Heyd 2002.

30. If the "best" and the "ought" are not trading in the same currency there will be no such entailment: plausibly what is morally best is not what one ought *rationally* or prudentially to do.

considering those same acts to stem from an erroneous judgment of their duty![31] But I also doubt that moral saints are the only people who have these moral intuitions; many of us feel shamed when we contemplate acts of moral heroism. To quote a friend of Zell Kravinsky, "I don't think I'm a bad person. I give money to charity, and I think I'm fairly generous, but on the other hand, when I look at what he's done, I can't help but notice a little voice in the back of my head saying, what have you done lately, why haven't you saved someone's life?" (Strom, "An Organ Donor's Generosity Raises the Question of How Much is Too Much", *New York Times*, August 17, 2003). A great many more people who are not moral saints themselves share the moral saints' judgments about what they morally ought to do.

Still, we have a conflict of intuitions; many people deny vehemently that we are subject to such stringent moral requirements. Given the aim of capturing the ordinary conception of morality, and the subsequent need to defer to ordinary judgments, ought we not at least concede that we may have here two separate moral communities and two separate concepts of "morality"? I suggest rather that there is here a single moral community, but that proponents of a nonstringent morality are in error, and those who share the moral judgments of the moral saints are correct. One reason for suspecting this arises from consideration of *motive and character*. For one thing, moral saints are more likely to have thought long and hard about the requirements of morality, while those on the other side of the dispute have typically reflected on it less, are more inclined to take for granted everyday assumptions about moral requirements, and are less able to defend their position by articulating a theory of moral dictates. For another thing, there is a clear motive for self-deception in the proponents of a nonstringent morality: they typically desire strongly not to act "beyond the call of duty", but also desire strongly to be in good standing with morality, given the social and personal stigma attached to moral failings.[32] It is therefore to be expected that they would resist any claim that their moral obligations are uncomfortably stringent.

The problem has to be addressed, however, of how it can be that the concept of "morality" is determined by ordinary usage, but that ordinary judgments are wrong most of the time. The idea here is simple enough: ordinary usage applies a criterion for what counts as morally required and permitted. But it misapplies this criterion, such that it judges actions to be morally permitted that in fact are not.[33] Consider analogously the cases of witches and of knowledge. The (traditional) concept *witch* is determined by the referential intentions of the linguistic community as applying to any woman with supernatural powers. But they judge incorrectly that certain women meet this criterion, and hence systematically misapply their own word. Consider now

---

31. Urmson, "Saints and Heroes," suggests this. For similar criticism see Susan C. Hale, "Against Supererogation," *American Philosophical Quarterly* 28, no. 4 (1991).

32. If the stringent view is correct, however, this motivation is misguided; there is no reasonable social stigma for these moral shortcomings.

33. For a similar diagnosis of moral error, see Richard Joyce, *The Myth of Morality* (Cambridge: Cambridge University Press, 2001) (the witch example is his). Joyce, however, goes further and argues that all positive moral claims are false. The rationale for this error theory is that (unlike myself) he takes moral concepts to be committed to morality's necessarily possessing rational authority for us, which (like me) he denies it does.

this (plausibly fictional) story about knowledge: the concept of knowledge is determined by the referential intention to pick out cases of infallible belief. The community then judges incorrectly that numerous beliefs meet this criterion, and erroneously ascribes knowledge willy-nilly. Now, why think that such an analysis is correct, if it has the result that our ascriptions of witchhood or knowledge are systematically incorrect? One very good reason is if, were it to be brought to their attention that the alleged witches or knowledge do not satisfy the proposed criterion, a significant proportion of the intelligent membership of the community would then form the judgment that those persons and beliefs are not, respectively, witches or knowledge after all, which is clearly the case with witches, and arguably the case with knowledge.

Is the analogy to morality plausible? There are close parallels. Most people spend most of their time mindless of the concurrent sufferings endured by others or the actions they themselves could be performing to alleviate those, and many intelligent people do have the response, when confronted with this fact, that their lives are far less in conformity with morality than they ordinarily like to believe. Of course some do not have this response, but if as I have suggested there is a plausible story of self-deception to tell about those people, then we may be justified in dismissing their opinions. However, it remains possible that we should, after all, ultimately concede that some people mean something much narrower by "morality" than the rest of us.

Taking this line does not require that we *reject* the existence of supererogation or acts "beyond the call of duty", because arguably the concept of moral obligation is narrower than the concept of what we morally ought to do. Many people resist direct inferences from "You morally ought to do A" to "You have a moral duty/are morally obligated to do A". One possibility is that an act you ought to perform is obligatory in this narrower sense just in case others have a right to force you to perform it or bring sanctions (including blame and criticism) against you for failing to perform it. Duties are then acts, omissions of which in some way legitimize force or sanctions against you.[34]

This line of thought suggests a response to the insistence that we just do not consider that acts of extreme self-sacrifice are *morally required* of us. The person who gives hundreds of dollars to tsunami relief when she could have given hundreds of thousands of dollars is plausibly not appropriately blamed or criticized for not having made the larger sacrifice; she may well feel that she has done everything required of her, and feel justifiably guiltless. I suspect that here we need a further distinction: between (a) what morality requires of us, and (b) what level of conformity with morality is socially required of us.[35] First, failure to act as one morally

---

34. Roughly similar views of supererogation are offered by Urmson, "Saints and Heroes"; Dancy, "Supererogation and Moral Realism"; Walter Pfannkuche, "Supererogation als Element moralischer Verantwortung," in *Analyomen* 2, *Volume* 3, ed. Georg Meggle (Hawthorne: de Gruyter, 1997); and Mary Forrester, "Some Remarks on Obligation, Permission, and Supererogation," *Ethics* 85 (1975). See also Falk's discussion of H. L. A. Hart's views (243–44).

35. The contractualist tradition in moral philosophy as represented by T. M. Scanlon (*What We Owe to Each Other* [Cambridge, Mass.: Harvard University Press, 1998]), for example, claims that moral requirements are constituted by the requirement to behave toward others in a manner that one is able to justify to them. In my view, this corresponds to (b) rather than (a). Indeed, Scanlon himself acknowledges that it is only part of morality.

ought is not always or necessarily blameworthy. We excuse people many of their moral imperfections, recognizing the difficulty of the moral straight and narrow, without withdrawing our judgments that they failed to act as they morally ought to have. Second, "Let he who is without sin cast the first stone": it is hypocritical for people to criticize others for falling short of moral standards where they themselves fall short, and hence others generally will not hold us blameworthy or open to criticism for failures to act as we morally ought when they know themselves to be just as prone to such failures.[36] There is therefore a difference between what morality itself (and a moral conscience) requires, and the level of moral conformity that our neighbors and community require of us. I can excuse my moral shortcomings to my neighbors if they are shortcomings to which my neighbors are similarly susceptible. But I insist they are nonetheless moral shortcomings; confronted with the moral saint or the victim in need of my help, my self-righteousness will evaporate and I will find myself morally ashamed. (Among most people I feel no shame about eating meat, but when surrounded by conscientious vegetarians I find myself without excuse; I suggest that virtually all of us, confronted by actual disaster victims, would find ourselves hard pressed to justify the meager amount of our charitable giving.)

I should briefly address another line of objection to this view of morality that focuses on the psychological ramifications of accepting it. If we find compliance with morality too unattractive and difficult, would this not undermine all commitment to morality altogether? If so, then oughtn't we reject this view of morality?[37] But this view of morality *need not* undermine commitment; so long as morality and others' interests matter to us at all, we will have personal reasons to be committed to some level of compliance with morality. Nevertheless, undermining of commitment is a likely psychological result. But it is also a real phenomenon in our moral experience that as moral demands on us multiply, our dedication to morality can wane (e.g., "disaster fatigue"). Furthermore, unwelcome psychological consequences are no proof of a doctrine's falsity. The reaction that we ought to reject a stringent view of morality in fact looks like a *moral* judgment: we ought to encourage a less stringent view of morality, as a normative code that people are comfortably able to comply fully with, *in order that* people's commitment to beneficence is bolstered rather than undermined. Perhaps so, but that is no objection to the truth of the view of morality advanced here.[38]

The considerations I have offered do not prove that morality requires a radical level of beneficent action, but they do present a robust prima facie case. To make the

36. Urmson ("Saints and Heroes") himself supports his contention that the supererogatory is a real phenomenon solely with the observation that nobody else could reasonably demand that we act in these exemplary ways or criticize us for our failure to do so.

37. Urmson, ibid., seems to argue like this.

38. Nonstringent views of morality are commonly defended on the grounds that successful institutions do not require more of people than will seem reasonable to them: (Urmson, ibid.; Samuel Scheffler, *Human Morality*; David Schmidtz, "Reasons for Altruism": David Schmidtz, "Self-Interest: What's in It for Me?" *Social Philosophy and Policy* 14, no. 1 [1997]). In my view this overestimates the role convention plays in determining the content of morality.

case that morality conflicts radically with self-interest, however, an account is needed of the nature of self-interest. And while it may appear trivial to demonstrate this conflict once we're granted such a stringent conception of morality, there remains redoubtable philosophical opposition to overcome, which attempts to show that self-interest and other-interest largely coincide.

What Is Self-Interest?

The notion of self-interest may seem straightforward, but its analysis is highly contested. A simple account identifies it with the objects of the self's considered and informed interests; that is, my self-interest is whatever I most desire under privileged conditions.[39] But on this account any successful action I perform under these conditions is in my self-interest, and rational self-sacrifice or neglect of my self-interest turns out to be impossible.[40] If I take an interest in the interests of others, then the interests of others are on this account ipso facto part of my self-interest. But whatever is ordinarily meant by "self-interest", it is something we are supposed to be able to sacrifice and disregard; this account of self-interest is too broad. Among theories that make room for self-sacrifice, hedonistic theories are historically predominant; self-interest consists in pleasure. This view, however, derives much of its appeal from psychological hedonism, the theory that the only object of our intrinsic desire is pleasure—which is almost certainly false. A person's good consists in much more than merely pleasure. A tempting strategy, therefore, is to say simply that a person's self-interest consists in her possession of her good. For my purposes, however, this shortcut is unacceptably vague; it can be and has been argued, for example, that moral virtue is itself a basic element of human good,[41] and on this basis it can be argued that conforming with morality is always best for us, no matter what else it might cost us.

As with morality, self-interest has both a subjective and an objective side. Being (subjectively) self-interested entails taking an interest in the *self*, or being *self-focused*. We can define self-focus as intrinsically desiring an end that includes an ineliminable reference to one's self. (Consider my motivation to give to charity. Whether this motivation is self-focused depends on whether the intrinsic desire motivating me is self-referring—e.g., the desire that *I give to charity*—or not; e.g., the desire that *charitable*

---

39. Harry Frankfurt ("The Dear Self," *Philosophers' Imprint* 1 [2001]: http://www. philosophersimprint.org/001000), for example, claims that one's interest is defined by what one loves.

40. Mark Overvold, "Self-Interest and the Concept of Self-Sacrifice," *Canadian Journal of Philosophy* 10 (1980); Stephen Darwall, "Self-Interest and Self-Concern," *Social Philosophy and Policy* 14, no. 1 (1997). As Joseph Raz ("The Central Conflict: Morality and Self-Interest," in *Well-Being and Morality: Essays in Honour of James Griffin*, ed. Roger Crisp and Brad Hooker [Oxford: Clarendon, 2000]) observes, however, strictly speaking self-sacrifice has to do with compromising our personal goals, not our self-interest.

41. For example, Philippa Foot, *Natural Goodness* (New York: Oxford University Press, 2001).

causes are well supported.) Self-focus is, however, not sufficient for being self-interested; the former encompasses self-loathing and self-destructive desires, whereas being self-interested requires concern for one's own good or objective "interest".

Neither self-focus nor (subjective) self-interest are necessary or sufficient for being *selfish*. To label just any form of concern with oneself or one's own good "selfish" is an inappropriately broad use of the word, as some paradigms of selfishness are motivated by desires that are not self-focused (infants, e.g., are paradigmatically selfish, but do not even have a concept of a self to focus on). Rather, our concept of selfishness has to do merely with the lack of concern for others' interests, and is significant here because I suspect it is the case that when people inquire into the conflict of morality and self-interest, they often really mean to be asking about the conflict between morality and (what in the case of its disregard would be) our *selfish* interests; that is, the satisfaction of our nonbenevolent desires. The focus here will nonetheless remain on self-interest proper.

Self-interested desire is intrinsic motivation toward your life's going well for you from your own point of view over the course of your whole life.[42] Objective self-interest or what is *in your self-interest* is whatever promotes this end. As an approximation to a definition of self-interest, therefore, I offer the following: an action is in my self-interest (good for me) just in case and to the degree that it promotes a life containing intrinsically rewarding pursuit and/or accomplishment of goals that I strongly and intrinsically care about at the time of my pursuit/accomplishment of them.[43] I therefore *ought* from the point of view of self-interest to perform some action A in some situation S if and only if performing A in S promotes such a life *better* than any other action I can perform in S.

On this account it remains significantly indeterminate what self-interest counsels us to do. It does not tell us, for example, what relative weight to assign to a pursuit's temporal location, duration, or likelihood of eventuating, or how to weigh a shorter life of intensely rewarding pursuits against a longer life of moderately rewarding pursuits. This is welcome to me, however, as self-interest is contestable in precisely these respects, and the account does provide all the determinacy my argument will need.

The Conflict

The conflict that is the subject of this essay lies between what we morally ought to do and what we self-interestedly ought to do. It is clear that the most extreme positions

---

42. There is a commonsense distinction between short-term and long-term self-interest, which corresponds to the distinction between the present or short-term self and the temporally extended or long-term self. My treatment is concerned only with the latter.

43. Some philosophers require that such goals be "objectively" worthwhile (Raz, "The Central Conflict"; Susan Wolf, "Morality and the View from Here," *Journal of Ethics* 3 [1999]). I'm skeptical about any robust notion of objective worth, but even if there is such a thing, I doubt it is a necessary component of a person's self-interest. If the emperor Tiberius's life of cavorting sexually with children on Capri was for him a life maximally filled with the intrinsically rewarding pursuit and accomplishment of goals that he cared fundamentally about then, I'm sorry to say, such activities were in his self-interest.

can be ruled out for all but artificial persons. There are circumstances where the action that best promotes the interests of others coincides with the action that best promotes a life for oneself of intrinsically rewarding pursuits (e.g., saving one's plane from a bomb)—unless someone is so psychologically constituted that (e.g.) having saved other people's lives would cause him such ongoing misery that it would be better for him if he had been blown up. There are circumstances in which the action that best promotes the interests of others coincides with the action that is among the *worst* from a self-interested point of view: for example, where one can save the lives of many others by falling on a grenade that otherwise you could escape—unless someone is so constituted that having *failed* to save others' lives would cause him such ongoing misery that it would be better for him if he had been blown up.

What is in our self-interest depends largely on how we are psychologically constituted, because what is intrinsically rewarding for us depends on our dispositions to desire or care. Questions of whether and to what degree morality and self-interest conflict for any person accordingly call for empirical psychological investigation.[44] But given my characterization of morality and self-interest, I think we can safely draw the following conclusion: doing what we morally ought is not, for virtually all of us most of the time, what we self-interestedly ought to do. Most of us have basic altruistic dispositions; we care, largely indiscriminately, about other people and their misfortunes. There is always therefore some personal cost to us in not acting as we morally ought (insofar as we are aware of this): we miss out on the full extent of the intrinsic rewards of benefiting others, and we may suffer guilt. But the personal costs of complying with the full extent of morality's requirements are most of the time much greater. We care about other things, such as ourselves, our loved ones, personal projects, countries, possessions, hobbies, religious faiths, reputations, and hedonistic indulgences—we care at least as much about various of these and similar things, and most of us care more. Complying with the moral "ought", in most circumstances, would involve wholesale sacrifice of these, reducing the quality of one's life much more than would failure to conform fully with morality's requirements.

Eyebrows will be raised over the claim that concern for loved ones is in competition with morality. Philosophers such as Bernard Williams (1981) and Michael Stocker (1976) have argued that morality must allow us to give special regard to those close to us. Our loved ones are of course others, and caring about them is morally good motivation, but it comes into conflict with morally right action, in my view, when we pursue their benefits at morally excessive cost to others, as is typically the case. This is notwithstanding the fact that we have particular moral obligations to our loved ones in virtue of their particular dependence upon us. The view is well expressed by Zell Kravinsky: "I love my children, I really do. But I just can't say their lives are more valuable than any other life". The dispensations for caring for loved ones urged by Williams and Stocker, I believe, are not a matter of limits on the impartiality morality requires of us, but rather a matter of the limits on the level of conformity with morality that is socially required of us. In any case, as Williams himself observes, taking care of our loved ones out of a sense of moral duty is "one thought too many".

---

44. This is not to deny that the results may turn out to converge substantially for us in virtue of our shared biology.

Given all the concerns competing with morality that each of us have, my hypothesis that morality and self-interest conflict radically may seem trivial and obvious. But self-interest is not strongly tied to present concerns. Suppose, for example, that I am a fan of the Chicago Cubs, baseball's "lovable losers", while I detest the New York Yankees, a perennial powerhouse. Foreseeably, my life would contain more intrinsically rewarding activities if I were to switch my allegiance to the Yankees than if I retain my allegiance to the Cubs. It seems that self-interest counsels me to switch my allegiance. Similarly, it can be argued that the fact that we presently care so much about ourselves, our loved ones, and our personal projects does not show that acting as we morally ought is not in our self-interest, for were we to relinquish or weaken these nonmoral concerns and cultivate our dispositions for general benevolence, a life of morally right action would turn out to be much more intrinsically rewarding than it would be for us as we presently are.[45] It may then be argued that this path of moral asceticism[46] would be *better* than any other path open to us with respect to promoting a life of intrinsically rewarding activity, and since there is no better way to cultivate such dispositions than to act accordingly and thus habituate ourselves to benevolence, it is, in fact, in our best interests to resist our nonmoral inclinations and act as we morally ought.

The strategy is coherent: *were* it the case that the morally ascetic life promises the most such rewarding activity, self-interest and morality would coincide. But I think most people would concur that it is very implausible that this is the case, and we can support this judgment with the following two considerations. First, a life guided by perfect moral virtue is by (our) definition not in any way a life guided by self-interest, and its goals are not chosen with an eye to what will conduce maximally to a lifetime of intrinsically rewarding pursuits. Despite the fact that what will be intrinsically rewarding is largely determined by one's dispositions to care, any convergence between the perfectly moral life and the best life for oneself will be serendipitous.[47] (In a worst-case scenario, the needs of others would dictate that one expend all one's resources in a single moment, rather than in a lifetime's worth of gratifying service.) It would therefore be highly surprising if the best possible life for us is the life of moral perfection, as opposed to a life where some conscious concern is directed toward its own quality.

Second, existing desires and dispositions are not wholly irrelevant to the question of which life is best for us. In order to acquire sufficiently moral dispositions that our life of moral sainthood would not be burdensome for us, these existing desires and dispositions must first be weakened or extinguished. The cost, in life quality, of this ascetic training in combating nonmoral desires will be significant, giving a presumption to lifestyles that chafe less against the dispositions we already possess. Indeed, we have reason to doubt that most of us *could* relinquish or weaken our nonmoral dispositions

---

45. Singer, *How Are We to Live?* 235; Shelly Kagan, *The Limits of Morality*, 390–93.

46. I intend the term here in the original significance of "ascesis" as *training*, although the connotation of *self-denial* is not unwelcome.

47. See Susan Wolf, "Moral Saints,": 425; Raz, "The Central Conflict."

to the requisite degree that a life of perfect moral virtue wouldn't be onerous for us. For these reasons it is most implausible that the life of moral asceticism is better stocked with intrinsically rewarding activity than any other available to us.[48]

How Ought We to Live?

For most of us for most of the time, I have argued, what we morally ought to do is incompatible with what we self-interestedly ought to do. This leaves us with the question, given such a conflict between morality and self-interest, to which ought we conform and give precedence, and which ought we to flout? As I indicated, however, this question has no clear answer. The reason for this is that it is not, in my view, a clear question. There is a difficulty regarding how we are to understand this "ought". As we have encountered it up until now, "ought" has always presupposed some perspective or standpoint, identified with the standpoint of being oriented toward some end. We have "ought" from the standpoint of morality and "ought" from the standpoint of self-interest. Clearly the "ought" is not here asked from either of these standpoints: it is trivially true that we morally ought to conform with morality and self-interestedly ought to conform with self-interest. The intended question, it will be said, is rather about which of morality and self-interest we ought simpliciter (all things considered, from the standpoint of practical reason as such) to conform. But it is a serious question whether there is such an overarching standpoint, the standpoint of practical reason as such.[49] Given the teleological view of normative standpoints adopted here on which "ought" always presupposes an end, there is no "ought" simpliciter. (As I do not have the space to argue for this view here, this section aspires merely to present a point of view.) Instead, on this view, there are a variety of different, contingent perspectives from which the question, "Ought we conform with morality or with self-interest?" can be asked.

This rejection of a unified standpoint of practical reason may seem untenable. Don't we deliberate over and choose between conflicting ends, and don't we ponder over what we ought, all things considered, to do? But although it is clear we often ask simply, "What ought I to do?" it is not so obvious that these queries do not always presuppose some implicit end or ends.[50] We can always evaluate even our fundamental ends from the standpoint of other ends; arguably, for example, a significant

48. These claims are not so far from Peter Singer as it may appear: I have not denied that we would be much better off adopting a morally *better* life than we presently lead, and Singer concedes that he has not "dissolved" the clash between morality and self-interest (*How Are We to Live?* 223).

49. The existence of such a standpoint is also denied by David Copp, "The Ring of Gyges: Overridingness and the Unity of Reason," *Social Philosophy and Policy* 14, no. 1 [1997]. Contrast Wolf ("Moral Saints," 439), who appeals to a need to "raise normative questions from a perspective that is unattached to a commitment to any particular well-ordered system of values."

50. A number of philosophers argue that practical reasoning has a constitutive aim: for Christine Korsgaard (*The Sources of Normativity* [Cambridge: Cambridge University Press, 1986]), for example, practical reasoning aims to discover something like what I ought to do *in order that I conform with my practical identity*. See also David Velleman "What Happens When Someone Acts?" reprinted in *The Possibility of Practical Reason* (New York: Oxford University Press, 2000), 139.

component in our practical thought is deliberating over what we ought to do in order not to act in a manner we will later regret, or what we ought to do in order to promote the ends that are most important to us. But also, deliberation between fundamental ends is often not deliberation about what I *ought* to do, but rather deliberation over what I *shall* do: there are no "oughts" in weighing incommensurable ends.[51] Sometimes we can adjudicate a conflict of ends by turning to some further end that is better served by one than the other (e.g., when someone chooses a relationship over a career opportunity on the grounds that the relationship promises more happiness than does career advancement), but sometimes we just have to choose; in the latter circumstance at some point we just prefer one end to another.

We can simply prefer, and in doing so choose for no reason that we can give to justify our choice to ourselves. But we can also choose to pursue a certain end *for the reason* that we prefer it: in this case we may judge that it is what we *ought* to choose, in order to satisfy our all-things-considered preferences. The best approximation to the question intended by the sentence, "Which ought I, all things considered, to choose?" is "Which matters more for me?" What matters, or is important *for* a person, is a function of what can matter or be important *to* a person. In my view, something is important for a person just in case and to the degree that it promotes something that the person would find intrinsically important if fully aware of it. There are two fundamentally different ways of understanding what it is to find something intrinsically important. On a *cognitivist* model, to find something intrinsically important is to perceive or judge it to have an objective property of value or worth.[52] On a *conativist* model, it is rather to care intrinsically about it. It is this latter view that I think is correct: to adopt the former is to allow an answer to the all-things-considered normative question that looks beyond our subjective preferences, contrary to my claims in this section. To say that morality is more important for me than self-interest, therefore, is just to say that living as I morally ought is more promotive of states of affairs that I would care intrinsically about if fully aware of them, than living as I self-interestedly ought, or in other words, that I have an all-things-considered preference under conditions of full information for the well-being of anonymous others over my own well-being.

This standpoint of personal importance differs significantly from that of self-interest in that it is based solely on *present* dispositions to care.[53] If I am presently disposed to care more about the fortunes of the Chicago Cubs than I am to care about a small increase in my future happiness, for example, this standpoint directs me not to switch my allegiance to the Yankees, and if I am presently disposed to care more about the well-being of some other person than my own well-being, it directs me to sacrifice my interests to the other's in a situation where they conflict. It may also direct the spurned

51. There is no answer to the question, "Which pile of hay *ought* Buridan's ass choose?" but if the ass is to have any hay, he must settle the question, "Which pile shall I choose?" (here, of course, the goods are equal rather than incommensurable).

52. For example, Raz, "The Central Conflict"; Susan Wolf, "Happiness and Meaning: Two Aspects of the Good Life," *Social Philosophy and Policy* 14, no. 1 [1997]; Raz, "Morality and the View from Here."

53. It corresponds closely to the standpoint of rationality on what Derek Parfit (*Reasons and Persons* [Oxford: Oxford University Press, 1984]) calls the "critical present-aim theory".

lover to choose revenge over benevolence, or suicide over self-maintenance. The standpoint of personal importance is not dictated to us by either psychological or rational necessity. It is possible to deliberate and choose without regard to what we would prefer if fully informed (we can embrace our ignorance, and sometimes with good reason), and hence our choices need not be informed by what is important for us, although it is unavoidable that they are shaped by what we find important.

On this picture there is no objective or impersonal issue over whether morality or self-interest is more important. Questions of importance and normative priority are subjective or personal questions, although if we are all sufficiently alike in our dispositions of concern, the answers for us all will largely coincide. So in addressing the normative question, "Ought we comply with morality or with self-interest?" we are left with the psychological question: Which do we care more about, anonymous others' interests or our own?

Even the answer to this psychological question is far from simple, however. First, it's vital to note that for virtually all of us *both* moral and self-interested ends are relatively low in our order of priorities, ranking well below our personal projects, be they our families, professions, intellectual quests, hedonistic indulgences, and so forth. We care more about having a nice house, car, or lawn, for example, than we care about distant human misery; more for our favorite foods and sports teams than for some level of health or future happiness. For virtually none of us, therefore, is it the case that doing what we morally *or* self-interestedly ought to do is what matters most for us in most circumstances. "Morality *or* self-interest" is a false dichotomy.

Second, even where we care more about one kind of end than another, this usually doesn't result in a simple ordinal ranking where the demands of one kind always take priority over those of the other. We care both about ourselves and about others, even if not equally, but a greater degree of promotion of a lesser concern may be more important for us than a lesser degree of promotion of a greater concern; while few philosophers are willing to abandon their careers in philosophy in order to devote themselves to improving conditions in the Third World, most are more than willing to divert some amount of time and money away from philosophical pursuits for charitable causes.

Third, regarding the relative priority in our lives of morality and self-interest, I can only say from my unexceptional observation of the world that humans differ greatly. Some people care greatly about their self-interest, but many seem hardly to care at all (witness all the carefree substance abuse and other willful self-destructive behavior). Some people care greatly about the welfare of anonymous others, while many seem hardly to care at all (witness widespread attitudes in the United States toward wars on foreign soil), and a casual glance delivers no evidence of a statistical relationship between the degree of people's self-concern and the degree of their other-concern: some care little about self or others, some care a lot about self and others; some care much about themselves and little about others, some care much about others but little about themselves. We can, however, conclude this much: even virtually all self-disregarding people have nonmoral concerns that for them are more important than most of their moral requirements, and so it is fair to say that for virtually all of us, most of what we morally ought to do—like what we self-interestedly ought to do—is less important than the pursuit of certain of our *selfish* concerns.

II

MORALITY WITHIN SELF-INTEREST

A. Morality as Necessary to Self-Interest

8

Scotus and the Possibility of Moral Motivation

T. H. IRWIN

1. Sources of the Dualism of Practical Reason

Henry Sidgwick claims that the "dualism of practical reason" is unknown to ancient moralists. In his view, the ancient moralists agree on the supremacy of a single principle of practical reason, enjoining the rational pursuit of one's happiness. Joseph Butler rejects this ancient view by distinguishing two supreme principles, so that practical reason enjoins morality as well as self-love.

> Butler's express statement of the duality of the regulative principles in human nature constitutes an important step in ethical speculation; since it brings into clear view the most fundamental difference between the ethical thought of modern England and that of the old Greco-Roman world, — a difference all the more striking because Butler's general formula of "living according to nature" is taken from Stoicism, and his view of human nature as an ordered polity of impulses is distinctly Platonic. But in Platonism and Stoicism, and in Greek moral philosophy generally, but one regulative and governing faculty is recognized under the name of Reason — however the regulation of Reason may be understood; in the modern ethical view, when it has worked itself clear, there are found to be two, — Universal Reason and Egoistic Reason, or Conscience and Self-love. This dualism, as has been noticed, appears confusedly in Clarke's account of "reasonable" conduct, and implicitly in Shaftesbury's account of the obligation to Virtue; but its clear recognition by Butler is perhaps most nearly anticipated in Wollaston's *Religion of Nature Delineated* (1722). Here, for the first time, we find "moral good" and "natural good" or "happiness" treated separately as two essentially distinct objects of rational pursuit and investigation; the harmony between them being regarded as a matter of religious faith, not moral knowledge.[1]

Sidgwick's claim deserves further clarification and exploration, but for the moment we may concentrate on his suggestion that we find no explicit duality of ultimate practical principles in moral philosophy before Butler. Is this suggestion correct?

1. Sidgwick, *Outlines of the History of Ethics*, 3rd ed. (London: Macmillan, 1892), 197f.

If it were correct, it would be significant; for we might reasonably wonder why the duality emerges in modern moral philosophy, after two millennia of moral reflexion. We might try to explain its emergence by referring to the special concerns or circumstances of modern philosophy or of its historical or intellectual context. Sidgwick's explanation is part of his account of the distinctive characteristics of modern ethics, and his account is certainly worth discussing. But before we consider explanations of the phenomenon, we ought to ask whether it is a genuine phenomenon.

I will not look for counterexamples in ancient philosophy, where I think Sidgwick's claim is broadly correct. But I want to consider a possible counterexample in medieval philosophy. Sidgwick devotes only half a page to Duns Scotus, whom he takes to present an important criticism of Aquinas's views on morality and free will. He mentions that Aquinas "is scarcely aware" that his position raises "the old pagan difficulty of reconciling the proposition, that will or purpose is a rational desire always directed towards apparent good, with the freedom of choice between good and evil that the jural view of morality seems to require". Against Aquinas Scotus argues "that will could not be really free if it were bound to reason, as Thomas (after Aristotle) conceives it; a really free choice must be perfectly indeterminate between reason and unreason".[2]

Sidgwick does not mention the fact that Scotus's criticism of Aquinas on this point leads him to question Aquinas's eudaemonism. Aquinas follows Aristotle in accepting both psychological and rational eudaemonism, holding that one's own happiness is both the ultimate actual object of desire and the appropriate object of a rational agent's desire. Sidgwick does not mention Scotus's disagreement with Aquinas on this point, nor the fact that Scotus's arguments against eudaemonism are distinct from his claims about free will. If we examine these arguments, we should be able to see whether Scotus expresses belief in the sort of duality of practical principles that Sidgwick ascribes to Butler.

I will argue that Scotus rejects eudaemonism and affirms the independence of moral practical reason from self-love. But I will also try to show how they support a conclusion that casts doubt on the existence of the moral motivation that he tries to defend.

2.   Scotus's Case against Eudaemonism

To find the source of some of Scotus's objections to eudaemonism we may begin with some of Augustine's objections to self-love. In Augustine's view, our will is wrongly directed if it is directed toward ourselves, and rightly directed if it is directed toward God; this is why self-love underlies the earthly city and the love of God underlies the heavenly city. The self-love of the earthly city is the source of its conflicts, because our arrogance refuses to accept others as our equals (*De Civitate Dei*, xv 5; xix 12). We might infer that we are free of these conflicts only when we abandon self-love for the love of God. From the moral point of view, we might take Augustine's

<hr>

2. Ibid., 146f.

position to imply that we have genuine moral motivation only if we abandon self-love. This is the conclusion that Scotus draws.

It would be one-sided and misleading to take these remarks as a summary of Augustine's view on self-love. But they summarize an aspect of Augustine that is prominent in Scotus. Following Augustine, he takes the city of the devil to rest on "love of self that goes as far as contempt of God" (*2Sent.* d6 q2 = OO vi 1, 535 = W 464).[3] In contrast to the city of the devil, the city of God rests on love of God that goes as far as contempt of self. The right direction of one's will, therefore, seems to rest on the limitation of self-love by the love of God. If self-love ought to be limited, it can be limited, and hence the pursuit of one's own happiness is neither psychologically nor rationally supreme.

Scotus believes it is clear that the pursuit of happiness is not psychologically supreme. If the will necessarily pursued happiness, it would follow that whenever I believed both x and y were open to me and that x rather than y would promote my happiness, I would choose x rather than y. But Scotus replies that sometimes we are aware that x rather than y promotes happiness, but we can simply choose to pursue neither x nor y. If we suspend further action, we choose to be indifferent toward happiness.[4]

Even when we act, we do not always act with a view to happiness, and hence we do not necessarily will happiness.[5] Since we sometimes aim at particular ends without reference to happiness, and we do not always stop to think about how they bear on happiness, eudaemonism is false. In such cases, we choose "negatively" not to pursue happiness, because we have a good reason for pursuing something without considering happiness. In other cases, we choose "contrarily" not to pursue happiness, because we recognize that our action is contrary to happiness, but we still choose to do it.[6]

3. In references to Duns Scotus, "OO" refers to *Opera Omnia*, 12 vols., ed. L. Wadding (Lyons: Durand, 1639); "W" refers to *Duns Scotus on the Will and Morality*, trans. and ed. A. B. Wolter (Washington, D.C.: The Catholic University Press of America, 1986). Scotus's quotation from Augustine is inexact. Augustine actually speaks of the earthly city (civitas terrena), not the city of the devil (civitas diaboli) as the one that is guided by excessive self-love (*De Civ. Dei*, xiv 28). Augustine also speaks of the earthly city with its angels as being founded on self-love (xiv 13).

4. "[I]t [sc. the will] can suspend itself from every act, when happiness is shown to it. Hence, for any object, the will is capable of neither willing nor rejecting it, and of suspending itself from any act in a particular case about this or that object. And this anyone can experience in himself, when someone offers him some good, even if <the other> were to show him a good as a good to be considered and willed; he is capable of turning away from this, and of eliciting no act of will about it" (*4Sent.* d49 q10 = OO x 514 #9 = W 194).

5. "If the will necessarily willed happiness, it would determine [determinabit; Wolter reads "necessario determinaret"] the intellect to consider about happiness always, which is false (*4Sent.* d49 q10 = OO x 513 #5 = W 188).

6. "Even if one recognizes that fornication cannot be directed towards happiness, one may choose it none the less, without directing it towards happiness" (*4Sent.* d49 q10 = OO x 540 #15 = W 194–96; Wadding's text differs from Wolter's here, though the main point is the same).

To explain how we both can and should limit our pursuit of our own interest, Scotus introduces two primary affections of the will. He follows Anselm in distinguishing the affection for justice from the affection for advantage.[7] According to Anselm, if we had only the will to happiness, we could not be blamed for pursuing happiness through unjust means; for if we believed that these unjust means promoted happiness, we could not avoid pursuing them.[8] In order to be open to praise and blame for acting justly and unjustly, we must have a will to justice that is independent of the will to happiness.[9] Anselm assumes that if we act unjustly because of a false belief about the means to happiness, we cannot be responsible or blameworthy for acting unjustly. Since we are sometimes responsible for acting unjustly, our acting unjustly cannot always depend on our belief about the means to happiness. Similarly, if we are responsible for acting justly, our acting justly cannot always depend on the belief that acting justly promotes our happiness.

Scotus agrees with Anselm's argument from responsibility. In his view, the affection for justice is nobler than the affection for advantage, because it causes us to will something that is not directed toward ourselves. It manifests freedom in the will, because an agent who is capable of choosing the just rather than the advantageous is not necessitated by nature to pursue only his own advantage. If we pursued everything with a view only to advantage, we would not have a free will; we would only have a "natural desire belonging to an intellectual nature" just as a nonrational animal has a "natural desire belonging to a sensory nature" (*2Sent.* d39 q2 = OO vi.2, 1021 #5 = W 202).

Anselm suggests a further argument against eudaemonism besides this argument from responsibility. He understands a just person as one who "preserves correctness of will not because of anything else, in so far as he is to be called just, than the correctness itself" (Anselm, *De Veritate* 12). The description of the just person's reasons, "not because of anything else than the correctness itself", might be understood so as to be consistent with eudaemonism; then it would mean that the just person regards correctness of will as worth preserving even if no further benefit results from it. This is what Aristotle means in saying that the virtuous person acts for the sake of the fine itself. But Anselm might also be taken to intend a more restrictive interpretation that excludes eudaemonism, so that the just person cannot value correctness of will for anything other than itself, and hence cannot value it for the sake of happiness. He maintains that we are not just if we will the action we ought

---

7. For Anselm's distinction see *3Sent.* d26 q1 = OO vii.2, 635 #17 = W 178; *2Sent.* d6 q2 = OO vi.1, 537 #5 = W 464.

8. "If Satan willed these base and impure advantages (commoda) that delight nonrational animals, would his will not be both unjust and blameworthy? [Answer] How could his will be unjust and worthy of reproach, because he willed what he had received the inability not to will?" (*De Casu Diaboli* 13; this is translated in Anselm, *Truth, Freedom, and Evil*, ed. and trans. J. Hopkins and H. Richardson [New York: Harper & Row, 1967], 174f.).

9. "[J]ust as the will [sc. for happiness alone] would not be unjust if it willed unfitting things, since it would be unable to avoid willing them, so also the will [sc. for justice alone] would not be just if it willed fitting things, since it would have received [this will] in such a way that it would be unable to will anything else" (*De Casu* 14).

to will only because we are led to it by force or by external reward.[10] But he does not make it clear whether the prospect of happiness is necessarily an external reward that excludes choosing correctness of will for its own sake. If the prospect of happiness counts as an external reward, the just person does not always choose for the sake of happiness.

Scotus accepts this restrictive interpretation of Anselm's description of justice. He takes the existence of an affection for justice to refute eudaemonism, because he identifies the pursuit of happiness with the pursuit of advantage (*3Sent.* d27 q1 = OO vii.2, 651 = W 434). If our happiness were our supreme end, we would not be free to choose justice over our own advantage, and we would not be free to love God above everything. "Everyone who loves out of charity loves himself as directed towards the infinite good, because he loves the act or state by which he tends towards that good, and in this respect his love tends towards another, because his act is towards God as its principal object, and then he has charity to himself not as the final object, but as a proximate object directed towards the final and first object which is distinct from himself" (*3Sent.* d29 q1 supp = OO vii.2, 667 #4 = W 456). The appropriate sort of love for God requires self-love to become subordinate to the love of God, and so requires our desire for our happiness to become subordinate to the love of God.

Once we recognize that justice requires the choice of right action without reference to one's own happiness, we can understand the basis of Satan's sin against God. When Satan asserts himself against God, he does not act out of love of God, which cannot be excessive; hence he does not act on the affection for justice, which would require the love of God above all else. He must, then, be acting on excessive affection for the advantageous, which Scotus identifies with desire for one's own happiness (*2Sent.* d6 q2 = OO vi.1, 537 = W 464: "the greatest advantage is one's complete happiness"). Lucifer ought to have preferred justice over his own advantage, but he sinned by preferring his own advantage.

We might be inclined to answer Scotus by pointing out that Satan has the wrong conception of his happiness. But Scotus is not satisfied with this answer, because he does not believe it captures the motivation of the virtuous person. He argues that brave people who sacrifice their lives will the nonexistence of themselves and their virtue for the good of the community; they act for the sake of the community, not for the sake of their own virtue.

> The Philosopher maintains in Ethics III that the person with the bravery of a citizen ought to expose himself to death for the good and advantage of the commonwealth. But the philosopher would not suppose that such a person would have any reward after this life.... And so, setting aside all future reward, this is in accord with right reason, that every person with the bravery of a citizen should will his own non-existence to prevent the perishing of the good of the commonwealth. Now according to correct reason, the divine good and the good of the community (*politicum*) are

---

10. "[S]omeone who wills what he ought to will only if he is forced to, or when induced by an external reward, does not preserve correctness for its own sake, but preserves it only for the sake of something else—if he can be said to preserve it at all" (*De Veritate*, 12; this is translated in Anselm, *Truth, Freedom, and Evil*, 114).

to be loved more than the good of some individual. Therefore a given person, in accordance with correct reason, ought to will his own non-existence because of the divine good. (3*Sent.* d27 q1 = OO vii 2, 652 #13 = W 436)

In his view, brave people choose the common good without reference to their happiness, even while they recognize that it conflicts with their happiness.

In these claims Scotus implicitly answers the objection that a correct account of happiness would show that brave people promote their happiness by acting bravely. He implies that even if this were true, it would be irrelevant; whether or not brave people promote their happiness by their action, the desire to promote their happiness ought not to be any motive for them to act bravely. His argument might be expanded as follows: (1) The desire for happiness is directed toward oneself. (2) Virtuous people's choice is not directed toward themselves. (3) But their choice is rational. (4) Therefore, some rational choice is not directed toward oneself. (5) Therefore, some rational choice is not directed toward one's own happiness.[11] The argument depends on the claim that some choices are or are not "directed to oneself" (ordinatum ad se). If Scotus is right, eudaemonism is incompatible with admitted facts about the virtuous person's rational choices (stated in [2] and [3]). The eudaemonist position is mistaken because it fails to make room for the non-self referential character of the choices required by morality.

Scotus does not simply argue that a virtuous person must have a motive distinct from the desire for happiness, but also insists that virtue requires the absence of any motive that directs one's choice to oneself. And so he seems to accept the more restrictive interpretation of Anselm's account of justice as preserving correctness of will "not because of anything else". We may express his point by saying that he requires not only a pure motive, but also pure motivation. We might satisfy the demand for a pure motive provided that one of our motives is sufficiently pure, even if it is combined with other motives; but we lack pure motivation unless the pure motive moves us without any others.

As far as I know, Scotus does not explain why he takes pure motivation to be necessary for the virtuous person. But if his demand is justified, he is right to claim that the affection for the just must be independent of the desire for one's own happiness.

3.   Is Scotus a Dualist?

Scotus's attack on eudaemonism shows that he does not take the supremacy of self-interest for granted, and that he does not treat this as the only principle of practical reason. On this point, he rejects the main tradition of ancient and medieval ethics. Since he anticipates Butler and Sidgwick, it is reasonable to ask whether he also anticipates some of the questions that they raise.

---

11. "The affection for justice is nobler than the affection for the advantageous, where "justice" is understood not only as acquired and infused justice, but as innate justice, which is the inborn freedom in accordance with which one [or "it"?] can will something not directed toward oneself [or "itself"?]" (3 *Sent.* d26 q1 = OO vii.2, 635 #17 = W 178).

One of Sidgwick's claims about Butler raises a worthwhile question about Scotus as well. Since Butler rejects the primacy of self-love, we may say that he accepts a "duality" of practical reason, marked by the irreducible principles of self-love and conscience. Sidgwick also claims that Butler recognizes a "dualism" of practical reason; not only are there two irreducible principles, but neither is subordinate to the other or to any third principle. But Butler does not seem to treat his duality as a dualism. He maintains that self-love and conscience are distinct superior principles, but conscience is supreme. He therefore denies that they are equally ultimate principles.

Where does Scotus stand on this question? Does he regard the affection for advantage and the affection for justice as two ultimate and equal principles, or does he take the affection for justice to be superior? One interpretation of his account of the will suggests that the affection for justice is the supreme principle. If the will is a rational capacity, and the two affections of the will are two aspects of the application of practical reason to our actions, perhaps they express the same general principle. In deliberating with a view to our own happiness, we impose the appropriate rational order on our desires with reference to our own good; in deliberating with a view to justice, we impose the appropriate rational order on the desires of the different people affected. Deliberation with reference to happiness imperfectly embodies practical reason for only one person's desires, whereas deliberation with reference to justice embodies it more fully.

If this is Scotus's view, he anticipates Butler, but he does not anticipate Sidgwick's belief in a dualism of practical reason. But since Butler does not anticipate Sidgwick's dualism, either, we should not ascribe to Butler any insight (or error) on this point that goes beyond Scotus.

This is a reasonable conclusion to draw if we consider only the role of the affection for justice in explaining morality. If we take account of its role in explaining free will, we may well have grounds for ascribing to Scotus a position that is much closer to Sidgwick's dualism. But since I am not exploring that role of the affection for justice, I will not develop the comparison between Scotus and Sidgwick any further.

4.   Later Objections to Self-Love

It would be appropriate at this point to consider what one might say on behalf of the eudaemonist position that Scotus rejects. Since his arguments to show that eudaemonism conflicts with the motive required for moral virtue are by no means conclusive, one might fairly doubt his reasons for recognizing a duality of practical reason. But I will pass over that question, and try to say a little more about the significance of Scotus's position for the outlook of modern moral philosophy.

If Scotus's recognition of noneudaemonist practical reason had been an isolated exception with no influence on modern moral philosophy, we might say that Sidgwick's omission of Scotus is unimportant for his main purpose. We have no reason to suppose that Butler knew anything about Scotus's views. If the considerations that move modern moral philosophers to recognize a duality in practical reason are unconnected to Scotus's reasons, we might still believe that Sidgwick is right to regard the duality as a modern discovery (or invention), even if it had been anticipated.

A proper historical treatment of this question would require me to know more than I actually know about seventeenth-century Scotist writers. The publication of the *Opera Omnia* in 1639 testifies to considerable interest in Scotus, and the elaborate commentaries included in these volumes reflect the vigor of Franciscan studies in theology and philosophy. In the same century John Caramuel y Lobowicz relied on the authority of the Scotists in moral theology, claiming that they were more numerous than all the other schools put together.[12] But I will leave this potentially important source to one side.

Even if we take no account of Scotus in particular, we can easily identify the influence of one of Scotus's themes, his Augustinian attack on self-love. Luther exploits the Augustinian objections to self-love in order to prove that human beings, in their fallen condition and without divine grace, are incapable of virtue. He argues that since all the alleged virtues of pagans rest on self-love, they are really vices and not virtues.[13]

This line of argument from the pervasive presence of self-love to the impossibility of virtue is not confined to writers of a Lutheran or Reformed outlook. Among Roman writers of the sixteenth century, Michael Baius relies on the same argument in order to oppose Aquinas's view that pagans are capable of acquiring the moral virtues. Baius discusses these issues at length in *De Virtutibus Impiorum*, where he often appeals to Augustine. Baius argues that if we allow virtue to pagans, we fail to recognize that the motivation of human beings without divine grace is fundamentally flawed. Since pagans act on self-love, not on the love of God, they are incapable of genuine virtue. Once we recognize Augustine's alternatives, "either charity or cupidity",[14] we recognize that anyone who is moved by self-love cannot be moved by charity, and hence cannot have a genuine virtue.[15]

12. On the source and context of this remark see F. Bak, "Scoti schola numerosior est omnibus aliis simul sumptis," *Franciscan Studies* 16 (1956): 144–65.

13. Luther, *Lectures on Hebrews*, on Heb. 1:9: "Therefore, since love of oneself remains, it is quite impossible for a human being to love, speak, or do justice, even though he may simulate all these things. It follows that the virtues of all philosophers, indeed of all human beings, whether jurists or theologians, are virtues in appearance, but really vices". (*Luther's Works* [St. Louis: Concordia, 1955], xxix 119).

14. "Aut cupiditate aut caritate," *De Trinitate*, ix 13.

15. "St Thomas...thinks they are virtues because they are referred to some particular genuine good, which can be referred to the universal good, even if these states are found in those who are ignorant of the one true God because of blindness, or who despise him because of arrogance....Here one must especially wonder how St Thomas thought this possible reference of a proximate end to the universal good could be enough to constitute a virtue....A human being is made, and is required, to love God with all his might and to serve him alone; now anyone who lives in accord with virtue does what he is required to and what he is made for; therefore, anyone who does not serve God and seeks to do the duties belonging to the virtues not because of something else but for their own sakes, does not live in accord with virtue" (Baius, *De Virtutibus Impiorum* 4, in *Michaeli Baii Opera* [Cologne: Egmont, 1696], 65). I have discussed Baius further in my "Splendid Vices? Augustine for and against Pagan Virtues," *Mediaeval Philosophy and Theology* 8 (1999): 105–27.

The Pope condemned Baius's views in 1567.[16] But they reappear in the Jansenist movement in seventeenth-century France. First, Cornelius Jansen's *Augustinus* presents a long defense of an extreme interpretation of Augustine's views on the impossibility of pagan virtue. If we are moved by self-love, we cannot be moved by the love of God, and hence we cannot have genuine virtues, even if we do what a virtuous person would do. Jansen agrees with Baius in alleging that if we believe in pagan virtue, we concede too much to the Pelagians. The Pope condemned the errors of the Jansenists in 1690.[17]

A second controversy in seventeenth-century France also involved the Augustinian attack on self-love. Fénelon and the Quietists rely on a strict interpretation of Augustine's contrast between self-love and the love of God, and they argue that Christianity requires an entirely self-forgetful love of God in which believers even forget that they achieve their own happiness in the love of God. The Quietists attack any outlook that gives any place to self-love as a perversion of Christianity. Bossuet argues against Quietism by reaffirming the legitimacy of eudaemonism within a Christian outlook.[18]

While it is easy to see that these controversies turn partly on different reactions to an Augustinian view of self-love, it is not so easy to see any influence of Scotus's views. Those who agree with Scotus's demand for pure motivation might have reached their position by independent reflexion on Augustine, just as Scotus did. But if the revival of Scotus's demand rests on independent reflexion, that is a further reason for believing that Scotus captures a central element in an important line of thought about morality. We can grasp the philosophical significance of this line of thought if we trace its influence in English moral philosophy.

5. Mixed Motives

This controversy between Fénelon and Bossuet influences English moral philosophers as well. Shaftesbury—according to his opponents, at any rate—uses the Augustinian test for genuine morality, but rejects the Quietists' conclusion. The Quietists infer that since the Christian outlook requires the love of God above all, it rejects any appeal to one's own happiness. Shaftesbury, however, infers that since the Christian outlook appeals to one's own happiness, it does not allow genuine morality.[19]

One of Shaftesbury's opponents, John Balguy, quotes one of Shaftesbury's attacks on self-love:

16. Pius V, 1567, *Errores Michaeli Baii*, in *Enchiridion Symbolorum*, 36th ed., ed. H. Denzinger and A. Schönmetzer (Freiburg: Herder, 1976), §§1925, 1933, 1937.

17. See *Enchiridion Symbolorum* §§2308–9. N. Abercrombie, *The Origins of Jansenism* (Oxford: Clarendon, 1936), 125–58, gives an account of the contents of Jansen's *Augustinus*. At 3–51, he describes the relevant aspects of the dispute between Augustine and Pelagius.

18. Most of my slight acquaintance with Jansenism and Quietism is derived from R. A. Knox's fascinating account in *Enthusiasm* (Oxford: Oxford University Press, 1950), chaps. 9–12.

19. I do not believe that this is an accurate account of Shaftesbury's position, but for present purposes I will not contest it.

Nor can this fear or hope…consist in reality with virtue or goodness if it either stands as essential to any moral performance or as a considerable motive to any act, of which some better affection ought alone to have been a sufficient cause.…In this religious sort of discipline…the principle of self-love, which is naturally so prevailing in us, being in no way moderated or restrained but rather improved and made stronger every day by the exercise of the passions in a subject of more extended self-interest, there may be reason to apprehend, lest the temper of this kind should extend itself in general through all the parts of life. For, if the habit be such, as to occasion in every particular, a stricter attention to self-good and interest, it must insensibly diminish the affections towards public good, and introduce a certain narrowness of spirit.[20]

Shaftesbury's views encouraged his opponents to accuse him of the "enthusiasm" (i.e., fanaticism) that they found in Fénélon. George Berkeley, for instance, implicitly accuses Shaftesbury of endorsing the enthusiasm of the French Quietists because of his emphasis on disinterested moral motivation. Berkeley compares the Quietists to the Stoics who "have made virtue its own reward, in the most rigid and absolute sense".[21] According to these critics, Shaftesbury's demand for disinterested motives is unrealistic and inappropriate.

Shaftesbury's critics differ, however, about where he goes wrong. They put forward two different kinds of objections: (1) He ought not to demand disinterested motives at all, because these are irrelevant to virtue; (2) he ought not to demand disinterested motives that are not combined with self-interested motives, because such a combination still allows genuine virtue.

Balguy takes the second view.[22] He considers someone who is benevolent, but at first does not believe in God or an afterlife. He argues that if such an agent becomes convinced of the truths he previously rejected, we have no reason to suppose that his benevolent impulses will thereby be weakened.[23] The opponent of self-love gives no reason for believing that the motives produced by divine sanctions

20. Anthony Ashley Cooper Shaftesbury, *Characteristics of Men, Manners, Opinions, Times*, ed. L. E. Klein (Cambridge: Cambridge University Press, 1999), 184. Balguy quotes this passage (not exactly), and comments: "Whether by this the author did not mean to show or insinuate the inconvenience and damage that virtue sustains from the future and invisible motives of religion, let the reader judge. My business is to show, if I can, that these apprehensions are groundless; and that in some cases a strict attention to self-good is of great service to the public" (*A Collection of Tracts Moral and Theological* [London: Pemberton, 1734], 9).

21. George Berkeley, "Alciphron," in *The Works of George Berkeley*, ed. A. A. Luce and T. E. Jessup (London: Thomas Nelson and Sons, 1948), iii 136.

22. In his "First Letter to a Deist" Balguy defends the appeal to divine sanctions: "Though interest can never enter into the nature and constitution of virtue, yet why may it not be allowed to accompany and stand beside her. Notwithstanding all that has been granted, I can see no reason why virtue and the rewards of virtue must needs be separated and set at variance" (Balguy, *A Collection of Tracts Moral and Theological*, 7).

23. "However the new motives may operate, they cannot hinder the efficacy of the old one. Whatever good they may produce over and above (as indeed much may be expected from their conjunction with the former principle), yet still the benevolence being supposed the same in degree must, I think, remain the same in force and influence" (Balguy, *A Collection of Tracts Moral and Theological*, 8).

necessarily undermine the motive of benevolence. Contrary to Scotus and to later Augustinian arguments, a genuinely virtuous outlook does not require the renunciation of self-love. We might express Balguy's point by saying that he takes pure motives without pure motivation to be sufficient for moral virtue, so that he rejects the Augustinian and Scotist demand for pure motivation.

In the light of this objection to the Augustinian demand, it is quite surprising to find that some of Balguy's descriptions of moral virtue seem to rest precisely on the Augustinian demand. His conception of virtue seems to exclude the possibility of coincident virtuous and self-interested motives in a virtuous person.[24] He seems to deny that we could remain virtuous while we acquire self-interested motives for virtuous action, in addition to the properly virtuous motives that we already have. He argues that the presence of the self-interested motive subtracts from the worth of the action to the extent that it influences the agent.[25]

Balguy defends this principle of subtraction by offering two examples: (1) A mother rescues her drowning child "in the transports of her fear, grief, and tenderness"; (2) a brave soldier is challenged to a duel without having given any offense, but "conscientiously and resolutely refuses to fight" despite "many vile reproaches, insults, and outrages".[26] In Balguy's view, the virtue and moral merit of the two actions "will bear no comparison"; the second action is clearly superior to the first on these points.

But these examples do not support the principle of subtraction. Balguy implies that the mother acts solely from the motives that he mentions, and that the soldier is not acting simply from shame, or fear of punishment, in refusing to fight a duel. If, therefore, the mother lacked these specific emotions, she would have no rational convictions moving her to save her child. If that is how we describe the case, it is the mother's lack of these rational convictions, not the soldier's lack of nonrational incentives, that explains our comparative judgment.

To justify the principle of subtraction, we need to suppose that both the soldier and the mother have an equal tendency to act "conscientiously and resolutely", and that the only difference between them in these two cases is that the mother's instinct agrees with her conscientious motive and the soldier's instinct disagrees with it. Balguy seems to assume that an action has a fixed quantity of motivation that can be taken up either by the moral motive or by some other motive. If we have a liter jug, we have it filled purely with wine if it is filled with wine and nothing else. If we fill it with half a liter of wine and half a liter of methylated spirits, we have adulterated the

---

24. "The perfection of moral goodness consists in being influenced solely by a regard to rectitude and right reason, and the intrinsic fitness and amiableness of such actions as are conformable thereto" (Balguy, *A Collection of Tracts Moral and Theological*, 33).

25. He seems to accept this consequence of his position, when he discusses the concurrence of reason and instinct: "[H]owever actions may be mixed or compounded, as flowing from the united principles of reason and instinct, I cannot but suppose that the worth of such actions is in proportion to the share of influence which reason has in the production of them. The force of the natural impulse, whatever it amounted to, must, I think, be subtracted in the estimate" (Balguy, *A Collection of Tracts Moral and Theological*, 192).

26. Balguy, *Tracts*, 193.

wine, and someone who wants to buy a liter of wine has been cheated if he buys the mixture we have produced. If this is the right way to think of motivation, we would be justified in complaining that the moral motive has been adulterated and is not present in the pure form we expected, if it has been mixed with nonmoral motives.

This "Kantian" conception of motivation supports Balguy's principle of subtraction.[27] But it also casts doubt on his objection to Shaftesbury's view about the moral motive and self-interest. For if we act both on the moral motive and on self-interest, the Kantian view tells us that the influence of self-interest has to be subtracted from the influence that the moral motive would have if it were acting alone. Hence the more convinced we become that morality is in our interest and the more we care about that aspect of it, the less influence we allow to the moral motive. That is exactly the position that the "enthusiasts" defend.

Is it credible that Balguy's claims about moral motivation conflict on this basic point? The conflict is perhaps easier to understand if we notice that he rejects the demand for pure motivation when he argues against Shaftesbury, but he accepts it when he argues against Hutcheson's view that a benevolent sentiment is sufficient for moral virtue. He does not seem to notice that in these two argumentative contexts he relies on inconsistent assumptions about virtue. For the purposes of his argument against Hutcheson it would be enough to show that moral virtue requires something more besides benevolence. But Balguy goes further, and argues that the presence of nonrational benevolence actually reduces moral virtue, because of the principle of subtraction. Had he revised his position to eliminate the conflict, he would have been well advised to drop his demand for pure motivation.

On this issue, then, a Kantian conception of motivation supports the Augustinian objection to self-love, and the Scotist objection to eudaemonism. Balguy seems to state the basic principle underlying Scotus's demand for purity of motivation; the basic principle is the principle of subtraction.

6.   Skeptical Doubts about Moral Motivation

But if we rely on a Kantian claim about motivation to support a Scotist demand for pure motivation, we offer an opening to skeptical doubts. Bernard Mandeville exploits this opening in his inquiry into the origins of moral virtue. By arguing that astute legislators have cultivated the virtues through an appeal to pride, he suggests that virtuous people are often moved partly by the pride that has been cultivated. In reply to an objector who claims that some people act virtuously even when no one knows about it, and therefore are not moved by pride in their reputation, he suggests that a closer scrutiny of the motives of allegedly virtuous agents may change our minds about them. In some cases they may be moved by a motive that is not always morally good.

27. This subtractive view is often attributed to Kant, on the basis of his example of the "honest" shopkeeper, in Kant, *Groundwork of the Metaphysics of Morals*, trans. H. J. Paton (New York: Harper, 1964), chap. 1. See, for example, W. D. Ross, *The Right and the Good* (Oxford: Clarendon, 1930), 170–73. However, I do not believe Kant holds this view.

> It is impossible to judge of a man's performance, unless we are thoroughly acquainted with the principle and motive from which he acts. Pity, though it is the most gentle and the least mischievous of all our passions, is yet as much a frailty of our nature, as anger, pride, or fear....There is no merit in saving an innocent babe ready to drop into the fire; the action is neither good nor bad, and what benefit soever the infant received, we only obliged our selves; for to have seen it fall, and not strove to hinder it, would have caused a pain, which self-preservation compelled us to prevent: nor has a rich prodigal, that happens to be of a commiserating temper, and loves to gratify his passions, greater virtue to boast of, when he relieves an object of compassion with what to himself is a trifle.[28]

But even if we consider someone who is not moved by these morally ambiguous motives, we may find that he takes pride in the purity of his motives. If this pride encourages him to act virtuously, his motives are mixed and he is not virtuous after all.

> But such men, as without complying with any weakness of their own, can part from what they value themselves, and, from no other motive but their love to goodness, perform a worthy action in silence;...yet even in these (with which the world has yet never swarmed) we may discover no small symptoms of pride, and the humblest man alive must confess, that the reward of a virtuous action, which is the satisfaction that ensues upon it, consists in a certain pleasure he procures to himself by contemplating on his own worth: which pleasure, together with the occasion of it, are as certain signs of pride, as looking pale and trembling at any imminent danger are the symptoms of fear.[29]

Careful scrutiny of possible motives for virtuous action raises doubts about whether any allegedly virtuous people really act from the appropriate motives. Mandeville assumes that a virtuous character requires the "enthusiastic" attitude that renounces all nonmoral motives for virtuous action.

We might answer Mandeville by arguing that it does not matter whether virtuous people act out of sympathy or pity or pride, as long as they also act from the moral motive and this motive is sufficient for their actions. But this reply is not open to us if we accept the Kantian conception of motivation and the Scotist objection to self-interest. For these doctrines imply that any sort of self-interested motive subtracts moral worth from the action and the agent. Hence any contribution by any other motive casts doubt on the agent's claim to virtue.

Mandeville's argument is not purely sophistical, then, if it is aimed against opponents who accept Balguy's principle of subtraction. It suggests that the enthusiast's pursuit of virtue without self-interest is self-defeating; for as soon as we have achieved it, we will find satisfaction in it, and thereby we will reintroduce the self-interest we thought we had eliminated.

---

28. Bernard Mandeville, *The Fable of the Bees*, in *British Moralists*, ed. D. D. Raphael (Oxford: Oxford University Press, 1969), §270.

29. Mandeville, §271.

7.   Replies to the Skeptical Doubts

Butler formulates his views about moral motivation in the light of the controversies about enthusiasm. He alludes to the "enthusiastic" view that the love of God should be entirely disinterested and self-forgetful, so that any thought of the benefits one gains from the love of God is entirely out of place, and incompatible with the proper love of God.[30] This attitude of the French Quietists provokes a sharp reaction from other Christian moralists, who believe that the self-forgetful attitude advocated by Quietists is psychologically impossible and morally dangerous.

Butler agrees with Shaftesbury in rejecting this extreme opposition to enthusiasm about the love of God. He believes that, just as benevolence and self-love can and should coexist, so also the disinterested love of God can and should coexist with self-love. Those who deny the possibility of disinterested love of God reduce religion to purely self-interested calculation.[31] The disinterested love of God is legitimate and appropriate, both from a religious and a moral point of view; it is no less appropriate than love of a good moral character and of a human being who embodies it. Such reasonable and disinterested love is demanded by any sound, moral outlook.

We might be surprised to find that Butler's defense of disinterested moral motivation did not persuade most of his contemporaries and immediate successors. But we can perhaps explain why they did not listen to him if we notice that he does not deal with questions raised by the principle of subtraction. He suggests that we can answer objections to the disinterested love of God by observing that this is simply a case of the disinterested affection that we have to recognize in any case in order to understand the character of desire. Butler uses his answer to psychological egoism to show that we do not impose unrealistic demands on moral motivation if we require it to include a disinterested concern for morality.

> It is plain that the nature of man is so constituted as to feel certain affections upon the sight or contemplation of certain objects. Now the very notion of affection implies resting in its object as an end. And the particular affection to good characters, rever-

30. "The question, which was a few years ago disputed in France, concerning *the love of God*, which was there called enthusiasm, as it will every where by the generality of the world; this question, I say, answers in religion to that old one in morals now mentioned. And both of them are, I think, fully determined by the same observation, namely, that the very nature of affection, the idea itself, necessarily implies resting in its object as an end" (Joseph Butler, *Sermons*, in *The Works of Bishop Butler*, 2 vols., ed. J. H. Bernard [London: MacMillan, 1900], preface §43).

31. "Everybody knows,...that there is such a thing as having so great horror of one extreme as to run insensibly and of course into the contrary; and that a doctrine's having been a shelter for enthusiasm, or made to serve the purposes of superstition, is no proof of the falsity of it....It may be sufficient to have mentioned this in general, without taking notice of the particular extravagances which have been vented under the pretence or endeavour of explaining the love of God; or how manifestly we are got into the contrary extreme, under the notion of a reasonable religion; so very reasonable as to have nothing to do with the heart and affections, if these words signify anything but the faculty by which we discern speculative truth" (Butler, *Sermons*, xiii 1).

ence and moral love of them, is natural to all those who have any degree of real goodness in themselves. This will be illustrated by the description of a perfect character
in a creature; and by considering the manner in which a good man in his presence
would be affected towards such a character. He would of course feel the affections
of love, reverence, desire of his approbation, delight in the hope or consciousness of
it. And surely all this is applicable, and may be brought up to that Being, who is infi-
nitely more than an adequate object of all those affections; whom we are commanded
to love with all our heart, with all our soul, and with all our mind…there is nothing
in it enthusiastical or unreasonable. (Butler, *Sermons*, xiii 3–4)

Butler assumes that we have satisfied a reasonable demand for disinterested moral
motivation once we can show that moral motivation requires no greater degree of dis-
interest than we already have to recognize in many other desires and affections. But
this answer does not cope with the demand for pure and unmixed motivation in a
morally virtuous person. Butler believes that morality requires a pure motive, but he
does not mention the demand for pure and unmixed motivation. Perhaps he assumes
that the demand for unmixed motivation is unwarranted; but he does not explain
why it is mistaken. If the demand is legitimate, the sort of motivation that Butler takes
to be possible is open to objections derived from the principle of subtraction, since he
takes the virtuous person to act on a pure but not unmixed motive.

Reflexion on Butler, therefore, might persuade some readers that he has missed
the main point, and that he has not shown unmixed moral motivation to be possible.
Since the extent of disinterested motivation that he allows is not wide enough to
show that we can act on unmixed disinterested motives, it might seem wiser to deny
that morality requires disinterested motivation. This is the solution that persuades
many of Butler's contemporaries.

The apparent weakness in Butler's position helps to explain why a version of
theological voluntarism is so popular among eighteenth-century English moral philosophers. This voluntarist position maintains three major claims: (1) an imperative
account of morality as consisting in obligations imposed by commands; (2) a utilitarian account of the content of morality; and (3) an egoist account of moral motivation. These claims are logically separable, but voluntarists pass easily from one to
the other. They are especially prone to combine the first claim, about the metaphysics of morality, with the third claim, about moral motivation. They are influenced
by the different aspects of obligation, which they take to include both metaphysical
and motivational elements.

For present purposes, the most relevant aspect of the voluntarist position is its
account of moral motivation. Despite Butler's warning, the English voluntarists take
the more extreme position, and try to avoid any appeals to disinterested motives.
Perhaps they are impressed not only by the dangers of enthusiasm but also by the
skeptical doubts that Mandeville expresses about disinterested motivation. Mandeville
suggests that since true virtue depends on pure and disinterested motivation, and
since we can usually find some mixture of self-interest in the antecedents of allegedly
virtuous actions, we may reasonably doubt the reality of true virtue. One might suppose that the safest reply to Mandeville is to concede his point, on his understanding
of true virtue, but to deny its relevance. If we can defend morality without assuming
disinterested motives, we need not worry about his skeptical doubts.

This is an extreme reaction to Mandeville. His doubts rest on observations about mixed motives. He generalizes from cases in which someone who gives a charitable gift is also attracted by the thought that he will gain a good reputation for his charity, so that it will be good for business. But such cases show only that mixed motives are common. Mixed motives do not threaten the reality of disinterested motives; they show only that disinterested motives often cooperate with self-interested motives. Such cooperation is no threat to the reality of moral virtue, unless we assume that virtue requires pure and wholly unmixed motivation. Some moralists, however, including Balguy, assume this about virtue, and so leave themselves open to Mandeville's doubts. Balguy's position makes it easier to understand why voluntarists prefer to avoid any reliance on claims about disinterested motives.

The voluntarist position is usefully summarized in William Paley's influential textbook *The Principles of Moral and Political Philosophy*. Paley recognizes that we may oppose voluntarism if we trust our intuitive judgments about the difference between moral requirements and commands backed by threats. But Paley believes that no intelligible alternative to the voluntarist analysis can be offered, and so we should simply reject the relevant intuitive judgments. The supposed obscurity of claims about disinterested motivation encourages Paley to conclude that these claims are spurious.

He therefore supposes that he has cleared up an unnecessary air of mystery surrounding morality and obligation.[32] His argument implies that there is nothing distinctive about obligation in contrast to other types of inducement. In his view, "A man is said to be obliged when he is urged by a violent motive resulting from the command of another" (ii 2 = R §848). In the case of morality, the commander is God, and the violent motive results from the prospect of reward and punishment.

The theological voluntarism represented by Paley is important not because Paley is a great philosopher, but because his basic principles are the same as Jeremy Bentham's, with the exception of the theological element. Bentham's normative theory is utilitarian, but he agrees with Paley's account of moral motivation as a response to a command backed by a sanction. The removal of the divine sanction leaves utilitarians with some difficulty in explaining why we have any reason to do what utilitarian morality requires of us. The later history of utilitarianism includes a series of efforts to resolve this difficulty.

---

32. "When I first turned my thoughts to moral speculations, an air of mystery seemed to hang over the whole subject; which arose, I believe, from hence,—that I supposed, with many authors whom I had read, that to be obliged to do a thing, was very different from being induced only to do it; and that the obligation to practise virtue, to do what is right, just, etc., was quite another thing, and of another kind, than the obligation which a soldier is under to obey his officer, a servant his master; or any of the civil and ordinary obligations of human life" (William Paley, *Principles of Moral and Political Philosophy*, ii 3, in *British Moralists*, ed. D. D. Raphael [Oxford: Oxford University Press, 1969], §851).

8.   From Scotus to Mandeville

I have traced this historical sequence in order to suggest the rather surprising result of the Augustinian objection to self-love. We can sum up the main steps in the sequence through this argument:

1. Moral virtue requires pure and unmixed motivation.
2. Morally virtuous people do what is right because it is right, irrespective of their own happiness.
3. Hence moral virtue requires motivation by consideration of the right, without any admixture of self-love.
4. But if we achieve this motivational state, we will take pride in it, and therefore will mix self-love in our motivation.
5. Hence we cannot act from the motive required of a morally virtuous person.
6. Hence, moral virtue is impossible.

Scotus's arguments help to show why it is difficult to avoid the unwelcome conclusion once we accept Augustinian doubts about self-love. For his confidence that there must be motives and rational principles that are not subordinate to the eudaemonist principle rests on the assumption that virtuous people must act on moral principles that are not subordinate to the eudaemonist principle. This assumption about virtuous people rests on a demand for unmixed motivation. Once we demand unmixed motivation, we leave room for Mandeville's argument against virtue.

One might want to resist Mandeville's argument by rejecting his claim about pride. Perhaps the growth of pride can be resisted, or perhaps we can take pride in acting from the virtuous motive without making this part of our motivation for being virtuous. But even if either of these replies to Mandeville is correct, it does not completely remove the difficulty. For Mandeville's argument reaches the very strong conclusion that the pursuit of unmixed motivation is necessarily self-defeating. We need not defend this strong conclusion if we want to show that the demand for unmixed motivation is unreasonably "enthusiastic". Most people in many situations have reasons both of morality and of self-interest for doing what morality requires; and we may reasonably suspect an account of moral motivation that requires virtuous people to remove any influence of self-interested motives from the actions required by morality. Even if the pursuit of unmixed motivation is not self-defeating, it may well appear unhealthy. If this is true, Mandeville seems to win the main point.

It is not too surprising, therefore, that the Augustinian suspicion of self-love leads to the voluntarist outlook that makes self-love the basic motive and denies any place for disinterested moral motives. For since the suspicion of self-love leads to the unreasonable demand for unmixed motives, it provokes the response that morality has nothing to do with unmixed motives, and that we should try to get on without them.

I don't believe that the demand for unmixed motives is reasonable or that the quantitative conception of motivation is plausible, and so I have not tried to defend them. But I have mentioned them in order to show how Augustinian and Scotist claims are difficult to defend without a demand for unmixed motives. If that is right, doubts about the demand for unmixed motives may reasonably lead us to doubt the Augustinian and Scotist claims.

The voluntarist rejection of the demand for unmixed motives leads to the denial of the disinterested character of moral motivation. We may reasonably agree with Butler that this denial goes too far, and that it misses something important about the moral outlook. Scotus's assertion of the independence of morality from happiness is intended to recognize the disinterested character of moral motivation. If it fails in its intended purpose, we should consider the possibility that we can safeguard disinterested moral motivation more effectively if we take moral motivation to be compatible with the supremacy of the desire for one's own happiness. If this is right, one aspect of Aristotelian eudaemonism is not simply compatible with disinterested moral motivation, but is actually the best defense of it.[33]

33. I read a version of this paper at the University of Virginia, and I have benefited from helpful comments by the audience there. Paul Bloomfield, the editor of this volume, has also suggested several improvements.

9

Butler on Virtue, Self-Interest, and Human Nature

RALPH WEDGWOOD

In his *Sermons*, Joseph Butler argued for a series of extraordinarily subtle and perceptive claims about the relations between virtue and self-interest.[1] Unfortunately, there has been a great deal of controversy among Butler's interpreters about what exactly these claims amount to, and about what role these claims play in the overall project of his *Sermons*. In this essay, I shall set out and defend a new interpretation of Butler's argument. Although I shall argue that in the end, Butler's argument is not completely successful, I hope that my interpretation will make it plausible that Butler's argument is both more distinctive and original, and also more defensible, than most commentators have supposed.

1.   Butler's "Naturalist" Project

Butler announces his project at the very beginning of the preface. It is to answer "the important question, What is the rule of life?" (P1). In particular, his answer is that we have "obligations to the practice of virtue" (P12). By this he seems to mean that we have *overriding reasons* to live virtuously and to comply with the requirements of morality. However, the ultimate aim behind Butler's project is not philosophical at all. He is a preacher, and his arguments are sermons. Thus, his ultimate aim is homiletic and therefore pastoral. He argues that we have "obligations to the practice of virtue" as a way of exercising spiritual care for his congregation, by strengthening their disposition to lead a virtuous life.

Butler believes that he will be following a distinctive *method* to argue for this answer to the question. As he says: "There are two ways in which the subject of morals may be treated. One begins from inquiring into the abstract relations of things;

---

1. References to the *Fifteen Sermons* are to sermon and paragraph number, according to *The Works of Bishop Butler*, ed. J. H. Bernard (London: Macmillan, 1900), vol. 1. "P" refers to the preface to the *Fifteen Sermons*.

the other from a matter of fact, namely, what the particular nature of man is, its several parts, their economy or constitution; from whence it proceeds to determine what course of life it is, which is correspondent to this whole nature" (P 12). These two methods, he says, "both lead to the same thing, our obligations to the practice of virtue; and thus they exceedingly reinforce and strengthen each other" (P 12). But as he goes on to explain, in his *Sermons* he is chiefly following the second of these two methods: "The following discourses proceed chiefly in this latter method. The three first wholly" (P 13).

Commentators generally agree that the first method is the *rationalist* method, which Butler almost certainly associated with the work of Samuel Clarke and William Wollaston.[2] The characteristic feature of this rationalist method is that it seeks to discover *necessary truths* by means of *a priori reflection*. By contrast, the second method starts out from *contingent facts* that are known on the basis of *empirical observation*. So Butler is claiming that the arguments of his *Sermons* are largely based on the contingent facts of empirical observation.[3] However, he does not make this claim because he is an empiricist who rejects the rationalist method; on the contrary, he explicitly accepts the validity of the rationalist method. He follows the empirical method simply because it better suits his homiletic purposes; as he says, the empirical method "is in a peculiar manner adapted to satisfy a fair mind, and is more easily applicable to the several particular relations and circumstances of life" (P 12).

Specifically, Butler's empirical method is based on an inquiry into *human nature*. Here it becomes crucial to understand exactly what Butler meant by speaking of human nature. One good way to understand what Butler means is to look at the earlier works of moral philosophy that are clearly influencing him.

First, Butler explicitly claims that in saying that virtue consists in following nature, he is repeating the view of "the ancient moralists" (P 13). He seems to be thinking chiefly of the ancient Stoics here. When he says that the ancients had some "inward feeling...which they chose to express in this manner, that man is born to virtue, that it consists in following nature, and that vice is more contrary to this nature than tortures or death", he is giving a close paraphrase of a passage where Cicero presents the Stoic view (*De Officiis* iii.21). So in appealing to human nature in this way, Butler takes himself to be following these ancient Stoic philosophers.[4]

2. In his youth Butler had corresponded with Clarke; see the letters in *The Works of Joseph Butler*, vol. 1: 311–39. Butler refers to William Wollaston as "a late author of great and deserved reputation" in the preface to the *Sermons* (P 13).

3. Compare I.6, note: "Whether man be thus, or otherwise constituted, what is the inward frame in this particular, is a mere question of fact or natural history, not provable immediately by reason. It is therefore to be judged of and determined in the same way other facts or matters of natural history are: by appealing to the external senses, or inward perceptions, respectively, as the matter under consideration is cognizable by one or the other".

4. Besides Cicero, the only other obvious allusions to ancient authors in Butler's ethical works are in the "Dissertation upon the Nature of Virtue" (*The Analogy of Religion*, appendix 2), in *The Works of Bishop Butler*, vol. 2. Here too it is Stoic philosophers that he refers to—namely, Epictetus (§ 1, note) and Marcus Aurelius (§ 2, note). On Butler's use of Stoic ideas, see especially Terence Irwin, "Stoic Naturalism in Butler," in *Hellenistic and Early Modern Philosophy*, ed. Jon Miller (Cambridge: Cambridge University Press, 2003).

At the same time, Butler was obviously well acquainted with Shaftesbury's *Inquiry Concerning Virtue or Merit*, which he refers to explicitly in the preface (P 6).[5] Shaftesbury also seems to have been profoundly influenced by some of the ancients (including the Stoics Epictetus and Marcus Aurelius). Moreover, Shaftesbury bases his inquiry into virtue on an account of the "Constitution and Frame of *Nature*", and in general he believes that nature is known "by Study and Observation".[6] In general Shaftesbury's work seems clearly to appeal to empirical observations of human nature,[7] and largely to lack the attempts at formal demonstrative reasoning that are such a prominent feature of such works as Clarke's *Discourse concerning the Unchangeable Obligations of Natural Religion*. For these reasons, then, it seems plausible that Butler would also have regarded Shaftesbury as also employing this second method. This is not to say that Butler is just a slavish follower of Shaftesbury. Far from it. Butler clearly believes that his execution of this naturalist empirical method avoids a certain crucial "material deficiency or omission" that mars Shaftesbury's approach (P 6). But nonetheless at bottom it is the same method that both philosophers are employing.

Now it should be quite uncontroversial that both Shaftesbury and the ancient Stoics had a profoundly *teleological* conception of nature. This is quite explicit in Shaftesbury: "We know that every Creature has a private Good and Interest of his own; which Nature has compel'd him to seek by all the Advantages afforded him, within the compass of his Make. We know that there is in reality a right and a wrong State of every Creature; and that his right-one is by Nature forwarded, and by himself affectionately sought. There being therefore in every Creature a certain *Interest or Good*; there must be also a certain END, to which every thing in his Constitution must *naturally* refer" (I.ii.1, 167). Thus, the "constitution" or "make" of each individual creature involves some natural "end" or purpose toward which its nature is directed or oriented. Moreover, according to Shaftesbury, we should not just look to the natural end of the nature of each individual creature; we should look to the natural end of the whole species:

> If therefore in the Structure of this or any other Animal, there be any thing which points beyond himself, and by which he is plainly discover'd to have relation to some other Being or Nature besides his own; then will this Animal undoubtedly be esteem'd *a Part* of some other System. For instance, if an Animal has the Proportions of a Male, it shews he has relation to a Female.... So that the Creatures are both of 'em to be consider'd as Parts of *another System*: which is that of a particular Race or Species of living Creatures, who have some one *common Nature*, or are provided for, by some one *Order* or *Constitution* of things subsisting together, and co-operating towards Conservation, and Support. (I.ii.1, 168)

5. Passages in Shaftesbury's *Inquiry Concerning Virtue or Merit* are cited by book, part, and section number, and by the page numbers in Shaftesbury (Anthony Ashley Cooper, 3rd Earl of Shaftesbury), *Characteristics of Men, Manners, Opinions, Times*, ed. Lawrence Klein (Cambridge: Cambridge University Press, 2003).

6. See Shaftesbury, *An Inquiry Concerning Virtue or Merit*, I.i.1, 167.

7. See, for example, Shaftesbury's observation that even "ruffians" have a sense of honor, in ibid., I.ii.4, 177.

Thus, Shaftesbury thinks that "there is a System of all Animals; an *Animal-Order* or *Oeconomy*, according to which the animal Affairs are regulated and dispos'd"; indeed, he even speculates that the entire universe as a whole may form a single "System" that has some natural end or purpose (I.ii.1, 169).

Butler's *Sermons* seem to endorse the basic ideas behind Shaftesbury's teleological conception of nature. Thus, Butler says in the preface, clearly following Shaftesbury's idea that the "parts" of a "system" form an overall "economy" or "constitution":

> Whoever thinks it worth while to consider this matter thoroughly, should begin with stating to himself exactly the idea of a system, economy, or constitution of any particular nature, or particular any thing: and he will, I suppose, find, that it is an one or a whole, made up of several parts; but yet, that the several parts even considered as a whole do not complete the idea, unless in the notion of a whole you include the relations and respects which those parts have to each other. Every work both of nature and of art is a system: and as every particular thing, both natural and artificial, is for some use or purpose out of and beyond itself, one may add, to what has been already brought into the idea of a system, its conduciveness to this one or more ends. (P 14)

Butler famously illustrates this conception of "nature" with the example of a *watch*. To understand a watch properly (or to have the complete "idea" of a watch, as Butler puts it), one must not only know what its parts are but also what their mutual relations are, and how this arrangement of these parts makes the whole watch conducive to the "end" or "purpose" of the watch. In a similar way, Butler promises, his study of human nature will lead to an understanding or "idea" of a human being, and "from this idea itself it will as fully appear that this our nature, *i.e.* constitution, is adapted to virtue, as from the idea of a watch it appears that its nature, *i.e.* constitution or system, is adapted to measure time" (P 14). The same teleological conception of nature is set out at the beginning of Sermon II: "If the real nature of any creature leads him and is adapted to such and such purposes only, or more than to any other; this is a reason to believe the Author of that nature intended it for those purposes. Thus there is no doubt the eye was intended for us to see with. And the more complex any constitution is, and the greater variety of parts there are which thus tend to some one end, the stronger is the proof that such end was designed" (II.1).

Admittedly, there is one way in which Butler's teleological conception clearly differs from Shaftesbury's. Whereas Shaftesbury is uninhibited about speculating about the natural end or purpose of the whole species, or even of the whole universe, Butler—a vastly more cautious thinker than Shaftesbury in almost every way—avoids committing himself about such large questions, and focuses exclusively on the natural end or purpose of the constitution of the *individual* human being. Apart from this difference, however, Butler's teleology seems fundamentally similar to Shaftesbury's.

It might seem surprising to some readers that this teleological conception of nature plays such a fundamental role in the works of Shaftesbury and Butler. Teleological conceptions of nature are often thought to belong to a "premodern" worldview, which—it is often thought—was swept away with the rise of the new science that was typified by Galileo's *Dialogue Concerning the Two Chief World Systems* (1632). However, this is a very partial view of the period in question. It is true that

Galileo's new science inspired some philosophers—most notably, Hobbes—to turn their back on teleological thinking. But this was certainly not how all philosophers in this period responded. Most thinkers who had a serious interest in biology or medicine would have found it indispensable to appeal to natural ends or purposes in trying to understand the nature of living things. Even in the last decade of the eighteenth century, Immanuel Kant devoted the entire second part of his *Critique of Judgment* (1790) to an attempt to understand how it can be legitimate for natural scientists to take a teleological approach to understanding the empirical world. It was not the new science of Galileo that finally swept away the appeal to traditional teleology in natural science, but Charles Darwin's *Origin of Species* (1859) more than 200 years later.

Admittedly, the mechanistic forms of physics that came to be accepted in the seventeenth century did indeed avoid the sort of teleological theorizing that had been common in earlier attempts to understand the natural world. However, as recent historians of science have shown, whereas scientists in the first half of the seventeenth century were optimistic that their mechanistic form of physics would ultimately provide a *complete* explanation of the entire universe, the rise of Newtonian mechanics later in the century actually *discouraged* any such belief in the causal completeness of physics.[8] It seemed perfectly reasonable to the best-educated thinkers in the late seventeenth and early eighteenth centuries to hypothesize that in addition to the forces that were studied by Newtonian mechanics, there should be other fundamental forces (such as "vital forces") that were distinctive of living things, and that the best way to understand these forces would be by means of a teleological approach.

2. The Interpretation of Butler's Teleology

Clearly, it is crucial for interpreting Butler correctly, then, to understand exactly what this teleological conception of human nature amounts to. How exactly does Butler conceive of what it is for the constitution or nature of something to involve a certain "end" or "purpose"?

Different commentators have interpreted Butler's teleology in different ways. One simple and straightforward interpretation focuses on Butler's reference to what "the Author of nature intended"; according to this interpretation, for the constitution or nature of an object to involve a certain end or purpose is simply for the creator of that object to have *designed* it to promote that end. This is how Stephen Darwall interprets Butler's teleology, for example.[9] It is because Darwall interprets Butler's teleology in this way that he raises the following objection to Butler: "It is

8. For this point, see David Papineau, "The Rise of Physicalism," in *Physicalism and Its Discontents*, ed. Carl Gillett and Barry Loewer (Cambridge: Cambridge University Press, 2001).

9. See Stephen Darwall, *The British Moralists and the Internal "Ought": 1640–1740* (Cambridge: Cambridge University Press, 1995), 261–70.

difficult to see...how any facts about functional design can establish [Butler's conclusion], since no normative facts follow from them" (267).

Someone might offer the following reply to Darwall on Butler's behalf. Since Butler accepts the fundamental articles of traditional Christian belief, he believes that everything in the world is created by an all-knowing, almighty, and morally perfect God. Thus, if God designed us for a certain purpose, it must be right and proper for this purpose to be the supreme purpose of our existence. Thus, given these traditional Christian assumptions, facts about our functional design *do* imply normative facts.

Darwall might retort that this reply on behalf of Butler suffers from the following problem. Butler rejects a "voluntarist" interpretation of God's will.[10] If God intends us to lead a certain sort of life, His will is not arbitrary. On the contrary, if He intends us to lead a certain sort of life, He does so precisely *because* this is the life that there is overriding reason for us to lead. So it is not God's intending us to lead a virtuous life that *makes it the case* that there is overriding reason for us to lead a virtuous life. The fact that God intended us to lead virtuous lives is, at most, decisive *evidence* that there is overriding reason for us to be virtuous. It does not *explain why* there is such an overriding reason for us to be virtuous.

However, it is not at all clear to me that Butler is trying to give an *explanation* of *why* we have an "obligation to the practice of virtue". That question seems to be the topic for the sort of philosophical speculation that Butler would most likely regard as unnecessary for his ultimate homiletic project. It would be enough for this project if Butler can produce a compelling argument for the conclusion *that* we have such an "obligation to the practice of virtue", without also going on to speculate about *why* this is the case.

Be that as it may, however, it seems to me that from Butler's point of view, there is a more serious problem with the argument that Darwall ascribes to him. How could Butler think he knows anything about God's intentions? There are many passages where Butler seems extremely wary about speculating about God's intentions. For example, he describes the supposition "that the end of divine punishment is no other than that of civil punishment, namely, to prevent future mischief" as a "bold supposition", "which it would be very presumptuous to assert" (29). So what is different about those cases where he *is* willing to make claims about God's intentions with respect to a "system", such as the human eye (II.1)? It seems that Butler thought it perfectly *obvious* that a teleological conception of the human eye was correct: the nature of the eye essentially involves a certain end or purpose—namely, for us to see with. Given his traditional Christian assumptions, Butler can then infer from this conception of the eye, as having a nature that essentially involves this end or purpose, to the conclusion that God must have created the eye with this nature, and so must have intended it for this end or purpose.

However, if the claim that the nature of a system involves a certain end or purpose is to *support* the conclusion that God intended the system for that purpose, it must be possible to have *independent* reasons for accepting this teleological claim about this system—that is, reasons for accepting this claim that do not depend on

---

10. For evidence of Butler's rejection of theological voluntarism, see XIV.14, and *The Analogy of Religion*, I.v.12n.

any assumptions about the Creator's intentions with respect to this system. So the teleological claim that the nature of the system involves that end or purpose surely cannot just *mean* that the system was originally designed for that end or purpose. Indeed, it is clear that when the ancient philosophers made teleological claims of this sort, they were not just making claims about the Creator's intentions. Many ancient philosophers firmly believed that there are many things the nature of which involves an end or purpose, but did not believe that those things were designed by a Creator for that purpose.[11]

A different interpretation of Butler's teleology is suggested by the way in which Shaftesbury expresses his teleological conception: "We know that there is in reality a right and a wrong state of every creature; and that [the creature's] right one is by nature forwarded" (I.ii.1, 167). Moreover, this sort of teleological conception is true, Shaftesbury believes, of everything in the universe that has enough of a "constitution" to count as a "system".

This suggests a quite different interpretation of Butler's teleology. On this interpretation, a teleological conception of a certain "system" holds that there is a right or correct or proper way for that system to operate in, and it is a fundamental principle governing the behavior of that system that it is generally *disposed* to operate in the way that counts as the right or proper way for it to operate in. This way of operating is the "end" or "purpose" toward which the system is oriented or "adapted".

This sort of teleology can certainly allow that these dispositions that are conducive to the system's end or purpose may be inhibited or blocked by various interfering factors; these dispositions do not have to be manifested in every possible case. As Butler says, even a watch "is apt to be out of order" (P 14). This does not prevent it from being the case that the watch is generally disposed or "adapted" to tell the time. It is a common occurrence that a thing's dispositions are inhibited or blocked in this way; that does not prevent the thing from genuinely possessing the dispositions in question.[12]

This interpretation of Butler's teleology is, in effect, closely related to Mark Bedau's interpretation of what teleological explanations amount to.[13] According to Bedau, the defining feature of a teleological explanation is that it seeks to explain a contingent event by showing what is *good* about that event. On this interpretation, then, the proponent of such a teleological explanation is committed to the view that it is a basic feature of the natural system in question that contingent events can occur within that system precisely *because* it is *good* for them to occur. For example, the plants put out leaves because it is *good* for them to do so; predators grow sharp teeth because it is *good* for them to do so. (Some thinkers might even extend this teleological approach beyond the realm of biology, for example suggesting that the rain falls because it is *good* for it to help the plants to grow.) In general, according to

11. The most striking example of this is Aristotle, whose conception of nature was profoundly teleological, but was not based on any assumption about the Creator's intentions.

12. This point has been stressed by much recent work on dispositions. See especially Alexander Bird, "Dispositions and Antidotes," *Philosophical Quarterly* 48 (1998): 227–34.

13. See M. A. Bedau, "Where's the Good in Teleology?" *Philosophy and Phenomenological Research* 52 (1992): 781–806.

a teleological approach, the goodness of some possible event can make that event actually occur, because the natural system in question has a fundamental tendency to operate in the way that is right or best for it to operate in.

If this is the right way to understand Butler's teleology, then we can see that Darwall was quite mistaken to claim that "no normative facts follow from" a teleological conception of a system. On the contrary, a teleological conception of a system essentially incorporates a conception of what is the right or proper state for that system—that is, the state that the system ought to be in. In that sense, a teleological conception involves a normative conception. A teleological fact—a fact about what teleological conception is correct—does indeed imply a normative fact.

However, it does not follow that we can only discover the teleological fact on the basis of a prior knowledge of the normative fact. On the contrary, we may know that *some* teleological conception of a certain system is correct; then an investigation of the *dispositions* that seem most fundamental to and characteristic of that system may help us to see precisely *which* of the states that could be intelligibly regarded as the right or proper state for that system to be in is the "end" that those dispositions are conducive to.

To Butler, I propose, it must simply have seemed obvious that some teleological conception of the human mind must be correct. After all, Butler assumes that it will seem obvious to everyone that a teleological conception of the human *eye* must be correct (II.1); and would it not be extraordinary if the human eye had a natural end or purpose but the human *mind* did not? So, an empirical investigation of the most characteristic and fundamental dispositions of the human mind should help us to see which, out of all the many ways of life that could be intelligibly regarded as the right or proper way for a human being to live, is the natural "end" that these fundamental dispositions are conducive to. We may then conclude that it is not just our end or purpose to lead this way of life, but it is also the right and proper way for us to live; it is the way of life that we have overriding reason to lead.

Some philosophers might think that this teleological conception of the human mind is just too antiquated to take seriously. So perhaps Butler's moral philosophy belongs to those parts of the history of philosophy that the progress of science has rendered utterly obsolete.

We should agree, I think, that Shaftesbury's teleology, according to which whole species (and perhaps even the whole system of the universe as a whole) has a natural end or purpose, has indeed been rendered obsolete by the advances of contemporary natural science. Evolutionary biologists have incontrovertibly shown that the theory of evolution through natural selection provides vastly more powerful and empirically adequate explanations of biological phenomena than any traditional teleological appeal to a fundamental tendency of living things toward leading the sort of life that it is right and best for them to lead.

However, it is not so clear that the aspect of Butler's teleology that is most central to the argument of his *Sermons*—his teleological conception of the individual human mind—has also been shown to be obsolete by contemporary natural science. Indeed, Butler's teleological conception of the human mind could be defended on the basis of a philosophy of mind that accepts some version of the slogan that "the intentional is normative". For example, a Davidsonian philosophy of mind would insist that we must have some tendency to believe the truth, and to love the good, if we are to be correctly interpretable as having the attitudes of belief or love at all.[14] According to a philosophy of mind of this sort, it is essential to the various types of mental state that are characteristic of the human mind that there is a correct or proper role that these mental states should play in human thinking and reasoning, and in every human being, these mental states must have at least some disposition to play this correct or proper role, if the human being is to be capable of those types of mental states.[15] In effect, this philosophy of mind adopts a teleological conception of the mind, of the same general kind as I have ascribed to Butler. So the proponent of this sort of philosophy of mind should be able to welcome the naturalist project that Butler pursues in the *Sermons*.

3. Butler's Conception of Reasons for Action

In this section, I shall highlight a further feature of Butler's project, which sharply distinguishes Butler from many later philosophers of the modern era. This feature concerns Butler's conception of *reasons for action*.

As we have seen, Butler aims to base his argument for the conclusion that we have an overriding reason (or "obligation") to be virtuous on an account of *human nature*. So, according to Butler, *all human beings* have an overriding reason to be virtuous. This marks an important difference between Butler's approach and the approach of many other modern philosophers. On the one hand, Butler's approach differs from that of philosophers of a broadly Humean persuasion, such as Philippa Foot (at least in the 1970s) and Bernard Williams, since these philosophers hold that only human beings who have certain desires or interests (or who have appropriate elements in their "subjective motivational set") have a reason to be virtuous.[16] At the same time, Butler's approach also differs from that of philosophers of a broadly Kantian persuasion, such as Christine Korsgaard, who base their conclusion that we

14. As Donald Davidson put it, in interpreting someone we "will try for a theory that finds him consistent, a believer of truths, and a lover of the good"; see his "Mental Events," in *Essays on Actions and Events* (Oxford: Oxford University Press, 1980), 222.

15. For a defense of this sort of philosophy of mind, see my forthcoming paper, "The Normativity of the Intentional," in *The Oxford Handbook of the Philosophy of Mind*, ed. B. McLaughlin and A. Beckermann (Oxford: Oxford University Press, forthcoming).

16. See Philippa Foot, "Morality as a System of Hypothetical Imperatives," *Philosophical Review* 81, no. 3 (1972): 305–16; and Bernard Williams, "Internal and External Reasons," in *Moral Luck* (Cambridge: Cambridge University Press, 1981). For the Humean antecedents of this position, see David Hume, *A Treatise of Human Nature*, ed. L. A. Selby-Bigge (Oxford: Clarendon, [1740] 1978), II.iii.3. In her later work, Philippa Foot argues for a position that is closer to Butler's, in that it sees our reason to comply with moral requirements as ultimately grounded in human nature; see her *Natural Goodness* (Oxford: Oxford University Press, 2001). For another approach that also grounds our reason to comply with moral requirements in human nature, see Paul Bloomfield, *Moral Reality* (New York: Oxford University Press, 2001).

all have overriding reason to be virtuous not on an account of human nature, but rather on an account of the necessary structure of rational agency as such.[17]

Underlying this difference between Butler, on the one hand, and the Humeans and Kantians, on the other hand, is the fact that the Humeans and Kantians both seem to hold a purely *formal* or *procedural* conception of reasons for action. To the extent that these philosophers are willing to make sense of the notion at all,[18] they conceive of what there is "overriding reason for one to do" in terms of what it is *formally* or *procedurally rational* for one to do. First, these philosophers start with a notion of what it is for a process of practical reasoning to count as procedurally rational. Then, they propose, there is "overriding reason" for one to perform an action just in case, if one were adequately informed of the relevant nonnormative facts about one's situation, and went through a process of procedurally rational practical reasoning, one would choose to perform that action. Of course, the Humeans and the Kantians have strikingly different conceptions of what it is for a process of practical reasoning to count as "procedurally rational". But there are certain fundamental similarities: for example, both Humeans and Kantians believe that the conditions of procedurally rational practical reasoning have a similar status to the laws of *logic*.[19] I shall refer to these philosophers' conceptions of reasons for action as *procedural conceptions*.[20]

On the face of it, however, the Kantian claim—that, for absolutely all well-informed rational agents, it is procedurally irrational to violate a moral requirement, in essentially the same way as it is procedurally irrational to violate the laws of logic—is an awfully strong claim. Offhand, it seems possible for an agent to violate a moral requirement even if his reasoning is logically quite coherent and free from any error or ignorance about the relevant nonnormative facts. For example, we could imagine a brilliantly successful criminal. Suppose that this criminal is a genius at a priori reasoning—at mathematics, logic, decision theory, and so on—but he does not accept that moral requirements provide him with any reason to act accordingly, and has committed appalling crimes without compunction or remorse. Is it really necessary that this criminal's practical reasoning is either in some way *procedurally irrational*, or else *misinformed* or *ignorant* about some relevant nonnormative fact? The claim that there must be some such procedural irrationality or nonnormative error or ignorance in his

---

17. See Christine Korsgaard, *The Sources of Normativity* (Cambridge: Cambridge University Press, 1996). Even though Korsgaard appeals to our "practical identity" as human beings, she argues that any rational agent who is capable of reflective choice at all is committed to recognizing this practical identity; so she is not basing a defense of virtue on an empirical conception of human nature in the way that Butler is doing.

18. Arguably, Hume himself refused to make sense of this notion at all; see Elijah Millgram, "Was Hume a Humean?" *Hume Studies* 21 (1995): 75–93.

19. Thus, Humeans often speak of the "logic of decision"; see, for example, Richard C. Jeffrey, *The Logic of Decision*, 2nd ed. (Chicago: University of Chicago Press, 1983). And Kantians often compare their fundamental principle of rational practical reasoning to the laws of logic; as Christine Korsgaard puts it (*The Sources of Normativity*, 235), just as "if I am going to think I must think in accordance with the principle of non-contradiction," so too, "if I am going to will at all I must do so [in accordance with Kant's categorical imperative]."

20. For an argument against all such procedural conceptions of reasons for action, see my paper "Choosing Rationally and Choosing Correctly," in *Weakness of Will and Practical Irrationality*, ed. S. Stroud and C. Tappolet (Oxford: Oxford University Press, 2003), 201–29.

reasoning surely has a heavy burden of proof to bear. Many Kantians are willing to try to shoulder this burden of proof.[21] Prima facie, however, this burden of proof gives us a reason to try to find an acceptable alternative to this Kantian approach.

In general, the procedural conception of reasons for action seems to make it at least prima facie implausible that moral requirements must provide a consistent egoist with strong or weighty reasons to act accordingly. As the Humeans claim, with considerable prima facie plausibility, even if a criminal or an egoist is procedurally rational and ideally well informed about the relevant nonnormative facts, he could still lack any motivations that would lead him to choose to comply with moral requirements. So, the Humeans conclude, moral requirements would not provide such an egoist with any reasons to act at all.

However, this Humean view also seems open to prima facie serious objections. James Doyle puts it well:[22] "The point is not just that [on this Humean view] there will be nothing we can say by way of rational persuasion on behalf of morality to someone, such as the egoist, who just happens to lack the relevant motivation—although this is true.... The real problem with such a Humean view is that we will not even have anything to say *to each other* about what mistake, exactly, the egoist is making." On this Humean view, the egoist is making no mistake at all: he is quite right to deny that moral requirements provide him with any reasons whatsoever. Indeed, *you* would be right to deny that moral requirements provide you with any reasons, if you too came to lack the relevant motivations. But this is surely not an attractive way to conceive of morality. So if we embrace the procedural conception of reasons for action, it will be hard for us to give a satisfactory account of our reasons to comply with moral requirements: either we will have to shoulder the heavy burden of proof that the Kantians must bear, or we will be forced into the unattractive conclusion of the Humeans.

Butler does not accept the procedural conception of reasons for action. In his view, the egoist, in acting viciously, is acting in a way in which there is overriding reason for him not to act. But Butler never claims that the egoist is *procedurally irrational*. Unlike Samuel Clarke, Butler never claims that anyone who acts viciously is "guilty of the very same unreasonableness and contradiction in one case; as he that in another case should affirm one number or quantity to be equal to another, and yet that other at the same time not to be equal to the first".[23] For all that Butler says, there need be no procedural irrationality, and no logical incoherence, in the egoist's thinking at all.

---

21. Besides Korsgaard, the most notable Kantian who has attempted to shoulder this burden of proof in recent years is Thomas Nagel, in *The Possibility of Altruism* (Oxford: Clarendon Press, 1970).

22. James Doyle, "Moral Rationalism and Moral Commitment," *Philosophy and Phenomenological Research* 60 (2000): 1–22, especially 7.

23. See D. D. Raphael, ed., *The British Moralists* (Oxford: Oxford University Press, 1969), §232. (Strictly speaking, Clarke is only referring to *injustice* here, not to vice in general, although elsewhere he claims that there is a similar "absurdity and inconsistency" in other kinds of vice as well.) It is true that Butler concedes that Clarke's method of "inquiring into the abstract relations of things" is just as valid as his own method of inquiring into human nature (P 12). However, there is no reason to interpret Butler's endorsement of Clarke's method as an endorsement of Clarke's view that anyone who acts viciously is guilty of "absurdity and inconsistency."

Butler also never claims that the egoist is necessarily misinformed or ignorant about any *nonnormative* fact. Of course, if the egoist believes that moral requirements do not provide him with any reasons to act accordingly, then according to Butler, the egoist believes something *false*. But this is a false normative belief, not about a false belief about any nonnormative fact. Butler does not claim that this false normative belief must be explained either by procedural irrationality or by error or ignorance about any nonnormative fact.

Moreover, Butler may have a positive reason for being skeptical of any such procedural conception of reasons. Butler seems to be generally quite skeptical of attempts to give reductive definitions. Arguably, this is part of what he meant when he famously said, "Everything is what it is, and not another thing" (P39). Thus, Butler would be equally skeptical of attempts to reduce the notion of "what there is overriding reason for one to do" to the notion of "what one would choose to do if one were procedurally rational and adequately informed about the nonnormative facts". Butler could probably endorse the following elucidation of the notion of "what there is overriding reason for one to do". The judgment that there is "overriding reason" for one to do something expresses a *conclusion of practical reasoning*. So one would be being weak-willed or *akratic* if one simultaneously made the judgment that there is "overriding reason" for one to do a certain thing, and yet willingly failed to do it. But Butler would not accept any attempt to reduce the notion of an "overriding reason" to the notion of "procedural rationality". An overriding reason for action is just an overriding reason for action; it is what it is, and not another thing.

Of course, Butler can still claim that *one* way in which one might fail to recognize what there is overriding reason to do is by being procedurally irrational. But if he rejects the procedural conception of reasons for action, then he must regard it as possible, at least in principle, that even if one is procedurally rational, and ideally well informed about all relevant nonnormative facts, one could still fail to recognize what there is overriding reason to do. If such failures are possible, this must be because our most basic normative beliefs arise, not just from procedurally rational reasoning from nonnormative premises, but from a specific faculty that can malfunction even if one is procedurally quite rational.

Butler certainly believes in such a specific faculty. He calls this faculty "conscience" (I.8), although sometimes he also uses other names, such as "reflex approbation or disapprobation" or "reflection" (26). He acknowledges that there seems to be "some small diversity amongst mankind" with respect to the deliverances of conscience (II.1), which seems to imply that our conscience is fallible.[24] Someone whose conscience fails to inform them of a normative truth might have a corrupted or defective conscience, but he need not count either as procedurally irrational or as misinformed about any nonnormative truth.

---

24. Thus, Butler is not committed to denying that conscience is fallible—contrary to what G. E. M. Anscombe says in "Modern Moral Philosophy," *Philosophy* 33 (1958): 1–19. However, Butler does not develop this point. He clearly thinks that the main danger to our appreciation of moral and normative truths is *self-deception*, which he discusses at length in sermons VII and X.

In short, Butler's argument for "our obligation to the practice of virtue" differs from that of most later modern philosophers, in the following ways: Unlike the Humeans, Butler argues for the conclusion that moral requirements really do provide the egoist with overriding reasons to act accordingly; unlike the Kantians, Butler bases his argument for this conclusion in an account of human nature, not in an account of the necessary structure of rational agency as such; and unlike most later moral philosophers, including both the Humeans and the Kantians, he does not accept the procedural conception of reasons for action.

4. Butler's Rejection of Eudaimonism

Even though Butler's approach differs in this way from the approach of most later modern philosophers, there is also one crucial way in which his approach also differs from that of the "ancient moralists" whom he claims to be following. Unlike them, Butler *does not accept eudaimonism*. As I shall understand it, eudaimonism is a view about reasons for action, according to which it is universal principle, applying to all agents and all actions, that an agent has an overriding reason to perform an action if and only if that action *promotes the agent's happiness* more than any available alternative action.

It is important not to misread this formulation of eudaimonism. According to this formulation, eudaimonism does *not* make any claim about *why* one has an overriding reason to perform these actions, or about what is the proper motive for performing these actions. So, in particular, eudaimonism does *not* claim that the only reason that there is for performing these actions is that these actions will best promote one's own happiness, or that the proper motive for performing them is the desire to promote one's happiness. On the contrary, it is perfectly compatible with eudaimonism to claim that the fundamental reason for performing many of these actions, and the reason that ought to motivate one to perform them, is just that these actions are intrinsically fine or admirable. Eudaimonism only claims that whenever one has overriding reason to perform an action, that action will also promote one's happiness more than any available alternative; and conversely, whenever an action will promote one's happiness more than any available alternative, one has an overriding reason to perform it. Eudaimonism claims that overriding reasons for action perfectly *coincide* with the demands of one's own happiness; it does not claim that these reasons for action all *arise* from the demands of one's own happiness.

Even if we understand eudaimonism in this cautious way, however, Butler does not rest his argument for our "obligation to the practice of virtue" on this eudaimonist principle. Instead, he bases his argument on his own principle of the *natural supremacy of conscience*—that is, the principle that it is an essential part of human nature that our conscience should be supreme.[25]

---

25. This principle appears to imply that it is an essential part of human nature to *have* a conscience. Any member of our species (e.g., an infant) who lacked a conscience would not be a full-blown instance of "human nature" in the relevant sense.

This point emerges most clearly in a passage where Butler criticizes what he calls "a material deficiency or omission in lord Shaftesbury's Inquiry concerning Virtue" (26):

> [Lord Shaftesbury] has shewn beyond all contradiction, that virtue is naturally the interest or happiness, and vice the misery, of such a creature as man, placed in the circumstances which we are in this world. But suppose there are particular exceptions; a case which this author was unwilling to put, and yet surely it is to be put: or suppose a case which he has put and determined, that of a sceptic not convinced of this happy tendency of virtue, or being of a contrary opinion. His determination is, that it would be *without remedy*. One may say more explicitly, that leaving out the authority of reflex approbation or disapprobation, such an one would be under an obligation to act viciously; since interest, one's own happiness, is a manifest obligation, and there is not supposed to be any other obligation in the case.

Here, Butler seems to think that we must allow, at least for the sake of argument, that there are "exceptions" to the general rule that virtue and self-interest coincide;[26] and he seems to want to develop an argument for the conclusion that we have "an obligation to the practice of virtue" that could be accepted by "a sceptic not convinced of this happy tendency of virtue, or being of a contrary opinion". Such a skeptic presumably rejects the traditional Christian doctrine that we will all receive rewards or punishments in an afterlife that will ensure the perfect coincidence of virtue and happiness. So Butler's argument for his conclusion is designed to be acceptable to someone who rejects the Christian doctrine of an afterlife.

By an "exception" here Butler clearly means an exception to Shaftesbury's general conclusion that "virtue is naturally the interest or happiness, and vice the misery, of such a creature as man, placed in the circumstances which we are in this world". Now, in his *Inquiry concerning Virtue or Merit*, Shaftesbury is primarily concerned, not with a comparison between particular actions, but with a comparison between overall ways of life. Thus, Shaftesbury's conclusion is that virtuous ways of life are, in general, happier than vicious ways of life. So an "exception" to Shaftesbury's conclusion would be a case in which someone will be happier on the whole if he leads a certain vicious way of life than if he leads a virtuous way of life. Presumably, if there is a vicious way of life that will make this person happier than any virtuous way of life, then there will be cases in which some particular vicious action will make the person happier than any available virtuous alternative action. Butler's argument is designed to be compatible with the existence of such "exceptions". So his argument must be compatible with the existence of cases in which one has an overriding reason to act virtuously but the virtuous action does *not* promote one's happiness more than any alternative. Thus, his argument must be compatible with the falsity of eudaimonism.

---

26. There are other passages that seem to recognize such "exceptions." For example: "Self-love then, though confined to the interest of the present world, does in general perfectly coincide with virtue; and leads us to one and the same course of life. But, whatever exceptions there are to this, [they] are much fewer than they are commonly thought" (III.8).

In this passage, then, Butler is implying that once we take account of the natural supremacy of conscience, we can solve the problem that when faced with an "exception" to the general coincidence of virtue and self-interest, one would be "under an obligation to act viciously". Immediately after this passage, Butler considers an objection to this view, and then offers a rather unexpected reply to that objection (P 26):

> But does it much mend the matter, to take in that natural authority of reflection? "There indeed would be an obligation to virtue; but would not the obligation from supposed interest on the side of vice remain?" If it should, yet to be under two contrary obligations, *i.e.* under none at all, would not be exactly the same, as to be under a formal obligation to be vicious, or to be in circumstances in which the constitution of man's nature plainly required that vice should be preferred. But the obligation on the side of interest really does not remain. For the natural authority of the principle of reflection is an obligation the most near and intimate, the most certain and known: whereas the contrary obligation can at the utmost appear no more than probable; since no man can be *certain* in any circumstances that vice is his interest in the present world, much less can he be certain against another: and thus the certain obligation would entirely supersede and destroy the uncertain one; which yet would have been of real force without the former.

Here, Butler concedes, at least for the sake of argument, that there may be cases in which it is "probable" that it is in one's interest to be vicious. Nonetheless, even in those cases, it would still be "certain" that one has an obligation to be virtuous. Hence, the certain obligation to be virtuous completely trumps and removes what would otherwise have been an uncertain and merely probable obligation to be vicious.

Butler concludes this discussion of Shaftesbury's views as follows (P 27): "In truth, the taking in this consideration totally changes the whole state of the case; and shews, what this author does not seem to have been aware of, that the greatest degree of scepticism which he thought possible will still leave men under the strictest moral obligations, whatever their opinion be concerning the happiness of virtue." Thus, Butler clearly intends his argument to be completely *independent* of the eudaimonist view that overriding reasons for action always coincide with the demands of one's own happiness. Even though the conclusion of his argument is that every human being has an overriding reason to act virtuously at all times, his argument is designed to be compatible with the existence of cases ("exceptions") in which it is "probable" that one will promote one's own happiness more effectively by being vicious than by being virtuous. Butler's only concession to eudaimonism is to accept that if one has an overriding reason to pursue a certain course of action, then it cannot be *certain* that refraining from that course of action will promote one's happiness more. (We shall inquire later on exactly why Butler makes this limited concession to eudaimonism.)

As we shall see later, there is another feature of Butler's *Sermons* that also reveals Butler's refusal to accept eudaimonism. This feature emerges in the fact that he distinguishes sharply between *conscience* and *self-love*. It is conscience that makes us aware of, and inclines us to pursue, the way of life that we have overriding reason to lead, while it is self-love that makes us aware of, and inclines us to pursue, our own self-interest or happiness. Butler resists any attempt to identify conscience with self-love, or to view either of these two "inward principles" as merely a superfluous adjunct to the other. Since these two faculties are independent in this way, our judgments about what we have overriding reasons to do arise independently of our judgments about what will promote our own happiness; so there is no reason at this stage in the argument to assume that the two sorts of judgments will universally and perfectly coincide.

5.   The Supreme Authority of Conscience

As I have argued above, Butler's project involves arguing for a certain *teleological* conception of human nature. According to such a teleological conception, it is part of human nature that there is a certain sort of life that is the *right* or *correct* or *proper* life for any human being to lead. To deviate from this sort of life, Butler claims, would be "disproportionate to the nature of man", and so "in the strictest and most proper sense unnatural" (II.10). Butler appears to assume that it is a basic truth about reasons for action that the life that is, in this sense, the correct or proper life for human beings to lead is also the life that there is overriding reason for human beings to lead. What Butler aims to show is that this sort of life essentially involves living virtuously and complying with moral requirements. In fact, he aims to show that this sort of life is not only a virtuous life, but also a life that involves the effective pursuit of the agent's own happiness.

It is part of any teleological conception of human nature (according to my interpretation of Butler's teleology) that the human mind is a "system" in which various elements are structured in relation to one another in such a way that the whole mind is generally disposed or "adapted" to leading the kind of life that is the correct or proper life for it to lead. This is why an empirical investigation of our mental dispositions can help us to see what is the correct or proper life for us to lead.

Thus, Butler has to argue that in various ways, many of our mental dispositions are conducive to virtue, and many of these dispositions are also conducive to the effective pursuit of happiness. Butler gives an initial summary of this argument in sermon I (I.15): "The nature of man considered in his single capacity, and with respect only to the present world, is adapted and leads him to attain the greatest happiness he can for himself in the present world. The nature of man considered in his public or social capacity leads him to a right behaviour in society, to that course of life which we call virtue. Men follow or obey their nature in both these capacities and respects to a certain degree, but not entirely: their actions do not come up to the whole of what their nature leads them to in either of these capacities or respects." This point is also argued at greater length throughout the sermons. For example, in sermon IV, he focuses on our disposition to talkativeness—roughly, our tendency to like the sound of our own voices—and argues that our delight in idle chatter helps us to cement the social bonds between us. In sermons V and VI, he focuses on compassion, our tendency to feel the pain of others, and argues that this helps us to be charitable and inhibits us from cruelty. In sermons VIII and IX, he focuses on anger and resentment: here, he argues that the natural end or purpose of our tendency to "sudden anger" is "self-defence" (VIII.6); while "deliberate" or "settled resentment ... is to be considered as a weapon, put into our hands by nature, against injury, injustice and cruelty" (VIII.8). In sermon XI, he considers self-love, and argues that self-love is not essentially in tension with virtue, and can even play a role in supporting virtue. Finally, in sermons XII–XIV, he considers mental dispositions that have a more obvious role in supporting virtue—namely, the "principle of benevolence" (in sermon XII), and our disposition toward religious feeling or the "love of God" (in sermons XIII and XIV). In general, he says, "Every one of our passions and affections hath its natural stint and bound" (XI.9); within these natural bounds, none of these passions conflicts with virtue, and most passions help us, at least indirectly, either to be virtuous or to pursue our own happiness (or indeed to do both).

However, the most distinctive element in Butler's argument concerns the special role of *conscience*, which is his focus in sermons II and III. It seems to be part of Butler's teleological conception of human nature that the right or correct or proper sort of life for human beings to lead must involve all the various elements of human nature functioning in a certain way—as we might put it, it involves all these elements functioning "properly". The elements of human nature that Butler focuses on are what he calls the "internal principles" of the human mind, of which he gives a brief survey in sermon I (I.5–8). These "internal principles" include: the principles of benevolence and self-love (I.6); our various particular passions (I.7); and conscience (I.8).

In sermon I, Butler gives a preliminary description of how conscience actually operates (I.8):

> There is a principle of reflection in men, by which they distinguish between, approve and disapprove their own actions. We are plainly constituted such sort of creatures as to reflect upon our own nature. The mind can take a view of what passes within itself, its propensions, aversions, passions, affections, as respecting such objects, and in such degrees; and of the several actions consequent thereupon. In this survey it approves of one, disapproves of another, and towards a third is affected in neither of these ways, but is quite indifferent. This principle in man, by which he approves or disapproves his heart, temper, and actions, is conscience.... And that this faculty tends to restrain men from doing mischief to each other, and leads them to do good, is too manifest to need being insisted upon.... It is needless to compare the respect it has to private good, with the respect it has to public; since it plainly tends as much to the latter as to the former, and is commonly thought to tend chiefly to the latter.

There is a second description of the operations of conscience in sermon II (II.8): "But there is a superior principle of reflection or conscience in every man, which distinguishes between the internal principles of his heart, as well as his external actions: which passes judgment upon himself and them; pronounces determinately some actions to be in themselves just, right, good; others to be in themselves evil, wrong, unjust: which, without being consulted, without being advised with, magisterially exerts itself, and approves or condemns him the doer of them accordingly." Thus, Butler thinks of conscience as a faculty that reviews both our inner mental states (such as our feelings and intentions) and our external actions. Its deliverances are described sometimes as states of "approval" or "disapproval", and sometimes as "judgments"; it is also credited with the power to "restrain" us from some actions, and to "lead" us to do other things instead. Its general tendency is to approve of courses of action that are favorable either to the good of the community or to the good of the agent (or to both). The crucial point for our purposes is that even though Butler does not analyze the operations of conscience in full detail,[27] we can be confident that he believes that when our conscience is functioning properly, it will approve only of "external actions" and of "internal principles of the heart" that are compatible with virtue.

Butler's crucial move comes in sermon II, where he argues that when all these elements in our nature are functioning properly, they will form a *hierarchy*. First, our particular passions will be directed or regulated by self-love (II.10–11). That is, whenever there is a conflict between self-love and any particular passion, then if the elements of our nature are functioning properly, we will act in accordance with self-love, and not in accordance with the passion.

Second, when the elements of our nature are functioning properly, both the particular passions and self-love will be directed or regulated by conscience (II.12–17). That is, when these elements all function properly, we will always act as our conscience directs us to act, and we will presumably also try to cultivate the "internal principles of our heart" as conscience directs us to. As he puts it, self-love has greater *authority* than the particular passions, and conscience has even greater authority than self-love—even if the particular passions or self-love may on many occasions have greater motivational *strength* (II.14). As he also puts it, self-love is a *superior principle* compared to the particular passions, and conscience is a superior principle compared to both the particular passions and self-love (II.11). As he says, conscience "was placed within us to be our proper governor, to direct and regulate" all the other "principles, passions and motives of action" (II.15).

Butler argues for this point by claiming that conscience "is to be considered…as from its very nature claiming superiority: insomuch that you cannot form a notion of this faculty, conscience, without taking in judgment, direction, superintendency" (II.14). This argument seems to start from identifying certain features of conscience. One feature is conscience's "superintendency", which seems to consist in the way in which conscience considers and oversees all the other internal principles of the mind. Another feature is its capacity for "judgment", which may consist in the fact that it arrives at all-things-considered judgments about what is right or wrong, good or bad, aiming to take all relevant considerations into account. The final feature is its capacity for "direction", which may consist in the fact that we have a fundamental disposition to be moved to action by the directions of our conscience.

It is not completely clear why Butler says that a faculty that has these features "claims superiority from its very nature". But in the light of the teleological reflections that are so prominent at the beginning of sermon II, it seems plausible to read this as the claim that these features of conscience—"judgment, direction, superintendency"—make it clear that the natural end or purpose of the faculty of con-

---

27. For example, Butler does not tell us how the deliverances of conscience are related to the axioms of the rationalist method that he discusses in the preface (P 12). Do we have any way of knowing those axioms other than by relying on our conscience? If not, then how exactly is our "heart and natural conscience" (II.1) capable of informing us of such necessary truths about the fitness and unfitness of things?

science is precisely to serve as our "proper governor" in the way that Butler describes.[28]

Thus, Butler has argued that when the elements of our nature are all functioning properly, our conscience will only approve of external actions and internal mental states that are compatible with virtue, and we will only act as our conscience approves (and we will also try to cultivate our internal mental dispositions as conscience directs us to). So, when the elements of our nature are functioning properly, we will always act virtuously, and we will also cultivate virtuous internal mental dispositions in ourselves. Given the background assumption that the life that we have overriding reason to lead is the life in which all these elements of our nature are functioning properly, Butler's conclusion follows: we have overriding reason to be virtuous.

6.   Butler's Claims about the Harmony of Virtue and Self-Interest

Now that we have a clearer conception of Butler's overall project, we can return to the controversial question of how exactly Butler understands the relations between virtue and self-interest.

I have already discussed the passages where Butler seems clearly to reject eudaimonism, such as his discussion of Shaftesbury in the preface (P 26). But there are also some passages where Butler seems to come much closer to the eudaimonist position. The most notorious of these passages is the following (XI. 20):

> And to all these things may be added,…there can no access be had to the understanding, but by convincing men, that the course of life we would persuade them to is not contrary to their interest. It may be allowed, without any prejudice to the cause of virtue and religion, that our ideas of happiness and misery are of all our ideas the nearest and most important to us; that they will, nay, if you please, that they ought to prevail over those of order, and beauty, and harmony, and proportion, if there should ever be, as it is impossible there ever should be, any inconsistence between them: though these last too, as expressing the fitness of actions, are real as truth itself. Let it be allowed, though virtue or moral rectitude does indeed consist in affection to and pursuit of what is right and good, as such; yet, that when we sit

---

28. Darwall (*The British Moralists and the Internal "Ought,"* 256–61) argues that there is an altogether different line of thought in II.16–17, which he interprets as part of Butler's argument for "Kant's reciprocity thesis". This interpretation seems entirely misguided to me. Prima facie, the passage in question makes a fairly weak point: it would be absurd to claim "that there was no distinction to be made between one inward principle and another, but only that of strength" (II.16)—that is, there must be *some* distinctions between "superior" and "inferior principles". This point by itself does not tell us that conscience is the supreme principle, nor that conscience approves only of actions that are compatible with virtue (it provides some small degree of support to the conclusion that conscience is the supreme principle, because *one* way in which conscience might not be supreme is if absolutely no distinctions could be drawn between superior and inferior principles at all).

down in a cool hour, we can neither justify to ourselves this or any other pursuit, till we are convinced that it will be for our happiness, or at least not contrary to it.

Here, Butler asserts[29] that it is " impossible there ever should be...any inconsistence between" (i) "our ideas of happiness and misery" and (ii) our ideas of "order, and beauty, and harmony, and proportion", which express "the fitness of actions". He also implies that "it may be allowed, without any prejudice to the cause of virtue" that we cannot "justify" an "affection to and pursuit of what is right and good as such" unless "we are convinced that it will be for our happiness, or at least not contrary to it". It is not surprising that this passage has convinced many scholars that Butler is a eudaimonist after all.[30]

Thus, we must find an interpretation of Butler's language that enables us to reconcile all of the following four propositions:

1. Butler's ultimate conclusion, that all human beings have an "obligation", or overriding reason, to be virtuous;
2. The proposition (which Butler does not assert, but seems to regard as compatible with his argument) that no "pursuit" is justified if it is "contrary" to our happiness;
3. The proposition (which Butler also regards as quite compatible with his argument) that there are "exceptions" to the coincidence of virtue and happiness;
4. The proposition (which Butler asserts) that it is impossible for there to be any "inconsistency" between happiness and virtue.

Finally, we also need to understand how it can be that here Butler is asserting that it is "impossible" for there to be any "inconsistency" between happiness and virtue, whereas in the preface he seems to claim that his argument could be accepted by a "sceptic not convinced of this happy tendency of virtue" (P 26).

As we saw in discussing the preface (P 26), Butler's only clear concession to eudaimonism was to insist that we can never be *certain* that it is in our interest to be vicious, or to fail to be virtuous. It is possible to read these four troublesome propositions in the light of this claim. When Butler speaks of a pursuit's being "contrary to" our happiness, he may be using these terms in a special sense. Specifically, for a pursuit to be "contrary to" our happiness in this special sense would be for that pursuit to be *certain* to make us less happy than some available alternative. So, given that he insists that it is never certain that virtue will make us less happy than vice, he

---

29. It seems to me that the only natural way to read this clause is an assertion, parenthetically inserted inside a nonasserted sentence that is within the scope of "It may be allowed, without any prejudice to the cause of virtue and religion, that...".

30. For example, Butler is interpreted as a eudaimonist by H. A. Prichard, in *Moral Obligation* (Oxford: Clarendon, 1949), 96–97. Henry Sidgwick interprets Butler as viewing self-love as coordinate with conscience, so that an act can count as reasonable only if it is approved by *both* self-love and conscience, in his *Outlines of the History of Ethics*, 3rd ed. (London: Macmillan, 1892), 196.

can conclude that virtue is never in this sense "contrary to our happiness". Moreover, when he speaks of an "inconsistency" between happiness and virtue, he may mean a situation in which it is *certain* that being vicious will promote one's happiness more than being virtuous. Then the claim that there cannot be any "inconsistency" between virtue and happiness will be compatible with the idea that there could be "exceptions" to the coincidence of virtue and self-interest, if these "exceptions" have the feature that even if it is possible to be in such an "exceptional" case, one can never be *certain* that one is in such a case.

Finally, when Butler says that we must consider the case of a "sceptic not convinced of this happy tendency of virtue, or being of a contrary opinion", it may be that his aim is only to produce an argument that is acceptable to someone who thinks that there are "exceptional" cases where it is *probable* that the demands of virtue and of happiness diverge, not to produce an argument that is acceptable to someone who thinks that there are cases in which it is *certain* that the demands of virtue and happiness diverge. Butler's aim may only be to produce an argument that is acceptable to this more modest sort of "skeptic".

This reading will also help us to explain why Butler's claims about the harmony of conscience and self-love do not trivialize his claim that conscience has greater authority than self-love. The *certain* counsels of self-love will never conflict with the directions of conscience. However, there may be some cases in which self-love gives no certain counsels at all, but only *uncertain* counsels—possibly including uncertain counsels that conflict with the directions of conscience; in these cases, the supremacy of conscience implies we should always follow the certain directions of conscience. However, this reading still leaves us with two exegetical problems. First, why does Butler think he needs to argue for the impossibility of any "inconsistency" between virtue and happiness here? Second, how exactly does Butler think he can argue for this?

Butler never explicitly says why he thinks that he has to argue for the impossibility of any "inconsistency" between virtue and self-interest. But it is relatively easy to see what his main reason for wanting to argue for this must be.

Butler argues that self-love is a *superior principle* when compared to the "particular passions": as he says, "the passions...may be contradicted without violating [our] nature, but [self-love] cannot" (II.10). According to the interpretation that I have proposed, what this means is the following: if all the elements of our nature are functioning properly, then whenever there is a clear conflict between a particular passion and self-love, we will act in accordance with self-love rather than in accordance with the particular passion. This is why he says, "interest, one's own happiness, is a manifest obligation" (P 26). But Butler also wants to claim that when all the elements of our nature are functioning properly, we will always act virtuously. So, to avoid self-contradiction, he will have to rule out the possibility of cases in which all the elements of human nature are functioning properly, and self-love is in conflict with some particular passion because self-love clearly motivates us to act viciously, while the particular passion motivates us to act virtuously.

He cannot rule out such cases by arguing that when the elements of our nature are functioning properly, the particular passions never motivate us to act virtuously, since, as he stresses, many of our particular passions lead us, at least indirectly, to act virtuously. For example, "Desire of the esteem of others...naturally lead[s] us to regulate our behaviour in such a manner as will be of service to our fellow creatures" (I.7). Nor could he rule out these cases by arguing that when all these elements of our nature are functioning properly, self-love never conflicts with the particular passions: making that argument would risk draining the claim that self-love is a superior principle of all content whatsoever. So the only way in which he can rule out these cases is by arguing that when all these elements of our nature are functioning properly, self-love never clearly motivates us to act viciously.

In addition, Butler wants to argue, on the basis of his empirical survey of the "internal principles of the human heart", that the life that one has overriding reason to lead will not just be a virtuous life; it will also be a life that is reasonably effective at achieving one's own happiness (I.15). Since he assumes that one is guaranteed to lead this sort of life when all the elements in one's nature are functioning properly, he will also have to claim that when all these elements are functioning properly, one will be leading a life that is reasonably effective at achieving one's own happiness in this life. So it seems that he must argue that a whole life that involves all these elements functioning properly will never be certain to make one less happy than any alternative way of life.

Thus, there are really *two* claims that Butler has reason to make about the relation between virtue and happiness. The first claim concerns *particular external actions*, but is *restricted to cases in which all the elements of one's nature are functioning properly*: here the claim is that within this restricted range of cases, a vicious action is never certain to make one happier than all of the virtuous alternatives. The second claim concerns a comparison between the *whole way of life* that involves these elements' all functioning properly (including the overall "temper" or pattern of mental dispositions that is characteristic of that way of life), and alternative ways of life in which some of these elements are *not* functioning properly: here the claim is that the latter ways of life are never certain to make one happier than the former. Moreover, since he is aiming to produce an argument that is acceptable to a "skeptic" who does not accept the traditional Christian doctrine of an afterlife, he must argue that a virtuous life is never certain to make one less happy than a vicious life in *this world*.

Thus, we can sum up Butler's claims about the precise sort of harmony that exists between virtue and self-interest as follows: there may be "exceptions"—cases where someone leads a vicious way of life and turns out to be happier than he would have been had he led a virtuous way of life—but one can never be *certain* that one is in such an exceptional case oneself. Thus no one can ever be under a *certain* obligation of self-love to lead a vicious way of life. By contrast, because of the natural supremacy of conscience, one is always under a certain obligation to lead a virtuous way of life. Once one is leading a virtuous life, and all the "inward principles of one's heart" are functioning properly (so that all these inward principles remain within their "natural stint and bound"), then one's dispositions will be such that, when one is faced with the choice between particular alternative actions, it will never be certain that a vicious action will make one happier than all the available virtuous actions.

Even though Butler makes these claims about the harmony of virtue and happiness, he is *not* claiming that one's only reason to be virtuous is simply to promote one's own happiness. On the contrary, one's reason to be virtuous is simply that a virtuous life is the right or proper life for us to lead—as is shown by the fact that when all the elements of our nature are functioning properly, one's conscience will always direct one to act virtuously, and one will always follow the directions of one's conscience. Moreover, it is this reason that should motivate one when one acts virtuously: as Butler puts it, virtue consists "in affection to and pursuit of what is right and good, as such" (XI.20). Nonetheless, as a matter of fact, a virtuous course of life will never be certain to make one less happy than any vicious alternative way of life.

Even if this is the correct interpretation of the *content* of Butler's claims about the harmony of virtue and self-interest, we still have to deal with the second of the two exegetical problems that I identified above: How exactly does Butler think he can argue for this sort of harmony between virtue and self-interest?

7.   Butler's Arguments for His Claims about Virtue and Self-Interest

Butler presents his arguments for this sort of harmony between virtue and self-interest several times—for example, in sermon I (I.14), and in sermon III (III.7–8). These arguments are based on his fundamental conception of self-interest, which is first briefly explained in the preface (P 35–42) and in sermon I (I.7), but receives its fullest exposition in sermon XI.

Butler is particularly insistent that self-love, the steady calculating desire that each person has for his own self-interest or happiness, must be distinguished from the particular passions. The distinction is illustrated by a striking pair of examples:

> And as self-love and the several particular passions and appetites are in themselves totally different; so, that some actions proceed from one, and some from the other, will be manifest to any who will observe the two following very supposable cases. One man rushes upon certain ruin for the gratification of a present desire: nobody will call the principle of this action self-love. Suppose another man to go through some laborious work upon promise of a great reward, without any distinct knowledge what the reward will be: this course of action cannot be ascribed to any particular passion. The former of these actions is plainly to be imputed to some particular passion or affection, the latter as plainly to the general affection or principle of self-love. (I.7, note)

He analyzes this difference in the following way:

> Every man hath a general desire of his own happiness; and likewise a variety of particular affections, passions, and appetites to particular external objects....The object the former pursues is somewhat internal, our own happiness, enjoyment, satisfaction; whether we have, or have not, a distinct particular perception what it is, or wherein it consists: the objects of the latter are this or that particular external thing, which the affections tend towards, and of which it hath always a particular idea or perception. The principle we call self-love never seeks any thing external for the sake of the thing, but only as a means of happiness or good: particular affections rest in the external things themselves. One belongs to man as a reasonable creature reflecting upon his own interest or happiness. The other, though quite distinct from reason, are as much a part of human nature. (XI.5)

Here Butler insists that the object of self-love is one's own happiness *as such*; self-love need not involve any particular "perception" of what concrete external goods one's happiness will involve, as is shown by the case of the man who toils laboriously "upon promise of a great reward" without knowing what the reward will be. Moreover, he insists that one's happiness is something "internal": that is, it is purely a mental state, not a state of the external world. Self-love seeks particular external goods only as a means to this internal state of happiness.

By contrast, the objects of the particular passions are "external objects", which are desired simply for their own sake, and not merely as means to happiness or pleasure. He offers a famous but obscure argument for the conclusion that the particular passions must be conceived in this way: "That all particular appetites and passions are towards *external things themselves*, distinct from the *pleasure arising from them*, is manifested from hence; that there could not be this pleasure, were it not for that prior suitableness between the object and the passion: there could be no enjoyment or delight from one thing more than another, from eating food more than from swallowing a stone, if there were not an affection or appetite to one thing more than another" (XI.6). Butler is sometimes interpreted here as identifying pleasure or enjoyment or delight with the satisfaction of a desire.[31] Now, it certainly seems true that if there are to be any satisfied desires at all, there must be desires for something other than just for the satisfaction of desires as such. So if this identification of pleasure with the satisfaction of desire is correct, then Butler's argument is sound.

However, this identification of pleasure with the satisfaction of desire seems clearly incorrect. First, one can desire things of which one will never have any knowledge: for example, one might desire to be remembered after one's death; but even though this desire is satisfied (one *is* remembered after one's death), the satisfaction of this desire does not give one any pleasure since after death, one is no longer capable of pleasure at all. Second, even if one does know of the satisfaction of one's desire, this knowledge might just fail to bring any pleasure at all. Finally, pleasures can take one by surprise: one may just suddenly find oneself taking pleasure in something, even though one never desired it before one starts to feel the pleasure.

Fortunately, we do not have to interpret Butler in this way. In objecting to the identification of pleasure with the satisfaction of desire, I assumed that "desire" is a mental state that we have toward objects that we do not know to have been attained (such as objects that are absent or uncertain, or can be attained only in the future).[32] But Butler's use of the terms *affection* and *passion* need not be restricted in this way. It is plausible that these terms refer simply to any mental state or mental disposition that involves an element of *feeling*. When Butler speaks of an "affection for" a certain object, he means a state that involves a *positive* feeling that is *directed toward*

31. David Phillips interprets Butler in this way; see his "Butler and the Nature of Self-Interest," *Philosophy and Phenomenological Research* 60, no. 2 (March 2000): 421–38.

32. As Plato puts it, less precisely though more intuitively, we desire things that we lack, not things that we have (*Symposium*, trans. R. Waterfield [Oxford: Oxford University Press, 1994], 200a).

that object. So when he says, "The very idea of interest or happiness consists in this, that an appetite or affection enjoys its object" (P 37), he is saying that pleasure or happiness consists in any sort of positive feeling that is directed toward an object that one knows to have been attained.

Butler's basic insight, I believe, is that pleasure has an ("intentional") object, and that one's pleasure is in a sense "based on" the knowledge that this object has been attained. When we are pleased that *p* is the case, our pleasure is based on the knowledge that *p* is the case; when we are pleased by the sound of beautiful music, we know that we are hearing the music; and so on. Now, sometimes one might be pleased merely at the thought that one will be pleased by something or other. But this cannot always be the case: sometimes, the object of one's pleasure must be some object other than one's own pleasure. In short, it must sometimes be the case that the pleasure is a passion or affection toward a particular external object (specifically, a particular external object that one knows to have been attained).

Many of our pleasures, then, we get from the satisfaction of affections that are directed toward objects other than our own pleasure itself. Now, when all of the elements of our nature are functioning properly (within "their natural stint and bound"), we will still have a great many particular passions and affections. To focus on the particular passions and affections that are discussed most extensively in the later sermons: (1) we will feel a moderate delight in talking and chatting with other people; (2) we will feel compassion toward those who are suffering; (3) we will feel moderate resentment toward injustice; and above all, (4) we will feel benevolent goodwill toward other people. But then whenever we know that the objects of these affections have been attained we will feel a commensurate pleasure or satisfaction. Thus, we will feel pleased when we know (1) that we are chatting communicatively about topics of mutual interest with other people, or (2) that suffering has been relieved, or (3) that those have violated the rights of others have been brought to justice, or (4) that other people's interest or happiness has been promoted.

Moreover, when all the elements of human nature are functioning properly, in addition to these particular passions, we will also have an affection toward virtue as such: we will want to be virtuous, and will take pleasure in the exercise of virtue, purely for its own sake. Thus, when we have the attitudes and dispositions that are characteristic of virtuous people, virtuous conduct will also bring pleasure. This emerges most clearly in the passage where Butler distinguishes between benevolence "considered as a natural affection" and benevolence "considered as a virtuous principle" (XI.16):

> Happiness consists in the gratification of certain affections, appetites, passions, with objects, which are by nature adapted to them. . . . Love of our neighbour is one of those affections. This, considered as a *virtuous principle*, is *gratified by a consciousness of endeavouring* to promote the good of others; but considered as a natural affection, its gratification consists in the actual accomplishment of this endeavour. Now indulgence or gratification of this affection, whether in that consciousness or this accomplishment, has the same respect to interest, as indulgence of any other affection. ... Thus it appears, that *benevolence and the pursuit of public good hath at least as great respect to self-love and the pursuit of private good, as any other particular passions, and their respective pursuits.*

The "natural affection" of benevolence is simply the wish to promote the good of others; the "virtuous principle" of benevolence involves a tendency to be pleased by the consciousness of *one's own endeavouring* to promote the good of others. Since there is such a range of pleasures that are characteristic of the virtuous way of life, Butler thinks that there is no reason at all to think that these pleasures will be any less than those of the various vicious ways of life. He tries to make this point plausible by giving some rather anecdotal reflections on the unhappiness that tends to go along with certain forms of vice. For example, he enumerates the disadvantages of lives that are characterized by excessive covetousness, ambition, or intemperance: "[T]hat persons in the greatest affluence of fortune are no happier than such as have only a competency; that the cares and disappointments of ambition for the most part far exceed the satisfactions of it; as also the miserable intervals of intemperance and excess, and the many untimely deaths occasioned by a dissolute course of life: these things are all seen, acknowledged, by every one acknowledged" (I.14). He also makes similar observations about the drawbacks of lives that are characterized by envy, rage, and (excessive) resentment: "Let it not be taken for granted that the temper of envy, rage, resentment, yields greater delight than meekness, forgiveness, compassion, and good-will; especially when it is acknowledged that rage, envy, resentment, are in themselves mere misery; and the satisfaction arising from the indulgence of them is little more than relief from that misery; whereas the temper of compassion and benevolence is itself delightful; and the indulgence of it, by doing good, affords new positive delight and enjoyment" (III.8). Thus, if we compare these different "tempers", there is no reason to think that the expected benefits of the temper of virtue are any less than those of the various tempers of vice.

Moreover, once we have the temper that is characteristic of the virtuous, then performing a particular vicious action will secure us pleasures that will seem paltry and insignificant compared to the inevitable pains of self-condemnation and self-dislike: "[O]ne may appeal even to interest and self-love, and ask, since from man's nature, condition, and the shortness of life, so little, so very little indeed, can possibly in any case be gained by vice; whether it be so prodigious a thing to sacrifice that little to the most intimate of all obligations; and which a man cannot transgress without being self-condemned, and, unless he has corrupted his nature, without real self-dislike: this question, I say, may be asked, even upon supposition that the prospect of a future life were ever so uncertain" (P 28). Thus, Butler concludes: "Self-love, though confined to the interest of the present world, does in general perfectly coincide with virtue, and leads to one and the same course of life. But whatever exceptions there are to this, which are much fewer than they are commonly thought, all shall be set right at the final distribution of things.... Duty and interest are perfectly coincident, for the most part in this world, but entirely and in every instance if we take in the future and the whole, this being implied in the notion of a good and perfect administration of things" (III.8–9). In this conclusion, Butler reminds us, parenthetically, of something that he believes but does not rest his argument on — namely, the traditional Christian doctrine of the afterlife, which will ensure that in the end, virtue and happiness will coincide, without any of the "exceptions" that occur in this life, "entirely and in every instance".

8.   The Evaluation of Butler's Arguments about Virtue and Happiness

It seems to me that there are pressures arising from morality itself to accept something like Butler's claims about the general harmony between virtue and happiness. Virtuous parents presumably want to inculcate virtuous dispositions in their children, but they presumably also earnestly hope that their children will have lives characterized by a rich array of pleasures and enjoyments. It would be hard for such parents to accept that they can inculcate virtuous dispositions in their children only at the cost of depriving them of many of the pleasures of life. R. M. Adams makes this point well:[33]

> [It] is hard to deny the moral importance of believing that the moral life will be good, or is apt to be good, *for other people*. For it is part of moral virtue to care both about the other person's good and about the other person's virtue. Morality requires that we encourage each other to live morally. But how could we do that in good conscience if we thought living morally would be bad for the other person?… So it seems that, if we do not believe that living morally is at least normally good for a person, there will be a conflict in the very soul of morality that threatens to tear it apart.

It seems highly plausible to me that there is an important insight behind what Adams is saying here. But it is not clear that Adams's statement of this insight is exactly right. Perhaps all that morality requires of us is that we should not *harm* other people, and beyond that basic requirement of nonmaleficence, we should not attempt to promote their happiness in any way that might undermine their virtue. Perhaps we are also not required to encourage others to achieve the sort of supererogatory virtue that is characteristic of the saint or the hero. So perhaps all that it is morally important to believe is that people are not normally *harmed* by complying with what morality strictly *requires* of them.

Be that as it may, Butler's arguments for the harmony of virtue and self-interest seem to me pure wishful thinking. The anecdotal evidence that he adduces about the troubles of the various vicious ways of life provides only the flimsiest support to his conclusion. Moreover, a very little reflection will reveal the implausibility of what he says. Is it really true that "the temper of compassion and benevolence is itself delightful"? Butler himself takes the biblical passage where we are told to "weep with them that weep" (Romans 12:15) as the epigraph to his two sermons on compassion; and he surely cannot have forgotten that the man whom he regarded as his Lord and Savior "wept for Jerusalem" (Luke 19:41), apparently out of a sense of compassion for suffering and dismay at injustice.

Butler focuses on the extravagant forms of vice (intemperance, covetousness, and excessive ambition) that are no doubt very often conjoined with unhappiness. But he neglects one very common form of vice, which consists simply in a callous attitude toward those who are sufficiently distant from us that it is easy for us not to

---

33.   See R. M. Adams, "Moral Faith," *Journal of Philosophy* 92 (1995): 75–95, especially 80.

"feel the effects of their resentment"[34]—such as the poor and the oppressed in faraway countries of which we know little, or the future generations who will have to deal with the environmental degradation that we have left behind us. It is hard to see how this sort of vice deprives us of many pleasures, but easy to see how it will spare us the anxiety that more virtuous people will feel.

In short, Butler's claims about the harmony of virtue and self-interest seem implausible to me. Nonetheless, his claims about our "obligation to the practice of virtue" seem to me essentially correct. We must, I think, face the hard fact that a virtuous life is the right or proper life for us to lead—even though by living such a life we expose ourselves to various sources of pain and anxiety that the vice of callousness would spare us from.[35]

34. The phrase is from David Hume, *Enquiry Concerning the Principles of Morals*, ed. L. A. Selby-Bigge, revised by P. H. Nidditch (Oxford: Clarendon, [1751] 1975), sec. III ("Of Justice"), part I.

35. An earlier draft of this paper was presented to an audience at the University of Reading. I am grateful to members of that audience, and also to Paul Bloomfield, the editor of this volume, to Stephen Darwall, and to my Oxford colleagues Robert Adams, Bill Child, Antony Eagle, David Charles, Dorothy Edgington, and Oliver Pooley, for helpful comments on earlier drafts.

10

Virtue Ethics and the Charge of Egoism

JULIA ANNAS

We care about being generous, courageous, and fair. This looks as though we care about other people, since what we care about is having a disposition to help others, respect their rights, and intervene when they are threatened. But is it correct for concern for others to come in by way of my own dispositions? Is caring about virtue focusing too much on myself? This worry has been the basis of objections that virtue ethics, as a theory, is selfish or egoistic. In recent years defenders of virtue ethics have provided many responses, but the objection keeps coming up in revised forms. The objection can be met, and discussion of the issue is also useful in helping us to see what virtue ethics is, not just what it is not.

The egoism in question here is ethical egoism, the theory that holds that my own good is the ethical standard for what it is right for me to do, the dispositions I should have, and so on. The theory comes in several versions, depending on the many different possible interpretations of what my own good is. My own good might be held to consist in my having the maximum pleasure, or it might be given other content, such as my satisfying my desires, or achieving what is in my own interests. (And different versions will result from distinguishing what is actually in my interests from what I merely think to be in my interests.) Some versions of egoism are interested in my own good merely as a standard for "the rightness of action", while others think of it also as what justifies my having some dispositions rather than others. But for present purposes I don't think that it matters to distinguish these versions. The basic idea of ethical egoism is that what ethically justifies what I do, and the way I am, is my own good, where that is distinct from, and potentially in conflict with, the good of others. And we find at once a problem in the idea that this could be an *ethical* position, because of the very basic thought that ethics is fundamentally about the good of *others*, not my good.[1]

---

1. There are other problems with egoism as a theory, but what matters here is the point that intuitively ethics is thought to be about the good of others, so that focusing on your own good seems wrong from the start.

Why would anyone think that virtue ethics is egoistic?

What is a virtue? A minimal conception is that of a disposition or character trait. Virtues are not just character traits, however, since forgetfulness or stubbornness are not virtues. Virtues are character traits which are in some way desirable. But neither are they just desirable character traits; tidiness and punctuality are nice traits to have, but not yet virtues. A virtue is, at least, a character trait which is admirable, embodying a commitment to some ethical value. If we deny this, we are losing contact with everyday discourse about virtue and virtuous people, as we can see if we look at a typical list of virtues. Courage, fairness and patience are all virtues. They are not just character traits that are desirable to have—in fact, notoriously not everyone *desires* to be courageous, even when they think they ought to be. They are character traits which embody a commitment to some value, in a way which may benefit the agent, but equally may benefit others. The courageous person stands up for what is worthwhile against temptations to give in or compromise. This is a useful trait for the person to have in that it enables her to achieve her own goals without being sidetracked in various ways. But obviously this trait is also useful for others, in that it enables her to stand up for what is worthwhile when the interests of others are at stake.

Some accounts of virtue, stemming from Hume and the utilitarians, have thought that a virtue is just a trait which it is useful for me to have in that it promotes a value which might benefit me or equally well might benefit others. This does at least capture the thought that there is something worthwhile about the virtues, something explaining why we think it important, and not just nice, to have them. But reduced virtue theories of this kind leave the virtues as merely plastic dispositions whose shape is determined by what happens to benefit people; and this is wildly revisionary as an account of virtue.[2] Moreover, a virtue is not just a disposition which happens to have certain effects. It is a disposition which works through the agent's practical reasoning, built up from decisions and manifesting and expressing itself in decisions and choices which reflect the agent's deliberations.

The virtues, then, are dispositions which do not just happen to have the effect of achieving what is valuable for others as well as the agent; they are dispositions *to do* this—dispositions to choose actions that give others their fair share, treat others in considerate ways, stand up for the rights of others, and so on. These dispositions may also, of course, sometimes achieve what is valuable for the agent also, but that is not their point: they are dispositions to do what has value.

Where, then, does a charge of selfishness or egoism take hold?

One kind of virtue ethics holds that I should cultivate the virtues because they are valuable, in a number of different ways, and that these cannot be reduced or simplified down to one. (This might be the way we begin to teach the virtues.) There is nothing egoistic about such a position; but it is obviously unsatisfactory from a theoretical point of view. Why are just these dispositions virtues? Can we really say nothing about what the values of the different virtues have in common?

Any theory of virtue will have something to say about the way the different virtues are valuable by contributing in a unified way to a further end. Since they are

---

2. The problem is not just that it is revisionary, but that the revisions forced by the theory will be completely indifferent to any normal expectations about the virtues.

dispositions, they are ways that I am, traits of my character; they contribute to my living my life as a whole in a certain way. The reason it is worthwhile for me to cultivate the virtues is that they will make up or constitute my living my life as a whole in a way ·vhich it is valuable to live. The notion of "my life as a whole" is crucial here; the virtues make sense within a conception of living, which takes the life I live to be a unity.

Thus the virtues will contribute to the overall final end I have in living my life as a whole; this is variously called *eudaimonia*, following Aristotle, or flourishing, or happiness, though the latter is always risky because of potential confusion with modern feel-good notions of happiness.

It is at this point that charges of egoism begin to get a grip. The virtues are valuable because they contribute to my final end—but this is *my* final end, not yours, and so it looks as though it is my good, or interests, or whatever, which is justifying my acquisition of the virtues, and so they owe their ethical justification to their contribution to my good. So we have egoism?

No. This goes too fast. For the virtues are not just any old dispositions making up my life; they are courage, generosity, fairness, and so on. How does fairness, for example, contribute to my final end? The fair person will give others what is their due, sometimes to his own disadvantage. In what sense is this contributing to *his* good, interests, or whatever?

One answer is that it need not. Exercising the virtues is part of my living my life as a whole; they are dispositions whose exercise makes up the way I live my life, my life overall. But the exercise of the virtues need not *benefit* me, or contribute to my living a life we would call flourishing. Exercising the virtues is admirable, and we do admire people whose lives are lived in admirable and valuable ways. But these need not lead to flourishing, and in the case of some virtues, those which primarily benefit others, they characteristically will not. The virtues, then, will be pursued as part of my whole life, but they need not benefit me or lead to my flourishing.[3] This type of theory faces questions as to what does justify the distinct virtues, and why we think that the dispositions on our list are the virtues.

Many virtue ethicists have followed Aristotle and the rest of the classical virtue ethics tradition in holding that the virtues benefit their possessor. Not only are they dispositions whose exercise constitutes the living of a certain kind of life, they are (in the weak versions) necessary and (in the strong versions) sufficient for the living of that life to be good, for the life to be a good, flourishing one. Here we find a unified justification for the virtues, and do not have to rely on finding them valuable in a piecemeal way. However, accusations of egoism do begin to find a footing at this point. For it looks as though my flourishing is my good in a way which contrasts with the good of others, and if the virtues benefit me by leading to my flourishing, then my reason for acquiring and exercising them would seem to be my seeking my own flourishing. And how can this be a decently *ethical* reason for becoming virtuous? Shouldn't an *ethical* reason for becoming virtuous be that the virtues contribute to the flourishing of other people, not to my flourishing?

3. See Christine Swanton, *Virtue Ethics, a Pluralistic View* (Oxford: Oxford University Press, 2003).

Two versions of this objection are frequently made, but can be rapidly met. The first goes: if my reason for having the virtues is that they benefit me, contribute to my flourishing, then virtue ethics will come up with wrong recommendations as to what I should do. I should be brave, for example, in aid of my own flourishing, and thus only in the interests of what will benefit me. Courageous behavior in standing up for the interests of others would seem not to be virtuous, on this account, or at least not required by virtue. However, it is clear what is wrong with this. Courage is a *virtue*, that is, a disposition to stand up for what is worthwhile even against temptation to avoid danger, difficulty, and so on. I have not so far specified how we are to identify what is worthwhile, but it is clear that, however we do this, courage is not a disposition which can be switched off when my own interests are not at stake. The virtues are dispositions embodying a commitment to values, not to my self-interest. Thus the thesis that the virtues benefit their possessor cannot be interpreted in such a way that the virtuous person acts in an egoistic way. Rather, we have to take the virtues as they are, taking into account the point that virtuous action may often lead to loss of various kinds on the agent's part, and so is not egoistic. We need to find an account of what it is for the virtues to benefit their possessor which does justice to this.

A second objection holds that, even if someone is virtuous in the sense of acting virtuously, still, if their reason for so acting is that being virtuous benefits them and is in his interests, he cannot have the right ethical *motivation*. If I stand up for someone else's rights, act generously to a stranger, and so on, then I may have acted virtuously, but if my reason for so doing is that doing the virtuous thing leads to my flourishing, then it is my own good which is my reason for acting in the relevant way. Is this not egoistic? The obvious answer to this is that if my motivation is egoistic then I am not acting virtuously. I could, of course, do an action which is such that a virtuous person would do it, but do it only because I have an eye on my own flourishing. But then I would not be virtuous, because a virtue is not a disposition that can be exercised in the absence of the right kind of motivation. If I have my eye on my own flourishing, then I am not acting from courage, or generosity, or whatever. The thesis that the virtues benefit their possessor cannot show that the virtues themselves lead to deliberations with egoistic content, or egoistic motivation. In either case, all that would be shown would be that it was not a virtue that was in question.

However, these objections, particularly the second, can take a more sophisticated form. The objection that virtue ethics is at bottom egoistic has recently been reformulated by Thomas Hurka in a general attack on virtue ethics, and meeting this objection turns out to be revealing about virtue ethics and particularly the relation of being virtuous to flourishing.[4]

Hurka claims that a virtue ethics (at least of the kind we are considering here) is what he calls "foundationally egoistic."[5] The claim that the virtues are necessary for flourishing,[6] together with the claim that an ethics of virtue will give an account of

---

4. Thomas Hurka, *Virtue, Vice and Value* (Oxford: Oxford University Press, 2001), 219–55.

5. Ibid., 232.

6. Actually, Hurka on 232 of *Virtue, Vice and Value* introduces the claim as the claim that the virtues are "defined" as traits a person needs to flourish, and this is too strong; farther down the page we find the corrected claim that "the virtues are *needed for*…flourishing".

what it is right to do in terms of virtue,[7] leads, he asserts, to the thesis that for virtue ethics a person's reasons to act and be motivated in virtuous ways "derive ultimately from their own flourishing", and this will, he claims, show virtue ethics to be egoistic.

According to Hurka, two dilemmas for virtue ethics can be constructed. One goes as follows. Hurka tries to show that *either* virtue ethics is committed to accepting that it has an egoistic end, in which case it is not a satisfactory ethical theory, *or*, if not, it is committed to being a "two-level" theory, something that is problematic for virtue ethicists to accept.

This alleged dilemma starts from the assumption that a theory which holds that the virtues benefit their possessor is committed to egoism. "A flourishing-based theory...says that a person has reason to act rightly only or ultimately because doing so will contribute to her own flourishing. If she believes this theory and is motivated by its claims about the source of her reasons, her primary impetus for acting rightly will be a desire for her own flourishing. But this egoistic motivation is inconsistent with genuine virtue, which is not focused primarily on the self....Someone motivated by the theory's claims about reasons will therefore be motivated not virtuously but in an unattractively self-indulgent way".[8]

Hurka here lays out lucidly the claim that to act so as to achieve my own flourishing is to act from egoistic motivation, and the further claim that this is self-indulgence. The problem is that there is no argument for either of these claims.[9] The first claim in particular is obviously denied by a virtue ethicist who thinks that the virtues are necessary (or sufficient) for flourishing. For if this is true, then aiming at my flourishing is aiming at *acting and living virtuously*, living as a person who is fair, just, brave, generous, and so on. How is this egoistic? The claim that an agent's motivation is egoistic *merely* because she is aiming at her flourishing is not a claim from neutral ground between Hurka and the rest of us, including the virtue theorist. It assumes the truth of Hurka's own claim, that aiming at flourishing is egoistic. So it is not an independently powerful objection to the virtue theorist, who can reasonably deny it.

The same is even more clearly true of the second claim, namely that pursuing my flourishing in being virtuous is "focusing on the self" and thus being "self-indulgent". Again, this is hardly neutral ground between Hurka and the rest of us, including the virtue theorist. If I aim at living a good life, I am aiming at being just and generous, and thus "focusing" on others rather than myself. And it is particularly strange to hold that somebody living in a brave, generous, and just way is self-indulgent! The self-indulgent person is typically the person who cares too little for others.

---

7. I have stated this, deliberately, in a rather general way. Hurka, like many modern theorists, demands, without argument or considering alternatives, a "theory of right action." That is, he demands that an ethical theory come up with a universally applicable procedure for specifying the right thing to do, which in the case of virtue ethics produces this via "what the virtuous person would do." I have argued against this way of construing a virtue ethics account of right action, and suggested an alternative, in "Being Virtuous and Doing the Right Thing," *Proceedings of the American Philosophical Association* (November 2004).

8. Hurka, *Virtue, Vice and Value*, 246.

9. However, by the time we have worked through both dilemmas we shall have more insight into Hurka's assumptions, which lead him to see no need for argument here.

So Hurka has failed to show that the virtue theorist is forced onto the second horn of his alleged dilemma. This is so because, far from isolating a particular position of the virtue theorist, he has so far simply made theoretical assumptions with no argument for them.

However, even though the first horn of the dilemma lacks force, let us look at this second horn, for it turns out to be instructive. The thought here is that there is a problem in being required by the theory to be motivated by what, according to the theory, is one's aim. So, the theory has to tell you not to be motivated by what, according to the theory, is your aim, but by something else instead. In the present case, to avoid the alleged problems of being motivated by my own flourishing, the theory tells me to be motivated by the virtues themselves—to act, that is, from the motivation to be fair or generous, to give others their due, or to make them better off than they would otherwise be. For if I were to be virtuous with one eye always on my own good, I would not be properly *virtuous*. Hurka claims that "this requires the theories to be what Parfit calls *self-effacing*, telling agents not to be motivated by or even to think of their claims about the source of their reasons".[10]

A swift response by the virtue theorist here is that of course, if the virtues lead to flourishing, the agent would seek to have virtuous motivation—*how else* is she to flourish as a virtuous person? So there is no need for the theory to be self-effacing. Being virtuous is just what the theory tells you to do, not what it tells you to avoid—how could you flourish otherwise? This answer is correct, since the first horn of the dilemma has no force. But it does not get to the bottom of the issue of virtue and flourishing, so more needs to be said.

Self-effacingness is an issue which arises for consequentialism, one first clearly recognized in Sidgwick's *Methods of Ethics*. If our end should be to maximize some good consequence (happiness, pleasure, welfare, the good, or whatever) then it will soon become clear that if everyone tries to employ a method so remote from our everyday practical thinking, the result will not be much good—it will, in fact, be worse, from the theory's point of view, than if they do not.[11] It looks, then, as though in order for the aim of the theory to be achieved, this is best done by its not being aimed for directly. This at once forces the issue: *by whom* is the aim of the theory to be achieved? The answers uniformly have to divide into two the source from which the theory's inventors hope its achievement is to come.

One scenario is that some people have a clear view of the theory's aim, and they manipulate others (either by withholding information or by misleading them) into having motivations which have no reference to the theory's aim, but whose presence helps to bring it about. This is the version that Bernard Williams has aptly called "Government House" consequentialism; the colonials, rather than vainly trying to enlighten the natives, manipulate the natives into furthering the aims which the colonials consider enlightened.

This is an obviously unattractive scenario, and consequentialists have tended to prefer a less objectionable picture of most people's ability to be enlightened about

10. Hurka, *Virtue, Vice and Value*, 246.
11. Given the remoteness of consequentialist reasoning from the way we ordinarily think, it is independently reasonable to think that most people are not going to find it easy or acceptable to impose this form of thinking on themselves.

the consequentialists' aim. In this alternative, then, each individual is supposed to be capable, in principle, of understanding the consequentialists' aim, and also of understanding that ordinary practical reasoning will not bring this about. Assuming that they fail to regard this position as a reason to reject consequentialism, they are supposed to understand that most of the time they should forget about consequentialism and be moved by motivations whose effect, though not their content, is consequentialist. Thus the person's practical reasoning is fundamentally split: part is manipulating the other part into acting in a way with consequentialist effects, while the other part either is too stupid to notice, or dumbs itself down into forgetting, or not minding, that it is being thus manipulated. R. M. Hare is the frankest consequentialist in admitting that the individual on this view replicates inside himself the colonialist view of the native: he calls the manipulating part of the person the "archangel" and the manipulatee the "prole".

This problematic split in the agent's practical deliberation is not, it should be noted, at all like a situation to which it is sometimes compared, namely when we from time to time step back "in a cool hour" and reflect about the way we have been reasoning in the hurried course of everyday life. For that presupposes that reflection is prompted by felt difficulties at the everyday level. And this is very different from the situation where the everyday level is judged defective by an external authority precisely on the grounds that it is not aware of difficulties and feels that it is doing fine.

Consequentialists have been much criticized for the objectionable aspects of their view, which I will not rehearse here. I am merely concerned here with the problem which virtue ethicists have pressed in particular, namely that the split within the self (which mirrors the split between the two classes in consequentialist society) renders impossible an acceptable account of practical reasoning. For the archangel and the prole can, *ex hypothesi*, not share the same practical reasoning. A large advantage of virtue ethics over consequentialism has frequently been taken to be the point that the former is not driven to split the source of practical reasoning in such a way that two levels of reasoning are going on which, by definition, cannot unite to come to a practical conclusion, the conclusions of either having to be hidden from the other. Virtue ethics, by contrast, insists on the unity of the agent's practical reasoning.

Hurka is aware of these criticisms; interestingly, he actually tries to make them rebound on the virtue ethicist.[12] Allowing that the split in the self is a disadvantage, he claims that it also afflicts the virtue ethicist, and in a more "disturbing" way. For the consequentialist is put into the problematic position by a "contingent psychological fact", namely that if people try to achieve the consequentialist aim they will not succeed.[13] But

12. Hurka, *Virtue, Vice and Value*, 247.

13. Even if contingent, it is surely a rather important fact, since it implies that consequentialism has a mistaken moral psychology. Most people would surely accept that if an ethical theory is not livable—that is, it is impossible to put it into practice—then the theory is ruled out. It continues to surprise me that consequentialists fail to recognize this as an important point about their theory, instead resorting to "two-level" approaches, or distinguishing the truth of a theory from its applicability (as though the two were unconnected for a theory the point of which is to be put into practice).

virtue ethics, allegedly, *must* deflect attention from its own aim in order to avoid "self-indulgence".[14]

Fortunately, the way in which virtue ethics requires self-effacingness is perfectly harmless. First, there is a way in which virtue comes to efface itself from the virtuous person's motivation. A beginner in virtue will have to try explicitly to become a virtuous person, and to do so by doing virtuous actions; his deliberations will include such thoughts as that so and so is what a virtuous person would do, or what virtue requires. This is, indeed, how he guides his own deliberations. The truly virtuous person, however, will not explicitly think about, for example, being brave or performing a brave action. Rather, he will, as a result of experience, reflection, and habituation, simply respond to the situation, thinking that these people in danger need help, without explicit thoughts of bravery entering his deliberations. Thoughts about bravery, or the virtuous person, are no longer needed.[15] This does not, however, produce a problematic split in the self, for the reasonings about virtue and virtuous action could still be recovered if needed, and are thus still transparent to the agent. In fact, they are recovered when the brave person explains his action, as he does, for example, to a learner. The self-effacingness here is as harmless as it is with a practical skill. A skilled plumber or pianist will simply respond to a challenge, without explicit thoughts about good plumbing or playing; the occurrence of such thoughts notably marks the learner and it is a sign of expertise that they are no longer on the scene. Yet the expert can recover such thoughts to convey the expertise to a learner; no problematic split in the self, or in the agent's practical reasoning, has been introduced.[16]

What, however, of the virtuous person's thoughts about flourishing? On some theories of virtue the virtuous person would not need to have these. But we are considering theories in which the virtues are held to benefit the agent by leading to his flourishing, and it is hard to see how on this conception of virtue someone could be virtuous while having no, or the wrong, thoughts about flourishing. If bravery does benefit the agent and lead to his flourishing, then thoughts about flourishing have to play some role in the agent's becoming virtuous. Let us try to imagine someone who is brave, but has no thoughts about what it is to flourish, or who thinks that you flourish only by having a good time. We find a tension. If he really has no thoughts about his life as a whole, then what we called bravery looks more like a localized routine habit, and so not a virtue at all. If he really thinks that you flourish only by having a good time, then again what we called bravery looks shaky; if it really is the disposition to stand firm against danger only in the service of having a good time, then again we do not actually have a virtue.

14. The *tu quoque* form of the objection suggests that Hurka thinks that the schizophrenia objection actually is an important one against consequentialism; it is not clear how he proposes to meet it.

15. See Bernard Williams, "Acting as the Virtuous Person Acts," and Rosalind Hursthouse, "The Virtuous Agent's Reasons: A response to Williams," both in *Aristotle and Moral Realism*, ed. R. Heinaman (London: University College London Press, 1995), 24–33.

16. This very brief account presupposes that the development of virtue is like that of a practical skill, a point not argued here but in any case familiar from the mainstream virtue ethics tradition.

The virtuous person will, then, have thoughts about flourishing. These will be like the explicit thoughts about virtue and virtuous action; they will be explicit in the beginner, who needs to be taught the point of being brave, generous, or whatever. As he becomes more virtuous, he will no longer need reminders about the point of being virtuous; these thoughts will gradually, as they are no longer needed, become effaced from his deliberations, and he will simply act, think, and feel virtuously without explicitly thinking about the point of it. Still, this progressive effacement from his explicit thoughts does not mean that thoughts about flourishing evaporate and leave a blank. For, as with virtue itself, the thoughts can be recovered, when they need to be conveyed to a learner, and so they remain transparent to the agent. But, as with virtue itself, the progression is like that in a skill from a learner to an expert: explicit thoughts gradually become effaced from explicit deliberations, but can be reactivated if required without creating any split in the self, or problem for unified deliberation.

There is a complication, however, since eudaimonism, the kind of theory in which the agent's flourishing is basic, is not itself a theory; it is a family or cluster of theories, of diverse types. They have in common, of course, that the agent has a final end to which all her actions are, in one or another way, directed. Different theories of this type, however, have different positions as to what is the best way to achieve *eudaimonia* or flourishing. Aristotle says that being virtuous is necessary; the Stoics, that it is necessary and sufficient; and the Epicureans claim that flourishing is being in a state of pleasure.

We can agree, then, that our final end is flourishing while disagreeing as to what it is that constitutes flourishing, whether virtue, pleasure, or whatever. Whether this produces a problem depends on how flourishing is specified. It is arguable, though I shan't be arguing it here, that Epicurus, who is a hedonist, and thinks that we achieve our final end by seeking pleasure, does become liable to a problem of the same type as those that afflict consequentialism. For he tells us that we shall achieve flourishing by seeking pleasure, and, although he also tells us that this is strongly circumscribed in ways that thoughtless pleasure-seekers get wrong, it is still *my* pleasure that I seek as a way to my flourishing. And this does look egoistic — it looks like a claim that I will flourish only if I put my own interests first as against those of others. Epicurus tells us that as a matter of fact I will not get this pleasure unless I live according to the virtues, but it was pointed out already by ancient critics that this is not very plausible unless we reinterpret what the virtues are. Thus it does seem that an Epicurean's theory tells her to achieve her end in an indirect way. This way requires her to pursue virtue, if she is to do so properly, in a way which hides from herself the fact that she is trying to achieve her aim of flourishing by getting herself into the right state of pleasure; and, if she is clear about her pursuit of pleasure, it requires her to redefine the virtues and what they require. Obviously, there will be problems in producing a unified account of the Epicurean's deliberations.[17]

But this problem does not afflict versions of eudaimonism which claim that my flourishing is to be achieved through my being virtuous. For this is the claim that

---

17. I discuss the problem with Epicureanism in detail in *The Morality of Happiness* (Oxford: Oxford University Press, 1993).

being virtuous is the right way to achieve flourishing, and on this view flourishing is not a state of myself, as it is for hedonists, nor is it a matter of *my* good as opposed to yours, as it arguably has to be for Epicurus. For, if I achieve flourishing through being virtuous, my flourishing will be constituted by my virtuous activity, which is focused on others as much as on myself. In this it is unlike a pleasant state of myself, which I might well aim to produce in a way which focuses on me at the expense of others.

Thus those versions of virtue ethics which are forms of eudaimonism do not split the self or produce problems for deliberation, even though there is a sense in which a virtuous person's thoughts about flourishing are self-effacing; they disappear from explicit deliberation as the person becomes more virtuous and no longer needs them. Unlike the perpetually conflicting perspectives of the consequentialist, which can never be brought together in unified deliberation, the virtuous person's thoughts about virtue and flourishing can be recovered if needed, to convey to learners the nature and point of virtue, in a way which imports no conflict and creates no problem for the theory. This alleged dilemma, then, is no threat to the virtue ethicist.

There is, however, a second alleged dilemma in store, on the basis of Hurka's assertion that all virtue ethics is "foundationally egoistic" in aiming at flourishing. So we need to look further at the relation of virtue to flourishing.

According to Hurka, either flourishing is defined in a *substantive* way, in which case virtue ethics is committed to implausible claims, or it is defined in a *formal* way, in which case virtue ethics will give an unsatisfactory account of the virtues.[18] Either way, virtue ethics is supposed to be in trouble.

"A *substantive* conception equates flourishing with some determinate state F of people or their lives, where both the nature and the goodness of F are defined independently of the virtues".[19] This is a common way of stating the issue. The major objection to this, also common, is that we have to find such a state F (call it success) and a plausible list of the virtues (properly conceived), and show that having these will lead to achieving F, that is, success. And it is unlikely that we will succeed in this.

How much does this matter? *Of course* it is unlikely that being just, fair, and so on is a good bet for achieving success, *if* this success is defined independently of the virtues. A fairly common conception of success might be financial prosperity and security. A flashier definition might be, for example, being very rich and having a trophy spouse. These definitions are certainly "independent of the virtues". But whoever thought for a moment that being fair, generous, and so on was a good way to achieve *that*? Where success is defined independently of the virtues, it will always be hopeless to try to show that the virtues are a good way of achieving *that*.

This does show something about the virtues. It shows that problems are likely to lurk in any theory which as Aristotle's does, comes up with an account of flourishing which allows it to contain even some elements whose value for flourishing is defined independently of the virtues. But as far as concerns the general relation of virtue and flourishing, it shows only that no sensible virtue ethics works with a conception of flourishing which is substantive in this sense.

18. Hurka, *Virtue, Vice and Value*, 234–43.
19. Ibid., 235.

This is not to claim that the virtues are not useful in achieving some kinds of success defined independently of the virtues.[20] Brave people will achieve their ends more reliably, and can be trusted more, than the cowardly; people who are cruel and mean have difficulty sustaining the relationships needed for social cooperation; and so on. But it is a fact about the world that the virtuous are not guaranteed to succeed in worldly terms, and that virtue may even prevent it: brave people, for example, will protest against injustice rather than go along with it; honest people will refrain from taking advantage of a corrupt system plundered by the greedy; and so on. While it would be wrong to think of the virtuous person as always at a disadvantage in worldly terms, it is still true that no sensible virtue ethics works with a conception of flourishing which is substantive in the above sense. A virtue ethicist who defended such a substantive conception of flourishing would be committed to holding an unrealistic view of the extent to which the world will work in favor of the virtuous.

So we turn to the other option, which is that in virtue ethics, flourishing is defined formally (or, as Hurka puts it, "merely formally"). This "does not equate flourishing with any independent good F but only with the general idea of the human good, whatever its content".[21] Hurka's objection to this is odd. He claims that it abandons the "explanatory ambitions" which "we" have of a theory of virtue. Allegedly, "we" give an account of virtue a "task", which is that of using "one fundamental good F to explain simultaneously what unifies the virtues, what makes them good, and what distinguishes them from other goods that are not virtues".[22] The formal account of flourishing fails in this "task", he claims. Why? A virtue ethics theory can perfectly well explain all these things, and thus fulfill its Hurkan "task" of fulfilling explanatory ambitions for virtue. The oddity is in the demand that they all be explained in terms of one fundamental good F, which is defined independently of virtue.[23]

But why should the virtue ethicist accept this constraint? No reason is ever offered. A plausible conjecture is that it comes from the demand that an ethical theory have a form such that there is a basic concept, defined in a way which is both substantive and independent, from which other concepts in the theory are "derived", as is presumably thought to be the case in whatever theories are the favored model.[24] But there is no reason why a virtue ethicist should accept this, and plenty of reason to be suspicious, since the "task" has been set up in such a way that virtue ethics is bound to fail it. Nor should the virtue ethicist be bullied by claims that this is a demand which "we" make of virtue ethics. The achievements of the whole classical tradition of virtue ethics serves rather to strengthen doubts that the "derivation" model for ethical theories is at all appropriate. We may reasonably ask, Which theories in fact have this structure? (It does not fit scientific theories, certainly.) And why are they

20. I am grateful to Dave Schmidtz for helpful discussion on this point.

21. Hurka, *Virtue, Vice and Value*, 235.

22. Ibid.

23. There might of course be something about *virtue* that explained the unity of the virtues, their goodness, and so on, but this is clearly not what Hurka has in mind.

24. Hurka, in *Virtue, Vice and Value*, uses the language of "derivation" elsewhere, for example, 239, and on 246 talks of virtue ethicists "complet[ing] their derivations" (another "task"?) but never gives any reason why an ethical theory should be thought of in this way.

supposed to be a good model for ethics? Until we have convincing answers to these questions, we have no reason to let the "derivation" model be foisted on us.

Still, even if we reject the demand that flourishing be an independent concept from which we can "derive" the unity and value of virtue, we might reasonably wonder what role a formal account of flourishing can play in an ethics of virtue. Here we have the advantage of having, in the classical tradition, a large body of material consisting of theories which do develop accounts of virtue within a formally defined account of flourishing, so we can see what some of the possibilities are.

The basic assumption which needs to be made at the start of such a theory is that each of us has a final end or *telos*—some overarching aim in whatever we do. This is not a philosophers' theoretical demand; it is a very ordinary and everyday way of thinking of our lives. We get to it simply by reflecting on the fact that our actions can be thought of not only chronologically, in a linear way, as we perform one action after another. They can also be thought of, and frequently are, in a "nested" way, as happens whenever we ask *why* we are doing something. The answer to why I am doing a particular action will typically make reference to some broader concern, and this in turn to some even broader concern. Given that I have only one life, I will eventually come up with some very broad conception of my life as a whole, as that to which my actions are at any given point tending. This is my final end. A few points need to be stressed here. This is a very ordinary way of thinking, one in which everyone engages except people who are severely conflicted about their aims, or in denial about the way their actions fit into broader patterns in their lives.[25] We do not typically, when we think in this way, come up with a very *specific* characterization of such a "final end". We just think of it as "my life going well" or the like, where we are thinking of the life as a whole and not just the way it is now.

Although so far it is specified without reference to content, the conception of my final end has significant formal constraints. Most important, it is *complete*—all my actions are done for the sake of it, in a way that I do not seek it for the sake of anything further. My final end includes all my purposeful endeavors. All the classical ethical theories assume, with Aristotle, that everybody thinks of their life going well, in this way, as happiness, *eudaimonia*. Nowadays it is controversial to make this claim about happiness (at least in English). I think that reflection shows that we do have this conception of happiness,[26] but it is entangled with other thoughts about happiness that have come in from other quarters, such as the thought that it is pleasure or feeling good. Moreover, we are used to the idea that happiness might be a local aim in my life, so that I can do my duty and neglect my happiness, whereas the conception of happiness as my final end demands that it be complete, not just one local aim among others for my deliberations. It is, then, problematic for us to use the notion of happiness at this point, and many modern virtue ethicists avoid confusion by talking of flourishing instead. But in any case Aristotle at once remarks that people disagree as to what *eudaimonia* is, some calling it virtue, others pleasure, and

25. Also, perhaps, existentialists who deny that their life has any meaning or final end.
26. In "Happiness as Achievement," *Daedalus* (Spring 2004): 44–51, I argue that we do in fact have the notion of happiness as an achievement as well as the more familiar "subjective" notion of feeling good.

so on; it is not a concept which could be supposed to give a substantive conception of our final end.

The kind of theory which begins in this place, from *eudaimonia*, is unsurprisingly called eudaimonism, which is, as already remarked, a family or cluster of theories, not a theory itself. This is because different theories develop at this point, analyzing and giving a theoretical account of what *eudaimonia* is. It is perfectly possible for a eudaimonist theory to be egoistic. Above, I pointed out that a hedonist theory like that of Epicurus does risk becoming egoistic. Also, many people think of achieving *eudaimonia* as a matter of what I earlier called success—having a good job, a big house and car, and so on. (These versions are very liable to breakdown, and for reasons for which eudaimonist theories can give a good explanation.) But other versions are available, in particular versions which give a role to virtue.

The whole eudaimonist approach to ethics has been queried, for a reason which is worth a brief mention here. The objection is that thinking of ethics in terms of a final end, however specified, "has outrageously paternalistic implications: they see looming the specter of people's imposing 'the good life' on others".[27] However, this response rests on three misconceptions.

First, no theory imposes anything on anyone; people respond to theories by using their minds to think about them and then to accept or reject them. People can misuse theories to impose their own priorities on others, but this is an abuse that can happen with any theory, so it is irrelevant to mention this possibility with respect to virtue ethics.

Second, this objection forgets that theory does not find us blank slates. By the time we think about ethical theory at all, or even ethical alternatives, we *already* have views about our lives and how they are going, namely, the views we have acquired from our parents, schools, TV and general culture. Ethical theory helps us to reflect about the views of our lives that we already have: consequentialism urges us to throw them out (and then take them back); other theories urge us to rethink them for ourselves. So we have another sense in which eudaimonism doesn't, because it can't, impose anything on us. By the time eudaimonism comes into the picture, nobody fails to have views about their life except people who are pathological or seriously in denial about important aspects of themselves. Eudaimonism does not impose those views, but helps us to think about them for ourselves.

Third, many of the views people have about their lives prior to encountering ethical theory are themselves repressive and contain paternalistic elements imposed on them by parents or society. Thinking about their lives for themselves in terms of eudaimonist theory is empowering, not repressive. This will be especially true of forms of virtue ethics which stress, as the classical account does, the importance of the agent's practical reasoning in living her life.

This general objection to eudaimonism is, then, without force. We still, however, face the issue of showing how virtue has a role in my achieving *eudaimonia*, living well. But is this really puzzling? As Rosalind Hursthouse has recently stressed,[28]

27. Brad Hooker, "Is Moral Virtue a Benefit to the Agent?" in *How Should One Live? Essays on the Virtues*, ed. Roger Crisp, 141–55 (Oxford: Oxford University Press, 1996).

28. Rosalind Hursthouse, *On Virtue Ethics* (Oxford: Oxford University Press, 1999).

when we bring up children, we teach them to be brave, generous, and so on, and we do so in their own interests, not just ours: we take it that to have a character of a certain kind is a good way for them to live. Few people in fact doubt that the virtues are goods which a person has reason to want.

Virtue ethics wants more than this, of course; it claims that virtue is, more weakly, necessary, or, more strongly, necessary and sufficient for flourishing. It must, as Hurka puts it, "give these virtues priority over other goods, by stating that they are uniquely necessary for flourishing".[29] Many critics have tried to show that this is not going to succeed, because it depends on showing that virtue is important and central to a person's good, a view which is, it is asserted, "not plausible". This kind of objection is very familiar; virtue ethics is held to flout common sense when it holds that virtue is at least necessary for leading a life which is a flourishing, good one.[30] For if this claim is true, then the wicked are not leading flourishing lives, however wealthy and glamorous they are. And is this not completely counterintuitive?

Surprisingly many critics have thought that defenders of virtue ethics hold *both* that virtue is at least necessary for flourishing *and* that wealth, glamour, and other indications of success are acceptable as indications of a flourishing life. Of course, this combination of positions is doomed to be hopelessly implausible. In fact, defenders of virtue ethics strongly reject the second position. Wealth and the like are quite unreliable as indications of flourishing. What matters for flourishing are a range of concerns, engagements, and commitments which are available to people with a virtuous character and unavailable to the vicious.

Criticism is generally renewed at this point on the grounds that claims about flourishing are now including claims about virtue, and are thus no longer common ground to the defender and the critic of virtue ethics. But virtue ethics has never held that they are, so this is not a problem. It is only to be expected that the virtuous will differ from the nonvirtuous in their assessments of flourishing, because we are dealing here with virtue in the context of a formally characterized conception of flourishing. Virtue ethics is not telling us that virtues are a good bet to achieve an independently defined flourishing, but rather telling us that the virtuous life is the *best specification* of flourishing. This is *already* a claim which the nonvirtuous dispute, since they think that wealth (etc.) matters more. How could we expect that such competing specifications of flourishing would agree as to how to achieve it? They are not disputing about means to an agreed end. Many critics have failed to see this point, because they have assumed that virtue ethics must have a substantive account of flourishing which is common to their opponents, defining flourishing in a way that is independent of the virtues. So they have cast the virtue ethicist in the

---

29. Hurka, *Virtue, Vice and Value*, 240.

30. I have very often seen and heard cited Bernard Williams's claim that there are horrible people who are "not miserable at all but, by any ethological standard of the bright eye and the gleaming coat, dangerously flourishing" (Williams, *Ethics and the Limits of Philosophy*, [Cambridge, Mass.: Harvard University Press, 1985], 46). However, these citations generally fail to note that Williams immediately adds that it is unclear whether there really are such people, or whether they are just our own projection, generally as figures in the past, where they are more plausible than in the present.

thankless and clueless role of arguing that the virtues are the best means to an end agreed on by virtuous and nonvirtuous alike.

It is often thought to be a fault in virtue ethics that it rejects the idea that virtue can be assessed as a means to an agreed-on substantive final end. But what would such an assessment actually look like? Another consequentialist critic of virtue ethics, Brad Hooker, sets up what he calls the "sympathy test". Take two people, Upright who has led a virtuous life and Unscrupulous who has not. Both have unsuccessful, wretched lives. Would we be sorrier for Unscrupulous—that is, would we think that Unscrupulous missed out on something worth having in not being virtuous?[31] Astonishingly, Hooker thinks that it is obvious that "we would *not* feel *sorrier* for Unscrupulous". Who, however, are "we"? Are we ourselves upright, or unscrupulous? (Assuming that we cannot be both, or neither.) Obviously, which we are, and the degree to which we are, makes all the difference in what our judgment is.[32]

Moreover, there is no need for virtue ethics to be concessive about this point. For it is a positive theoretical advantage, in that it answers to the way we actually think about our lives, and thus shows the theory to be well grounded empirically. Suppose that there is a disagreement as to whether someone ruined his life by acting virtuously, or rather should be admired for the way he did the right thing. We do not expect that people who disagree radically as to what ways of life are worth living will nevertheless agree, in this dispute, on a neutral list of indicators that a life is ruined or worth living. This is because such a dispute is recognized as not being a simple dispute about means to an agreed-on end, and not reducible to one. It is a more complex kind of dispute, in which a wider range of issues are in debate.

This point about virtue ethics has been argued convincingly in depth by Rosalind Hursthouse in her recent book, and I cannot do justice to it here. It is relevant to the present argument, however, in that a prominent reason why critics underestimate the resources of a formal conception of flourishing is that they tend to think of disputes about flourishing as having the form only of debates about means to an agreed-on end, while they can see that this is not what happens when a formally constrained conception of flourishing gets its content specified by a theory claiming that virtue is at least necessary for one to flourish.[33]

---

31. Hooker, "Is Moral Virtue a Benefit to the Agent?" 149 (emphasis in original).

32. Who *could*, in fact, make the judgment from a neutral point of view? Hooker goes on to admit that the argument "is addressed only to those of us who (a) do not know what we think about whether moral virtue is a fundamental category of prudential value and (b) do not feel sorry for the immoralist". This appears to imply that the judgment already embodies a commitment to the conclusion Hooker wants. It is indeed hard to think of someone making the judgment from a viewpoint that was completely neutral as to virtue's having any kind of value at all. And why should such a person's judgment have any authority, in any case?

33. We can see, though I cannot go into the issue further here, that the move to claiming the necessity of virtue for flourishing is fairly intuitive; Hursthouse carries this out elegantly. The move to claiming that virtue is also sufficient for flourishing is more complex, and relies on more theoretical grounds, including theoretical difficulties that the necessity view falls into.

Virtue, then, relates to flourishing in that living a virtuous life is claimed to be either necessary (in weaker forms of virtue ethics) or necessary and sufficient (in stronger forms) for flourishing; virtue ethics is one way of specifying our final end of flourishing. So there is no conflict latent in living a virtuous life as a way of achieving flourishing. If virtue ethics is correct, it is the only way to go. Holding the virtues to be a way of achieving flourishing, and thus benefiting their possessor, is in no way egoistic.

What becomes of the claim that virtue theories are "foundationally egoistic" in taking our reasons for acting to relate, ultimately, to our flourishing? Now that we have looked at the substantive and formal accounts of flourishing, we are in a position to see what this charge comes to. We have seen that Hurka is right in holding that a virtue ethics will have problems if it accepts what he calls a substantive account of flourishing. (Some versions of virtue ethics may have done this, but it is clearly an unpromising way to go.) In fact, a long tradition of virtue ethics has taken the form of a version of eudaimonism which characterizes our final end formally, and specifies it as being a life in which virtue is necessary (in weaker versions) or necessary and sufficient (in stronger versions). This is not an attempt to produce an account of flourishing whose characterization is independent of the virtues and thus acceptable to virtuous and nonvirtuous alike. Nor is it a point about "foundations" in the modern sense. Finally, we have seen that egoism is in no way involved.

We can appreciate, by the time we have seen even sketchily how a eudaimonistic virtue ethics actually works, that the point that I am aiming at my flourishing does not make the theory egoistic in any sense. If I am aiming at flourishing by living virtuously, I am aiming at being a just, generous (etc.) person. The formal point, that I am aiming at my flourishing, just comes down to the point that I am trying to live my life virtuously. If you point out that I am doing this as *my* way of flourishing not yours, the retort is that I am trying to be virtuous in living *my* life, not yours, because my life is the only life I can live. It would be objectionable, as well as ill advised, for me to try to live your life, but this is not egoistic of me.

There is one final misunderstanding that needs to be mentioned. Hurka claims at one point that even virtue ethics within a formal framework of flourishing is egoistic because he "assum[es that the agent's] flourishing is a state of him".[34] But my flourishing is obviously not a state of me, as we have already seen. It is the way I live my life, my activity as a (hopefully) virtuous person. We misunderstand eudaimonist conceptions of happiness and flourishing if we construe them as states or static conditions. To flourish, to be happy in the ancient understanding of that, is to live your life actively, not to be in a state as a result of what you (or possibly even someone else) does. This is a peculiarly modern misunderstanding, which perhaps derives from thinking of happiness or flourishing as a state of pleasant feeling.

---

34. Hurka, *Virtue, Vice and Value*, 232, note 28. It is odd that Hurka *assumes* this in the context of referring to my book *The Morality of Happiness* (Oxford: Oxford University Press, 1993), since there I *deny* this at length, and develop the point that *eudaimonia* is not a state but the agent's activity in living his or her life, a point implicit in the framework of eudaimonism.

We can see that the issue of whether or not virtue ethics is egoistic cannot even be properly discussed until we clarify the way in which being virtuous relates to our final end, *eudaimonia* or flourishing. Getting this clear removes the misunderstandings which have led to thinking of virtue ethics, at least in its classical version, as egoistic. We are brought back to our original thoughts: when I care about being generous, courageous, and fair, I am caring, quite straightforwardly, about other people.[35]

35. This paper derives from and includes material that I presented as lectures, and I am very grateful to my audiences, whose comments have enormously improved it. I gave the material as an Erskine Lecture at the University of Canterbury, Christchurch, New Zealand; as a Hägerström Lecture at the University of Uppsala, Sweden; and as a David Ross Boyd Lecture at the University of Oklahoma. I am also grateful to colleagues who discussed the paper at the University of Arizona. Among very many debts I would like to single out are those due to David Schmidtz, Frans Svensson, and Linda Zagzebski. I am particularly grateful to Paul Bloomfield for very helpful comments at several stages of the paper's development.

B. Morality as Indistinguishable from Self-Interest

11

Morality, Self, and Others

W. D. FALK

1

In: And how can you say that I never had a moral education? As a child, I was taught that one ought not to maltreat other children, ought to share one's sweets with them, ought to keep tidy and clean; as an adolescent, that one ought to keep one's word, to work, to save, to leave off drink, not to waste the best years of one's life, to let reason govern one's emotions and actions. Nor did I simply learn that one is *called upon* to act in these ways by paternal authority and social custom on pain of censure. I learned to appreciate that one *ought* to do these things *on their merits*, and that what one ought to do on its merits does not depend on the requests or enjoinders of anyone. The facts in the case themselves make one liable, as a reflective person, to act in these ways of one's own accord: they provide one with choice-supporting reasons sufficient to determine one if one knows them and takes diligent account of them.[1]

Out: I know you were taught all this. But why did your teacher say that you ought to act in these ways?

In: Why? For very cogent reasons. My tutor was a student of the Ancients. The moral man, "the man of practical wisdom", he kept quoting Aristotle; "is the man who knows how to deliberate well about what is good and useful for himself". And surely, he would say, you can see for yourself: if you don't act sociably, who will act sociably toward you? Uncleanliness breeds disease. Without work, how are you to live? Without savings, what about your future? Drink leaves one a wreck. Indulging one's sorrows makes them worse. The wasted years, one day you will regret them

---

1. For the use of "ought", compare my "'Ought' and Motivation" (1947–48) in *Readings in Ethical Theory*, ed. W. S. Sellars and J. Hospers (New York: Appleton-Century-Crofts, 1952), pp. 492–510; "Goading and Guiding," *Mind*, n.s. LXII (1953), 145–171; and "Morality and Convention," *The Journal of Philosophy*, LVII (1960), 675–685. Parts of the last paper have been incorporated in the present essay.

when it is too late. People who cannot govern themselves are helpless before fortune, without the aid and comfort of inner strength.

Out: And so you think that you had a moral education? Let me tell you, you never even made a start. For what were you taught? That there are things that you ought to do or to avoid on your own account. But one does not learn about morality that way. What one *morally* ought to do is what one ought to do on account of others, or for the sake of some good state of things in general. Now had you been taught to appreciate that you ought to keep clean so as to be pleasing to others, and that you ought to do what moral custom requires for the sake of the general good, then, and then only, would you have learned the rudiments of moral duty.

In: Very well, my upbringing was too narrow. One would hardly be a human being if the good of others, or of society at large, could not weigh with one as a cogent reason for doing what will promote it. So one has not fully learned about living like a rational and moral being unless one has learned to appreciate that one ought to do things out of regard for others, and not only out of regard for oneself.

Out: No, you have still not got my point, I am saying that only insofar as you ought to do things—no matter whether for yourself or for others—for the sake of others, is the reason a moral reason and the ought a moral ought. Reasons of self-regard are not moral reasons at all, and you can forget about them in the reckoning of your *moral* obligations.

In: But this seems artificial. A moral education surely should teach one all about the principles of orderly living and the reasons which tell in their favor. And if there are also perfectly good personal reasons which tell in their favor, why suppress them? To be sure, in talking to people in ordinary life, we do no such thing. If they say "Why ought I to act sociably?" we say "For the general good as well as your own". If they say "Why ought I to be provident?" we say "For your own good as well as that of others". In short, we offer mixed reasons, and none of these reasons can be spared. One ought not to lie because this is a good social rule, and equally because the habit of evasiveness is destructive of oneself as a person. And one ought not to take to drink or indulge one's sorrows, or waste the best years of one's life primarily out of proper regard for oneself, much as there may be other-regarding reasons as well. If morality were all social service, and one had no moral responsibilities towards oneself or toward others, the moral inconveniences of life would be far less than they are. So I don't see the point of saying. "But one has no *moral* commitment to do anything except insofar as one ought to do it on account of others". To say this seems like encouraging people not to bother about doing things insofar as they ought to do them only for personal reasons, as after all this is not a moral ought.

Out: But one does not speak of a moral duty to do things for one's own sake. If one ought to save in order to provide for one's own future, one regards this as a precept not of morals but of prudence. It would be different if one ought to save in order to provide for one's dependents. Moral commitments are those which one has as a moral being, and what makes one a moral being is that one has commitments towards others and does not evade them.

In: Not everyone will agree that as a moral being one has only commitments toward others or that only such commitments are properly "moral". The Greeks, for example, took a wider view. For Plato the equivalent of a moral being was the just or right-living person, and of a moral commitment the right and just course—the one which the right-living person would be led to take. And this right-living person was one who would keep himself in good shape as a sane and self-possessed being, and who would do whatever good and sufficient reasons directed him to do. This is why for Plato and the Greeks temperance and prudence were no less among the just man's commitments than paying his debts and not willfully harming others, and why the one was not treated any less as a moral commitment than the other. The Greeks placed the essence of man as a moral being in his capacity to direct himself on rational grounds; and his commitments as a moral being were therefore all those which he seriously incurred as a properly self-directing being.

Out: Citing the Greeks only shows how distant their concept of morality is from ours. We will not call every rational commitment "moral" or equate the moral with the rational man.

In: This is broadly so, although not entirely. Our concept of morality vacillates between the Greek and the Christian tradition. We associate "moral" with "social" commitment, and the "morally good man" with the "selfless man". But we also speak of man as a "moral agent", of his "moral freedom" and "moral powers"; and here we refer to his whole capacity of self-direction by good and sufficient reasons. One may speak without strain of a personal and a social ethic, and refer to the negligent disregard of oneself as a vice, and a sign of moral defect. We call the improvident man "morally weak", and we call the man who can resist drink in company on account of his health or who sticks to his vocation in adversity a man of "moral strength and character". There is certainly little difference in the qualities needed to live up to a social or a personal ought. It takes self-denial to provide for one's future, moral courage to stick to one's vocation. One may show one's mettle as a moral agent here no less than in selfless care for others. There are contemporary moralists who call "moral" any "authentic" commitment of a self-governing person, whether its grounds are social or personal. What justifies them is the broader use of the term which is also part of our language and tradition.

Out: And how eccentric this use is. Our very concept of a moral being is inseparable from the notion of submission of self to a good other than one's own. It is not conceivable that a man should have moral duties on a desert island, devoid of man or beast. Would one say that he still had a moral duty to do what was good for him? You may as well go on and say that if a shipwrecked fellow arrived to share his vegetables, it might be his moral duty to let him starve rather than starve himself.

In: The good of others need not always have the overriding claim on one, if this is what you mean. One could say to a good-hearted and weak-willed person, "For your own sake, you ought to stop neglecting your future, even if this hurts others". This would not be a typically "moral" ought, but one may be giving sound moral advice.

Out: And so, if beneficence had the better of this person, you should call him morally irresponsible and blameworthy. On your showing, he has evaded a moral commitment, and for such evasions one is held morally responsible and liable to censure. But surely, even if I granted your case, one would not call him blameworthy and a morally bad man; as indeed in any case where a person fails to do what his own good requires we do not call him morally bad, but only imprudent, unwise, rash. It is quite a different offense to be slack about brushing one's teeth, than to be negligent about providing dentures for others. And this is so precisely because the second is a moral offense and the first is not and because one is blameworthy for the one and not for the other.

In: I agree that there is a difference. One is only called morally bad and is held answerable to *others* for neglecting what one ought to do out of regard for them. And this is understandable enough. After all, insofar as one fails to do only what one's own good requires, the failing is no one's concern but one's own. But then I should not say that such self-neglect was in no sense morally irresponsible and blameworthy. If it does not call for blame by others, it still calls for self-reproach. A rational person is responsible to himself for not being evasive about anything that he is convinced that he really ought to do. And the lack of moral strength and courage in personal matters, although commonly viewed as an amicable vice, is an amicable vice only in the estimation of others since it is not directly a threat to them.

However, we are not making headway. You find it repugnant to call a commitment "moral" unless its grounds are social and unless its non-observance makes one liable not only to social censure but also to self-reproach; and so be it. Perhaps our disagreement is only verbal, and despite some misgivings, I am ready to settle for your usage. Let us only speak of a moral ought where one ought to do things on account of others. But let us not be misled. For it still does not follow that if one ought to do things on one's own account, this ought may not still be otherwise functioning *like* a moral ought.

Out: How could it be like a moral ought if it is not a moral ought?

In: Because when one thinks of a moral ought, one thinks not only that its grounds are social but also that it has a special force and cogency. A moral ought commits one in all seriousness and in every way, without leaving any reasonable option to act otherwise. Your view comes to saying that if an ought is to be moral it must satisfy two conditions: it must seriously bind one in every way, and it must do so for other-regarding reasons. On your showing, a personal ought cannot be moral, as it cannot satisfy one of these conditions simply by having personal grounds. But it may still satisfy the other condition, and be as cogently binding and action-guiding in its force and function as a moral ought. This is why I can only accept your usage with one proviso: that one may also say that there are other than strictly moral commitments which a right-living person may have to reckon with no less than his strictly moral ones.

Out: Surely you don't expect me to fall for this. When I say "Don't count the purely personal ought as moral" I am not saying "Count it as well, but call it by another name". My point is precisely that it does not function like a moral ought at all. Personal reasons do not commit one to do anything with the same cogency as social reasons. In fact, in calling them reasons of prudence or expediency, we depreciate them. We regard them as inferior, and often disreputable, guides to action. So I won't let you reduce my position to triviality. That only the social commitments are essentially moral must be taken as implying that only they have the characteristic moral force.

In: I thought that this was at the back of our discussion all along. It usually is so with people who are so insistent on your usage, although part of the trouble is that one can never be sure. First one is told that a moral ought is one that commits one on other-regarding grounds and that a personal ought is not a moral ought *for this reason*. But then comes the further suggestion that it is not only different from a moral ought in this way, but is also otherwise inferior. It gives directives, but directives of a somehow shady kind. One way or other, the idea is that a commitment that has personal grounds is either not properly a commitment at all, or, if one in any way, then one that belongs in some limbo of disrepute. But your argument so far has done nothing to prove this point. From your language rule, it only follows that the personal ought must be unlike a moral ought in one essential respect, but not, except by way of confusion, that it must be therefore also unlike a moral ought in other respects too. You might as well say "Surely a lay-analyst is not a doctor", as one is not a doctor without a medical degree, and take this to be proof that a lay-analyst cannot otherwise cure like a doctor either. "No lay-analyst is a doctor" is strictly and trivially true in one way, and may be misleading and tendentiously false in another. And the same with "No personal ought is a *moral* ought". Your language rule makes this strictly and trivially true; but it does not go to show that a personal ought cannot otherwise be *like* a moral ought by being seriously committing or by taking precedence in a conscientious calculus of action-guiding considerations. My point is that, even if this were so, your appeal to usage cannot settle this matter. Logical grammar can decree that only social reasons are properly called "moral". But it cannot decide what reasons can, or cannot, be seriously committing for human beings.

Out: But what I am saying seems substantially true. What one ought to do on account of others is the prototype of the categorically binding ought. Personal reasons have not got the binding cogency of other-regarding reasons, and one deprecates them as inferior and disreputable.

In: And there is some truth in this. Personal and social reasons are not on the same footing in the economy of action-guiding considerations. Personal reasons are very commonly less thoroughly committing, they are often inferior reasons, and not rarely discreditable. But why this is so is a different matter and has not yet been touched on in any way. What is more, personal reasons need not always be in this inferior position. They are often not intrinsically discreditable, and become inferior guides to action only where there are other reasons in the case deserving of prior consideration. Take someone concerned for his health, or future, or self-respect. Surely these are respectable aspirations and there may be things which he ought to do on account of them without violating other claims. His health requires that he be temperate, his self-respect that he live without evasion. Would it not then be positively remiss of him not to act in these ways? If he did not, one would say that he had failed to do what a man in his position really ought to have done, and precisely for the reason which he had. And, if one can say this, what remains of the blemish?

This is why it remains perplexing to me why commitments on personal grounds should be excluded from the orbit of moral teaching, and why modern moralists, unlike the Ancients, should disdain to mention them as an integral part of the moral life. For they may also be cogent and sometimes overridingly cogent commitments to action. And if they are not the whole of morals, why not count them as part of them? For it also seems natural to say that to teach someone all about morality is to teach him about all the valid directives for action; about all those things which he might not otherwise do readily but which, for good and compelling reasons in the nature in the case, he ought to do and would have to break himself into doing whether for the sake of others or his own.

There is, I agree, one tendency to say that the moral man acts in accordance with precepts of selflessness. But there is also another tendency to say that he is the man to organize his life in accordance with all valid precepts. Our disagreement has exhibited the kind of shuttle-service between rival considerations better known as the dialectic of a problem. It may be that this shuttle-service is maintained by a cleft in the very concept of morality. This concept may have grown from conflicting or only partially overlapping observations, which are not fully reconciled in ordinary thinking.

Out: If this is so, I would have to be shown, for common sense still seems to me right in its disparagement of personal reasons.

In: Very well, then we shall have to consider why personal reasons should function as a less cogent guide to action than social ones. I shall admit that in more ways than one the personal ought presents a special case, but not that it presents a case for disparagement except in special contexts. After this, the question of whether the personal ought is properly called moral or not will appear less important, partly because it will have become plainer why there is a question. Nor shall I try to offer a ruling on this point. With a background of discourse as intricate and full of nuance as in this case, discretion is the better part of valor, and clarification is a safer bet than decision.

2

Whenever one remarks that clearly there are things which one ought to avoid or do if only for one's own sake, someone is sure to say, "No doubt; but any such ought is only a precept of prudence or expediency". It is a textbook cliché against Hobbes that his account of morality comes to just this. And this is said as if it were an obvious truth and enough to discredit all such precepts in one go. This assumes a great deal and settles nothing.

What it assumes is this: that everything that one ever does for one's own sake, one does as a matter of prudence *or* expediency; that there is no difference between these two; that morality always differs from prudence as a scent differs from a bad smell; and that everyone knows how so and why.

None of this will do.

In the first place, not everything done for oneself is done for reasons of prudence. That one ought to insure one's house, save for one's old age, not put all one's money into one venture, are precepts of prudence. But it is not a precept of prudence, though it may be a good precept, that someone ought to undergo a dangerous operation as a long shot to restoring his health rather than linger under a disability forever after.

The point is that prudence is only one way of looking after oneself. To act prudently is to play safe, for near-certain gains at small risks. But some good things one cannot get in this way. To get them at all one has to gamble, taking the risk of not getting them even so, or of coming to harm in the process. If one values them enough, one will do better by oneself to throw prudence to the winds, to play for high stakes, knowing full well the risk and the price of failure. Explorers, artists, scientists, mountaineers are types who may serve themselves better by this course. So will most people at some juncture. Thus, if someone values security, then that he ought to save in order to be secure is á precept of prudence. But that someone ought to stick to his vocation when his heart is in it enough to make it worth risking security or health or life itself is not a precept of *prudence*, but of *courage*.

One says sometimes, "I ought to save, as I *want* to be prudent", but sometimes "as I *ought* to be prudent". One may also decide that in one's own best interests one ought to be prudent rather than daring, or daring rather than prudent, as the case may be. Now, that one ought to do something as it would be prudent is a dictate of prudence. But that one really ought to be prudent, in one's own best interests, would not be a dictate of prudence again. One then ought to play safe in order to serve oneself *best* and not in order to serve oneself *safely*.

A dictate of prudence where one wants to be prudent but ought to be courageous in one's own best interests is a dictate of timidity. A dictate of courage, where one feels reckless but ought to be prudent, is a dictate of foolhardiness. Both will then plainly be morally imperfect precepts. But there is nothing obviously imperfect about a dictate of prudence where one ought to be prudent, or a dictate of courage where one ought to be daring. Such precepts seem near-moral enough to allow one to call the habit of acting on them a virtue. The Ancients considered both prudence and courage as moral virtues. Oddly enough, in our time, one is more ready to view courage on one's own behalf as a moral virtue than prudence. It needs the reminder that precepts of self-protection may be precepts of courage as well as of prudence for one to see that any precept of self-protection may have a moral flavor. I think that the dim view which we take of prudence corresponds to a belief that to be daring is harder than to be level-headed, a belief most likely justified within our own insurance-minded culture. But such belief would have seemed strange to Bishop Butler and the fashionable eighteenth-century gentlemen to whom he addressed himself. Prudence in Butler's time, as throughout the ancient world, was not yet the cheap commodity which it is with us; and the price of virtue varies with the market.

There are other precepts of self-protection which are not "just a matter of prudence" either. That one ought not to take to drugs or drink, indulge oneself in one's sorrows, waste one's talents, commit suicide just in the despair of the moment, are precepts made of sterner stuff. One wants to say, "Surely, it is more than just a matter of prudence that one ought to avoid these things". And rightly so. The effect on oneself of taking to drugs or drink, or of any of the others, is not conjectural, but quite certain. To avoid them is therefore more than a matter of *taking no risks*. Sometimes, when one looks down a precipice, one feels drawn to jump. If one refrains, it will hardly be said of one, "How prudent he is, he takes no chances". The avoidance of excesses of all kinds in one's own best interests is in this class. The habit of avoiding them the Greeks called temperance, a virtue distinct from prudence.

Another error is to equate the prudent with the expedient, and, again, the expedient with everything that is for one's own good. To save may be prudent; but whether it is expedient or convenient to start now is another matter. With a lot of money to spare at the moment it will be expedient; otherwise it will not. But it may be prudent all the same. Again, one marries in the hope of finding happiness; but marriage in this hope is not a marriage of convenience. The point is that reasons of expediency are reasons of a special sort: reasons for doing something on the ground that it is incidentally at hand to serve one's purpose, or because it serves a purpose quite incidental to the purpose for which one would normally be doing this thing. One marries for reasons of expediency when one marries for money, but not when in hope of finding happiness. Hobbes said that "men never act except with a view to some good to themselves". This would be quite different from saying that "they never act except with a view to what is expedient".

There is also this difference between the prudent and the expedient: one can speak of "rules of prudence", but less well of "rules of expediency". The expedient is what happens to serve. It is not therefore easily bottled in rules.

The word "prudence" is used too freely in still one more context. When one wishes to justify the social virtues to people, a traditional and inviting move is to refer them, among other things at least, to their own good. "You ought to hold the peace, be honest, share with others". "Why?" "Because an order in which such practices were universal is of vital concern to you; and your one hope of helping to make such an order is in doing your share". The classical formulation of this standard move is Hooker's, quoted with approval by Locke: "If I cannot but wish to receive good . . . how should I look to have any part of my desire herein satisfied, unless I myself be careful to satisfy the like desire: my desire therefore to be loved of my equals in nature, as much as possible may be, imposes upon me a *natural duty* of bearing to themward fully the like affection".

Now, it is said again, "So defended, the social duties come to no more than precepts of prudence"; and this goes with the veiled suggestion that it is morally improper to use this defense. But, even if so defended, the social duties are not necessarily reduced purely to precepts of prudence. For they may be recommended in this way either as mere *rules* or as *principles* of self-protection; and as principles they would be misdescribed as mere precepts of prudence. The distinction is this: When one says, "People ought to practice the social virtues, if only for their own benefit", one may be saying, "They ought to practice them for this reason as a *rule*, i.e., normally, as much as each time this is likely to be for their own good". Or one may be saying, "They ought to practice them for this reason not merely as a rule but as a *matter of principle*, i.e., every time, whether at that time this is likely to be for their good or not". And one might defend the adoption of this *principle* by saying, "Because your best, even if slim, hope of contributing to a society fit for you to live in lies in adding to the number of principled people who will do their share each time, without special regard for their good at that time".

Now this seems to me a precept of courage rather than one of prudence. The game of attempting by one's actions to make society a place fit for one to live in is a gamble worth the risk only because of the known price of not attempting it. This gamble is a root condition of social living. One is sure to give hostages to fortune, but again, what other hope has one got? Hence, if a man practiced the social virtues, thinking that he ought to as a matter of principle, and on these grounds, one will praise him for his *wisdom*, his firm grasp of vital issues, his stead-fastness, his courage. But one will not necessarily congratulate him on his prudence. For many times the prudent course might have been otherwise. It may be wise to persist in being honest with cheats, or forbearing with the aggressive, or helpful to those slow to requite helpfulness; but it might have been more prudent to persist for no longer than there was requital, or not even to start before requital was assured.

Now would it be a moral precept or not that, if only out of proper care for oneself, one ought to act on principles of wisdom and courage? That one ought to risk life in order to gain it? And, assuming a society of men acting fixedly on these principles but no others, would it or would it not contain men of moral virtue? One might as well ask, "Is a ski an article of foot-wear"? There is no more of a straight answer here than there. One may say, "Not quite"; and the point of saying this needs going into. But it would be more misleading to say, "Not at all". For it is part of the meaning of "moral precept" that it prescribes what a man would do in his wisdom—if he were to consider things widely, looking past the immediate concerns of self and giving essentials due weight before incidentals. As it is also part of what is meant by one's moral capacities that one can live by such considerations, it becomes fruitless after a time to press the point whether such precepts are properly called moral.

There are then varieties of the personal ought, differing in the considerations on which they are based and the qualities needed to follow them; and they all seem at least akin to a "moral" ought in their action-guiding force and function. But I grant that one does not want to speak of more than a kinship, and the point of this needs considering. One's hesitancy derives from various sources which have to be traced one by one.

Some of the hesitancy comes from contexts where one can say disparagingly, "He did this *only* for reasons of prudence, *only* for reasons of expediency, *only* for himself". This plainly applies sometimes, but it does not apply always. One would hardly say of someone without dependents, "He thought that he ought to save, but *only* for reasons of prudence"; or of someone, "He thought that he ought to have the carpenter in along with the plumber, but *only* for reasons of expediency or convenience"; or "He thought that he ought to become a doctor, but *only* because the career would suit him". "Only" has no point here. Why else should a man without dependents save, except to be prudent? Why else should anyone have the carpenter in along with the plumber, except for convenience? What better reason is there normally for choosing a career than that it will suit one? On the other hand, there is point in saying, "He held the peace only because it was prudent". "He saved only because it was convenient", "He practices the social virtues only for self-protection". It is plain why "only" applies here and is disparaging. One says "only" because something is done for the wrong or for not quite the right reason—done for *one* reason where there is *another* and nearer reason for doing it anyway. Personal reasons are often in this position, and then they are disparaged as inferior. One saves "only" because it is expedient, if one ought to have saved anyway for reasons of prudence. One holds the peace "only" because it was prudent when one ought to have done so anyway as a matter of principle and even if it had not been prudent. And one practices the social virtues "only" for self-protection when one does not *also* practice them for the general good.

The last case is different from the others. Plainly, one ought to practice the social virtues as principles of general good. But on none but perhaps pure Christian principles would it hold, or necessarily hold, that one ought to practice them on this ground unconditionally, however great the provocation to oneself. The case for the social virtues is weakened when the social environment becomes hostile and intractable by peaceable means; it is correspondingly strengthened where they can also be justified as wise principles of self-protection. That someone practices for-bearance "only" as a wise principle of self-protection is not therefore to say that he practices it for a reason which is neither here nor there; but rather for a reason which falls short of all the reason there is. This was, in effect, the view of the old Natural Law moralists—Hooker, Grotius, Puffendorf: the social virtues derive joint support from our natural concern for our own good and for that of society. Hobbes streamlined this account by denying the second, which provoked subsequent moralists to deny the first. Both Hobbes's sophistical toughness and the well-bred innocence of the academic moralists since are distorted visions which are less convincing than the unsqueamish common sense of the philosophers and divines of earlier times.

3

So far we have met no reason for deprecating every personal ought. Men often have cause to be temperate, courageous, wise for their own good. This is often the only, or the nearest, reason why they should. It is then pointless to go on complaining, "But they still only act so for their own sakes". "Only" is a dangerous word.

Even so one feels that somehow a commitment that has only personal grounds is morally inferior. "One ought to risk one's life in order to gain it" seems near-moral enough. But compare it with "One ought to risk one's life in order to save others". This still seems different. And this is so not only because the one has a personal reason and the other has not, but also because where the reason is social rather than personal, the ought itself feels different—more binding, more relentless, and more properly called "moral" for this reason. The real inferiority of the personal ought seems here to lie in a lack of formal stringency.

There are such differences of stringency between "I ought to save, as I *want* to provide for my future" and "I ought to save, as I *ought* to provide for my children". The first prescribes saving as a means to an end which one *is* seeking; the second as a means to an end which in turn one *ought* to seek. The first therefore commits one formally less than the second. It leaves one at liberty to escape the commitment by renouncing the ultimate end, which the second does not. One may, as Kant did, call the first ought hypothetical and nonmoral, and the second categorical and moral on account of this difference. The distinction is made to rest on a formal difference of the binding force and not at all on any material difference in the justifying grounds. The formally "moral" commitment is to an ultimate end or rule of life and to what one ought to do on account of it in any particular case.

Now the personal ought comes more typically as non-moral and the social ought as moral in form. One says, "You don't *want* to make your misery worse, so you ought not to dwell on it"; "You *want* to secure your future, so you ought to be prudent and save". One might also say "You *want* to provide for your children, so you ought to save"; and then formally this too would be a nonmoral ought although its grounds are other-regarding. But this is the less typical case. One is often more grudging about the needs of others than one's own. So there is here less occasion for saying, "You ought to do this on account of an end which you *are* seeking"; and more for saying, "You ought to do it on account of an end which in turn you *ought* to seek".

This typical difference between the personal and the social ought raises two questions: one, whether it is an inherent feature of the personal ought to be never more than non-moral in form; the other, whether, even if this were so, it would be any the worse as a possibly serious commitment. Both of these positions have been taken. One's own good one always seeks. It is not therefore among the ends which one ever ought to seek in the absence of a sufficient inclination. But with the good of others, or the avoidance of harm to them, it is different. Here are ends which one does not always seek, but ought to seek all the same: ends which one may still have reason for seeking on their own account; which one would be led to seek on a diligently comprehending and imaginative review of them (of what doing good, or harm, inherently amount to). Only the social ought, therefore, may bind one to the choice of the final end as well as of the means, while the personal ought binds one only to the means on account of an end which one wants already. The personal ought is therefore only nonmoral in form, and "only" once again signifies a defect. But all this is misleading. One does not always seek one's own good as much as one has reasonable ground for seeking it, and about this I shall say more later. But even supposing that one did, then all precepts of self-regard would prescribe what one ought to do consistently with an already desired end. But they would not therefore be negligible or improper all the time.

It is true that what one ought to do consistently with a desired end need not be what one really ought to do at all. The end, or the means toward it, may prove undesirable on further scrutiny either by reason of what it is in itself or of the special circumstances of the case. I ought to save as I wish for security, and there is nothing inherently wrong with the end or the means, and so far so good. But I also ought to support my mother, and I cannot do both. Then maybe I ought not to do *all told* what otherwise I ought to have done. But in this case, the precept of prudence would have been less than "only" nonmoral. It would have been invalid all told, and countermoral altogether. But surely not every case is like this.

For often there is nothing wrong with the things which one cares for on one's own behalf, and one really does care for them. Even if one had the abstract option to give them up, one has no serious wish to do so. One often does care for one's life or health or career or the regard of others, and one often *may* without violating other claims. And one always *may* care, if one does, for one's peace of mind or self-respect. And so what one ought to do as far as these ends go one really ought to do. As one wants to live, one really ought to look after one's health. As one wants to be liked by others, one really ought to keep a civil tongue. As one wants to live after one's own fashion, one really ought to stick to one's vocation in adversity. As one wants to be able to respect oneself or, in Hume's phrase, "bear one's own survey", one really ought to conduct oneself as one thinks that one has good reasons for doing. All these precepts tell one what one ought to do consistently with a personal end which one actually has at heart; and where they hold after scrutiny, they hold no less validly and conclusively than any fully "moral" precept. The conscientious man would have to take notice of them no less than of the others. They deserve to be called "semimoral" at least.

I keep allowing that a distinction remains. "I ought to work hard, as I *want* to succeed" is still a different kind of commitment from "I ought to work hard as I *ought* to provide for others". The difference is partly in the end, personal in the one case, impersonal in the other. But this quite apart, there is another reason for the difference. The second ought has a quality of sternness which is lacking from the first, and which is a product of its *form*, not of its *content*. For the second is an ought twice over. It says that one ought to take steps for an end which one ought to pursue ultimately. The first is an ought only once; it says that one ought to take steps for an end with regard to which one is at liberty as far as it goes. So the second ought subjects one to a regimen which is complete. It commits one *through and through*, whereas the semimoral ought does not. And this through-and-throughness gives to the moral ought its notoriously stern flavor. It makes it more imposing and often more onerous. One is having one's socks pulled up all over. And additional qualities are required of one for appreciating it and acting on it: not only forethought and consistency, but also the ability to appreciate an end as committing by reason of its own nature, which, among other things, requires sympathetic understanding and imagination. No wonder that a moral ought inspires those confronted with it with awe. The semimoral ought cannot compete with this, though when it comes to the precepts of wisdom and courage on one's own behalf they come near enough.

However, having given the formally moral ought its due, I want to add that respect for it should be no reason for slighting the other. For in the first place, and as a reassurance to those who regard lack of onerousness as a defect, though the semi-moral ought is not so bad, it may be bad enough. How hard it is to pull up one's socks does not necessarily depend on their number; two commodious socks may respond more readily than one shrunken one. One semimoral and one moral case may serve as examples. If one really *wants* to do a thing and do it well, one ought to take trouble. And if one really *ought* to do good to the sick, one ought to telephone and inquire how they are getting on. The first requires a lot: putting oneself into harness, forgoing all sorts of things which one would rather do, particularly at that moment, coping with aches and pains and anxieties, playing the endless game of snakes and ladders with achievement, and yet going on, nursing one's purpose. The second, though in form a commitment through and through, requires nothing but getting up and dialing a number. It may need a great deal not to put things off, not to dwell on one's miseries, not to spend improvidently, all simply because one really ought not to in one's own best interest. The ought that lays down the law on these things may be little imposing in form. But such is the bulk of the stuff which compounds the "moral" inconveniences of ordinary life. And one also measures oneself and others by the show that is made on this front.

But then it is not the lack of onerousness as much as that of formal stringency that is felt to discredit the semi-moral ought. It still is not binding like the moral ought, simply as it is not committing through and through. Moreover, its very subservience to an end which is only desired seems something amiss, as if a man should rather act always for the sake of ends which he ultimately ought to seek, and not just of ends which he happens to be seeking even if nothing is wrong with them.

This sense of guilt about the non-obligatory rests partly on excessive zeal for original sin. What the natural man in one desires never can be quite as it should. It is always "Tell me what you want to do, and I shall tell you what you ought to do instead". But there is also a failure to see that not every semi-moral commitment is renounceable at will. Not every situation need confront one with a commitment through and through, and it is improper to demand that it should or to deplore that it does not.

When one ought to do a thing on account of some desired end, then one need not always be at liberty to escape the commitment by renouncing the end. It depends on whether one is free to give up the end itself, and this is not always so. One says of some ends, "If you want to seek it you may, and if you don't want to you need not". There is here no reason against seeking the end, nor reason enough to tell one to seek it in the absence of a desire for it. And one is free to escape a commitment on account of such an end simply by giving up the end. But in the case of other ends one will say, "If you want to seek it you may, but if you do not want to you still ought to all the same". Again there is no reason against seeking the end if one wants to, but here there would be still reason for seeking it even if one did not want to. A commitment on account of such an end one may not escape at will as one is not here free to give up the end. It is arguable whether commitments on personal grounds are not often in this position. One ought to be temperate as one wants to preserve one's health. And although this is a semi-moral ought as far as it goes, one need not be free to get out of it at will. For even if one ceased to care about the end, one might still here have reasonable ground for caring, and ought to care all the same.

An ought of this kind commits one on account of an end which one seeks as well as ought to seek. And this makes it like an ought through and through, but still not quite. There can be ends which one seeks and ought to seek. But insofar as one *is* seeking such an end, it is strained to say that one also *ought* to seek it at the same time. One would rather say that if one were not seeking it already, then one ought to be seeking it all the same. This is why, if someone is perfectly willing about an end, a commitment on account of this end would still not for him have the form of a commitment through and through; and this although it is potentially such a commitment and would turn into one as soon as he ceased to be readily inclined toward the end.

The point is that ought applies only where there is a case for pulling one's socks up. The same action may be viewed in otherwise the same circumstances either as one which one ought to do, or as one which one wants to and may do, according to the psychological starting point. One normally wants to have one's breakfast, and one would find it improper to have it put before one with the remark, "You ought to eat this morning". "Why ought I? Don't I eat every morning anyway?" But if one were convalescent, the remark would be in place. Nor would one say to a notoriously indulgent parent, "You ought not to be harsh with your children" (though one might wonder whether he *may* be so indulgent). The remark applies to a parent bad at controlling his temper. If I resolved to become an early riser and succeeded, I might report in retrospect, "For the first month it was a duty, but afterward it ceased to be a duty and became a habit, if not a pleasure."

None of this should be surprising. Ought is an action-guiding concept. It expresses the notion that one is liable to direction by reasons in the case which would motivate one if one gave them due consideration. And one cannot be *liable* to direction by reasons except in a matter of doing what one is not fully motivated to do already. This is why it cannot be an obligation for one to do what one wants to do anyway, much as it might become an obligation for one to do it if one ceased to want to. This is also why, when one really wants to do something, the natural question to ask is not, "And *ought* I to do this thing?" but rather, "And *may* I do it?" or "Would there be anything wrong with it?" or "Ought I perhaps *not* to do it?" One looks for possible reasons against, not for possible reasons for. And what point would there be in doing anything more? When one really wants to do something, one already has, *for* doing it, all the reason one needs. And this is also why one only says "You ought to" to others when one takes it that there is a case for changing their present frame of mind. But to wonder whether one ought to (as distinct from wondering whether one may, or perhaps ought not to) where one already wants to would be like wondering whether to sit down when seated; and to say "You ought to" to someone quite ready to, would be like advising a sitting man to take a seat. *There is no ought for those blessed with wants which are not wrong.*

One may object: "But surely one can say that everyone ought to do good, and if there were benevolent people this would not make this false". And this is correct, but no refutation. What raises a problem are general statements like "People ought to do good". "One ought to be tolerant". But one may make a general statement without having to specify all the conditions when it shall or shall not hold. One says in general, "Butter will melt in the sun"; and if someone interjected, "But *not* when one has just melted it on the kitchen stove", this would be no rebuttal. "*This* butter will melt in the sun", when I am bringing it dripping from the kitchen, would be different. This particular butter is not *liable* to melt, even though it remains true that butter is. The same with "People ought to do good". This is a general statement, and one need not state the obvious: that it will not apply to someone whose heart needs no melting as it is soft already. Nor does one use "one ought to" directively to people, except for general purposes of propaganda. "I ought to" and "you ought to" are in a logically different class.

One makes general ought-statements about standard ends and practices toward which people commonly have no sufficient inclination. These ought-statements apply particularly to doing things for others, and less so to doing things for oneself. And this alone could explain why one normally does not say that people ought to care for their own good. For the question of whether they *ought* to does not here normally arise. They can be trusted with a modicum of well adjustment toward this end—they seek it, and, within limits, they may seek it. Hence, what one ought to do on account of one's own good is commonly a commitment on account of a desired end, much as it might also turn into a commitment through and through with a loss of immediate interest in the end. Nor could one reasonably hope that such commitments were more imposing in form than they are. On the contrary, one may say that the less imposing the ought, the better designed for living the man.

4

We are nearly out of the woods, but not quite. For the picture now before us still gives *Out* more than he can have. *Out* could say at this point:

By and large you have vindicated me. All your personal oughts are at best semimoral. Only what one ought to do on account of others is in any way like what one morally ought to do. In fact, you have explained why this is so. Men are more immediately and unreflectively drawn towards their own good than toward that of others. So the pursuit of their own good as an end never comes to them as an obligation. But in the matter of considering others they need the full treatment. Here they must learn to care for the end as well as the means, and to care for the end even at cost to themselves. To do what serves social ends therefore comes as obligatory on one through and through. And this is the moral ought, the one that pulls one up without further question all along the line. However, you have convinced me on one point. Personal commitments need not always be negligible or discreditable. Sometimes one really ought to be prudent or courageous in one's own best interest, and the conscientious man ought to take notice of this and to conduct himself accordingly. So in a sense perhaps there is a personal as well as a social morality. But I still insist that the two are not on the same level, that only the social commitments are in every way properly "moral,", and that only their neglect is a properly "moral" failing.

This statement calls for two comments. The first is that *Out* is already loosening the hold on his position. He has to speak of morality in a strict and in a broader sense, and of the conscientious man as doing his share by both. And this rightly so. By a conscientious person one understands someone who will not be evasive about anything that he is convinced he really ought to do. He is the right-living man of the Greeks whose first commitment is to the principle of self-guidance by good and sufficient reasons. To observe his socially grounded commitments will be an imposing part of his job. But the whole job will be to conduct himself in line with all valid commitments, no matter whether they are imposing in form or not. One may say if one wishes that his properly "moral" commitments are only those which commit him through and through and out of regard for others. But then it must be granted that there is more to being a right-living person than only observing one's "moral" commitments; and that the neglect of a nonmoral commitment, even if not strictly a "moral" failing, is nevertheless like one by being the evasion of a known commitment supported by valid reasons.

The second comment is that the case against *Out* needs pressing still further. It is also not the case that only the social commitments are ever fully moral in form. Commitments on personal grounds are less commonly so, because of the greater immediate regard which one has for oneself. One's own pain or unhappiness are closer to one than these same states in others. Unless they lie in the future it requires no effort of understanding and imagination to enable one to respond to them. But this immediate regard for oneself has its limits. Men may feel as unreasonably unconcerned for their own good as for that of others. Hume rightly spoke of "that narrowness of soul which makes us prefer the present to the remote"; and there are sick drives towards self-effacement and self-denial, so much so that it has been said that "man's inhumanity towards man is only equalled by his inhumanity towards himself". One meets the suggestion that everyone is at liberty to act as he will in the matter of his own life. But it would be odd if in this matter one were not liable to correction from a reflective appraisal of the nature of what one is doing. Men who are separated from their own good as an end may still have reasonable ground for seeking it in the absence of sufficient inclination. Their own good will then become something that they ought to seek and stand up for more than they are wont to or can readily bring themselves to; and to do the things which their own good requires will for them then become a commitment through and through.

It may also be that in a case like this someone ought to stand up for his own good even to the detriment of another. It could be sound advice to say to a woman in strife with herself and tied to a demanding parent, "You ought to consider yourself, and so break away now, hard as it may be on the parent". One is then saying more than simply, "If you wanted to you would have a right to." One is saying, "I know you are shrinking away from it, but this is what you ought to do, and above all else." In form this is an ought through and through, and an overriding one at that, but its ground is not other-regarding. And even true Christian charity might not here prescribe anything different. One cannot love one's neighbor as oneself if one has not also learned to accept one's own wishes as a proper object of respect and care, as one's own wishes are the paradigm of all wishes. There is a profound sense in which charity begins at home. For some this acceptance of themselves is hard, and it may confront them with a personal commitment as categorical and as onerous as any. Is this then a "moral" commitment or not? Here language fails one. For the usual conjunction between the categorical and the socially grounded commitment has come apart and turned into a clash. It is to strain the usual associations of language to the limit to speak of moral commitment to put one's own good before that of another. But the unqualified refusal to call this a moral commitment is strained too and may be tendentiously misleading. For apart from not being grounded in regard for others, such a commitment may be precisely like the typical moral commitment in its cogency, its form and its action-guiding relevance.

There is still another type of case. One's own good comprises not only one's states but also the possession of one's self as a mind. One cannot carnestly wish to lose hold of oneself, to be reduced to a shaky mess when in trouble; one needs to be in control and to be able to cope with whatever may come. And this preservation of onself as a capable ego is also something that one may find that one ought to care for when one is too driven or despondent to be inclined to care for it. Kant spoke of the duties of self-perfection, the commitments which subserve the protection of one's rational nature; and he did not hesitate to include them among one's moral duties along with the social ones. And this quite consistently so, as here is a type of concern for oneself for which one has reasonable ground though one is not always ready for it by inclination. Moreover, this type of personal commitment is morally relevant in a special way. For among the duties of self-perfection is the conscientious man's commitment to live without evading any issue — to seek out and weigh what cogent reasons would lead him to do, and to submit himself without self-deception or evasion to their determination. One cannot derive that one ought to live in this manner from one's special obligations toward others. For one may never duly confront any of one's special obligations unless one is already willing to live that way. All principled conduct which is reasoned practice and not just well-bred habit turns on this commitment as its pivot. It involves the acceptance of the principle of nonescapism as an over-all rule of life. And this commitment has the most intimately personal reason. It rests on an individual's inmost concern to preserve himself intact as a living and functioning self: mentally in possession of himself and of his world, able to look at himself and what he is doing without having to hide himself from himself. The penalty for slighting this need is his undoing as a person.

And now is one still to say that only what one ought to do with a view to the good of others can have the *cogency and force* of the "moral" commitment? The claim has been further reduced. Only most commitments which are committing through and through rest on other-regarding considerations. There can also be such commitments which rest on personal considerations, and they may on occasion take precedence over one's social commitments. And there is one commitment whose ground is intimately personal and which comes before any other personal or social commitment whatsoever: the commitment to the principled mode of life as such. One is tempted to call this the supreme moral commitment, but if no commitment may count as "moral" unless one has it on account of others, then the commitment to the practice of non-evasive living cannot properly count as a "moral" commitment at all.

That the social commitments make up the bulk of the formally imposing ones is, of course, a fact which one has no reason to deny. The good of others is the standard case of an end towards which men commonly find themselves less drawn by inclination than committed to on due reflection, through the exercise of understanding and imagination. But it illuminates the logic of the case that this is so as a matter of fact and of none else. Suppose that we were made the opposite of the way we are: that we were concerned about the good of others as immediately as we are now concerned about our own, and were concerned about our own good no more readily than we are now about that of others. Then the whole moral machine would be working busily in reverse. The bulk of the formerly imposing duties would be those which prescribe the subordination of our excessive regard for others to a proper regard for ourselves. Morality, in effect, would no longer serve primarily an order of mutual consideration, but the protection of the individual from being overwhelmed by his social sentiments. Nietzsche's transvaluation of all values was the claim that the hidden facts were such as to make this morality's real task. "Men are too weak-minded to be self-seeking". Their besetting vice is morbid pity, a guilty fear of their own wishes, self-hate, and resentment against others under the guise of concern. The moral machine needs putting into reverse.

I am not saying with Nietzsche that it does, though it may well with some. My point is rather to insist that a morality, if by this we mean a reasoned body of action-guiding principles and commitments, is always a morality for someone; and a morality for humans is one for humans. This is why in our morality, and in spite of Nietzsche, the socially grounded commitments have a special place. They are, even if not the only, the standard case of what reflective human beings meet as committing through and through. But this is so because men are what they are and their situation is what it is: because they do not live alone; because they can identify themselves with the concerns of others and of the communities of which they are members and can care about them; and because they can learn to care as much as they are able to by learning to comprehend. One commonly takes it that materially moral or social reasons are in some measure ought-implying for everyone. And this is fair enough if taken as a regulative principle, or presumption, with a massive, if incomplete, backing in experience. The presumption is that such reasons can be treated as standard reasons; that anyone can be taken to be accessible to them (although to an extent for which there is no standard measure) unless he is willfully uncomprehending, mentally disordered, or immature for reasons of age or cultural background. But there can be no demonstrative certainty of this being so. The case of an otherwise human being congenitally inaccessible to other-regarding considerations may be treated as *incredible*, but not as *inconceivable*.

There is also, however, the suggestion that one means by "moral" reasons more than this. "Moral" reasons are considerations of social good which are always binding, and in case of conflict with personal good, always *overridingly* binding on every reflective human being alike. But while one may *conceive* of moral reasons in these terms, there is nothing gained by doing so. For no conceptual gerrymandering can settle what will then be the crucial question, namely, whether what is here termed a "moral" reason is a concept applicable to human beings; and, if so to any extent, then by way of anything but a massively grounded presumption.

One may still say that the social commitments are the only "moral" ones properly so called. One is then making a *material* criterion a necessary condition for applying "moral" to a commitment. A "moral" commitment must not only be validly action-guiding and committing through and through; it must also be incurred on account of others. By this language rule, "moral" is used to mark off the species of social grounded commitments from the genus of validly action-guiding commitments in general. That there is this language rule is not disputed. The sole point at issue is that one should not be misled by it. The rule entails that none but the socially grounded commitments are properly "moral", but only for a reason which does not imply that they alone are seriously cogent, or committing through and through, or that they alone can take precedence in a proper calculus of action-guiding considerations. No answers to the questions, "How ought one to live?" and "What ought one to do?" must be taken as prejudged by the semantic taboo on calling a personally grounded commitment strictly "moral". No real-life possibility is excluded by the insistence that a Nietzschean "morality" would not properly be a "morality" at all. The question of what can or cannot be validly action-guiding principles and commitments for a reflective and human being is not settled by appeal to a linguistic convention.

5

I have argued that one may say that only the socially grounded ought is properly "moral"; but that, if the only reason for this is semantic, nothing substantial follows. Personal considerations, though not called "moral," could still be as seriously choice-supporting and binding on one as properly moral ones. But this conclusion may still seem unconvincing. One may object that we simply do not think that doing the right thing by oneself is ever *binding* on one in the same way as doing the right thing by others. In the matter of acting as we ought on our own account we consider ourselves free and not responsible to anyone. But in the matter of acting as we ought on account of others we consider ourselves obligated and responsible to them. This suggests that the personal and the social ought are not after all on the same footing; that the social ought carries with it an added authority which derives from the very fact that it is social, and that this is implied in calling it alone "moral".

It remains to be shown that here is another line of argument for the nonformalist, like *Out*, to follow; that this line of argument is indispensable to the understanding of the complex phenomenon that morality is; but that its ultimate relevance must not be overrated.

One may argue as follows. There is one plain difference between ought-abiding conduct in social and in personal matters. Other people have a stake in the first which they have not in the second. Their legitimate interests are involved in our social conduct; they hold us accountable for doing the right thing by them. This applies particularly to those rules and practices which, in a given society, are regarded as the backbone of the social order. Society credits its mature members with the ability to appreciate that they ought to respect these rules for their social merits. If they violate them without valid excuse they act counter to what others have a stake in their doing; and they are made responsible for their conduct. One may ask them to justify themselves, admonish and censure them. And this is why it may be said that the social ought alone is called moral; not only because it is social, but also because it has a special authority. When it comes to respect for social rules and the good of others, society obligates one to act as one ought on pain of moral sanctions. One is here, as it were, doubly bound; by the voice of reason and by the majesty of the law; by the knowledge that one ought to, and by one's accountability to others for doing it. None of this applies to one's conduct in the matter of acting as one ought on one's own account. One is not here socially obligated; one is a morally bad and socially guilty person for not acting as one ought.

Contemporary writers like Hart[2] are inclined to make this point more strongly. They suggest that the sense in which social ought-abidance is *obligatory*, and personal ought-abidance not, is the only proper sense of this term. Traditional philosophy, it is said, has ignored that "ought" and "obligation" are different concepts. Ought-language is "teleological"; only obligation-language is "deontological". That one ought to do something is to say that it is the "best" or "reasonable" thing to do, but not yet that one is obligated or bound to do it. Words like "obligation" or "duty" are at home in legal or quasi-legal contexts and apply only to social injunctions or prohibitions. Any other use of them is a philosopher's extension of language, a use which is as unwarranted as it is misleading. "Duties" are something assigned to one, "obligations" something imposed on one. Both are liabilities created by a public rule or requirement, or liabilities which one incurs by giving rise to claims against oneself as in giving a promise, or becoming a husband or father. It will then follow that a moral *obligation* can be only a liability created by a social rule or demand on one; and that what makes this liability "moral" is that its force derives from moral sanctions or from an internalized sense of moral propriety. The definitive authority which one associates with moral injunctions and prohibitions will then derive solely from this source. There may be things which one ought to do even on a desert

2. H. L. A. Hart, "Legal and Moral Obligation," *Essays in Moral Philosophy*, ed. A. I. Melden (Seattle: University of Washington Press, 1958), p 82.

island; but one is not bound, let alone morally bound, to do them outside a social context which alone can create an obligation.

Here, then, seems to be another way of diagnosing the formalist's error. He assumes correctly that moral judgments have a special authoritative role. And he argues from this that every authentic and definitive ought-judgment is a moral judgment. But it now turns out that no ought-judgment, whether its grounds are personal or social, has the characteristic force of a moral judgment. Moral judgments relate to obligations; ought-judgments only to what is "reasonable" or "best". Even what one ought to do on account of others is a *moral* ought only insofar as one is socially answerable for doing it. What falls within morality is only a segment of ought-abiding conduct. And what segment this is, what will count as *morally* obligatory or permissible, will be settled exclusively by our looking over our shoulders for the frowns and smiles of the social order. I doubt that those who press for a sharp distinction between "ought" and "obligation" would wish to go all the way with this conclusion. But this conclusion is implicit, and, given the premises, not easily avoided. If the conclusion seems extreme, the question is, Why?

There is rarely smoke without a fire: social ought-abidance plainly is of social concern, and blame and admonition have a place in it. Equally plainly, personal ought-abidance is treated differently. Our evasions here count as amicable vices, and not as moral turpitude. We may take the censure of others amiss, and require them to mind their own business. And the same with their admonitions. To say "you ought to" to another is always a kind of interference; and the propriety of *saying so* (as distinct from having a judgment about it) varies with the case. Ought-judgments and ought-speech, ought-judgments and judgments of blame or of praiseworthiness have different and variable functions. Again, the language of "ought" and "obligation" is infected with these distinctions. There is a sense in which obligations are social liabilities, and moral obligations such liabilities as are morally sanctioned. In this sense one has no obligation, moral or otherwise, to do the right thing by oneself. Nor has one, in this sense, a moral obligation to do everything that one's social conscience may tell one to do. Society only requires our conscientiousness in standard situations; it treats deeds which only an exceptionally sensitive regard for others would prescribe as acts of superarrogation. To devote one's life to the care of lepers is praiseworthy but "beyond the call of duty". But, true as this may be, this fashionable observation also shows the limitations of the view. We do not conceive of moral obligations as only dependent on social requirements and their external or built-in sanctions. Saints and heroes go beyond these in what they judge they must or ought to do. And it would be farfetched to say that, when they follow their judgment, they are not doing what they think is their duty. "Duty" and "obligation" are not words unequivocally tied to the socially obligatory.

Nor is the "morally permissible" tied only to the socially welcome. There may be occasions when someone may validly judge that he ought to put his own good before that of another. Here others may not readily welcome his ought-abidance. They may have a stake in discouraging it and be tempted to censure. But, granted that one accepts the authenticity of his judgment, one will here forbear censure, and consider him morally justified. The measure of moral justification is here his conviction that he ought to. But it is well to note how this case puts the social orientation of our moral thinking under stress. The upright deviant from social norms and interests is not judged "morally bad", but not "morally good" or "praiseworthy" either. We have to grant to others, as we must insist on for ourselves, that conscientious ought-abidance is the supreme moral rule for any agent in the situation of choice. But, socially, such conduct need not be an unmixed blessing. And if we may not condemn it on moral grounds, we need not bless it either. "Moral goodness" is a term of appraisal so geared to socially welcome conduct that not every morally *correct* choice makes one a morally *good* man.

There seems to be, then, a sense in which "ought" and "moral obligation" are not sharply separable; though there also is another in which they are distinct, and in which social ought-abidance has the added force of an obligation. How then do these two senses relate to one another? The question may be answered by considering the view that what gives to the social ought the force of a special *obligation* adds significantly to its action-guiding authority. For while this view is correct in one way, it is false in another. While social ought-abidance is required of us socially, we are surely not bound to it *only* on this account. The social ought differs in this respect from the obligations created only by law or custom. One has a legal obligation simply by being required by an appropriate public rule. But with the things which one ought to do on social grounds this is not so. What is here socially required of one is moral conduct: conduct in line with what one ought and can be reasonably expected to know that one ought to do. The very requirement presupposes that one has already an antecedent obligation to do it, insofar, namely, as one knows already that one ought to do it.

This would have seemed plain language in the past. What then is at issue in debarring us from using it? The traditional philosopher may have been guilty of an unidiomatic extension language in speaking here of an antecedent commitment or obligation. He may well have made light of the common or garden use of these terms for a liability created by an external rule. But sometimes an unidiomatic extension of language is less misleading than a narrow insistence on linguistic propriety; and if there is cause for complaint here the cure seems worse than the disease. The traditional philosopher wanted to bring out that if a deliberative person ought to do a thing he is to this extent also bound to do it *in some manner*. He is facing, if not a conventional, then a "natural" duty or obligation. And this extension of language has a warrant. Where one has an obligation or commitment to do something one is up against a characteristic constraint or limitation of one's freedom to act otherwise. And some language is needed to make the point that the demands or assignments of others are neither the only nor the most decisive form in which this constraint can be incurred.

A person who is obligated to do something is under a constraint which is not purely psychological or physical. He need not feel impelled to do it, he is not made to do it by main force, it is not causally impossible for him to act otherwise. The constraint is conceived as latent rather than actual, and as arising not from causes, but from reasons. The situation has features which *tell* for or against some action: they need not determine a person's choice, but they would if he knew them and took careful account of them. A deliberative person who can appreciate that he has such reasons will meet in them a latent limitation of his freedom to act otherwise.

Obligations in the common or garden sense are a special case of this. One meets a constraining reason in a social rule or demand on one which one can ill afford to ignore. Such obligations are imposed on one from without. The rule or demand issues from others; their insistence is the feature in the situation which supplies as well as creates the reason which limits one's freedom of action. But not all liability to direction by known reasons is like this. There are choice-guiding considerations which are not first imported into the situation by others with a view to direct one: they exist and can be found in the nature, effects, and implications of actions and principles themselves. A deliberative person need not wait for others to bring them to his notice; nor in being guided by them is he doing their bidding. That he is up against such reasons for doing things is equivalent to saying that he ought to do them, of his own accord and prior to being asked. This is why one may speak of a "natural obligation": of an *obligation* because a person is up against a latent limitation of his freedom by reasons; of a *natural* obligation because the limitation is the work here not of *anyone*, but of reasons to be found antecedently in the nature of the case.

Where one *ought* to do things on account of others, one is therefore *socially obligated* to do only what one has an antecedent natural obligation to do already. One is answerable to others, as someone against whom they have legitimate claims, precisely because one ought, and can know that one ought, to give them consideration to begin with. And this is why one's answerability to them cannot here significantly add to the weight and authority of one's commitment. It may do so de facto. When a person hesitates to do what he has no doubt that he ought to do, the reminder that he is accountable to others is a potent consideration. The mere thought of incurring recrimination and blame evokes apprehension and guilt. But these are not considerations to increase the force of a moral commitment de jure. A reflective person has no need of coercive reasons for acting as he ought. He does not require the fear of blame as a reason for not evading his own better judgment. And this is also why the absence of coercive reasons, where one ought to do things on one's own account, or on account of others, but beyond the call of conventional duty, could not allow one seriously to breathe a sigh of relief. Whatever one judges that one seriously ought to do, whether the reasons for doing it are ultimately social or personal, whether one is socially blameworthy for the omission or not, one is sufficiently committed to do and responsible to oneself for doing unasked. It is inconsistent with the concepts of mature moral thinking to keep looking for the differentia of the authority of the moral commitments in one's social answerability for observing them.

6

I am saying "with the concepts of mature moral thinking" advisedly. For the complex fabric of moral thinking contains still another notion of the moral bond. And the view that moral commitments have a special authority which derives from the sanctioned demands of the social order keeps drawing support from it. In fact, here is the primary concept of the moral bond, the one from which it derives its name, and the one which comes first, not only in the history of the race, but also in that of the individual. For as one grows up this is what happens. Father says, "Don't lie, don't be slovenly". Mother says, "This is what father says". The world says, "Don't be promiscuous". Father says, "This is what everyone says, this is also what God says". Father also says, "Do what God says", and, he says, "God says, 'Do what father says'." Here is a mixed barrage of requests made on one or reported to be made on one. They specify what one is to do or not to do. They come from "out there", though their precise imponent is obscure. They are addressed to one not without heat and are backed not by main force, like the law, but by moral suasion—smiles or frowns, approval or disapproval, the promise of bestowing or the threat of withdrawing love. And in these requests everyone first meets the demands of "morality". They are the first model for the notions of "moral law" and "moral duty", the first standard of "moral right" and "moral wrong". They create the moral obligations in their primary sense: as restrictions on one's freedom of action by the "mores" or "manners" of a social group. These obligations are like the legal obligations in being barriers against license maintained by social consensus for the protection of the social order. They only differ from them by the kind of sanctions employed, and by the absence of institutional procedures for their promulgation, codification, and administration.

Confusion keeps arising from the complex relations between the primary moral bond and the commitments of a reflective person by cogent considerations. As one's understanding develops one becomes acquainted and learns to live with both, yet without learning to keep them distinctly apart. One's moral commitments, in the mature sense, may oblige one to defer to the same rules on which the mores insist. In fact, this is how they come to be called "moral" commitments. The notion of the natural moral commitment arrives on the logical scene when it comes to be understood that a person who can use his own judgment does not need the insistence of the mores to defer to the rules which they prescribe. There are reasons why he ought to do so unasked, and, if not, then there are reasons why he ought to defer to other rules more adequate to the underlying social purposes of the moral code. This is how the word "moral" is transferred from the one level to the other. The commitments of a reflective person, by social considerations especially, are called "moral" because they incorporate and supersede the obligations by the mores in their role of protecting the social order. Social reasons become "moral" reasons, and the powers of mind and agency on which unforced self-direction by reasons depends, become "moral powers" on account of their continuity of function with the purposes of primary morality. But these new connotations are acquired at the loss of others. The newstyle moral commitment is no longer a creation of the social order. To call it "moral" is no longer to imply that its *authority* depends on the apprehension of guilt for the violation of a public rule. It is "moral" as backed by considerations which, while prior to the demands of primal morality, are favorable to its purposes; and it has authority if and when these considerations prove cogent on a due appraisal of the case.

This is how the word "moral" acquires its multiple associations. Such notions as the "moral order", or "moral rule", may all be viewed in *two ways*: as a body of rules or a rule publicly maintained by moral force; and as a body of rules or a rule which the members of a group ought, and can be expected to know that they ought, to respect unasked. Each time, the moral commitment to defer to the rule may be said to arise from the "requirements of the social order". But the ambiguities of this expression easily pass unnoticed. In the one case, the commitment arises from what the *will* of society "requires", i.e., insists on. In the other, it arises from what the *needs* of society "require", i.e., causally presuppose for their satisfaction, and from what a due appraisal of these needs "requires" one to do, i.e., provides one with telling reasons for doing. Both notions are settled parts of ordinary thought, in which the mind moves hazily from viewing the morally right or wrong as being so by a rule whose violation makes him socially guilty to viewing it as being so by a rule to which he ought to conform anyway. Moreover, the primary associations of "moral" are so ingrained that it is hard to appreciate that there really is a level on which public demands and the apprehension of incurring social guilt are irrelevant to the authority of a commitment considered as "moral". There is a standing temptation for the philosopher no less than for the ordinary person to import the quasi-legal features of the primary model into the mature one and to expect them to persist where they no longer have a place.

What furthers confusion is that even in the mature perspective the action-guiding role of the mores is not entirely superseded. There is a presumption (of which one can make too much as well as too little) that a rule strongly insisted on by the mores will also have valid prior reasons in its favor. And there is ground for caution in pitting one's own judgment too readily against the presumptive wisdom of the moral code. A commitment to a rule of the mores on this ground is still, in a way, created for one by the moral code. But there is a difference. The existence of the moral code is here no longer the *ratio essendi* of a moral commitment viewed as primal. It is rather that the moral code has become the *ratio cognoscendi* of a moral commitment on the level of maturity. A moral education is commonly a training in the mores as a first guide to what one is to do or not to do. But it will be a moral education in quite different senses, depending on whether one is introduced to the moral code simply as a body of morally sanctioned demands, or as a first, though by no means the last, ground for the determinations of mature moral thinking.

I have argued that the mature moral commitments are incurred through the unforced appreciation of cogent reasons in the case. Their authority owes nothing to the coercive moral pressures. They are roughly called "moral" because they are commitments which supersede the primary moral law in its action-guiding role. But the question of why and when they strictly deserve this name cannot well be settled.

We are inclined to conceive of morality by the joint application of two criteria. "Moral" principles commit one in a special and cogently authoritative manner; and they commit one in this manner to conduct which is, or is held to be, socially desirable. This concept is applicable well enough to primary morality. The primary moral law (on its own level and by its own means) supplies an authoritative rule of life which obligates everyone alike, and in the social interest. The coincidence between rules with moral force and in the service of social ends can here be counted on: it is contrived, albeit unwittingly, and where it is wanting it can be mended. One can define morality, on the primary level, as authoritative action-guidance whose function is to regulate the social order. But morality, on the mature level, is less well-conceived in this way. There are difficulties in uniting the authoritative and the social associations of "moral" in one concept.

It is plainly not the principal function of mature morality to protect the social order, if by the "function" of a practice is meant the reason why it exists and is carried on. The commitments by cogent reasons in the case are not imposed on one from without for social ends. One incurs them, if through anyone's doing, through one's own: as someone willing to seek direction from the counsel of cogent reasons. The involvement of human beings in this practice is personal: it turns on their stake in the kind of self-preservation which requires that one should be able to bear before oneself the survey of one's own actions. Responsibly reason-guided and ought-abiding living exists, in the first place, for the sake of sane and ordered individual being, and not for the regulation of the social order. Nor is the coincidence between ought-abiding living and the social interest axiomatic.

The fact—which traditional moral philosophy seems almost to exist to dispute away—*is that primary morality has no unequivocal successor on the level of autonomous choice*. The "moral law" (whether the actual law of the tribe, or the ideal law that would best suit its needs) has no identical counterpart in a "law of our own nature". It is true that the commitments by non-coercive reasons (like the primary moral law) supply a *definitive* guide to conduct on their level; and that where they have other-regarding grounds, they are in the *social interest*. But the agreement between the definitive commitments on this level and those typically geared to the social interest is not here guaranteed. The agreement is not contrived; the social order cannot lay down what reflective choice shall bid a mature person do, or for what reasons. Nor is the agreement logically necessary. Valid ought-judgments rest on the backing of choice-supporting reasons: of facts in the case which can dispose those who know and review them in favor of or against the choice. There is therefore no logical limit to what may be a valid ought. The care of others may be a valid ought for one, and so may be the proper care of oneself. Either end may manifestly direct one to seek it on a diligently comprehending view of it. Either, or both, may be valid premises for a particular ought-judgment. One may be conscientiously ought-abiding in serving one's community, or in seeking personal salvation behind the walls of a Buddhist retreat. Considerations of prudence and wisdom may relevantly add to the reasons why one ought to practice the social virtues, along with reasons of humanity and compassion. What is judged a valid ought, on a due appraisal of the facts and their force for one as deciding reasons, may have all manner of grounds; it may protect individual as well as social needs; it need not be the same for everyone alike. Nor need every ought be an ought for one through and through in order to be a seriously cogent ought, and among one's responsibilities as a right-living, reason-guided person. The ought-judgments which are formally imposing and backed by materially moral considerations are the standard case for human beings of the formally imposing ones; but they are no more than a species of the broad genus "definitively action-guiding ought-judgments".

Is one to say then that the mature moral enterprise is the general practice of conscientiously ought-abiding living? Or that it is only the part of it which is socially beneficial and a matter of active social concern? Are the mature moral commitments those which *formally*, or only those which *formally and materially*, continue the job of the primary moral law? Usage here leans uneasily either way. That man is a "moral agent" with "moral freedom" is associated with his power for responsible self-direction. "Moral strength" or "moral weakness" are terms which relate to the exercise of this power. But the "morally good man" connects with the "selfless man." The "moral" commitments of a mature person are conceived as essentially self-incurred through the responsible exercise of his moral powers and also as grounded in regard for others. There are those who insist that mature morality is socially beneficial ought-abidance: that language prescribes a material as well as a formal criterion for the use of "moral". There are others who will call "moral" any definitive and "authentic" commitment of a self-directing person, whether its grounds are social or personal.

Here is a semantic issue which it is far more important to understand than to take sides on. For whatever one says—whether it is the more consonant with ordinary language or not—must be semantically disquieting. Usage (at any rate, current English usage) backs the nonformalist more than the formalist. The mature moral commitments are those to conduct which is of social concern: they are properly called "moral" *as they supersede the primary moral law in its social role*. This usage is unexceptionable as long as its implications are faced. The *moral* and the *definitive* commitments on the mature level need not then coincide. One must grant that "morality" on this level is demoted from its accustomed place of being the sole and final arbiter of right and wrong choice. This is why, much as the nonformalist has semantically a case, the formalist has one too. He is opting for the other horn of the dilemma. The moral commitments on the mature level are *those which supersede the primary moral law in its role of supplying an authoritative and supreme rule of life*. And this rule is in the definitive—but not necessarily only materially moral—commitments which a reflective person incurs on a non-evasive appreciation of all the reasons in the case; and, in the last analysis, in his first commitment to the "authentic" way of life itself.

If both alternatives are repugnant, it is because both fall short of expectations. The unequivocal successor to the primary moral law should be a commitment by noncoercive reasons, manifestly binding on everyone alike, to give precedence always to the claims of beneficence and the requirements of social living. But there is no warrant for assuming such a commitment on the level of autonomous choice. The rules of language cannot furnish it any more than pure reason, or intuition. The hard fact is that the rational and autonomous mode of life overlaps, but no longer necessarily coincides, with the moral mode of life as conceived from the point of view of the social interest. The autonomous agent can be a debatable social asset. It is vain to expect morality on all levels to do the same kind of job as the institution of the law. The concept of morality itself bears the accumulated scars of conceptual evolution. Its multiple associations are a bar to summing it up in any one way.

12

Why It's Bad to Be Bad

PAUL BLOOMFIELD

The perennial question regarding the relationship between morality and self-interest may be broken down into two halves: the question of whether or not it is good to be good, and whether or not it is bad to be bad.[1] In the end, the former question proves to be even more complicated and subtle than the latter, and will have to be addressed elsewhere. Here, we will stick to the still quite formidable challenge of becoming clear on why it is bad to be bad.

The question "Why is it bad to be bad?" might seem either tautologous or poorly formed.[2] It may seem like a tautology because it seems logical to think that badness is necessarily bad and so it must, of course, follow that it is bad to be bad. It might seem to be malformed because it may seem like anyone who asks the question, "Why is it bad to be bad?" must fail to understand the meaning of the words they are using: generally, if something is X, it cannot fail to be X. If so, then it may seem as if there must be something wrong with the question itself or with the linguistic abilities of the person asking it.

Nevertheless, the question, "Why is it bad to be bad?" turns out to be a good question, indeed, a very important question when it is treated as elliptically incomplete.

1. I'd like to thank Richard Joyce, Stephen Finlay, Donald Baxter, Michael Lynch, Diana Meyers, Joel Kupperman, Margaret Gilbert, Sonia Michel, Walter Sinnott-Armstrong, Stephen Darwall, Marvin Belzer, Sangeeta Sangha, Harvey Siegel, Michael Slote, Mitchell Joe, Glendon Good, and Paul Beatty for their help and encouragement.

2. In his essay, "Why Not Be a Bad Person?" (in *Moral Literacy* [Indianapolis: Hackett] 1993) Colin McGinn begins his discussion of some of these matters by suggesting that "goodness is good" is a tautology. Though not cast explicitly in the terms above, H. A. Prichard famously argued that asking for a justification for morality shows that one must not understand what morality is ("Does Moral Philosophy Rest on a Mistake?" *Mind* 21 [1912]: 21–37). D. Z. Phillips argues that we must not attempt to give nonmoral reasons for being moral ("Does It Pay to Be Good?" *Proceedings of the Aristotle Society* [1964–65]: 45–60); see also, John Hospers, *Human Conduct*, 3rd ed. (Fort Worth: Harcourt Brace, 1996).

On the other hand, see, David Schmidtz's contribution to the present volume.

The question seems most likely to come up in discussions about the justification of morality in the face of objections to its (supposedly deleterious) effect on self-interest. It emerges when asking what appear to be reasonable, and hopefully answerable questions, such as, "Why should I not profit from this act of injustice?" Asking such questions may assume that "profit" is whatever is in the asker's (perceived) self-interest and that acts typically thought of as "unjust" are those prohibited by the conventionally accepted moral theory. Framing these issues without making assumptions both about what is in a person's self-interest, as well as about what morality requires, is part of the problem. At least, it seems reasonable to think that common sense rightly assumes a modest fallibilism with regard to the capacity of members of *Homo sapiens* for knowing about self-interest and morality. A neutral way of casting the discussion is that it concerns the proper relationship, whatever it may be, of morality to self-interest, whatever they may be. Given that this sort of discussion seems typical of when the question comes up, it seems natural to fill out its ellipsis with the terms of the relationship of morality and self-interest: if someone asks why it is bad to be bad, one important question they may be asking is, "Why is it bad for me, all things considered, to be morally bad?"

The inclusion of "all things considered" is crucial (though it will often be left out below). Some think that there is a problem with the idea of an all-things-considered point of view since it seems to them that the plurality of values one attempts to bring together in a single perspective may be incommensurable, so there is a problem in the idea of engaging such a perspective.[3] And while there may be problems regarding the rational commensurability of different values, these issues can be sidestepped by focusing on the normatively neutral yet fully practical issue of how we actually succeed in making real-life decisions about what to do. All that is meant here by the "all-things-considered perspective" is the point of view that is adopted by people when faced with real-life, difficult, practical decisions that must be made, where some action (or inaction) is required, and they determine what to do through fallible deliberation upon all the relevant and available aspects of the case. In such cases, when "all things have been considered", people make decisions as best they can that this, as opposed to that, is to be done. Similarly, even moderately reflective people occasionally make decisions about how they wish to live their lives, deciding what sort of people they wish to be and in so doing, they may want to know what is best for them when all relevant considerations have been made salient. They want, in other words, to know what is best for them, all things considered. Alternatively, we can ask whether something is bad for a person, all things considered, and if it is, then it seems fair to say of that something that it is harmful to a person's self-interest. When people ask "Why is it bad to be bad?", they want to know what the harm to them is, all things considered, in acting immorally, in being immoral.

3. See Stephen Finlay's contribution to this volume. See also David Copp, "The Ring of Gyges: Overridingness and the Unity of Reason," *Social Philosophy and Policy* 14, no. (1997): 86–106. For further discussion, see Michael Stocker, *Plural and Conflicting Values* (Oxford: Clarendon Press, 1990). For another contrasting view, see Ruth Chang, "'All Things Considered,'" *Philosophical Perspectives* 18 (2004): 1–22. I thank Ruth Chang for discussion on this topic.

Traditionally, there have been two sorts of answers to the question of why it is bad to be bad. The first is to say it is not, in fact, bad to be bad; that is, it is not harmful to be immoral. Such an answer generally comes, however, with the proviso that the person is not caught or punished for being bad.[4] Such an answer is generally given by people who think that the only valid reason for being morally good is that most people who are morally bad end up being punished for it; as a matter of fact, most people are better off if they are morally good. These people think that the green bay tree does occasionally flourish. Most of them go on to think that if a person were truly stronger than everyone else and, as such, could not be harmed or punished by others, that person would then have no reason to be moral; other than the harms of punishment, there are no harms incurred to one's self-interest by being morally bad. Views belonging to this roughly characterized family can be found in the thoughts and/or writings of Thrasymachus, Callicles, Epicurus, Machiavelli, Hobbes, Hume, Nietzsche, and, more modernly, Gauthier and other rational choice theorists.[5] For simplicity's sake, we can call this "Thrasymachus's view".

The second traditional answer to the question is that there is in fact harm done to a person by being morally bad. For example, in *Gorgias*, Socrates argues that it is worse for a person to harm others who are innocent than it is for that person to be harmed if he or she is innocent. The argument, however, does not say exactly what the harm is in harming others and being clear about this has been the traditional dif-

---

4. If one gets caught at being bad, then (in one sense) one is being bad at being bad. It is necessary for being good at being bad (in this same sense), that one does not get caught. This reads "being bad" as a success term, and Thrasymachus can be read as thinking of "being bad" in this way. He says "Do you suppose I would describe someone who makes mistakes as the stronger party when he is making a mistake?" (*Republic*, 340c). See also the following discussion between him and Socrates regarding technical mistakes in ruling, medicine, and math. On Thrasymachus's view, getting caught at being bad implies making a mistake.

5. I do not mean to imply that the philosophers listed here take Thrasymachus's view as their final and settled normative position; rather, all these philosophers have, at least, seriously entertained such a position. Some comments I have received registered surprise by the presence of Epicurus and Hume on the list. The former is present given that he thought that the virtues are only instrumentally valuable for the way they make long-lasting pleasure/tranquility more likely. The latter I include because of the following paragraph from the *Enquiry into the Principles of Morals*, sect. 3, part 1:

> Were there a species of creatures intermingled with men, which, though rational, were possessed of such inferior strength, both of body and mind, that they were incapable of all resistance, and could never, upon the highest provocation, make us feel the effects of their resentment; the necessary consequence, I think, is that we should be bound by the laws of humanity to give gentle usage to these creatures, but should not, properly speaking, lie under any restraint of justice with regard to them, nor could they possess any right or property, exclusive of such arbitrary lords. Our intercourse with them could not be called society, which supposes a degree of equality; but absolute command on the one side, and servile obedience on the other. Whatever we covet, they must instantly resign: our permission is the only tenure, by which they hold their possessions: our compassion and kindness the only check, by which they curb our lawless will: and as no inconvenience ever results from the exercise of a power, so firmly established in nature, the restraints of justice and property, being totally useless, would never have place in so unequal a confederacy

ficulty. In the end of *Gorgias*, Plato has Socrates appealing to rewards and punishments in the afterlife. He famously tries to give a different answer in *Republic* in terms of "psychic harmony", but it is generally agreed that the metaphor does not have much success. He gives another attempt, perhaps better, though less well known and very undeveloped, in the *Theatetus* digression (176a–177b). Let's call "Socrates' view" all which claim that there is a harm in being morally bad. The present essay falls within this tradition.

As noted, in this debate between Thrasymachus's and Socrates's view, there has been a recurring problem with the meanings of the terms of the debate: each side seems to talk past each other in their uses of normative terms like "moral" and "immoral". It is best then to renew the debate by first settling some neutral usage for these terms.

The words "moral" and "immoral" have many connotations and denotations, and often what happens is that questions are begged at the normative level when the debate is being pressed over whether it is harmful to be immoral: when giving answers it is common to assume the content of a particular moral theory not necessarily shared by those who disagree about the harmfulness of immorality. Both sides assume an appearance/reality contrast, both thinking the other sees only appearances. For example, Thrasymachus, who thinks that it is not bad to be bad, can be read as telling us that being "morally good" is for the dupes or the sheep and is not truly in a person's interest; rather, given his understanding of what is "truly in a person's interest", what is called "moral" or "immoral" is determined by those with power in order to serve the true interests of those powerful people.[6] When Thrasymachus prescribes a life of "immorality", he does so with an understanding that the meanings of "moral" and "immoral" are conventionally fixed and so come only with an illegitimate, merely conventional authority attached to them. In rejecting "morality", Thrasymachus sees himself as rejecting the illegitimate normative authority of social convention. Famously, Thrasymachus thinks that "clever and good" people reject morality (349d). On the other side, those who defend morality also often make assumptions about "self-interest" and "morality" in discussions of "amoralism" or "immoralism". On some understandings of "morality", a theory prescribing full-fledged egoism may not even count as a moral theory, though it may be prudential.[7] As a result of these normative assumptions, theoretical questions end up being begged on both sides of the debate.

---

6. While Thrasymachus does not put his point in explicitly semantic terms, see *Republic* 359a for Glaucon's statement of how moral terms gain their meaning. See also Nietzsche's *On Genealogy of Morals* (Cambridge: Cambridge University Press, 1994), First Essay.

7. It is not uncommon to find philosophers who seem to be asking purely metaethical questions about what morality is and answering them while employing a particular normative theory about what counts as moral, as opposed to immoral, behavior. See, for example, Prichard ("Does Moral Philosophy Rest on a Mistake?"), who seems to be assuming some deontological moral theory in his essay on why morality cannot be justified, or D. Z. Phillips ("Does It Pay to Be Good?"), where he argues against giving nonmoral reasons for being moral while assuming that self-interested reasons are nonmoral reasons. For a discussion of similar issues, see William Frankena's "The Concept of Morality," *Journal of Philosophy* 63, no. 21 (Nov. 10, 1966): 688–96.

We can, however, establish the debate neutrally by distinguishing two senses of "morality", a descriptive sense and a normative sense.[8] A descriptive sense of "moral" contrasts it to whatever is "nonmoral". This sense is at play in discussing moral agents or moral theories when setting these up against a nonmoral contrast class: so children and the insane are not moral agents, while (roughly) sane adults above a minimal level of intelligence are responsible moral agents; quantum theory is a nonmoral theory while ethical egoism and deontology are moral theories. The normative sense of "morality", on the other hand, is the one in which "moral" contrasts with "immoral". In this sense, we make normative distinctions among those theories which we descriptively call "moral theories", and say that one of the descriptively called "moral theories" is normatively the most *moral* of these theories, and it is the best or true moral theory (in the descriptive sense). The true moral theory (whatever it may be) is subscribed to by those who are truly good people (whomever they may be). Other descriptively moral theories are bad, to one degree or another, and lead to immorality or are themselves perniciously immoral. So, in the descriptive sense of "moral", bad moral theories or theories that lead to or prescribe immorality are still moral theories; in the normative sense, those theories that prescribe immorality are not moral theories at all. In the normative sense, having "bad morals" is having no morals at all; in the descriptive sense, one can have bad morals and still be a moral agent, since immoral agents still count as responsible "moral agents"; normatively immoral agents are descriptively bad moral agents.

It then makes sense to say, in a descriptive sense, that Thrasymachus's view represents a moral theory.[9] We can avoid begging any questions against his view at the normative level by leaving it open as to whether Thrasymachus has a bad, immoral, or harmful moral theory or, on the other hand, a good, moral, or beneficial moral theory. Given the descriptive sense of the term moral, both Thrasymachus and Socrates have moral theories and the debate proceeds by trying to determine which (descriptively) moral theory is the (normatively) good one, and which are the (normatively) bad ones; which is what a person should subscribe to, all things considered, and which should be avoided "at all cost". The situation can be pictured as if Thrasymachus and Socrates have moral theories that are at opposite ends of a continuum of descriptive moral theories with one end labeled "Good Moral Theories" and the other labeled "Bad Moral Theories"; the debate is over whose theory belongs on which side of the spectrum. Or one may imagine Thrasymachus and Socrates standing with their backs to each other, both pointing forward and saying a person ought to go in the direction they are pointing. We need to get our moral bearings straight and only one of our two guides can be correct. What is needed to determine who is right and who is wrong is a consideration that everyone agrees is relevant to what is bad for a person, which could show that one of these moral theories is bad for people, taken as individuals, all things considered.

8. I am not the first person, of course, to point out this distinction; see, for example, William Frankena, ibid.

9. This is to read Thrasymachus as being a eudaimonist and is similar to the reading of him given by Julia Annas in her *An Introduction to Plato's Republic* (Oxford: Clarendon, 1981). Philippa Foot takes a similar line toward Nietzsche in the final chapter of *Natural Goodness* (Oxford: Oxford University Press, 2001).

The answer proffered here is that only one of these theories makes it possible, in principle, to have self-respect (in a sense of "self-respect" to be discussed below). It is hard to imagine someone denying that a way of life that makes it, in principle, impossible for a person to have self-respect could be anything but bad for a person, all things considered. Happiness or living well, whatever it is, requires self-respect. It may not be impossible to deny this, and below a response to this denial will be given. The important conclusion is that if one lives in accordance with Thrasymachus's moral theory, then one will be kept from having self-respect: adopting an immoral lifestyle, such as one quintessentially characterized by injustice or unfair dealings with other people, establishes a moral psychology (in the descriptive sense of "moral") that is, to coin a phrase, "divided against itself" in such a way as to prevent that person from having self-respect. Let us now begin the argument for this conclusion.

The strategy is Platonic. We imagine the best-case scenario for the immoral person, namely one in which an individual "gets away" with every immoral deed. We then inquire about whether or not the immoral person has harmed himself or herself, despite not being caught by others. What we are to imagine as our paradigm of immorality is someone who acts unfailingly for his or her own perceived benefit, attempting to maximize it. This is, I take it, someone who fully lives the theory that Thrasymachus espouses. Such people try to gain the upper hand over everyone else whenever possible (349c). This person may be called the "pleonectic", based on the Greek "pleonexia", which literally translated means "having more", though it is often poorly translated as "greediness" or "covetousness". *Pleonexia* is a Greek contrast to *dikaiosyne* as intemperance is a contrast to temperance. *Dikaiosyne* has traditionally been translated as "justice", and it is for this reason that the *Republic* is often thought of as a work in political theory. But a number of scholars of Greek philosophy have noted that *dikaiosyne* is less legalistic and broader than our idea of justice, applying to all our interactions with other people, and is captured more by the idea of "right or fair dealings with others".[10] On some understandings of the meaning of "morality", it is apt to translate *dikaiosyne* as "morality".[11] Pleonectics do not deal fairly with others: they try

10. For example, Gregory Vlastos writes, "I shall use 'justice' and 'just' merely as counters for *dikaiosyne* and *dikaios*, whose sense is so much broader, covering all social conduct that is morally right". See his "The Argument in the *Republic* That 'Justice Pays,'" *Journal of Philosophy* 65, no. 21 (1968): 665–74. For more discussion on this point, see Julia Annas, *Platonic Ethics: Old and New* (Ithaca, N.Y.: Cornell University Press, 1999).

11. This is on a narrow reading of "morality" in which a theory does not count as a moral theory if it does not concern itself with the claims of others in determining what the agent ought to do. This seems to be the sense best captured by Robin Waterfield's translation of *Republic* (Oxford: Oxford University Press, 1993). It is markedly better than any which translates *dikaiosyne* as mere "justice", since it is natural on even Thrasymachus's view to understand *dikaiosyne* as being broader than justice per se. Typically, on such views, "morality" is taken to be opposed to self-interest, if we assume that "getting more" is in a person's self-interest. In fact, however, there is reason to think that Socrates' view of morality is even broader than its being concerned with *dikaiosyne* or "right or fair dealings with others": morality for him is intrapersonal as much as interpersonal; temperance and courage would count as "moral virtues" just as much as *dikaiosyne* does. Articulating this view in full goes far beyond the scope of this essay. Here, the concern is with the harms of Thrasymachus's view.

to "get the better" of everyone else, or to "set themselves up as superior" (*Republic*, 349b); they want as much as possible, whenever resources are to be divided among all. Like all character traits, pleonexia comes in degrees, but in its most extreme form, pleonectics are willing to do "whatever it takes" to "get what they want" and are bound only by their fear of punishment; they do not blanch at the thought of using or manipulating people as pawns or instruments in their own schemes or at acts of disloyalty and betrayal; in fact, such behavior may be their typical *modus operandi*. This is what Thrasymachus thinks "clever and good" people will do.

It is crucial to see that pleonexia comes in degrees. The argument given below is intended to cover cases in all degrees; the conclusion is that the degree to which one is immoral is the degree to which one's self-respect is harmed. So it is intended to capture the harms of immorality that are due to even infrequent acts of immorality. The harm done by immorality will be proportional to its frequency and intensity. Following Aristotle, we may note that one swallow does not make a summer, and conclude that very small, highly infrequent acts of immorality will not ruin a life: one may yield, now and then in one's life, to the temptation to say something cutting or perhaps even cruel without this ruining one's life. On the other hand, torturing just one baby for fun would be an indication that one's psychology is so twisted that one's life cannot be a good and admirable, or envious life, regardless of what other beneficent acts one performs.[12]

As familiar as pleonexia might be as a human characteristic (at least in many less severe cases), little positive account about the moral psychology of the pleonectic has been written.[13] Luckily, there has been a small literature on another character trait that

---

12. In many of the conversations I've had about this topic with philosophers, Woody Allen's movie *Crimes and Misdemeanors* has come up. In the movie, a seemingly good and philanthropic doctor has his inconvenient mistress murdered and seems to be unaffected, in the long run, by this evil act. The argument presented here has been constructed with cases such as this in mind.

13. The little that has been written is inconclusive. Both Bernard Williams and Philippa Foot deny that unjust acts have any single or systematic cause; they agree that both lust and greed can be the motive of people to act unjustly. In view of this, it may seem apt to deny pleonexia as the vice opposed to justice, though in their writings on justice as a virtue neither say anything substantive about pleonexia itself. In any case, I think both are mistakenly concerned with particular "motives" (in Williams, 192) or "springs of action" (in Foot, 9) that lie behind just acts and unjust acts and to this degree are chasing red herrings instead of character traits: pleonexia leads to unjust acts through the greed and lust it inspires. David Sachs makes the beginnings of a positive account of pleonexia as a character trait in his "Notes on Unfairly Gaining More: Pleonexia," in *Virtues and Reasons*, ed. R. Hursthouse, G. Lawrence, W. Quinn (Oxford: Clarendon, 1995). For Williams, see "Justice as a Virtue," in *Essays on Aristotle's Ethics*, ed. A. Rorty (Berkeley and Los Angeles: University of California Press, 1980); for Foot, see "Virtues and Vices," in *Virtues and Vices* (Berkeley and Los Angeles: University of California Press, 1978).

Though he does not refer to it as pleonexia, F. H. Bradley, in his *Ethical Studies* (Oxford: Oxford University Press, [1876] 1927), seems onto the same idea in defining "selfishness":

> The selfish man, so far as he is selfish, has objects of desire that are not subordinated to any principle higher than his private satisfaction. If you ask what is the general end which includes his ends, you can point to none; but you find that he treats all objects as means, that he cares

is similar to pleonexia insofar as it is characteristic of people who think they deserve more than others, namely arrogance. Arrogant people think they deserve more respect or better treatment than others, and insofar as this is true they are guilty of a "double self-deception": they judge themselves indulgently and they take their own motives to be the motives of duty.[14]

Before pulling apart these two self-deceptions, explaining what is meant by "self-deception" is necessary. I roughly follow the analysis of it given by Robert Audi, wherein a person is self-deceptive with regard to the truth of a proposition if the person who asserts its truth also knows or has good reason to believe that it is false, while simultaneously having a desire for the belief to be true that explains why the reason to think it is false is not given any credence or is ignored outright.[15] So, if one (consciously or unconsciously) recognizes that one has reason to disbelieve a proposition that one wants to believe, and as a result (consciously or unconsciously) ignores this evidence, perhaps because of its undesirable consequences, then this constitutes self-deception about the truth of the proposition.

We can distinguish the two self-deceptions involved in arrogance by noting that in judging themselves indulgently, on the one hand, arrogant people overlook their own deficiencies and weaknesses, ignore their failures and inadequacies while inflating the deficiencies, weaknesses, failures, and inadequacies of others. On the other hand, they inflate the quality and worth of their performances and contributions while discounting those of other people. One way of seeing this failure is as one of not judging in accordance with supervenience: arrogant people do not judge like cases alike. Rather they are prejudiced toward themselves; they think their actions are better than those of others just because their actions are theirs, so underlying

---

for none in itself, but will sacrifice any with readiness; and when you inquire what is common to them all, you find that they minister to his personal comfort; this comfort being a certain quantum of the pleasant and absence of pain, which satisfies him, and which he either consciously aims at or unconsciously uses as a measure of all objects of desire. (274–75)

14. I take much from Robin Dillon's excellent "Kant on Arrogance and Self-Respect," in *Setting the Moral Compass*, ed. C. Calhoun (New York: Oxford University Press, 2004) 191–216. See 208 of Dillon for the phrase "double self-deception". I also found the following helpful in understanding arrogance: Lewis White Beck, *A Commentary on Kant's Critique of Practical Reason* (Chicago: University of Chicago Press, 1960) 219–22; and "Arrogance" by V. Tiberius and J. Walker in *American Philosophical Quarterly* 35 (1998): 379–90.

Dillon's work on arrogance is informed by Stephen Darwall's important essay "Two Kinds of Respect" (*Ethics* 88, no. 1 (October 1977) 36–49). The literature on respect is quite deep. I found helpful Elizabeth Telfer's, "Self-Respect" in *Philosophical Quarterly* 18 (1968): 114–21. In a fashion similar to Darwall, she also distinguishes two kinds of self-respect, one based on what one has done or accomplished and the other based on a conception of some minimal standards of humanity or decency below which one's actions ought not to slip. Here, I am concerned with this latter form of self-respect.

15. Robert Audi, "Self-Deception, Rationalization, and the Ethics of Belief" in *Moral Knowledge and Ethical Character* (New York: Oxford University Press, 1997); see also his "Self-Deception and Rationality" in *Self-Deception and Morality*, ed. Mike W. Martin (Lawrence: University Press of Kansas, 1986). I have also greatly profited by reading Joseph Butler's "Sermon X—Upon Self-Deceit" in *The Works of Bishop Butler*, 2 vols. Edited by J. H. Bernard. London: MacMillan, 1900

their judgments is a belief that they are better or superior to others.[16] The second self-deception of arrogant people is that they fool themselves into believing that their judgments have moral rectitude. They take their own subjective will and judge it to be in accord with the moral law, so they attribute a false authority to their own maxims and desires. It is this that makes arrogance a moral vice. Arrogant people think their judgments have objective validity, when in fact these judgments are only a projection of their desire to think well of themselves. Arrogant people see their own agendas as having moral probity. This misconception can be aptly illustrated by the Euthyphro contrast: they fool themselves into thinking that their wants and desires are formed according to what is right and correct when in fact what they think is right and correct is formed according to what they want and desire. Quite literally, they arrogate to their own will moral correctness and authority.

Arrogant people are mostly concerned with their own self image, maintaining their overinflated sense of self-respect by demanding more respect than they accord to others: arrogant people want more than their fair share of respect. Their arrogant behavior is an expression of their desire for others to see them, and for them to see themselves, as superior and as more deserving of respect than everyone else. In fact, arrogant people cannot claim to have genuine self-respect since the object of their so-called "self-respect" is a falsely inflated picture of who they are and of their place in the world. They do not respect themselves, rather they respect who they wish they were.

The mental life of arrogant people lacks integrity insofar as they are consistently failing to judge themselves and others consistently. They must refuse to others what they demand for themselves, yet such refusals and demands are unwarranted and insofar as this is true, arrogant people cannot integrate all their judgments into a consistent whole. They must compartmentalize the justifications of their moral judgments of others from the justifications of their moral judgments of themselves. And to the degree that they must hide the truth about these judgments from themselves, they all cannot be made into a consistent whole. Consistency can only be gained by unjustifiable rationalization (cf. Audi, "Self-Deception, Rationalization, and the Ethics of Belief"). As Oscar Wilde says, "hypocrisy is the homage vice pays to virtue".

It is worth noting how great a source for "evil" Kant thought arrogance is.[17] In the *Lectures on Ethics* (Schneewind and Heath, 216) he claims that it is a tendency

16. From the point of view of moral psychology, perhaps the most important point is that the belief of arrogant people that they are superior to others is often actually a defense mechanism to compensate for a truly poor self-conception. On such a reading, arrogant people behave as they do in order to buttress a flagging sense of self-esteem. This is perhaps the most common form of arrogance, though there are also, undoubtedly, a few who are arrogant because they truly think they are better than others. For related comments, see Tiberius and Walker, "Arrogance."

17. Kant actually uses many words to describe the family of psychological characteristics described roughly here as "arrogance", "Arroganz", *arrogantia*; "eigenliebegen Selbstschätzung", egotistical self-esteem; "Stolz", pride; "Hochmut", haughtiness; "moralische Eigendünkel", moral self-conceit. For more detail, see Dillon, "Kant on Arrogance and Self-Respect".

to evil, and in *Religion within the Limits of Freedom Alone* (VI 36; Wood and diGiovanni, 66–67), he calls it the root of moral evil. And given this understanding of arrogance, we can see pleonexia as being a character trait very similar to arrogance. The differences between arrogance and pleonexia are subtle and complex, and explaining them fully would be a (very interesting) paper in its own right. Here we must settle for noting a few important differences. Arrogant people think they are more deserving of respect than other people (whether or not they actually get it); they want better treatment than others get, and this may amount to having more of some resource than they would otherwise get were it to otherwise be distributed equally among all. But what arrogant people are after, more than worldly goods or resources, is being treated by others as superior, where, importantly, these others are accorded some (albeit lesser) amount of respect in return, so the respect they give to the arrogant ones will be of value. Pleonectics do not, typically, care much about respect in this sense; indeed, they tend to think and act as if others do not deserve respect, except, perhaps insofar as a person is in a position to punish; the only respect they understand is the respect born of fear. Otherwise, they "respect" other people instrumentally as wolves "respect" sheep. They may want others to see themselves as superior, but only because they think this will help them with their real goal of getting what they want. Pleonectics want things, profits, and benefits; they typically want beautiful things, diamonds, cars, and houses. And, most important, they think and behave as if people are things too: they want flattering friends and beautiful lovers and the power to do as they please. If respect helps them get these things, that is fine, but respect, in the end, is not their end. The end for people with pleonexia is composed of having either "material goods" or the power to get or do what they want, and they judge their success in such measurable terms.

It seems likely that pleonectics think they are superior to others, but not in the way that arrogant people do. Pleonectics will think they are superior to others because of what they can "get away with". Where arrogant people respect others but are unfairly partial toward themselves, pleonectics seem willing to respect themselves in a way they are not willing to respect others.[18] They manipulate, politic, and betray. Loyalty, like everything else, is only of instrumental value and is honored only as long as it is profitable. In the *Republic*, Glaucon was able to make immorality look as attractive as he did because of the luxuriousness of the things with which successful pleonectics can surround themselves. On top of the luxury, successful pleonectics appear to avoid any punishment or detriment for their behavior: to be truly successful, they must hide their true self from others, acting in secret, whenever need be, to obtain more than they could justify to others. To use the normative, conventional sense of the terms *moral* and *immoral*, pleonectics are immoral though they do their best to appear moral: as Glaucon notes (*Republic*, 361b), though it

---

18. I'd like to thank Michael Slote and Sam Wheeler for independently bringing up the difference between how pleonectics behave toward themselves and an otherwise acceptable way in which agent-centered prerogatives may justify one in being (at least somewhat) partial toward those whom one cares about (perhaps including oneself). Of course, this is not to suggest that the partiality involved in arrogance is somehow justifiable.

might seem as if a magical ring of invisibility would be required to get away with it, the consummately immoral person will have a colossal reputation for being moral. The ends justify means which themselves appear to be of no harm at all. And so, given the luxury when combined with the lack of punishment, there seems to be all reward and no cost to pleonexia.

Now, it is not uncommon for philosophers to argue that because they need to hide their true selves from others, people are harmed by pleonexia because they are unable to keep and establish true, faithful, and loyal interpersonal relationships like those found in love, friendship, or family.[19] Unfortunately, this response only "preaches to the choir" and would most likely fail to have much effect at all on a committed and successful pleonectic. As pleonectics see it, what is being pointed to as a harm, namely the loss of *true* friendship or love, is more than made up for by the "quality of life" that they can achieve as successful pleonectics. (Of course, the scare quotes around "quality of life" point to exactly the final issue.) People with pleonexia do not value what they do not know or have or even want, namely true love or real friendship, so they do not miss it in the least. And, from their point of view, they may, if they are lucky, have a semblance of love and friendship. By combining these appearances of love and friendship with the houses on the beach, the beautiful lovers, and the feel of the Ferrari on the road, pleonectics think they are coming out at the better end of the deal. Insisting to them they are not amounts to no more than shaking one's fist at the wind.

It is for this reason that pointing to loss of "Aristotelian external goods", like friendship, will not be useful in arguing against immorality. Plato saw this and in *Republic* tried to argue that the harms of immorality are to the person's psychology. Unfortunately, he did not seem to have the psychological vocabulary to make his point convincingly: trying to defend morality by claiming that there is a benefit of "psychic harmony" conferred by it is going to sound pretty thin and unconvincing to the pleonectic living large in the lap of luxury.[20] But more modern ideas of self-respect, self-deceit, rationalization, and integrity open up new, and heretofore unex-

---

19. See, for example, Philippa Foot, "Moral Beliefs," (1958–59), in *Virtues and Vices* (Oxford: Clarendon Press, [1978] 2002): 129; Nancy Sherman, "Aristotle on Friendship and the Shared Life," *Philosophy and Phenomenological Research* 47, no. 4 (1987): 589–613; Laurence Thomas, *Living Morally* (Philadelphia: Temple University Press), 1989. A similar, though metaphysically more robust, attempt can be found in David Brink, "Self-Love and Altruism" in (*Social Philosophy and Policy* 14 [1997]: 122–57).

For a counterargument to such attempts, see Joseph Raz, "The Amoralist" in *Engaging Reason: On the Theory of Value and Action* (Oxford: Oxford University Press, 1999). Raz is here considering the consistency of thinking that people are not "ends in themselves". He does not go on to question the self-conception of a person who holds such a view, and this is precisely the issue that I am engaging.

20. The account offered here of the harms of pleonexia is similar to Plato's insofar as both take it that "psychic harmony" is understood as "each part of one's psychology being as it ought to be". But Plato interprets psychic harmony as a proper balance of passion, appetite, and reason, whereas here it requires the modern ideas of self-respect and integrity. For problems with Plato's interpretation of psychic harmony, in relation to the argument of the *Republic*, see David Sachs, "A Fallacy in the *Republic*" in *Plato II*, ed. Gregory Vlastos (Notre Dame, Ind.: University of Notre Dame Press, 1971). Vlastos responds to Sachs on this point.

plored, argumentative possibilities. One would think that certainly Glaucon and perhaps even Thrasymachus would be moved to adopt morality if it could be shown that one cannot be both immoral and have what we now call self-respect. The fact is that pleonectics cannot have genuine self-respect while also harmfully manipulating and taking advantage of innocent people; or, at least, this is the claim.

Arrogant people were seen to lack self-respect because the foundations for what they see as their self-respect are faulty in a way that shows their "self-respect" to be a sham. Below, I will make the case for thinking that pleonectics are self-deceptive, but for now the claim just made is defended by showing that the "self-respect" of pleonectics is similarly faulty in its foundations. To begin, we may remind ourselves that pleonectics treat other people as things, as pawns to be manipulated so that their ends can be obtained. To apply some basic jargon to this, we may say that those living immorally treat others as objects with only instrumental value. The real question is that, given how they value others, how do pleonectics value themselves? Either they see themselves as special with regard to the value of their lives or they do not. This establishes a dilemma. If they do, then they are just wrong (as well as self-deceptive) since any reason they can give for their life having value can be given by others as well; saying "I'm special because I am me" or "I'm special because I'm clever" provides no rational warrant to the pleonectic. (These points will be taken up at length below.) On the other hand, maybe they do not see themselves as special, in which case they must rationalize or compartmentalize the justifications of their attitudes toward others from the justifications of their attitudes toward themselves. Either way, they can be convicted of mistakes that, when manifested in their immoral behavior, prevent them from having self-respect.

We may pursue these convictions by looking further into why it is correct to say that pleonectics do not view others as having more than mere instrumental value. This can be seen by again comparing pleonexia to arrogance. As noted above, arrogant people accord to others some sort of value beyond instrumental value so that these others can give arrogant people their sought after respect; arrogant people will not be satisfied by getting respect from mere things or animals, like sheep, rather, they want to see others as being respectable but themselves as being more respectable than others. Only in this way will the honor done to them by others confirm their falsely inflated sense of self. Aside from respect of others based on fear (to be discussed more below) pleonectics do not accord others any respect whatsoever. If they did, then they would have to acknowledge that it is, in some way, wrong of them to harm these respectable innocent people: if pleonectics allowed themselves to recognize others as respectable, and thereby deserving of respect from the pleonectic, then even the pleonectic would have to admit that those being harmed are not "mere sheep" or "the dupes" who deserve no better. There would then be reason for pleonectics to not behave as they do. In order to justify their behavior in the face of these reasons to avoid it, they discount the worth of other people in a way that forces them to hide some aspects of their psychology from other aspects. If pleonexia is a condition in which one sees oneself as a wolf and other people as sheep, then these others are seen to have merely instrumental value.

It is reasonable, however, to think that pleonectics do not act as if they see themselves as having merely instrumental value. If we understand instrumental value as
the value something has when it is good for the sake of something else, then people
cannot view their own lives as having purely instrumental value unless they see themselves as being instruments in something other than their own lives. While this may
be possible, and perhaps even required at times by true love and friendship, it is not
plausible to say that it is consistent with pleonexia.[21] Pleonectics want as much as
possible for themselves. There is no higher or ulterior purpose they are in it for, rather
they are in it for their own sakes. It seems that pleonectics see their own self-interest
as their final end and everything else as means to that end. If so, then one horn of the
dilemma mentioned above becomes apparent. People who knowingly try to "profit"
from being morally bad, seeing themselves as justified while harming those who are
innocent, may see themselves differently than they see those whom they harm: others
are instruments to be used for the sake of improving the lives of pleonectics who see
themselves as different in kind, and not just better in terms of degree, by virtue of
their lives having a kind of value which others are seen as lacking.

This first horn of the dilemma is that immoral people deny to others a sort of value
that they attribute to themselves; they treat themselves as being deserving of respect
while denying this to those they harm.[22] By so doing, it would then be easy to justify
harming people for the sake of something better, namely themselves. But what then are
the sources of a pleonectic's sense of self-worth? How can pleonectics ground their sense
of "self-respect" while denying the possibility of such self-respect, and the treatment it
warrants, to others? The answer is the same here as it was for the arrogant people, though
it comes a fortiori. Any reason pleonectics can give to justify their own self-respect must
be generalizable and hence available to others: any reason pleonectics can give for having their self-interest treated with respect is a reason other people can give as well. The
pleonectic must claim some sort of ontological distinction for himself or herself and
base this solely on an unwarranted first-person claim. Only in this way is the sort of value
pleonectics reserved for themselves kept from being warranted for others as well. The
pleonectic must say, "I deserve more because I am me" and when spelled out explicitly
in this fashion, the charade the pleonectic has created is revealed for what it is: absurd
and ridiculous, pitiful, were it not so harmful. (Other possible responses the pleonectic
might give, such as "I deserve more because I am clever" will be discussed below.)[23]

21. Aristotle's argument (concluding at *Nichomachean Ethics*, 1094a18–24) that eudaimonia is the final end of living may show that one must view something as being valuable for
its own sake. In modern parlance, it makes no sense to think that all value is instrumental "all
the way down". For a good discussion of this often discussed and misunderstood argument,
see Julia Annas's *The Morality of Happiness* (Oxford: Oxford University Press, 1993), 27–34.

22. One might think that one pleonectic might see another pleonectic differently than
everyone else is seen, but this seems unlikely. Pleonectics want to get the better of everyone,
each other included. I will discuss below a further possibility of pleonectics valuing all people
in virtue of having some other property than being a "person as such".

23. The argument here bears some similarity to various arguments Thomas Nagel has
made against egoism. See, for example, *The Possibility of Altruism* (Oxford: Clarendon, 1970),
as well as his contribution to this volume. I see myself as trying to take a step beyond Nagel's
linking respect toward others to self-respect, by linking self-respect to happiness.

Still this does not substantiate the charge of pleonectic self-deception, the case for which builds as we notice that others, even arrogant people, are open to awarding respect to others simply based on the fact of their shared humanity; the idea being that equal status as members of the same biological species itself establishes some low standard or minimal level of humane behavior below which one must not fall. Given this sort of respect, people deserve respect because they are "persons as such".[24] Even if everyone sets this standard at slightly different levels, there is still, nevertheless, respect due to people just because they are "up to scratch".[25] What this sort of respect does is set people apart from being mere things; people, in this sense, have more than instrumental value and deserve to be treated as if they are intrinsically valuable or are, in the familiar phrase, ends in themselves.

We can contrast this sort of respect with one based on fear that Thrasymachus and pleonectics apparently do understand. When we respect people because we fear them, it is because we think they may harm us in a way that makes it harder for us to live well: they are people we fear because we think they can have a negative instrumental impact (or disvalue) in our lives. The sort of respect we are concerned with, respect for people "as such", is based on appreciation and not fear, where appreciation is seeing the value of a person independent of that person's instrumental value in one's own life. In recognizing (or detecting) this sort of value, we appreciate people for who they are in themselves and not for their instrumental impact on us.[26] This form of respect is based on an appreciation of what we can call "the human condition", shared by all *Homo sapiens*: "cut us and we bleed", we can all feel pain, we get hungry and thirsty, we all, as children, were at the mercy of those that cared for us, and so on, and, on top of these facts, life can often be indiscriminately unfair and, sadly, sometimes remarkably cruel. Merely muddling through life, at a minimal level, is hard enough and filled with challenges we all, as human beings, must face. It is in virtue of our attempts to get through life as best we can that we are each deserving of this minimal sort of respect, which we ought to accord to one another for reasons independent of how we instrumentally impact one another's lives.

The crux of the entire matter is here. The problem for people with pleonexia is that they act as if they treat themselves as if they have self-respect based on who they are as people, while failing to respect others for who they are as people. When pleonectics harm others, they harm individuals who are the same as them in important,

---

24. This does not seem to indicate explicitly what Darwall ("Two Kinds of Respect") calls "recognition respect", since he sees this form of respect as requiring that it be taken account of in deliberation. Here, I leave open the externalist possibility of being able to recognize others as "people as such" while failing to consider this in deliberation.

25. This phrase is from Telfer, "Self-Respect."

26. I take it that the difference between detecting and recognizing that people are more than instrumentally valuable amounts to a difference between a realist and a nonrealist metaethic. I am doing my best to construct the argument so that it will be equally acceptable to both realists and, say, expressivists. Insofar as this is the case, the account given here about the harms of immorality is intended to be metaethically neutral. For more on this point, see Richard Joyce, review of *Moral Reality*," by Paul Bloomfield, *Mind* 112 (2003) p. 94–99.

indeed essential, ways: in virtue of our common origin as members of the species *Homo sapiens*, we share a variety of essential properties (aspects) without which we could not be who we are as individuals (Kripke, 1971). When one person immorally harms another, the harm is manifest disrespect for all the aspects of the victim that make the victim the individual that he or she is. It is a given that both perpetrators and victims of immorality are humans; they share the property of *being human*; they have humanity in common. Insofar as these aspects of them are shared in the same way by both the perpetrator and victim (they each necessarily instantiate the given universals), they are equals in this respect. Insofar as both are human beings, they are identical. Perpetrators of immorality who disrespect their victims manifest disrespect for those aspects of themselves that they share with their victims. Immoral behavior shows that these people do not take being human by itself as sufficient warrant to refrain from immorally harming others, despite the fact that it is their humanity which in part makes the perpetrators who they are. What this shows is that pleonectics, in perpetrating immoral harm upon others, do not properly respect those aspects of themselves that they share with their victims. They may try to focus their attention on ways in which they are dissimilar to their victims (by saying "I'm me" or "I am clever"), but these many essential similarities nevertheless obtain. In disrespecting the victim, the pleonectic manifests self-disrespect since the personal identities of the pleonectic and victim are essentially based on possessing the very same properties. Pleonectics are willing to disrespect others who share essential properties with them, and insofar as this is true, they demonstrate disrespect for themselves. The pleonectics disrespect for humanity is self-disrespect, given their own humanity. Ultimately, perhaps, they are in denial of their humanity. In any case, pleonectics have fooled themselves into thinking they are special when, at bottom, they are not and have thereby only fooled themselves into thinking they have self-respect when in fact they do not.[27]

So, consider confronting the pleonectic, or someone committed to behaving in ways not bound by the demands of morality, especially when these are inconvenient, in a situation in which morality would proscribe the only behavior that would allow these people to satisfy their personal preferences. The defender of morality can say to such a person,

27. I was led to formulate the argument in this paragraph as the result of comments from Walter Sinnott-Armstrong on an earlier draft of this essay. I am grateful for his helpful encouragement. I pursue the argument more explicitly in a manuscript now entitled "The Harms of Immorality." The argument rests on three assumptions intended to be acceptable to all parties in the debate: (1) a theory making it impossible for a person to be happy is a bad, harmful, self-defeating theory by which to live; (2) it is impossible for a person to be happy without self-respect; and (3) one lacks self-respect, if one disrespects oneself. It has three premises: (a) individual moral agents have the identities they do (they are who they are) because each instantiates a unique set of properties, though some of these properties are essentially instantiated by more than one moral agent; (b) if x immorally harms y, then x disrespects y; and (c) when x disrespects y, and one of the properties that makes y whom she or he is is also a property that makes x who she or he is (as described in [a]), then x disrespects herself or himself. Given these assumptions and premises, the conclusion that immorality prevents happiness follows fairly simply.

We have the same origins, you and those you are willing to harm at your convenience. You cannot deny it. You were born from the womb as were all of us: living, innocent, harmless, and completely vulnerable. We are only alive because others took care of us, only fed because of someone else. Like it or not, at bottom, there are ways in which we are essentially equals in this world, peers. Morality prescribes behavior that recognizes and respects these undeniable ontological facts. Like casese ought to be treated alike. Your way of living flouts this, and as a result, your sense of self-respect is based on a fallacious way of thinking about reality and your place in it. In fact, you do not respect yourself, rather, you respect who you wish you were but cannot be. True self-respect requires a true or accurate conception of the self, and of the self's proper place in the world. You have convinced yourself that you are better for your way of thinking, but here you are wrong. Even if you can find a (self-deceiving) solution to problems that arise from your denial of what you share with your victims, allowing you to be satisfied with yourself from a subjective point of view, you must, at the very least, acknowledge that the defender of morality you disagree with does not have this problem to contend with. The foundations of self-respect that result from living morally are superior to yours. You are fooling yourself about who you are.

In keeping with the understanding of self-deception that was given above, the best explanation for a person's belief in the truth of a proposition in the face of (i) evidence to believe it is false and (ii) a desire to believe it, is self-deception. If a pleonectic's sense of self-respect is based on the belief that he or she is superior to others, then this satisfies (i) and (ii): given manifold essential similarities with others, there is good reason to think that the pleonectic is, in fact, not superior to others, while the belief that "I'm special because I'm me" provides no rational warrant at all for believing that one is superior to others. The reason for this is as follows. Saying or believing "I'm me" only secures for one the property of *being unique*. It is of a piece with believing in haecceities. Of course, however, everyone is unique, since everyone has a haecceity (if anyone does), so this alone cannot justify special treatment compared with others. What pleonectics need to justify their behavior is a property that makes them *special* and it is the pleonectics' perennial inability to say what does make them so special that belies their belief in their special status. The fact is that they are just mortal fallible humans, just like the rest of us. Finally, the belief of pleonectics in their own superiority is simply too convenient to them to see it objectively as being driven by something other than a desire to believe it is true. Thus, the pleonectic's belief in his or her own self-respect is based on self-deception. (And even if pleonectics were able to specify a sense in which they were special, they would nevertheless still have to be in denial of all the ways in which they are *not* special, all the ways in which they are essentially just like everyone else, in order to deceive themselves into thinking they are justified in treating others as not being worthy of *any* respect.)

Perhaps, however, pleonectics do not see themselves as ontologically special in this way, but still see themselves as deserving whatever they can get away with by appealing to their cleverness, their very ability to get away with what they do. We could imagine them claiming, for example, that despite not being "special", clever people deserve respect but unclever people are "sheep" who deserve the treatment they get at the hands of the clever.

How ought one respond to the idea that some particular property that some people have and others lack, like cleverness, is the only true basis for respect? Since we are supposing Thrasymachus is clever and others are not, perhaps he does no wrong by treating unclever people as he does. Well, one response is to note that whether or not one is clever is in part dependent upon how many people are "less clever" than one is. And it seems wrong to base one's self-respect on the characteristics of others in this way. But perhaps Thrasymachus will rule out such a response as being too stipulative or procedural. If so, then one may still point out to him that for any character trait he can point to, which could serve to distinguish respectable from nonrespectable people, is one so contingent that can be lost due to illness, accident, or plain old age. Then one may ask Thrasymachus if he really thinks that he would deserve to be treated as badly as the way he now treats those who are not clever, were he to lose his cleverness. Presumably, he would think it wrong, he would feel indignant resentment, if someone were to treat him badly simply because he is not clever enough to keep that from happening. It may be, however, that consistency would drive Thrasymachus to say that he *would* in fact deserve to be treated badly, were he to stop being clever. And while this answer might be consistent, it bears all the marks of, to coin the phrase, being "too clever by half". People who are dumb do not feel that they deserve to be maliciously maltreated just because they are dumb, and there is no reason to think that Thrasymachus would not feel similarly were he to become dumb. Regardless of how cleverly consistent his answers might be, they ring of disingenuousness.

And even if they do not sound disingenuous, the following problem still remains. Consider the claim "the only genuine basis for respect is cleverness" in relation to the person, like Thrasymachus, who thinks it is true. Following Thrasymachus's line of thought, we may understand "cleverness" in terms of how much a person is able to get away with. The first thing to note is that there is good reason to doubt such a claim, for were it true, then we all ought to act in accord with it. If we did, then our common desire for respect from others, as well as for self-respect, would yield a Hobbesian war of "all upon all". And there is nothing clever about thinking of respect in a way that would make it so much more difficult to get away with anything: if everyone believed this truth of Thrasymachus's, he personally would be worse off, since everyone would be that much more vigilantly on guard against being taken advantage of. Everyone has someone whom they are more clever than. How clever would it be if we all took advantage? Ultimately, believing that only cleverness justifies self-respect is self-defeating, unless one is lucky to be the one (or one of the few) to believe it and this is good reason to doubt it. How remarkably convenient for Thrasymachus, of all people, to believe its truth. And he thinks fear and envy are the only reasons people might have for disbelief. Once again, we find that Thrasymachus's belief in the truth of his claim about respect fill the conditions laid out for self-deception: there are both recognizable reasons to think the claim is false and he has desires to believe it is true. It is only through self-deceptive rationalization that Thraysmachus can convince himself that his behavior is justified.[28]

---

28. I'd like to thank Sonia Michel and Don Baxter for discussion on this issue.

So, it seems most likely that pleonectics see themselves as being something special, in one way or another, which, of course, ultimately, they are not. On the other hand, we may finally attend to the second horn of the dilemma introduced many pages above. It is still possible that pleonectics see others as being just as worthy of respect as themselves, but do not care about it or ignore it. If so, then, as noted above, they must ignore how they justify to themselves their other-regarding behavior while justifying their own self-regarding behavior. If we can understand "psychological compartmentalization" of attitudes, beliefs, or the justifications of either of these as a conscious or subconscious denial of the contradictions between them, for the purpose of reducing what psychologists call "cognitive dissonance", then we can see that pleonectics who do not view themselves as something special must be guilty of this compartmentalization. They must hide their sense of "self-respect" and its justification from other aspects of their psychology, and as such their sense of "self-respect" is again fraudulent and self-deceptive.

So, we are led back to the conclusion that whether or not pleonectics think of themselves as special, they cannot have a nonself-deceptive sense of self-respect due to the disrespectful way in which they treat others who are essentially like them. Whether or not they care about this is the final issue. It seems safe to assume that some pleonectics may be moved by the argument just given and others are, de facto, "lost causes" who will not listen. Leaving the lost causes aside for just a moment, and assuming the argument just given about pleonexia, self-respect, and self-deception is sound, the obvious move for the pleonectic to make is to deny the importance of genuine self-respect to a person and to assert that lacking self-respect is of no true harm to a person. Only in this way will the person subscribing to Thrasymachus's moral theory be able to deny the claim that it is bad for a person, all things considered, to be morally bad. But it must be noticed what a difficult position the argument just given has put him in. Being able to do without external goods like "true love" or "real friendship" might be a bullet that a person could bite for the sake of gaining extravagant luxury or large amounts of power, but being forced to recognize how one disrespects oneself, and to give up seeing oneself as possessing self-respect is another thing altogether. The reason it is bad to be bad, is because if one is bad, then one disrespects oneself. And the degree to which one disrespects oneself, one is not happy. And the thought is transitive: the degree to which one is immoral is the degree to which one is not happy.

The pleonectic is now in the position of defending the idea that it is not in one's self-interest to maintain one's self-respect. If this is not a reductio ad absurdum of immorality, then it at least shifts a large burden of proof from the shoulders of the defender of morality to the defenders of immorality. It is no longer the moral people who look like the dupes that have bought into a false bill of goods. It turns out that only moral people are in a position to say, "I have genuine self-respect, the real thing. And I don't think a person can be happy without this". Thrasymachus and his lot are forced to argue against the self-interestedness of self-respect, and this will be at best, a tough argumentative row to hoe. Before the argument, it seemed reasonable to think that Thrasymachus would find it in his self-interest to maintain his self-respect as much as possible. Indeed, prior to the argument, he would argue that the only way to maintain one's self-interest is by being immoral. The dialectical position shifts, the table turns.

What responses are left to those who think it isn't bad to be bad? Let us distinguish two different types of people to who might not already see why it is bad to be bad. The first are people like Glaucon and Adeimantus, who are at the early stages of their moral education and who ask the question "Why is it bad to be bad?" because they genuinely do not know and are looking for guidance about how to live. When people such as this hear that it is only by avoiding injustice that they even stand a chance of having self-respect, it is most likely that they will then appreciate the harms that accrue to those who are morally bad, thereby answering their original question.

Others, however, may already have the character trait of pleonexia or are already prone to immoral behavior, and even if they are willing to listen, the argument above is nevertheless less likely to be effective than it is for Glaucon and Adeimantus. These people may be lost causes. Committed pleonectics are more likely to claim that whatever harm they must endure by not having self-respect is outweighed by the benefits that accrue to them by way of their unpunished immorality. After all, if one were to ask a pleonectic if he or she were happy, perhaps not knowing the person's true character, the pleonectic might sincerely answer in the affirmative. Pleonectics might *think* that they are happy since they might feel satisfied with themselves, never having had any genuine self-respect. As Plato puts it in *Symposium*, "The trouble with ignorance is precisely that if a person lacks virtue and knowledge, he's perfectly satisfied with the way he is. If a person isn't aware of a lack, he can't desire the thing which he isn't aware of lacking" (204a).

What then are we to say to such a person? Is there any possible way to salvage people, presumably like Thrasymachus, who are committed to acting in ways that prevent them from having self-respect, for the sakes of their victims as much as for their sakes? Perhaps all pleonectics are "lost causes." There is at least some reason to think that Aristotle took this to be the case.[29] He thought that if people were not exposed in youth to the noble or the fine (*kalon*) so that they could recognize *that* moral quality of particular actions, they will never be in a position later on to understand the *because* of what makes virtuous actions noble, thereby explaining why *that* is the best way to live. Rather, what Aristotle is doing in *Nicomachean Ethics* is lecturing to those who already want to be virtuous and who also want to understand virtue better, so that they will know what they ought to do and why they ought to do it. Aristotle does not even attempt to respond to Thrasymachus.

And this might be because no adequate response to people who are lost causes will be possible if they are adamant about staying the way they are and are determined to not let anything get in the way of them gathering about themselves all the power and/or gewgaws they possibly can. The dialectic grounds to a halt upon encountering a real lost cause who would refuse to participate in the give and take of reason. But perhaps not all committed pleonectics are lost causes. Let's optimistically imagine that Thrasymachus is not a lost cause and instead responds as follows: "Fine, let's assume your argument is sound and my sense of self-respect is fraudulent. So what? I still *feel* like I have self-respect and that's good enough for me. What

---

29. I take my reading of Aristotle on this point from Myles Burnyeat's "Aristotle on Learning to Be Good," in *Essays on Aristotle's Ethics*, ed. Amelie Rorty (Berkeley and Los Angeles: University of California Press, 1980), 69–92.

harm am I suffering by my self-deception?" Responding fully to Thrasymachus on this point would probably require something along the lines of a full course of psychological and philosophical therapy for him, since it would eventually have to be tailored to suit the etiology of Thrasymachus's own self-deception. It would involve his personal history and psychology, and its content would go far beyond the scope of a philosophy essay. Still, we can close by doing little more than listing five things that could be said to Thrasymachus, each of which could be expanded in some detail. In the end, however, he would only be able to comprehend the first three of these five.

The first is that Thrasymachus suffers the harms suffered by the dupe: if a dupe is someone who is sold a false bill of goods, then Thrasymachus has sold himself just that. When one must dissemble oneself in one's own conscience, one is in fact not doing as well as one is telling oneself one is. And this gap, between what is in fact the case and what one tells oneself, surely need not be consciously recognized by the dissembler. If the situation were not so lamentable from every angle, it would be humorous. Like the ignorant person who figured above in the quote from *Symposium*, the immoral person is being cheated out of the best that life has to offer since, like all dupes, he does not even know the best stuff is on the menu, and, as a result, he does not really know what he is missing. Despite his protestations to the contrary, Thrasymachus is the real dupe. The second response is that there is a type of pleasure or satisfaction that only comes from a job well done (Aristotle discusses this sort of pleasure, see *Nichomachean Ethics* 1174b14). Presumably, even Thrasymachus would have some grasp of this sort of satisfaction and we can point out to him that this satisfaction is particularly strong when it attends "doing a good job in living one's life well" by maintaining properly one's sense of self-respect and integrity. Thrasymachus cannot wholeheartedly enjoy this satisfaction since there will be some aspects of his psychology that are not in accord with others. Third, related to this alienation just mentioned, his deceptive sense of self-respect implies that Thrasymachus's moral theory engenders a literal schizophrenia far more acute and advanced than what Michael Stocker points out in his famous criticisms of deontology and consequentialism.[30]

The fourth and fifth responses to Thrasymachus are actually beyond his comprehension since they concern the benefits of living well and morally, and these are benefits of which he is deprived.[31] Insofar as he is deprived from receiving these benefits, there is a sense in which he is being harmed. The fourth is what we have heard from other philosophers (see note 19): Thrasymachus does not know either the joy of loving someone else for that person's sake instead of for his own, nor does he know what

30. Michael Stocker, "The Schizophrenia of Modern Ethical Theories," *Journal of Philosophy* 73 (1976): 453–66.

31. This "point of view defense" is discussed and criticized by both John McDowell in "The Role of Eudaimonia in Aristotle's Ethics," reprinted in *Essays on Aristotle's Ethics*, and by Stephen Gardiner in "Aristotle, Egoism and the Virtuous Person's Point of View," in *Power and Pleasure, Virtues and Vices: Essays in Ancient Moral Philosophy*, ed. D. Baltzly, D. Blyth, H. Tarrant (June 2001): 243–65.

it is like to truly deserve to be the beloved of someone else. The joys of genuine love and friendship, arguably the finest life has to offer, are beyond him. Thrasymachus cannot understand any of the other benefits of a moral life since all he has experienced is what comes from doing a poor job of living; he cannot recognize the harms of lacking those benefits since, tautologically, all he knows is all he knows. Some people who have lived morally have also experienced the luxuries that pleonectics value above all else and these nonpleonectic people who have experienced both know which is more valuable: appreciating people for what they are truly worth beats treating them as tools or instruments and using them "for all they're worth" every time. But finally, and most crucially, the problem is not as much about how to live with others as it is about how to live with oneself. Thrasymachus has no familiarity with the peace of mind that comes from not having to dissimulate in front of others and that brings a tranquility to life and to one's sense of self that is unavailable to someone who is vigilantly "on guard" as any pleonectic must be. Even if dissimulation has become the pleonectic's "second nature" and requires no real work, as we have seen, it must still be accompanied by a motivational structure that prevents sincerity and fosters self-deception and disrespect. Not recognizing that other people have "more than instrumental value" is harmful because one ends up being deprived of one of the only things in life that can make it truly worth living: this is the joy of seeing things as they actually are, of living in the real world, of forthrightly interacting with other living creatures in full recognition of who and what they are, of having an accurate conception of one's place in the world, and of the value of living in a manner truly respectful of one's own inner worth. Immorality is first-person degradation made manifest.

In conclusion, the harm of being immoral is that it keeps one from seeing the value of human life, and if one is human, then one is kept from seeing the value of one's own life.

13

Classical and Sour Forms of Virtue

JOEL J. KUPPERMAN

It is often tempting to look for a general solution to a philosophical problem. This paper will not yield to the temptation. The argument will be that there is more than one moral psychology of virtue, and hence more than one set of relations between virtue and self-interest. Further, circumstances, including the state of the society one lives in, can make a significant difference. Pressed to take a side on the question of whether there is a strong connection between virtue and self-interest, the paper will answer "mostly yes". But there will be many qualifications.

Two lines of thought on the moral psychology of virtue will be explored. One will be called the classical line of thought, because its major exponents include classical philosophers such as Aristotle and Confucius. The other is one associated with modern European philosophy, most strikingly that of Immanuel Kant. It allows for a virtue that can see itself (in this life at least) as going against self-interest. This can amount to the "sour virtue" of the title.

I will argue that there are forms of life that correspond to the philosophies, and also that some of what each of the philosophies extols as virtue does genuinely count as virtue. Hence, there can be a strong connection between virtue and self-interest in some kinds of cases, and also one that is less strong in others cases. Further, the kind of society one lives in makes a difference; so that there could be cases in which the correlation between virtue and self-interest is negative.

What Is Virtue?

Ordinary discussions of the virtuousness of specific people often follow a pattern. They start with casual observation: so-and-so certainly seems to behave well. For the "respectable" part of society there can be a presumption of virtuousness, rather like the presumption of innocence in the law. In both cases, the presumption can be defeated, as we learn more and get into specifics. Sometimes it can look as if the presumption has been defeated for a number of people at once. Take, for example, the Milgram experiments, in which most experimental subjects were induced to give what they thought (or half-thought) were dangerous electric shocks to someone who appeared to be another experimental subject. There could be a strong inclination to think that those people, whatever their ordinary lives had been like, were not indeed really virtuous people.

There is a contrast here between "virtue" in the casual observation/benefit-of-the-doubt sense and "virtue" in the more stringent and considered sense in which we might judge someone, knowing a great deal about him or her (at the imaginable extreme, knowing everything, including how that person would be likely to behave in certain situations). When "virtue" or "genuine virtue" is spoken of in this paper, it will be in the latter sense. To say this, however, is not entirely to clarify its meaning, and indeed the standards for what should count as "virtue" in a more stringent and considered sense are contestable. In what follows I will defend a series of positions in relation to what can count as genuine virtue.

The starting point will be the claim that there is no specifiable set of necessary and sufficient conditions for being virtuous. If so, we are left, as Wittgenstein argued for the word "game", with a set of overlapping family resemblances rather than an essence. Of course, there are some necessary conditions for something to count as a game. It must be, for example, an activity. There also are necessary conditions for being virtuous. We can begin by exploring some of these, returning then to the question of whether we can specify necessary and sufficient conditions.

To be virtuous you cannot have frequent and recurring moral lapses. Even sporadic lapses of a clear and very serious sort could disqualify you. We would not say "He really is a good person. There is the occasional mass murder, but he hasn't been doing that for a while".

Could we simply equate being virtuous with having a perfect record of behavior? There are two strong objections against this. One is that it is widely assumed that no one is perfect, and that even a good person can have what look like lapses of moral behavior (e.g., the occasional promise broken for no very good reason, the occasional cutting remark that badly wounds someone's feelings). The other is that in many traditions it is thought that repentance or regret in relation to misbehavior can make a major difference, especially if as a result the misbehavior is not repeated. This allows someone who has done things that, by his or her own lights, were morally wrong to be held to qualify as a genuinely virtuous person. Think of St. Augustine.

All the same, it is widely agreed that there are tests of virtue, situations in which it is not at all easy to make the virtuous choice. These may involve considerable temptation or disorientation. It is generally thought that how someone behaves in these situations would count heavily in assessing how virtuous the person is—and for that matter, whether the person genuinely had been virtuous (or merely untested) before. The thought that genuine virtue requires being able to pass tests of virtue, and that some people whose record of behavior is good nevertheless are not genuinely virtuous, goes back to Plato.

In the tenth book of the *Republic* the near-death experience of Er is reported (or invented) to illustrate a point.[1] Er traveled to the underworld, where he witnessed

---

1. Plato, *Republic*, trans. G. M. A. Grube, rev. C. D. C. Reeve, in *Plato Complete Works*, ed. John M. Cooper (Indianapolis: Hackett, 1997), 614b–621, 1219–23.

the souls of the dead choosing new lives. Someone who in his previous life had had a record of good behavior chooses the glittering, but ultimately ruinous, life of a tyrant. How could someone who had behaved virtuously have chosen such a life? The answer is that he had lived in a well-regulated state. It is understood in this story that in a well-regulated state, habits of good behavior can simply represent the easiest and most convenient path of life. But this man's "virtue" had been founded on habit, and not on philosophy. In this, and in his likely motivations for having behaved virtuously, he is like the "honest villager" who Confucius says spoils true virtue.[2]

Let me suggest that a virtue that is founded on "philosophy", in this context, must be understood as a set of policies that has a thought out justification. One element in this justification surely will be the connection between the policies on one hand, and values that are thought to be most important in one's life. These values will include, as we say, being able to live with yourself, and more generally an enjoyment of the workings of one's thought and of social relations that are going well. Someone who has deeply internalized these values will not be greatly tempted to misbehave.

Someone whose virtue is founded on habit, on the other hand, can slide into bad behavior in unusual circumstances in which different rules seem to apply, and there seem to be unusual reasons (which may take the form of incentives or threats, or simply a sense of a different situational etiquette) for behaving differently from one's normal manner. The unusual circumstances can be disorienting, seeming almost unreal. There can be little more disorienting than being dead, as in the case witnessed by Er or those for which the *Tibetan Book of the Dead* was intended as guidance.

There certainly are many illustrations of the idea that great temptations can change behavior that has been (merely) conventionally virtuous, an idea explored with some flair in Mark Twain's story "The Man Who Corrupted Hadleyburg". Twain's idea seems to have been that most people's "virtue" would not withstand such temptations, but that in some cases the temptations might have a strengthening effect. In the end the town changes its motto from "Lead us not into temptation" to "Lead us into temptation".

Previously "virtuous" behavior that yields to threats can be abundantly seen in the record of what happened in Nazi-occupied Europe, or in China during the Cultural Revolution. What appears to be an early example is reported in Plato's *Apology* (32c, 29–30). The Thirty Tyrants who were ruling Athens ordered five citizens, including Socrates, to arrest Leon of Salamis (presumably an innocent man) and bring him to them (presumably to be killed). Socrates, telling about this, remarks that the Thirty Tyrants liked to implicate others in their crimes. Four of the five citizens complied; Socrates simply went home; and as luck would have it (the Thirty Tyrants fell from power soon afterward) was unharmed.

The power of situational etiquette has been illustrated by the results of the Milgram experiments. There were no incentives or threats; but there was a sense that the psychologists in charge must know what they were doing, and it was their world and not one's own normal world. One recent commentator has compared the

---

2. Confucius, *Analects*, trans. Arthur Waley (New York: Vintage, 1938), book XVII, no. 13, 213.

behavior of these experimental subjects to the actions of corporate employees who produce unsafe products but believe that the company could not really be endangering consumers just to make a profit.[3]

All of these real or imagined cases add up to a powerful argument for (a) the view that a record of good behavior, absent real tests of virtue, does not imply the possession of genuine virtue, and (b) that tests of virtue provide a much better indication of how virtuous someone really is. There also is the result (which Plato, Aristotle, and Confucius all clearly accepted) that the number of genuinely virtuous people is much smaller than is generally supposed.

If a record of good behavior is not the criterion for genuine virtue, then can we say exactly what is? Perhaps a necessary and sufficient condition for being genuinely virtuous is that (whatever one's behavior has been in the past) one can pass all tests of virtue. This clearly is sufficient, but is it necessary?

Those who regarded St. Augustine as genuinely virtuous would have expected this of him. Let me nevertheless express skepticism at this point. There could be a variety of unusual, protracted tests of virtues far more difficult than those represented by the occasional temptation, serious threat, or psychological experiment. It seems doctrinaire to insist that a genuinely virtuous person (even a saint) would have to be able to pass every one of these tests. Even the sort of person who walked out of the Milgram experiment, and who readily would sacrifice her or his life for others, might imaginably have some weak point and fail one or two such tests.

We still might insist that to be genuinely virtuous is to be able to pass the more familiar sorts of tests of virtue, and to be reliably virtuous also in the ordinary business of life, especially in things that really matter. Something like this is a necessary condition for virtue. Is it a sufficient condition? There is room for doubt here. Factors of motivation, especially those related to what a person's basic concerns are, can vary enormously. Imagine an extreme case. Someone might be inherently indifferent to what happens to other people, and have no sense of the inherent dignity or worthiness of moral principles, but also be totally convinced that God is watching his or her every move, and that the prospects of heaven or hell depend heavily on one's following accepted morality at every step. To make the example even more extreme, imagine that it is a case far removed from, say, ecstatic love of God. Instead the attitude is "These are the rules; someone is in charge, and I had better play safe." Such a person could be, at least in broad outline, well behaved, even in difficult tests of virtue; but it is highly debatable whether he or she should be considered virtuous. It could be argued that resolute selfishness is not the same as virtue: motivations do matter.

The remarks thus far suggest that there may well be no set of necessary and sufficient conditions for being genuinely virtuous. The necessary conditions could be summarized as follows: performs well in matters of moral choice, and passes (or would pass) major and obvious tests of virtue. This is a very loose and imprecise formulation. Matters become more difficult if we ask whether a virtuous person would

---

3. Thomas Blass, *Obedience to Authority: Current Perspectives on the Milgram Paradigm* (Mahweh, N.J.: Lawrence Erlbaum, 2000), 46–47; V. L. Hamilton, "Thoughts on Obedience: A Social Structural View," *Contemporary Psychology* 37 (1992): 1313.

pass all or almost all imaginable tests of virtue, or what the general moral psychology of virtue would be like. Even if motivations do matter, there could be a variety of motivations that pass muster.

We can close this section of the paper by mentioning a tempting position, so that we can eliminate it from our inquiries. If no one would meet every conceivable test of virtue (i.e., if no one is perfect) then it could be argued that no one actually is genuinely virtuous. One might regard being virtuous as an ideal that no one in fact meets. This is not totally implausible, and would have been congenial to Puritans who stressed the importance of a personal sense of moral and spiritual inadequacy. But it can be argued to set an artificially high standard.

There are some people, both living and historical, who we do think are or were virtuous. Many people would nominate Socrates, Confucius, St. Francis, and the Buddha. We may think that some groups or subcultures attribute genuine virtue incorrectly. There is room for argument even about St. Augustine, and in our own era Mother Teresa and Ralph Nader have their critics. But it would seem very implausible to claim that all attributions of genuine virtue, throughout time, have been mistaken. This would be akin to insisting that true knowledge requires knowing everything. It would set an artificially high standard that does not match the ordinary uses of the relevant words.

Classical Forms of Virtue

What will be called classical forms of virtue can be associated principally with three philosophers: Confucius, Plato, and Aristotle. Their views on the moral psychology of virtue are not identical; but there are strong similarities, especially on the relation between virtue and personal well-being. Some other classical Greek philosophers, and Confucius's great follower Mencius (4th c. BCE), hold views that also are similar.

Confucius, Plato, and Aristotle would agree on three propositions: (1) genuine virtue represents a kind of second nature, a result of education such that patterns of choice become natural and predictable that would not be natural and predictable for the average person, (2) there are patterns of gratification attendant on genuine virtue, that involve deeper values than most of the things that people pursue in life, and (3) because of these, genuine virtue is always in a person's self-interest.

The word "gratification" here is deliberately broad. There can be brief periods of satisfaction, with performances that enjoyably are going well; these would amount to refined pleasures. But there also can be an agreeable sense of having come to terms with oneself, with no sense of self-disapproval or keen regret. This can be an important element in happiness. The prospect of these rewards can influence anyone to turn herself or himself into a genuinely virtuous person.

Plato and Confucius provide a more detailed account of education than Aristotle does, and indeed the education of a superior person is a central topic in the *Analects* of Confucius in a way in which it is not for Aristotle or even Plato. This is in part because the *Analects* is an account of Confucius close up, written by his students and their students.

The circumstances of Confucius's life made education especially central. He had a broad vision of social and political reform for China, keyed to a paternalistic vision of educated, altruistic officials who would protect the peasants from want and also promote educational and cultural development. The hope was that one of the kingdoms that comprised the remains of the old empire would allow Confucius to set up a demonstration model of such a politics.

In search of this opportunity, Confucius went from kingdom to kingdom, trying to persuade rulers that his reforms would be to their advantage. While waiting for his opportunity, Confucius accepted students, who lived and traveled with him. Some of these students doubtless hoped that Confucius's training would give them a better chance of gaining coveted official positions, but Confucius's educational role as a guardian and transmitter of traditional culture also would have been an attraction. In any event, his opportunity never came; and when he died he probably thought of himself as a failure.

Hence we have a portrait of Confucius mainly as an educator. His educational model was that a student who came with a serious desire to learn could be transformed by three elements. One was a knowledge of the classics, especially the *Book of Songs* (which was held to contain coded moral messages). A second was ritual, useful for anyone looking forward to a position at court, but also (in Confucius's view) a kind of social dance that gradually transformed one's emotional nature. (If this seems far-fetched, think of the ritual of thanking people for favors, which over time becomes natural and leads to incorporating an emotion of gratitude in one's emotional repertoire.) Finally, Confucius (like Plato) thought that music—at least the right kind of music—could shape emotional life in a positive way.

Confucius claimed that the result of education was an integrated personality, in which one naturally pursued a way (a *dao*) of virtue. One of the chapters of Herbert Fingarette's book on Confucius is entitled "A Way without a Crossroads": the idea is that there are matters in which a developed person would have no choice.[4] As an example of the point, if you were offered a lot of money to torture a small child, would you have a choice?

The path of developed virtue would be very gratifying; there would be little sense of personal sacrifice. There are two reasons for this. First, there is a link, established in psychological research, between happiness and one's sense of self.[5] Someone who cannot be positive about his or her self cannot be happy. To be virtuous, and know that one was virtuous, would however guarantee a positive sense of self.

Second, virtue in Confucius's (and also, incidentally, in Plato's and Aristotle's) view was not merely a coiled potentiality, waiting for the big moment of moral choice. Rather, virtue was an ongoing quality of mind, expressing itself in daily life in a variety of interactions. Because of Confucius's emphasis on ritual, there was a sense in which these interactions would be, for a developed person, highly skilled. At one point Confucius claims that getting the detail right in ritual is not as important as is one's emotional relation to the ritual: one should have *he* (variously trans-

4. Herbert Fingarette, *Confucius: The Secular as Sacred* (New York: Harper 1972), chap. 2.
5. See Michael Argyle, *The Psychology of Happiness* (London: Methuen 1987), 124.

lated as "harmony" or as "naturalness").[6] Mihaly Csikszentmihalyi's research[7] shows that the experiences that people most value are those in which they lose themselves in the flow of a skilled performance. This experience would be especially common in the life of a developed Confucian.

All of this would seem to create strong motivational support for the idea of being virtuous. A natural question then is whether this is the dominant motivation for virtue, and if so, whether being virtuous out of self-interest can count as being genuinely virtuous (as opposed to being shrewdly prudent). This is a problem for Confucius, Plato, and Aristotle, as well as for any religious system that promises great rewards after death for those who are virtuous (if at the same time it thinks of virtue as more than merely compliance with established norms).

The answer (I think for all of these cases) requires a distinction among the various stages at which, or ways in which, self-interest can enter into the assessment of being virtuous. If it enters into a response to questions like "Should I do the virtuous thing on this occasion?" or "Should I continue being virtuous?" there is something deeply corrupt about the question that elicits the appeal to self-interest; and most of us would regard the person willing to rest virtue on self-interest as indeed not really virtuous.

There are two places at which the linkage between virtue and self-interest need not be corrupt. The first is at a very early stage of the development of virtue. A parent imaginably could be influenced by the thought that becoming really virtuous is likely to produce a more rewarding life for her or his child, and an adolescent also can be influenced by the thought that becoming a really virtuous person is likely to have advantages in life. Normally, virtue will have other sources of appeal besides this, but there seems to be nothing corrupt in being influenced by a vision of what a happy, harmonious life marked by virtue would be like.

Second, at the stage at which someone actually has become a virtuous person, there seems to be nothing corrupt about a general sense that it was and is highly advantageous. Such a positive review is quite different from a calculating reconsideration that would be corrupt. The essential point is that to have become a virtuous person is to have internalized virtue. This entails that one's virtue is not up for reconsideration.

To return to Confucius: virtue not only is satisfying but also it would represent an unusually secure form of gratification. This contrasts with what most people desire most (money and reputation). These sources of gratification tend to be insecure. This is why "A true gentleman is calm and at ease; the Small Man is fretful and ill at ease."[8] Luck plays a much larger part in the view of life had by people who highly value wealth and reputation than in that of people who have internal sources of value.

Further, there is the disadvantage that desires for money and prestige tend to be addictive. Someone who greatly desires these things and is successful will after a

6. Confucius, *Analects*, book 1, no. 12, 86.

7. See Mihaly Csikszentmihalyi, *Flow: The Psychology of Optimal Experience* (New York: Harper & Row, 1990).

8. Confucius, *Analects*, book VII, no. 36, 131.

while become dissatisfied and desire even more. Hence only the good man can "for long enjoy prosperity."[9]

Because of all of this, Confucius regards it as entirely clear that virtue is in any-one's self-interest. Plato does also, chiefly because of an argument (that runs through the *Republic* especially) that vice is a form of mental illness, and that psychological harmony is far more desirable than are psychological disintegration or inner con-flicts. Aristotle's view is somewhat similar, although a bit qualified. This comes out in two passages centering on the figure of Priam, king of Troy, who is presumed highly virtuous but was in the end extremely unlucky in the "externals" of life. He lived to see the invading Greeks kill his sons and destroy his city. Aristotle contends that, despite this extremely bad luck, Priam's *eudaimonia* (best translated here as "well-being") still remained in the intermediate range.[10] Aristotle in another passage sounds less positive, but all the same regards values in Priam's life as not in the low range.[11]

Even though Aristotle does give "externals" some weight in *eudaimonia*, he also (like Confucius) places great emphasis on the gratification provided by one's own virtue. This has been criticized by Nancy Sherman,[12] as involving an element of something like narcissism. Aristotle also is the target of Kant's criticism. True virtue in Kant's view is guided by a sense of duty, which is respect for the moral law. Duty is contrasted with inclination, which is directed to what we want—usually to what we think would make our life better. Kant sees what Aristotle regards as virtue as being guided by inclination, and hence not as true virtue.

The differences here between Kant and Aristotle are a little more complicated than they may at first look. Aristotle's ideal, like that of Confucius and I think that of Plato, is someone who has acquired a second nature in which it simply is much more congenial to help those in need and follow the traditional mandates of moral-ity than it would be not to behave in this way. This needs to be spelled out carefully. From Aristotle's point of view, part of being virtuous typically is to be a good judge of what to do in difficult cases. But this does *not* mean that typically one, as it were, reads out what should be done by examination of one's own virtue. (Someone who proceeded that way would be almost certainly morally unreliable, and possibly dan-gerous.) Rather, one looks first and foremost at the circumstances of the case at hand, and attempts to judge it intelligently in the light of experience.

Nevertheless, a large part of the Aristotelian virtuous person's motivation is pro-vided by the sense that virtuous behavior is both congenial and gratifying. Kant cer-tainly would not regard someone of this sort as immoral. The view is rather that, in cases in which this person does the kind of thing that we consider morally right, but does it mainly because it is very congenial, the actions are in some sense beyond or outside of morality. This is connected to Kant's observation that someone who had no room at all for bad inclinations, someone who had a "holy will", would have no need for morality and in fact would not have morality.[13]

9. Ibid., book IV, no. 2, 102.

10. Aristotle, 4th c. BCE/1984, no. 1101a, 1739.

11. Ibid., no. 1100a, 1738.

12. Nancy Sherman, "Common Sense and Uncommon Virtue," *Midwest Studies* 13 (1988).

13. Immanuel Kant, *Grounding for the Metaphysics of Morals*, trans. J. Ellington (Indianapolis: Hackett 1785/1981), no. 414, 24.

The further complication is that (as Kant sees it) there is no human being like that. Kant takes human imperfection seriously. He surely would concede that many of us have moments when we do the right thing, not out of duty but rather because it is far more congenial and personally attractive. Kant's insistence that morality is not then in play is in tune with the ordinary way we speak of such cases. Think of the difference between (a) on a cold day diving into the water to save the life of someone you really despise, and (b) diving into the water to save the life of the person you most love in the entire world. Because of human imperfection, though, Kant would doubt that there is anyone who consistently does what is right for nonmoral reasons. We all have our weak points and temptations.

A final complication is that the contrasts here between kinds of motivation are all matters of degree. A finely developed sense of human imperfection underlies this point. Doing what is right in general will offer some rewards, even to someone who is strongly influenced by the Kantian view that one should do what is right out of a sense of duty (and even if the rewards are often, or usually, outweighed by difficulties or frustrations). There is the reward of feeling virtuous, along with that of feeling that admiration should be forthcoming (whether it is or not): there can be the thought "If only they knew!" Because of such factors, Kant remarks that he does not know of a single case in which something was done purely out of a sense of duty.[14] "Dear self," he says, will intrude.[15] The force of this can be appreciated when one takes in the fact that the cases considered include all of Kant's own behavior. Moral behavior (in Kant's view) then must be behavior in which a sense of duty is the leading (but not the only) factor.

Some Eighteenth-Century Views of Virtue and Self-Interest

We will want to look more closely into the possibility of a virtue quite different from that recommended by classical philosophers (such as Confucius, Plato, and Aristotle), one that may well take sour forms. Before focusing on this, let me register (and largely endorse) a modern line of thought about the relation between virtue and personal well-being. This is set forth in Hume's examination of the case of the "sensible knave."[16] Hume's view owes something to the pathbreaking anti-Hobbesian polemic of Bishop Butler.

Hobbes had relied on a straightforward and seemingly unproblematic conception of self-interest in constructing his view of what human life (absent the social contract) would have been like, and of what the motivation for agreeing to the social contract then would have been. You accept the social contract because, under it, your life is less nasty and brutish and more secure. There was an implicit contrast in all of this between self-interest (to which Hobbes assigns the motivational power) and altruism that was, and still is, largely endorsed by common sense. Part of Hobbes's appeal is the absence from his account of anything that borders on the

14. Ibid., no. 407, 19.
15. Ibid., 20.
16. David Hume, *Enquiry Concerning the Principles of Morals*, ed. L. A. Selby-Bigge, rev. P. H. Nidditch (Oxford: Clarendon 1751/1975), no. 232–33, 282–84.

sentimental and uplifting. The story works because of what looks like basic human selfishness.

Butler's breakthrough involved deconstructing the concept of self-interest, relating it more carefully to human desires and concerns. It was an ironic move, especially because Hobbes's account had seemed so matter-of-fact, dry, and astringent. But perhaps the facts are not so dry and astringent? The irony was echoed when G. E. Moore preceded *Principia Ethica* by quoting Butler's "Everything is what it is, and not another thing".

Given normal human affections, a major part of what we want in life is that the people we care about do well. Is this self-interest? It is not totally self-regarding, but on the other hand it does loom very large in our sense of how well our life is going or is likely to go. It therefore seems doctrinaire to exclude it from what counts as self-interest.

Further, anyone who lives in a community—who is not a hermit, or otherwise psychologically cut off from others—can gain satisfactions from friendly relations with others, and in general from horizons expanded beyond the boundaries of one's purely personal projects. In these settings, the facts of how people are gratified point to ways in which a degree of concern for others enhances what is in our self-interest. People who are psychologically cut off from others, on the other hand, seem by and large to lead narrowly constricted lives that are not at all enviable. All of this points to the conclusion that self-interest and moderate altruism are not (or at least, normally are not) opposed to each other.

Hume's view of human nature, even if one tries to imagine it prior to a social contract, is close to Butler's; and we know that there was a conscious debt.[17] The argument about the "sensible knave" though covers different ground. It is mainly concerned with the specific issue of what (if any) the relation is between someone's virtue and the way in which that person is likely to be treated by others.

The "sensible knave" is presented as someone who has no deep-dyed allegiance to virtue, but is very aware that others will react badly to someone whom they perceive as not virtuous. Such a person will not be trusted, and is less likely than most to benefit fully from social networks and cordial relations. Because of this, to be visibly nonvirtuous is generally a very poor strategy in life. What though about the strategy of always appearing to be virtuous, but being open to surreptitious nonvirtuous actions that promise great gain? This is the strategy of the "sensible knave".

Hume's argument is that it is in general—even viewed from the perspective of a very narrow form of self-interest—a poor strategy. This is because people tend to pick up a sense that so-and-so is not reliable, and is to an unreasonable degree "out for no. 1". Because of this, the "sensible knave" is likely to lose a great deal, even if no specific immoral act is witnessed. More current versions of a similar sort of argument have appealed to Paul Ekman's research on "micro-expressions", facial expressions that occupy so little time that they do not consciously register on the viewer, but that nevertheless are reflected in character judgments.[18] The point remains Hume's, that people usually, sooner or later, give themselves away.

---

17. See Ernest Mossner, *Life of David Hume* (Oxford: Clarendon 1970), 74, 110–11.

18. See Paul Ekman and E. L. Rosenberg, *What the Face Reveals*, 2nd ed. (New York: Oxford University Press 2004).

These arguments seem to me to be convincing. But how strong a conclusion do they establish? Hume does not maintain that there never is a case in which a sensible knave does not (as assessed in terms of narrow self-interest) come out ahead in life. The claim is merely that this is not frequent, and that the odds are in favor of someone whose strategy in life centers on virtue. If, early in life (and thinking in the most selfish terms imaginable), you ask whether it would be to your advantage to become a virtuous person (a truly virtuous person, who will not opportunistically discard virtue on convenient occasions), Hume's answer is "probably yes".

This does, however, leave some loopholes. We may put aside the case of the sensible knave who happens to be very lucky, succeeding in fooling almost all the people almost all the time. Whether we judge the "successful" life that results as a desirable one obviously depends most on the values to which we assign the greatest weight. It is abundantly clear that neither Plato nor Aristotle nor Confucius would consider the life of the lucky sensible knave to be truly enviable. It is clear also that many people would disagree with them on this, and that the disagreement hinges on contestable issues of what is most important in life.

Let us explore different worries, which may be more serious. Butler's and Hume's positions owe much of their strength to the implicit context of societies that, even if they are not perfectly just, do qualify as moderately decent and stable. What of a society or a subculture in which there is not much decency or stability? Could virtue sometimes be a poor strategy in such a society? Also, could there be a life that is genuinely virtuous but, all the same, not a desirable life to lead?

Again the great classical philosophers would answer "No" to both questions. We have to take seriously though the people who have answered "Yes" to one or both of them. The book of Job in the Bible implicitly says "Yes" to the second question. Job judges his life (once his misfortunes begin) to be quite undesirable; and no one, not even God, gives him any argument on that point.

Kant also dissents from the view of the great classical philosophers, seemingly not prepared to answer a simple "No" or "Yes" (for this life at least) to either question. His reservations may be even more deeply troubling than the view of the book of Job, because they are not limited to cases (like that of Job) of extreme bad luck. Kant specifically maintains that virtue by and large leads to less (rather than more) happiness in this life.[19] Part of his basis for this may be the thought that there will be more to worry about, and less spontaneous joy, if one is governed by the rationality of virtue. Rationality and careless rapture do not go very well together.

The point that Kant really cares about is that the appeal of virtue is not connected with happiness, but rather is a matter of the superior dignity of virtue. It is clear that Kant recommends a life that achieves this dignity, and in that sense he considers it desirable. But it is far from clear that he considers such a life to be usually enviable. Nor does he allow that anything that we normally would consider self-interest ideally will have a place in the decision to pursue such a life.

---

19. Kant, *Grounding for the Metaphysics of Morals*, no. 395–96, 398–99.

The Possibility of Sour Virtue

We may approach the concept of sour virtue by looking first at something that Kantian virtue and the virtue of Job share, and that separates them from the virtue of the great classical philosophers. We need to look closely at the differences between classical virtue and what Kant and the book of Job consider to be virtue. But we also need to ask whether both of these very different kinds of virtue really do count as genuine virtue.

What Kantian virtue and the virtue of Job share is the idea that virtue is first and foremost a matter of respect for moral laws, rules, or principles. None of these terms has an entirely precise meaning, but examples might help. The claim that one should not take another person's property or kill an innocent person can be taken to state a moral law or rule. A more sweeping (and also potentially vague) moral recommendation, such as that of respect for persons or the injunction that one always should be fair, would be more likely to be termed a moral principle.

I have argued elsewhere that interpretation of how a case and the possible courses of action should be construed is always a feature of ethical judgment.[20] Is killing Canaanites, or whatever other people one happens to be fighting against, a violation of the rule "Thou shalt not kill"? To answer this is to offer an interpretation of "Thou shalt not kill," as well as of what a full description of the present case of killing should be.

Principles especially are open to interpretation, and we may well judge that some interpretations that were accepted for a long time were in fact quite poor. Is it "respect for persons" to take a condemned murderer seriously enough to order his execution?[21] Was it fair throughout the Middle Ages that the oldest son inherited the entire estate, and was it also true (as was widely thought until less than 200 years ago) that fairness did not demand that women be allowed to attend universities?

Let us put to the side these inconvenient matters of interpretation, and concentrate on the view that moral laws, rules, and principles are the keys to virtue. It is made clear in the book of Job that Job scored high in being "upright" in relation to moral rules and principles. Certainly there have been many people throughout the centuries who have scored high in loyalty to the moral law, including many who lost their lives in Nazi Germany because they would not be complicit in what was wrong. Alan Donagan describes such a case of a pious Austrian Catholic farmer in 1943 who refused induction into the German army, on the ground that declaring war to seize other people's land and resources was immoral; the farmer was subsequently beheaded.[22]

We cannot know whether the man that Donagan describes got much joy out of his uprightness, but it seems quite conceivable that he did not. It certainly sounds as if Job did not receive gratification from his uprightness that outweighed the misery

---

20. See Joel J. Kupperman, *Ethics and Qualities of Life* (New York: Oxford University Press, 2007).

21. Kant evidently thought so. See Kant, *The Metaphysics of Morals*, trans. Mary Gregor (Cambridge: Cambridge University Press 1797/1996); *The Doctrine of Right*, no. 49, 106.

22. Alan Donagan 1977, 15–16.

brought on by loss of possessions, children, and normal good health. All the same, it seems hard to deny that what Job possessed, and what the Catholic farmer described by Donagan exhibited, was moral virtue.

There are respects in which someone who adheres to a classical conception of virtue might find the virtue of Job or that of the Catholic farmer to be inadequate. One concerns the ability to respond to unusual cases, in which following what look like the relevant moral rules in the usual way arguably can lead to poor and harmful decisions. Another concerns motivation.

It is true that Confucius had reservations about high-minded people who were rigid in their adherence to standards. He insisted that he himself was flexible.[23] We are all familiar with modern cases in which the kind of person who in many respects behaves very virtuously can become narrow and intolerant in an unusual case that seems to call for a different style of behavior. Because of such cases, we may wonder whether someone (like a good Kantian or like Job) who is guided simply by moral laws, rules, or principles can behave virtuously in all circumstances.

Part of the answer is that (because no one is perfect, and there could be many different kinds of rigorous tests of virtue) no one would behave virtuously in all imaginable circumstances, and (as was argued previously) it is unreasonable to set a standard for genuine virtue this high. An important part of the answer though is this: we can contrast someone who in effect has been handed a set of moral laws, rules, and principles and doggedly follows them in a fairly narrow way with someone of a similar ethical orientation who is more reflective and less narrow. It is possible for a Kantian, as Donagan has pointed out, to allow that our ordinary understanding of rules includes implicit exceptions.[24] To give an example: "Promises should be kept" does not mean that relatively trivial promises should be kept if a likely result is that lives will be lost or that the promiser's personal happiness will be wrecked. Further, a law/rule/principle approach to morality requires casuistry, as Kant points out in the second half of the *Metaphysics of Morals*. Judgment and reflection are part of the apparatus of Kantian virtue. Even if the narrow, dogged follower of a rule-governed morality lacks something relevant to virtue, it is far from clear that this will be true of everyone of this general orientation.

With regard to motivation: it is true that that of Job or a Kantian will be slightly different from that favored by classical philosophers. Devotion to moral rules, laws, and principles will loom larger. All the same, the required motivation on neither side will be either purely self-interested or entirely unselfish. On both sides, there will be elements of self-interest, having to do with self-respect, self-esteem, perhaps exercise of skills, and perhaps a sense that one could not live with oneself if one behaved very differently. Kant is surely right in holding that even a devotee of duty will not present any case of a moral choice made entirely out of duty, with no admixture of self-interest. Conversely, even Aristotle's magnanimous man, who derives satisfaction from his own virtue, is guided by a sense of what situations call for; and the importance of being so guided will be part of his motivation. In short, motivations generally will be mixed, on both sides of the contrast.

23. Confucius, *Analects*, book XVIII no. 8, 221–22.
24. Donagan 1977, chap. 2.

When all of this is considered, it seems implausible for anyone—whether Kantian, Aristotelian, or Confucian—to dismiss all cases of what is considered "virtue" by those of different philosophical orientations as not being genuine virtue. One can prefer one model of virtue to others without dismissing all manifestations of another model as failing to be real virtue.

This said, there remains a major difference between the Kant/Job model and the classical models. At the root is the view of what contributes most to the rewardingness of life, or subtracts most greatly from it. Confucius, Plato, and Aristotle all place most emphasis on what might be termed "internal" factors, including a sense of one's self, the harmony of emotions, and the enjoyment of activities of a high quality.

Kant certainly does not disregard such factors. He speaks glowingly of the dignity of rationality, and maintains that there is an "imperfect" duty to develop our talents. However, the account of happiness that accompanies his account of hypothetical imperatives suggests that there is an important link between happiness and getting what we want. In all, Kant's axiological remarks lend themselves to a picture of human life in which there are certain things (dignity, rationality) that are admirable, but in which what is desirable is not far removed from what the average person tends to think: happiness, and successes in the ordinary business of life. In this picture, the degree to which a life is admirable and the degree to which it is desirable (in the sense of being rewarding) can diverge.

This allows for the possibility, within an ethics dominated by rules, laws, and principles, that someone could be genuinely virtuous (and admirable in her or his dignity and rationality), and at the same time have a life that by her or his own standards was not especially desirable. "External" things that most people value greatly, and that such a moral agent might also value greatly, could simply go wrong. Such a person might well be sour, while continuing as a dedicated moral agent to be virtuous.

Why So Sour?

This paper is philosophy rather than cultural history, but let me suggest that a stock figure in Western culture, especially in the nineteenth and early twentieth centuries, was someone who very probably was genuinely virtuous, but all the same was disappointed in the rewards of life and was sour. The phenomena of sour virtue are complex. A number of factors can contribute to the sourness of the stock figure who is virtuous but sour.

One is this. If the things one values most are money, various pleasures of ordinary life, and prestige, then it is arguable that one will never be satisfied for long. The money, pleasures, and prestige trigger habits of desire. Each success will be followed by a brief period of contentment, and then one wants more. There is a nice example of this reported in the collection of retrospective comments on the Milgram experiment.[25] Philip Zimbardo (designer of the Stanford Prison experment, and also a high school classmate of Milgram's) reported meeting Milgram some time after they both had done their best-known work. Milgram said that he was disappointed that his work had not got more attention. Many well-respected people must feel this

25. See Blass, *Obedience to Authority*.

way, and there appear to be many very wealthy people who are disappointed that they are not more wealthy.

In short, the nonclassical value system that makes sour virtue a live possibility also makes it likely even if there is a fair degree of success in life. Another factor that can contribute to the sourness of that kind of virtue is this: there is a strong association, which can be found in the philosophy of Kant but also in much popular thought about virtue, between virtue and relative lack of (or the sublimation of) self-interest. Anyone who thinks that moral virtue cannot be motivated primarily by self-interest may feel more virtuous if life does not seem all that rewarding, and definitely will look more virtuous while saying this. Being sour, in other words, can be an unconscious strategy to bolster one's claim to virtue.

Finally, in an increasingly antielitist society it might arouse hostility if one were visibly virtuous to an unusual degree. One strategy would be to downplay or qualify one's virtue. A notable American example was Jimmy Carter's report, when he was running for president, that he had "lust in his heart." An alternative strategy could be to disarm the hostility by emphasizing that one's life was not enviable. Sourness would be a useful attitude to adopt for that purpose.

Finally, one does have to admit the possibility that someone who is genuinely virtuous in the nonclassical way could turn out to have a life that is genuinely rotten. The classical philosophers previously discussed would deny this possibility, even for someone as unlucky as King Priam, because they are focused on a form of virtue in which keen satisfactions derived from one's virtue are a norm. Someone whose virtue is of a different sort though might not have such keen satisfactions, and the balance of satisfactions and misery might be negative if there were horrible diseases or victimization in terrible ways.

Two questions were asked earlier: (1) Can there be a life that is genuinely virtuous, but all the same not a desirable life to lead? and (2) Could virtue sometimes be a poor strategy in life? It should be clear by now that the answers depend, at least in part, on what the form of virtue in question is, and also on the judgments of what is rewarding in life that we (in viewing the lives in question) are prepared to make. Someone whose value judgments fit the model associated with the classical form of virtue, and who is judging a life that exhibits that kind of virtue, would have to answer "No" to both questions. "Inner" values would seem to make the classical kind of virtuous life always, come what may, somewhat desirable; and any strategy that risked losing these values (and taking on their opposites) would be a poor strategy.

The first answer changes, if the questions are asked in relation to someone whose virtue is of the laws/rules/principles sort, someone whose virtue does not provide really deep sources of satisfaction. Even if it is conceded that this person is genuinely virtuous, he or she could have misfortunes comparable to those of Priam without having the virtue-derived deep satisfaction that Priam is presumed to have had. We might well consider such a life on balance not a desirable one.

The arguments of Butler and Hume do show, I think, that even for a person with those values it will be true that virtue is a good strategy for achieving a desirable sort of life. At least, these arguments work for a society, like theirs and ours, that is moderately decent and stable. If, however, one imagines a society that has fallen apart, it becomes imaginable that many people who are virtuous in the nonclassical way could find themselves having rotten lives (and becoming increasingly sour).

14

Shame and Guilt

Self-Interest and Morality

MICHAEL STOCKER

This work is about shame and guilt. It is also about self-interest and morality. I hope to illuminate some aspects of self-interest and of morality and some of their relations by examining shame and guilt and their deep interconnections. Some explanation of my strategy is needed before beginning my discussion of shame and guilt. First a group of general points and then some more focused on shame and guilt.

One avenue to understanding some of the relations between morality and self-interest involves understanding emotions "connected" with them. This would involve asking whether the same emotions are connected with both; and, if there are differences, what they show. Guilt and shame seem natural candidates here. Both seem connected to the person in ways important for self-interest and also for morality. To mention only some obvious points, both may be seen as emotions of self-assessment: witness the title of Gabriele Taylor's *Pride, Shame, and Guilt: Emotions of Self-Assessment.*[1] Both shame and guilt can seem bad in themselves because they are painful, though also useful, for example, for improvement, and to that extent good.

Guilt, because of its connections with doing what is wrong, seems to involve morality, especially other-regarding aspects of morality. Shame, too, seems to involve morality—for example, I can be ashamed of my immoral treatment of you. But it can also involve at least some sorts or aspects of self-interest—especially those that involve moral or moral-like evaluations. So, I can be ashamed of my letting myself go, of failing to live up to my standards. But absent a special story, my not getting all the pleasure I could does not seem to warrant shame, but it may, of course, evoke shame by calling into question one's self-conception as a devoted hedonist committed to hedonistic self-indulgence.[2] For a final point, it can be useful to look at (systems of)

1. Gabriele Taylor, *Pride, Shame, and Guilt: Emotions of Self-Assessment* (Oxford: Oxford University Press, 1985).

2. On some distinctions between what warrants and what evokes an emotion, see Justin D'Arms and Daniel Jacobson, "The Moralistic Fallacy," *Philosophy and Phenomenological Research* 61 (2000): 65–90. I owe my thanks to them for discussion on this and other aspects of shame.

ethics and cultures that are thought of as guilt-based or shame-based to see how these portray various relations between their understandings of morality and of self-interest. In these and still other ways, shame and guilt can be taken as involving both morality and self-interest: as one might say, the self's interest in morality and morality's interest in the self.

Now to some more specific connections between shame and guilt, on the one hand, and self-interest and morality, on the other. A number of complaints have recently been leveled against what are thought of as our dominant ethical theories.[3] In no particular order, here are only five interrelated complaints.

(1) These theories are too concerned with guiding action—with action guiding evaluations, such as "right to do", "duty to do", "wrong to do"—and not concerned enough with other evaluations: other evaluations, still, of acts, for example, those concerning "remainders" and reasons for regretting what is right; and evaluations that are not of acts, for example, of character and virtue. On this view, ethics is too practically minded.

(2) When they do take note of agent evaluations, they suggest that these have little if anything to do with act evaluations. Rather, they hold that there are no important conceptual connections between act evaluations and agent evaluations.

(3) They fail to give the agent's self-concern the importance it has. This comes out in a number of different ways. It underlies some charges that our ethics, as presented in those theories, are too demanding or too impersonal.

(4) They fail to give due importance to an individual's integrity, an individual's ground projects, and an individual's desires, what an individual wants to do.

(5) They give undue support to a (form of) guilt morality at the expense of (aspects of) shame morality. Perhaps they are right in portraying our society/ies—which generate and ground "what we say" and "how we do things"—as embracing (in word or deed) guilt-morality. But they fail by not examining what this sort of morality does to and for us; and they fail also by slighting or simply ignoring the values of, and the values for us of, shame-morality.

In what follows I will not be concerned with whether or not these complaints are accurate or fair to our ethical theories. What is important for this work is what is complained about, what, it is claimed, our theories omit or misunderstand.

One common theme—or background—for at least many of these is the failure to pay adequate attention to individuals from their own, personal points of view. As it might be stated, the failure is paying too much attention to the concerns of justice and too little to the concerns of the self's interests in itself.

The self's interests in itself is clearly not the same as what is often called "self-interest"—at least not where self-interest is seen as involving rough, uncivilized

3. Except for complaint (2), below, Bernard Williams will come immediately to mind here. His work is deservedly so well known that I hope that this note, offered in thanks and acknowledgment of our many debts to him, is all the bibliographical reference needed.

concerns and demands, as these were presented by, say, Thrasymachus. Rather, what I have in mind by the self's interests in itself has to do with the interests of a person "at home" in a civilized and tolerably decent society.

What is the connection between self-interest, so understood, and shame? One quick way to begin the answer to that is to quote Martha Nussbaum, who writes, "Shame, as is generally agreed by those who analyze it, pertains to the whole self, rather than to a specific act of the self. (Guilt...takes an act, rather than the whole person, as its primary object.)"[4] Put most simply, shame is of the person, guilt is of an act.

Without arguing for it, I want to claim that one group of these interests of the self concerns the person's self-evaluation and self-appreciation. Again without argument, I want to claim that shame—shame at oneself—is a "counter" interest to such a person: shame is against such a person's self-interest; shame is painful in a way and to an extent that (experiencing) it is against one's self-interest. (Perhaps I should say that this is so only if other things are equal, for just as even painful punishment by others may be in some-one's self-interest, so may shame.) In this way and to this extent shame can be seen as an element of self-interest and perhaps can thus be a stand-in for it in various arguments.

How do morality and guilt come into the story? How, that is, is guilt an adequate stand-in for morality? Put simply, morality, as portrayed in those complaints, is about what guilt is about and guilt is about morality (*immorality*). The beginning idea (which may well be challenged later) is that guilt is of acts. Obviously, not just any act, but an act that is wrong to do. Morality also deals with what is right (and what is supererogatory, according to even some of those complained-about theories). But we can simply take this as understood. As said, guilt is only a stand-in for morality; it involves only some of what even those complained-about theories see as morality.

My hope, then, is that by exploring some relations between shame and guilt, we will be exploring the relations between some constituents and elements of self-interest and morality. It must be remembered that "shame" stands not only for shame but also for other evaluative focusings on the individual, especially by the individual—including, but not limited to, self-understandings and self-appreciations.

I will be concerned to show some of the deep interconnections between shame and guilt. This will show, or at least suggest, various deep interconnections between self-interest and morality. For as noted, shame and guilt are elements and constitu-ents of self-interest and morality. Shame and guilt are, of course, only part of self-interest and morality. But even so, the discussion of the relations between shame and guilt is (meant to be) a discussion of some relations between self-interest and morality. It is also meant to provide what I hope is a usefully illuminating, even if only analogical, picture of these relations.

Shame and Guilt: How to Distinguish Them

For many reasons—only some of which have been discussed—the nature of shame and guilt, and the differences between them, are staples of moral, philosophical,

4. Martha Nussbaum, *Hiding From Humanity* (Princeton, N.J.: Princeton University Press, 2004), 184.

and moral psychological inquiry. They are of some (and growing) interest among psychoanalysts and other, especially clinical, psychologists. Philosophers should welcome studies of shame and guilt by psychologists and, in particular, by psychoanalysts, whose central focus, after all, is our emotions. *Shame and Guilt in Neurosis*[5] is such a study—and, I suggest, an indispensable one, by the eminent psychoanalytic theorist, Helen Block Lewis.

Many of us, including Lewis, differentiate between shame and guilt, thinking that there are clear and important differences between them and that it is easy enough to distinguish between them. It is, thus, significant that Lewis writes that she and many other therapists and theorists find it very difficult, often impossible, to distinguish between shame and guilt both in practice and in theory. Some of the reasons for this are that there is often a flow and oscillation between them, they are frequently present at the same time, and they are frequently evoked by the same things. She further holds that often enough, when she can determine which one of shame or guilt a patient is experiencing at a given time, the evidence is not given by the episode itself, and not by what is happening at that time or what it is like for the patient at that time, but only by other more global findings, such as the overall style and character of the patient.[6]

I agree that there are important differences between shame and guilt. I also agree with Lewis about the difficulties in distinguishing and even more in characterizing these differences. The difficulties she alerts us to may explain, and they are certainly shown by, the central focus of this work: the difficulties and failures philosophers and others have had in characterizing and distinguishing shame and guilt. One of the most important lessons philosophers can learn from Lewis is the centrality of character—put very briefly, to understand what shame or guilt is, what occasions or blocks them, as well as to identify whether it is shame or guilt that a person is experiencing, we have to start with character, working from the inside out, from character to circumstance.[7] As we will see, too many philosophers work from the outside in.

Before starting on this enterprise I should mention what struck me as a strange problem I encountered. These various works have both vignettes, meant to give us good examples of shame or guilt, and also characterizations of shame and guilt. I found almost all of the vignettes clear and convincing. What we are offered as examples of shame or guilt are, to my mind, clear examples of shame or guilt. Nonetheless, I have found—and I will try to show—that the characterizations, especially the differentiating characterizations, presented in these works are, almost uniformly, seriously mistaken. The features that are offered as showing the differences between shame and guilt fit both shame and guilt; or when offered as important features of shame or important features of guilt fail to fit (enough of) the clear cases of shame or guilt. The question that arises for me is how can the vignettes, the examples,

5. Helen Block Lewis, *Shame and Guilt in Neurosis* (New York: International Universities Press, 1971).

6. For recent discussions of these difficulties as seen by psychologists, see June Price Tangney and Ronda L. Dearing, *Shame and Guilt* (New York and London: Guilford, 2002), especially chap. 2, "What Is the Difference between Shame and Guilt?"

7. I owe my thanks to the psychoanalyst Elizabeth Hegeman for the discussion here.

be so accurate and the lessons drawn from them so inaccurate. Perhaps at least part of the answer has to do with the difficulties Lewis points to and with her emphasis on character.

To show these difficulties and failures I will focus on some writings of four philosophers—primarily Herbert Morris's "Guilt and Shame,"[8] as well as Gabriele Taylor's *Pride, Shame, and Guilt*, Bernard Williams's *Shame and Necessity*,[9] and Martha Nussbaum's *Hiding from Humanity: Disgust, Shame, and the Law*. I will also discuss some writings of various psychoanalysts.

Let us start by simply setting out what many think of as one of the primary distinctions between shame and guilt: shame is of the person, guilt of an act. As Martha Nussbaum puts it, "Shame, as is generally agreed by those who analyze it, pertains to the whole self, rather than to a specific act of the self. (Guilt, as we shall see later, takes an act, rather than the whole person, as its primary object.)"[10]

This is not how Herbert Morris puts it:

> A child hits a playmate; he is told that that is a bad thing to do, that it is wrong to hit others; the next time he does it, he may be punished; he meets with "you're a bad boy." This situation, provided other conditions are met, can lead to the child acquiring the concept of a rule, his accepting a rule, and in cases of infraction feeling guilt. He may come to see that when he does wrong, punishment is an appropriate response from others. But the parent may respond differently to the conduct. He may say to the child of whose conduct he disapproves, "that is what an animal does, not a human being" and then turn away from the child. The child in such situations may come, in time, to connect "being a human being" with what is valued, with what should be sought after and connect "animal" with what is inferior, that which, when a human being manifests it, results in others turning away in disgust, turning away because they cannot stand the sight before them. The child may come, provided other conditions are met, to understand the conception of a valued or model identity, accept this and feel shame when he fails to correspond to it. We have here the seeds of a morality, let us call it a "shame morality" which, to be sure, overlaps in our own moral world with guilt, but which is still distinct.[11]

Morris pictures the parents focusing on the child's act, saying that it is wrong, that it is a bad thing to do—thus, according to Morris, presenting and creating conditions for guilt. But Morris does not depict these parents who are presenting and creating conditions for guilt as focusing on the act. He also has the parents say, now focusing on the child, "You are a bad boy". This, Morris tells us, can lead to "the child acquiring the concept of a rule, his accepting a rule, and in cases of infraction

---

8. "Guilt and Shame" is appended, as 59–63, to "Persons and Punishment" that appears in Herbert Morris, *On Guilt and Innocence* (Berkeley and Los Angeles: University of California Press, 1976), and was excerpted from "Guilt and Punishment," *The Personalist* 52 (1971).

9. Bernard Williams, *Shame and Necessity* (Berkeley and Los Angeles: University of California Press, 1993).

10. Nussbaum, *Hiding from Humanity*, 184.

11. Morris, "Guilt and Shame," 60.

feeling guilt". So, on Morris's view, guilt can be of the person or at least aroused by views about the person.

He also holds that being told these things can be shaming, through an eventual "understand[ing of] the conception of a valued or model identity, accept[ing] this and feel[ing] shame when he fails to correspond to it". I find it puzzling that he does not say or also say that being told "You are a bad boy" can also be *directly* shaming.

In any case, his account of differences between guilt and shame does not rely on whether the act or, alternatively, the agent is said to be bad. Morris's account depends on the differences between rules and ideals, including the violation of them and what is to be expected from such violation. We might well wonder how the rules/ideals distinction could possibly explain or even agree extensionally with the guilt/shame distinction. For the violation of at least some ideals can engender guilt. And one can be ashamed of having violated a rule. But this is to get ahead of ourselves.

To evaluate Morris's claim, we must turn our attention to differences between rules and ideals. Some see the main differences in pretty much syntactic form: rules are cast in imperatival form and ideals in terms of goals to be strove for. Along these lines, Morris suggests that it is a sharp and clear enough matter whether a rule has been followed—you have followed it or you have not.[12] Ideals, on the other hand, can be met or violated in more graded and graduated ways,[13] So Morris says, "With guilt one has either done wrong or not; it is not a concept admitting of degrees of realization...connected with this contrast between the conception of a scale and a threshold is the fact that with shame we may focus on failure to achieve an ideal, perfection, some maximum whereas with guilt it is a minimum demand that has not been met".[14]

I do not think the rules/ideals contrast(s) help us understand the guilt/shame contrast(s). Contrary to what Morris suggests, many rules are fuzzy in themselves, needing considerable interpretation for their application; many rules can be more or less satisfied: partially satisfied, fully satisfied, or supererogatorily oversatisfied. In all respects, ideals can be like this, too. Of course, rules can be as Morris says: exact and exacting. But so can ideals.

Morris also says that "the critical concept associated with shame is failure, shortcoming, not violation."[15] But as I see matters, we can fail to obey a rule and show we are a failure by not obeying a rule. So too for shortcomings. At least some, if not many, occasions for shame—both what warrants and what evokes shame—are violations of propriety, honor, and so on.

At least many of these violations can be seen as violations of standards. These standards can, of course, be moral or nonmoral (however these are understood). To mention only two nonmoral categories, the standards—and thus guilt and shame—can be technical or aesthetic. A member of a woodworking team can feel "guilty" about making an error that sets the team back or that spoils the work and can feel ashamed of having done that.

---

12. Ibid., 61.
13. Ibid.
14. Ibid.
15. Ibid.

It might be suggested, although Morris does not do so, that what is important about rules is that they are, or can be felt as, more alien, more imposed, more external or objective; whereas, in contrast, ideals are internal or subjective. (The discussion of psychoanalytic theory below will touch on connections between ideals and the ego ideal.) These ideals "refer" to what is subjective. Here we might note the claim made by many psychoanalysts that it is for this reason that obsessive people, characterized by their fear of the subjective, create a false sense of objectivity for themselves—a false sense that they do not have to exercise judgment and make choices—by looking to rules, real or imagined.[16] The suggestion here (again, not made by Morris) is that guilt has to do with violations of what is external or objective, shame of what is internal or subjective.

However, the rules/ideals contrast does not match up with the outer/inner one. Obsessive people do look to rules, because they see the rules as objective. But they also look to various ideals, real or imagined, that they see, correctly or not, as objective. So, an obsessive person, trying to decide which job to take, might focus on which is best, rather than also which he wants to do.[17] Turning now to other (nonobsessive) sorts of people, for many people many rules are felt as self-chosen, expressing their innermost sense of values and self.

Ideals seem much the same on this score. I can be alienated from my own ideals—feeling them to be "not really mine", "imposed on me by society", and so on. As this suggests, alienation and identification are not well sorted or handled by the rules/ideals contrast.

Do rules and ideals, quite generally—or, for that matter, do guilt and shame, again quite generally—differ in stringency? I do not think so. In some cases, for some societies, for some people, rules are honored more in the breach than in the performance. Violating these rules in these circumstances need not involve much, if any, guilt. Ideals might also be treated in this easygoing way, perhaps because they are seen as extra, rather optional ornaments of value. But in other circumstances or other societies, violations of these or other rules can be very serious. But all this is true of ideals, too. This is to speak of rules and ideals, guilt and shame, quite generally. To be sure, for us here and now, and of course elsewhere, there are many rules that are or are felt as being more stringent than many ideals. But so too, there are many ideals that are or are felt as being more stringent than many rules. So too for guilt and shame.

I want now to suspend direct examination of Morris to consider some aspects of psychoanalytic theory. I do not think that this will be to move too far from our original focus, the nature of and differences between shame and guilt. Many philosophers, including many of those at the center of the present inquiry, rely on these and similar psychoanalytic views. Further, the psychoanalytic views in question are directly centered on the nature of and differences between shame and guilt and between rules and ideals.

16. See, for example, David Shapiro, *Neurotic Styles* (New York: Basic, 1965).
17. On compulsiveness, see David Shapiro, *Neurotic Styles*, and his *Autonomy and the Rigid Character* (New York: Basic, 1981).

The psychoanalytic view in question would have us understand guilt in terms of rules issued by the harsh and punitive superego and internalized fear of punishment for violating these rules; and shame in terms of the ego ideal, in terms of not living up to ideals (of and for oneself), and of thinking of oneself as defective, as lacking, as not lovable, because one has not lived up to these ideals.[18]

This set of claims is central to Gerhart Piers's *Shame and Guilt*.[19] Many philosophers, including, I think, Morris, rely on Piers's account. So too, many psychoanalysts accept this sort of account (not, however, relying on Piers's work). For the latter, we can turn once again to Helen Block Lewis, one of the major psychoanalytic theorists of shame and guilt. She writes, "the immediately relevant stimulus to the evocation of shame or guilt is the pathway of identification with parental figures which has been stirred. When the ego ideal, or positive identification figure, is stirred, shame of failure results; this shame may be moral or nonmoral. When the negative or castrating identification figure is stirred, the sense of guilt for transgression results".[20]

It is well known—some would say, notorious—that there are different and contending schools of psychoanalysis. So, it is not surprising that other psychoanalysts disagree with this (sort of) account. But, because of the light they throw on rules and ideals, there are some objections that deserve our attention. We can learn from them—without presuming to enter into disputes within psychoanalysis.

One way to start on these objections is to note that various psychoanalytic theorists—including Freud—see the superego not just as harsh and punitive, and not as working just through requirements, prohibitions, and fear of punishment, but also as being, in part, loving. Here I want simply to indicate some of the claims in two instructively entitled articles: Roy Schafer's "The Loving and Beloved Superego in Freud's Structural Thought"[21] and David Schecter's "The Loving and Persecuting Superego".[22] They argue that, contrary to what is often taken as settled psychoanalytic doctrine, the superego is not always punitive, but is sometimes and in some

---

18. On some of the understandings of, and disputes about, the superego and the ego ideal, see J. Laplanche and J.-B. Pontalis, *The Language of Psycho-Analysis*, trans. Donald Nicholson-Smith (New York: Norton, 1974) under "super ego" and "ego ideal".

19. With Milton Singer. The full title is *Shame and Guilt: A Psychoanalytic and a Cultural Study* (Springfield, Ill.: Charles C. Thomas, 1953). This work is frequently relied on by philosophers who often enough refer to it in ways suggesting that it is coauthored by Piers and Singer. It is more accurate to say that it is two distinct essays, the first, a psychoanalytic study, is written by Piers and the second, a cultural study, by Singer. Whether, as I am inclined to think, Singer's work tells against Peirs's is a question for other work.

20. Helen Block Lewis, *Shame and Guilt in Neurosis*, 82.

21. Roy Schafer, "The Loving and Beloved Superego in Freud's Structural Thought," *Contemporary Psychoanalysis* (1979): 15, 163–88.

22. David Schecter, "The Loving and Persecuting Superego," *Contemporary Psychoanalysis* (1979): 15, 361–79. In his paper delivered as the presidential address to the William Alanson White Psychoanalytic Society, May 23, 1979, Schecter refers approvingly to Schafer's work, citing it as appearing in 1960 (361). Although published in 1979, Schafer delivered his work to the Western New England Psychoanalytic Society on March 19, 1960.

ways loving, protecting, and rewarding. (It may be worth repeating that I present these claims to help us understand rules and ideals, not to enter into debates internal to psychoanalytic theory.)

It is worth quoting some of Schecter's characterization. He writes

> The concept of the loving superego represents a structuralized, relatively stable set of qualities, actions, thoughts, and feelings which can be observed in normal individuals as well as in the psychoanalytic treatment of children and adults. Moreover, the loving superego is essentially a strong, tough *protective structure* which must be able to overcome the tremendous hardness of which the condemning and persecuting superego is capable. Of course the loving superego can also be soft and comforting but these are not its essential qualities, for without protective strength, the loving superego is no match for its persecuting counterpart.[23]

To help show that Freud held this view, both Schafer and Schecter quote the same passage from Freud's *The Ego and the Id*, "The fear of death in melancholia only admits of one explanation: that the ego gives itself up because it feels itself hated and *persecuted by the superego instead of loved. To the ego, therefore, living means the same as being loved — being loved by the superego*; which here again appears as a representative of the id. *The superego fulfills the same function as protecting and saving* that was fulfilled in earlier days by the father and later by Providence and Destiny".[24]

Further, what is loving, including the ego ideal, can be understood as issuing directives. As Schafer says, identification with a "great man" (to use Freud's term) "may be considered an instance of ego identification, though once the process of superego identification reinforces it, it takes on an *imperative moral quality*".[25]

It would be an unwarranted stretch to hold that where there are directives, there must also be punishment — punishment for failing to carry them out. Such failures might, instead, be met just with disappointment, or consolation, or encouragement to do better next time. This could be used to suggest the following difference between guilt and shame put in terms of a difference between the punitive superego, on the one hand, and the ego ideal, perhaps joined by the loving superego, on the other hand: the punitive superego operates, it motivates, through fear, but the ego ideal and perhaps the loving superego operate, motivate, through love. The suggestion can continue that the superego operating through fear accounts for guilt. As Schafer says, "Guilt corresponds to feelings of the superego's hatred"[26] — while the ego ideal and perhaps the loving superego account for shame. The thought about shame would be that a person feels a failure, unworthy, by failing to satisfy an ideal. As Schafer says, inferiority feelings "correspond to feelings of the loss of the superego's love".[27]

23. Schecter, "The Loving and Persecuting Superego," 362–63, emphasis in original.

24. Sigmund Freud, *The Ego and the Id, Standard Edition*, trans. James Strachey (London: Hogarth, 1961), 19:3, 66, Schecter's emphases.

25. Roy Schafer, "The Loving and Beloved Superego in Freud's Structural Thought," *Contemporary Psychoanalysis* 15 (1979):179, my emphasis.

26. Ibid.

27. Ibid.

This confronts us with a problem of distinguishing between loss of love and punishment. After all, withdrawing love is one way to punish or threaten punishment—"If you do that again, we won't love you anymore". As Schafer says, "The strongest childhood need is for the father's protection against superior powers of fate…; and the dread of loss of love is the dread of losing this protection as well as of being punished".[28] As this suggests, losing love and its attendant protection, and the threat of this, can easily be seen, and used, as threatened or actual punishment.

Further, many goods contain within themselves "ought not's"—these are goods that ought not be foregone or scanted. As Schafer puts it in "Ideals, The Ego Ideal, and the Ideal Self", "Hartmann and Loewenstein deprive conscience of the functions Freud assigned to it; this step frees them to go on to equate the "good" and ideals with the ego ideal and the "ought not" with conscience. This…makes little sense on close examination, for every "good" has an "ought not" built into it (as every child soon learns) and vice versa".[29]

For our present purposes, there is no need to discuss whether Schafer should have said "*many* goods", not "*every* good". Even if only many goods contain ought nots, that is good enough for us.

To sum up, feelings of unworthiness, of failure, of inferiority—of shame—can be attendant on failure to obey requirements and prohibitions. Loss of love can be experienced or threatened as punishment. Failures to adhere to both rules and ideals, and more clearly dishonoring or violating both rules and ideals, can be met, or it can be feared that they will be met, with consequences of considerable force: for example, death, banishment, fines, being forced in still other ways to make amends, perhaps to one's family or group, or to cleanse one's besmirched character or soul.

I now return to Morris and some other ways he attempts to distinguish between shame and guilt. On his view, the distinction can be made out by looking at (1) the damage done by what evokes shame as compared with the damage by what evokes guilt, (2) what needs to be done to make things right, (3) who gets to punish the violator, and (4) who owes what to whom in the different cases. In two related passages, Morris writes, "We shall feel shame, then, in situations where we do not conceive of ourselves as damaging a relationship with others…what is valued in a shame morality is an identity of a certain kind and not, as is necessary with guilt, a relationship with others"[30] and "[D]iminishing harm to others [is the predominant goal of guilt and laws.]… [T]here is incentive put forward for restoring relationships…the relations are between individuals who do not ordinarily have close ties that would, apart from obligations or a sense of obligation, provide strong motives for satisfying the interests of others. It is, I think, whenever interests of this kind predominate that one is pulled to responses that generate the conception of guilt".[31] But many of us feel shame over harming others, even if they are strangers. So too, many of us feel shame over what damages a relationship with others, even if they are strangers. So too, many of us feel shame over what damages a relationship with others because of harm or for other reasons.

28. Ibid., 175.
29. Roy Schafer, "Ideals, The Ego Ideal, and the Ideal Self," *Psychological Issues* (1967): 5, 135n4.
30. Morris, "Guilt and Shame," 61.
31. Ibid., 63.

Bernard Williams devotes a good portion of his *Shame and Necessity* to describing and criticizing our current ethical theories' overemphasis of guilt at the expense of shame. I agree with much of what he says on these scores. But I disagree with his characterizations of guilt and of shame and of the differences between them.

Given his acknowledgment of learning from Morris, we should not be surprised that similar difficulties afflict suggestions made by Williams:

> [D]ifferences in the experience of shame and of guilt can be seen as part of a wider set of contrasts between them. What arouses guilt in an agent is an act or omission of a sort that typically elicits from other people anger, resentment, or indignation. What the agent may offer in order to turn this away is reparation; he may also fear punishment or may inflict it on himself. What arouses shame, on the other hand, is something that typically elicits from others contempt or derision or avoidance. This may equally be an act or omission, but it need not be: it may be some failing or defect. It will lower the agent's self-respect and diminish him in his own eyes. His reaction…is a wish to hide or disappear, and this is one thing that links shame as, minimally, embarrassment with shame as social or personal reduction. More positively, shame may be expressed in attempts to reconstruct or improve oneself.[32]

Let us leave aside the seeming difficulties of understanding shame in terms of both attempts to reconstruct or improve oneself and also the wish to hide or disappear. Perhaps shame is to be understood as offering us the option: reconstruct or improve yourself or, alternatively, hide or disappear. More importantly for us, I do not see much, if any, difference between shame and guilt in these regards. I do agree that there are systematic connections between shame and self-reconstruction or self-improvement and also between shame and hiding and disappearing. But I find it difficult to understand guilt as lacking these connections. After all, one way to acknowledge one's guilt is to commit oneself to self-improvement.

Similarly, I agree that there are systematic connections between guilt and reparations and between guilt and punishment. But again, as I see matters, shame, too, is systematically connected with both punishment and reparations. If I am ashamed of how I have treated a student, I may well think or be told that I should make amends, to make things right. And one way to (try to) expiate shame is by inviting and undergoing penance and punishment.

Williams talks about different things that typically arouse, not shame or guilt in a person, but other emotions in other people: "contempt or derision or avoidance" for shame and "anger, resentment, or indignation" for guilt. But often enough, as he recognizes, the very same thing arouses both elements of these pairs. He says, "An agent will be motivated by prospective shame in the face of people who would be angered by conduct that, in turn, they would avoid for those same reasons".[33] If, as Williams rightly claims, both shame and guilt can be aroused by what evokes the very same reaction in other people—here, anger—we cannot use these people's different reactions to distinguish between guilt and shame.

---

32. Williams, *Shame and Necessity*, 89–90.
33. Ibid., 83.

Various theorists, including Williams and Taylor, characterize shame and distinguish it from guilt, by holding that shame, but not guilt, involves, shows itself by, wanting not to be seen, unwillingness to meet the other's eyes, looking sideways, slinking and slumping, wanting to hide. This involves two main elements: an audience and how the person who feels shame is (or wants to be) toward the audience. I will take these in reverse order.

Taylor writes, "In feeling shame the actor thinks of himself as having become an object of detached observation, and at the core to feel shame is to feel distress at being seen at all".[34] She also writes, "It is because the agent thinks of herself in a certain relation to the audience that she now thinks herself degraded".[35]

Similarly, Williams writes, "The basic experience connected with shame is that of being seen, inappropriately, by the wrong people, in the wrong condition. It is straightforwardly connected with nakedness, particularly in sexual connections. The word *aidoia*, a derivative of *aidos*, 'shame,' is a standard Greek word for genitals and similar terms are found in other languages."[36]

But it seems common enough that those who feel guilty want to hide and avoid being seen. As claimed earlier, if a person does not want to hide, to be unnoticed and unremarked upon, it is difficult to sustain the claim that the person feels guilty—unless we also hold that the person is trying to brazen it out. But such brazenness seems possible in cases of shame, too.

Further, it seems common enough for people to be made to feel guilty—to ask, "What did I do wrong?"—by others staring, perhaps pointing an accusing finger at them. Sartre says that the man in the hotel corridor is shamed and made to feel shame by being seen peering through the keyhole. That is entirely understandable. But it is also entirely understandable that another person would be made to feel guilty by seeing that he is seen doing that. That person, too, can be expected not to welcome being seen, either then and there or later by that other person. (We can understand Lewis as holding that we may have to imagine our two people having different sorts of character.)

It is difficult to see how only shame, but not guilt, can be thought to require an audience. Here we should consider some remarks by the psychoanalyst Andrew Morrison:

> From the vantage point of…the demands or goals of a strict ego ideal (the ideal self), shame can be appreciated as an essentially intrapsychic, internal experience. Of course, internalization of objects and their representations in the formation of the ego ideal and ideal self, along with the need for the self-object function in self-development, ultimately puts these intrapsychic structures into an interpersonal, or intersubjective, framework. But this is true as well for all human development, including the identifications that generate the superego and lead ultimately to guilt as well as to shame.[37]

34. Taylor, *Pride, Shame, and Guilt*, 60.
35. Ibid., 68.
36. Williams, *Shame and Necessity*, 78.
37. Andrew Morrison, *Shame: The Underside of Narcissism* (Hillsdale, N.J.: Analytic, 1989), 15–16, my emphasis.

To my mind, Morrison's last claim is quite similar in import to Williams's "The internalised other [viz., the audience needed for shame] is indeed abstracted and generalised and idealised, but he is potentially somebody rather than nobody, and somebody other than me".[38] Or perhaps, it would be better to say that Morrison's claim helps explain and justify Williams's. In these various ways, then, Taylor and Williams join many other theorists in holding that shame requires an audience. I should say, rather, that Taylor and Williams at first join those other theorists. For despite what we have just read Taylor and Williams saying about shame needing an audience, they almost immediately withdraw their claims. In a passage incorporating the second quote above, Taylor writes, "It is because the agent thinks of herself in a certain relation to the audience that she now thinks herself degraded, but she does not think of this degradation as depending on an audience. Her final judgment concerns herself only: she is degraded not relatively to this audience, she is degraded absolutely".[39]

Williams's first sentence, quoted above, reads, "The basic experience connected with shame is that of being seen, inappropriately, by the wrong people, in the wrong condition". This sentence, asserting the need for an audience, ends with note 8, which reads, "For a rather more complex account of the basic experiences of shame and how they come to be elaborated, see Endnote 1".[40] In that endnote, he says that his earlier claim about shame and being seen, especially when naked, was too simple and misleading; and that the more accurate view is that nakedness and being seen naked are signs of being at a disadvantage and suffering a loss of power; and that recognition of disadvantage and suffering is what is central to shame.[41] Once again, we are faced with a claim of doubtful coherence, first asserting and then withdrawing and denying that need.

We must ask whether there is something about shame and guilt that invites, or at least allows, philosophers to make important claims that in the next sentence they then deny. Is there something about shame and guilt that "clouds people's minds", hiding this very obvious problem from them?

I am unsure what to make of Williams's use of nakedness. There are just too many ways that the body and nakedness are taken up—depending on circumstances, social expectations, customs, individual psychologies, to mention some of the determinants—that the usefulness of this characterization of shame must be called into question.

Further, if I understand what Williams is suggesting by his talk of being caught naked, and his claim about a "recognition of disadvantage and suffering", he seems to be thinking of serious, major cases of shame, cases of major shame—found in humiliations, narcissistic meltdowns, involving a severe loss of self-esteem and self-confidence, coupled with despair, active attacks on oneself, one's competence, "I'm no good at anything; I can't do anything right"—and the like.

---

38. Williams, *Shame and Necessity*, 84.
39. Taylor, *Pride, Shame, and Guilt*, 68.
40. Williams, *Shame and Necessity*, 194.
41. Ibid., 220.

Williams is hardly the only theorist discussing shame who focuses on major shame. Many psychologists and psychoanalysts do this.[42] An especially strong, even florid, claim to this effect is made the psychologists Merle A. Fossum and Marilyn J. Mason: "Shame is an inner sense of being *completely* diminished or insufficient as a person".[43]

Many philosophers also do this. Martha Nussbaum writes that shame, understood quite generally, involves the agent seeing herself or himself as wholly and utterly inadequate: "[W]hereas shame focuses on defect or imperfection, and thus on some aspect of the very being of the person who feels it, guilt focuses on an action (or wish to act) but need not extend to the entirety of the agent, seeing the agent as *utterly inadequate*".[44]

Richard Moran's "paradoxes of self-censure" seem to require something like this.[45] The paradox runs as follows: a person is ashamed of doing such-and-such; he then comes to think (recognize) that at least he is sensitive enough to feel shame over doing that; he then becomes proud of himself for being sensitive enough to feel shame over doing that—or better put, he becomes proud of himself and he leaves the shame behind; reflecting on that pride, he comes to feel that it is shameful to take pride in that—or better, he becomes ashamed of himself, leaving the pride behind; and so on.

I think the most plausible account of why the previous emotion is left behind, erased by the later one, is that the shame and pride are cases of major, overwhelming shame and pride. These are cases where there is, near enough, no "room" for other emotions, especially for the other emotions (shame or pride).

There are, of course, episodes of shame that, however they start, end up with the person feeling that she or he is wholly, not just in part, utterly inadequate. Hysterics are often like this. But if shame is like this—especially if it is over something minor—that shows a lot about the person and less about the general nature of

---

42. For theoretical or clinical reasons, some quite generally focus on the most intense cases, for example, rage rather than modulated anger or on pathological rather than unproblematic cases. Some hold that this is how shame is for adults since they hold both that this is how shame is for infants and also that adults' shame is just like infants' shame. For criticism of the latter claim, for denying developmental changes from infants to adults, see, for example, Roy Schafer, "Ideals, the Ego Ideal, and the Ideal Self," *Psychological Issues* 5 (1967): 131–74; and Daniel F. Jones "Diagnosis and Character" in *Handbook of Interpersonal Psychoanalysis*, ed. Marylou Lionells et al., (Hillsdale, N.J.: Analytic, 1995).

43. Merle A. Fossum and Marilyn J. Mason, *Facing Shame: Families in Recovery* (New York: Norton, 1986), 5. My emphasis.

44. Nussbaum, *Hiding From Humanity*, 207, my emphases. She cites Taylor, *Pride, Shame and Guilt*, chap. 4; and Piers, *Shame and Guilt*, chaps. 1–2.

45. Richard Moran, *Authority and Estrangement: An Essay in Self-Knowledge* (Princeton, N.J.: Princeton University Press, 2001), chap. 5, sect. 4, 170–82. He attributes this view to Samuel Johnson, 171 (referring to the entry for April 25, 1778, in *Life of Johnson*, ed. R. W. Chapman [Oxford: Oxford University Press, 1953]); Jean-Paul Sartre, 172–73 (referring to *Being and Nothingness*, trans. Hazel Barnes [New York: Washington Square, Philosophical Library, 1956] 109); David Hume, 181n18 (referring to *A Treatise of Human Nature*, book. 2, "Of the Passions," part 1, "Of Pride and Humility," sect. 2); and some others.

shame. It shows a disturbing lack of ego strength and that the person is in considerable trouble, in need of rest, help, or other succor. But not all people are like this; nor are all cases of shame like this. There is well-contained, moderate shame.

Williams and Nussbaum do recognize that shame need not be so major. Above, we read Williams as saying, "More positively, shame may be expressed in attempts to reconstruct or improve oneself." Nussbaum writes, "Shame of a specific and limited sort can be constructive, motivating a pursuit of valuable ideals".[46] Such constructive shame would be difficult, if not impossible, if shame had to be of the whole person, who feels utterly inadequate.

So, some cases of shame—of major shame—do fit Williams's characterization. So too, some cases of guilt are as extensive and as intense as this, too. But neither shame nor guilt need be like this. There are many cases of minor shame, minor cases of shame where both the occasion and the feeling are minor. And there are many such cases: I can be ashamed in a minor way of wearing a stained shirt to a department meeting or of having spoken somewhat too harshly to a colleague at that meeting. I find it difficult—really, impossible—to understand these minor cases in terms of what I think Williams had in mind when he talked of what it is like to be caught naked, or to involve a recognition of "disadvantage and suffering".

If I were to understand those cases of shame in either of these ways, I would not see that person as experiencing them as minor. My point here is not that someone's shame at wearing a stained shirt must be minor. It is that it can be minor. Further, if it is, instead, major—perhaps involving felt humiliation or a narcissistic meltdown— that would show at least as much about the person as it does about the general nature of shame.

It might be of interest to explore why in their general discussion of shame various theorists focus on cases of florid, pathological, major shame. But whatever their reasons for this, we must recognize that in mature adults of adequate ego strength, shame can be well contained and limited. We must recognize that we cannot understand all cases of shame in terms of what I have called major shame.

Concluding Remarks

This work has been largely negative, showing the inadequacy of various attempted characterizations of shame and guilt and especially of the differences between them. Nonetheless, I join most every theorist in thinking that they are different and that in many, if not most, cases we can tell whether they show shame, guilt, both, or neither. Perhaps it would not be out of place to conclude that the nature of and the relations between shame and guilt are as difficult to detail as are those of and between morality and self-interest. That, of course, remains to be shown. I hope, however, that this work has done something to help us understand the latter pair, if only by exploring some of the moral, and more generally the evaluative, emotions it is useful to understand if we are to understand morality and self-interest.

---

46. Nussbaum, *Hiding from Humanity*, 208.

Early in this work, I said that the discussion of the relations between shame and guilt is (meant to be) a discussion of some relations between self-interest and morality. It is also meant to provide what I hope is a usefully illuminating, even if only analogical, picture of these relations. What do I hope to have shown about those issues by these discussions of shame and guilt? Perhaps the best answer is found by returning to those five complaints. These discussions, I think, have shown that at least some of those complaints are well taken, at least on the surface.

They are well taken in that they can be seen as complaints against our ethical theories' overconcern with only certain, limited parts of evaluation and human life—for example, an overconcern with acts it is right or wrong to do. By "on the surface" I mean that it has to do with our understandings of those theories—really, our *mis*understandings embodied in and expressed by those ethical theories; as it might be put, by those theories' misunderstandings of themselves and their central notions. My claim is that these theories suggest and depend on misunderstandings of their central notions.

I can put an instance of this—one of many—in terms of shame and guilt and then in terms of self-interest and morality. An adequate understanding of shame and of guilt will show the deep relations between them. They are distinct, but to a significant extent, they come to us together and both must be understood to understand either. If this is right, then contrary to our ethical theories as portrayed in those complaints, an adequate morality will focus not just on acts, but will focus also on the self, from the person's own points of view. If it focuses just on acts, especially those acts, it will fail to see vital aspects of acts, themselves, and it will thus misunderstand the nature and proper evaluation of action. Correcting for these truncated views, an adequate ethics will of course focus on rightness (and other act evaluations) and it will focus on the self's interests in itself: both on morality and also self-interest.

At the outset, I claimed that shame and guilt and their interrelations can be seen as, or as giving, analogues to self-interest and morality and their interrelations. To conclude this work, I want to use some claims developed in the discussion of shame and guilt to help sustain this claim. To this end, I will give, without much discussion, three instances of what I have in mind.

(1) In the discussion of shame, various problems—debilities, really—of excess shame were discussed. One was being overwhelmed with, completely "filled" by shame. Another was a concern only with shame without concomitant guilt—being concerned only with oneself and not one's effects on others or the world. Self-interest, when not "handled" well, can generate or otherwise involve similar debilities. Witness some of the problems of overconcern with self and self-interest.

(2) Guilt and getting it wrong suggest, perhaps are, good analogues of problems of morality as listed in the complaints noted at the outset of this work. Here we can think of the problems for a morality that is said to trump all considerations, including the individual's integrity, projects, and desires. One of the more important analogues for guilt has to do with the sorts of dissociation and other lacks of self-understanding of attending only to one's acts and their effects and taking no account of the self that these show. At the extreme, it is (almost) as if the person is not aware of himself or herself as an agent with a character, but at most only as a producer of those acts and effects.

(3) Shame can take guilt as a ground or object: for example, I can feel guilty at having wronged you and I can be ashamed of myself for having wronged you. Proper self-interest can, similarly, take morality as its ground or object: for example, it is in my self-interest—enlightened self-interest—to be able to think well of myself and acting immorally can make that difficult, if not impossible.

These are only three of the ways that shame and guilt can enter directly into self-interest and morality, and that shame and guilt and their interrelations can be or give analogues to self-interest and morality and their interrelations.

Bibliography

Abercrombie, Nigel. *The Origins of Jansenism*. Oxford: Clarendon, 1936.

Adams, R. M. "Moral Faith." *Journal of Philosophy* 92 (1995): 75–95.

Annas, Julia. *An Introduction to Plato's Republic*. Oxford: Clarendon, 1981.

———. *The Morality of Happiness*. Oxford: Oxford University Press, 1993.

———. *Platonic Ethics: Old and New*. Ithaca, N.Y.: Cornell University Press, 1999.

———. "Happiness as Achievement." In *Daedalus* Spring 2004.

———. "Being Virtuous and Doing the Right Thing" *Proceedings of the American Philosophical Association* (November 2004).

Anscombe, G. E. M. "Modern Moral Philosophy." *Philosophy* 33 (1958): 1–19.

Anselm. *Truth, Freedom, and Evil*. Edited and translated by J. Hopkins and H. Richardson. New York: Harper & Row, 1967.

Argyle, Michael. *The Psychology of Happiness*. London: Methuen, 1987.

Aristotle. *Complete Works of Aristotle*, vol. 2. Edited by Jonathan Barnes. Princeton, N.J.: Princeton University Press, 1984.

———. *Nicomachean Ethics*. 2nd ed. Translated by T. Irwin. Indianapolis: Hackett, 1999.

Audi, Robert. "Self-Deception and Rationality." In *Self-Deception and Morality*, edited by Mike W. Martin. Lawrence: University Press of Kansas, 1986.

———. "Self-Deception, Rationalization, and the Ethics of Belief." In *Moral Knowledge and Ethical Character*. New York: Oxford University Press, 1997.

Augustine. *The City of God*. Trans. M. Dods, in Basic Writings of St. Augustine, ed. W. J. Bates, 2 vols. New York: Random House, 1948, vol. 2.

———. *On the Trinity*. Edited by Garth Matthews. Cambridge: Cambridge University Press, 2002.

Austin, J. L. *How to Do Things with Words*. Oxford: Oxford University Press, 1962.

Badhwar, Neera Kapur. "Altruism Versus Self-Interest: Sometimes a False Dichotomy." *Social Philosophy and Policy* 10, no. 1 (1993): 90–117.

Baier, Kurt. "The Point of View of Morality" *Australasian Journal of Philosophy* 32, no. 2 (1954): 104–35.

———. *The Moral Point of View*. Ithaca, N.Y.: Cornell University Press, 1958.

———. "Why Should We Be Moral?" *Readings in Contemporary Ethical Theory*. Edited by K. Pahel and M. Schiller. Englewood Cliffs, N.J.: Prentice Hall, 1970, 427–41.

———. "Moral Reasons and Reasons to Be Moral." In *Values and Morals*, edited by A. I. Goldman and J. Kim. Dordrecht: D. Reidel, 1978.

Baius, Michael. *De Virtutibus Impiorum*. In *Michaeli Baii Opera*. Cologne: Egmont, 1696.

Bak, F. "Scoti schola numerosior est omnibus aliis simul sumptis." In *Franciscan Studies* 16 (1956): 144–65.

Balguy, John. *A Collection of Tracts Moral and Theological*. London: Pemberton, 1734.

Beck, Lewis White. *A Commentary on Kant's Critique of Practical Reason*. Chicago: University of Chicago Press, 1960.

Bedau, M. A. "Where's the Good in Teleology?" *Philosophy and Phenomenological Research* 52 (1992): 781–806.

Berkeley, George. *The Works of George Berkeley*. Edited by A. A. Luce and T. E. Jessup. London: Thomas Nelson and Sons, 1948.

Bird, Alexander. "Dispositions and Antidotes." *Philosophical Quarterly* 48 (1998): 227–34.

Blackburn, Simon. *Ruling Passions: A Theory of Practical Reasoning*. Oxford: Clarendon, 1998.

———. *Spreading the Word*. Oxford: Clarendon, 1984.

Blass, Thomas. *Obedience to Authority: Current Perspectives on the Milgram Paradigm*. Mahweh, N.J.: Lawrence Erlbaum, 2000.

Bloomfield, Paul. Review of *The Evolution of Morality*, by Richard Joyce. 116 (2007): 176–80.

———. *Moral Reality*. New York: Oxford University Press, 2001.

Boswell, James. *Life of Johnson*. Edited by R. W. Chapman. Oxford: Oxford University Press, 1953.

Bradley, F. H. *Ethical Studies*. Oxford: Oxford University Press, [1876] 1927.

Bratman, M. E. "Practical Reasoning and Acceptance in a Context." *Mind* 101 (1992): 1–15.

Brink, David. "A Puzzle about the Rational Authority of Morality." *Philosophical Perspectives* 6 (1992): 1–26.

———. "Self-Love and Altruism." In *Social Philosophy & Policy* 14 (1997): 122–57.

Brock, Dan W. "The Justification of Morality." *American Philosophical Quarterly* 14 (1977): 71–78.

Burgess, J. P. "Against Ethics." In Ethical Theory and Moral Practice, [1978] 2007.

Burnyeat, Myles. "Aristotle on Learning to Be Good." In *Essays on Aristotle's Ethics*. Edited by A. O. Rorty. Berkeley and Los Angeles: University of California Press, 1980.

Butler, Joseph. *The Works of Bishop Butler*, 2 vols. Edited by J. H. Bernard. London: MacMillan, 1900.

Carlsmith, J. and A. Gross. "Some Effects of Guilt on Compliance." *Journal of Personality and Social Psychology* 11 (1969): 232–39.

Chang, Ruth. "All Things Considered." *Philosophical Perspectives* 18 (2004): 1–22.

———. "Putting Together Morality and Well-Being." In *Practical Conflicts: New Philosophical Essays*. Edited by P. Baumann and M. Betzler. Cambridge: Cambridge University Press, 2004.

Clark, Maudemarie. "Nietzsche's Immoralism and the Concept of Morality." In *Nietzsche, Genealogy, Morality: Essays on Nietzsche's Genealogy of Morals*. Edited by Richard Schacht. Berkeley and Los Angeles: University of California Press, 1994.

Clark, Maudemarie, and David Dudrick. "Nietzsche and Moral Objectivity." In *Nietzsche and Morality*. Edited by Brian Leiter and Neal Sinhababu. Oxford: Oxford University Press, forthcoming.

Clark, Maudemarie, and Brian Leiter. "Introduction." In *Daybreak: Thoughts on the Prejudices of Morality*, by Friedrich Nietzsche. Cambridge: Cambridge University Press 1997.

Cohen, L. J. *An Essay on Belief and Acceptance*. Oxford: Clarendon, 1992.

Coleman, Jules L. *Markets, Morals, and the Law*. Cambridge: Cambridge University Press, 1988.

Confucius. *Analects*. Translated by Arthur Waley. New York: Vintage, 1938.

Copp, David. "The Ring of Gyges: Overridingness and the Unity of Reason." *Social Philosophy and Policy* 14, no. 1 (1997): 86–106.

Crisp, Roger. "The Dualism of Practical Reason," *Proceedings of the Aristotelian Society* 96 (1996): 53–73.

Csikszentmihalyi, Mihaly. *Flow: The Psychology of Optimal Experience*. New York: Harper & Row, 1990.

Currie, G. "Visual Imagery as the Simulation of Vision." *Mind and Language* 10 (1995): 25–44.

Dancy, Jonathan. "Supererogation and Moral Realism." In *Human Agency*. Edited by J. Dancy. Stanford, Calif.: Stanford University Press, 1988.

D'Arms, Justin, and Daniel Jacobson. "The Moralistic Fallacy." *Philosophy and Phenomenological Research* 61 (2000): 65–90.

Darwall, Stephen. "Two Kinds of Respect." *Ethics* 88, no. 1 (Oct. 1977): 36–49.

———. *The British Moralists and the Internal "Ought"*: 1640–1740. Cambridge: Cambridge University Press, 1995.

———. "Self-Interest and Self-Concern." *Social Philosophy and Policy* 14, no. 1 (1997): 158–78.

———. "Ethical Intuitionism and the Motivation Problem," in P. Stratton-Lake, ed., *Ethical Intuitionism: Re-evaluations*. Oxford: Clarendon, 2002.

Darwin, Charles. *On the Origin of Species by Means of Natural Selection*. London: John Murray, 1859.

Davidson, Donald. *Essays on Actions and Events*. Oxford: Oxford University Press, 1980.

Davies, M., and T. Stone. *Folk Psychology: The Theory of Mind Debate*. Oxford: Blackwell, 1995a.

———. *Mental Simulation: Evaluations and Applications*. Oxford: Blackwell, 1995b.

Dillon, Robin. "Kant on Arrogance and Self-Respect." In *Setting the Moral Compass*. Edited by C. Calhoun. New York: Oxford University, 2004.

Donagan, Alan. "Consistency in Rationalist Moral Systems." *Journal of Philosophy* 81, no. 6 (June 1984): 291–309.

———. *The Theory of Morality*. Chicago: University of Chicago Press, 1977.

Doyle, James. "Moral Rationalism and Moral Commitment." *Philosophy and Phenomenological Research* 60 (2000): 1–22.

Ekman, Paul, and E. L. Rosenberg. *What the Face Reveals*. 2nd ed. New York: Oxford University Press, 2004.

Falk, W. D. "Morality, Self, and Others." In *Morality and the Language of Conduct*. Edited by Hector-Neri Castaneda and George Nakhnikian. Detroit: Wayne State University Press, 1963.

———. "'Ought' and Motivation." Reprinted in *Ought, Reasons, and Morality*. Ithaca, N.Y.: Cornell University Press, 1986.

Fingarette, Herbert. *Confucius: The Secular as Sacred*. New York: Harper, 1972.

Finlay, Stephen. "The Conversational Practicality of Value Judgement." *Journal of Ethics* 8, no. 3 (2004): 205–23.

Foot, Philippa. *Virtues and Vices*. Oxford: Clarendon [1978] 2000. Berkeley and Los Angeles: University of California Press.

———. "Nietzsche's Immoralism." In *Nietzsche, Genealogy, Morality—Essays on Nietzsche's "Genealogy of Morals."* Edited by R. Schacht. Berkeley and Los Angeles: University of California Press, 1994.

———. *Natural Goodness.* Oxford: Clarendon, 2001.

———. "Morality as a System of Hypothetical Imperatives." In *Virtues and Vices.* Oxford: Clarendon [1978] 2002.

———. "Moral Beliefs" (1958–59). In *Virtues and Vices.* Oxford: Clarendon, [1978] 2002.

Forrester, Mary. "Some Remarks on Obligation, Permission, and Supererogation." *Ethics* 85 (1975): 219–26.

Fossum, Merle A., and Marilyn J. Mason. *Facing Shame: Families in Recovery.* New York: Norton, 1986.

Frankena, William K. "The Concept of Morality." *Journal of Philosophy* 63, no. 21 (Nov. 10, 1966): 688–96.

———. "Recent Conceptions of Morality." In *Morality and the Language of Conduct.* Edited by H. Castaneda and G. Nakhnikian. Detroit: Wayne State University Press, 1963.

Frankfurt, Harry. "The Dear Self." *Philosophers' Imprint* 1 (2001): http://www.philosophersimprint.org/001000.

Frankish, K. "A Matter of Opinion." *Philosophical Psychology* 11 (1998): 423–42.

Freedman, J. "Trangression, Compliance, and Guilt." In *Altruism and Helping Behavior.* Edited by J. Macaulay and L. Berkowitz. Academic Press, 1970.

Freud, Sigmund. *The Ego and the Id, Standard Edition.* Translated by James Strachey. London: Hogarth, 1953–74.

Gardiner, Stephen. "Aristotle, Egoism and the Virtuous Person's Point of View." In *Power and Pleasure, Virtues and Vices: Essays in Ancient Moral Philosophy*; a supplementary volume of *Prudentia.* Edited by D. Baltzly, D. Blyth, H. Tarrant. (June 2001): 243–65.

Garner, R. T. *Beyond Morality.* Philadelphia: Temple University Press, 1994.

Gauthier, David, ed. *Morality and Rational Self-Interest.* Englewood Cliffs, N.J.: Prentice Hall, 1970.

———. *Morals by Agreement.* Oxford: Clarendon, 1986.

———. *Moral Dealing: Contract, Ethics, and Reason.* Ithaca, N.Y.: Cornell University Press, 1990.

Gibbard, Allan. *Wise Choices, Apt Feelings: A Theory of Normative Judgment.* Cambridge, Mass.: Harvard University Press, 1990.

Glass, Marvin. "Why Should I Be Moral?" *Canadian Journal of Philosophy* 3, no. 2 (1973): 191–95.

Goldman, A. "Empathy, Mind, and Morals." *Proceedings and Addresses of the American Philosophical Association* 66 (1992): 17–43.

Griffin, James. "On the Winding Road from Good to Right." In *Value, Welfare, and Morality.* Edited by R. G. Frey and C. W. Morris. Cambridge: Cambridge University Press, 1993.

Hägerström, A. *Inquiries into the Nature of Law and Morals.* Stockholm: Almqvist & Wiksell, 1953.

Haji, I. *Moral Appraisability.* Oxford: Oxford University Press, 1998.

———. *Deontic Morality and Control.* Cambridge: Cambridge University Press, 2003.

Hale, Susan C. "Against Supererogation." *American Philosophical Quarterly* 28, no. 4 (1991): 273–85.

Hamilton, V. L. "Thoughts on Obedience: A Social Structural View." *Contemporary Psychology* 37 (1992): 1313.

Hampton, Jean. "Selflessness and the Loss of Self." *Social Philosophy and Policy* 10, no. 1 (1993): 135–65.

——. "The Wisdom of the Egoist: The Moral and Political Implications of Valuing the Self." *Social Philosophy and Policy* 14, no. 1 (1997): 21–51.

Hare, R. M. *Moral Thinking.* Oxford: Clarendon, 1981.

Harman, Gilbert. *The Nature of Morality.* New York: Oxford University Press, 1977.

Hart, H. L. A. *The Concept of Law.* Oxford, Clarendon, 1961.

Heyd, David. "Supererogation." *Stanford Encyclopedia of Philosophy*, 2002. http://plato.stanford.edu/entries/supererogation/.

Hill, Thomas E. Jr. "Reasonable Self-Interest." *Social Philosophy and Policy* 14, no. 1 (1997): 52–85.

Hinckfuss, I. "The Moral Society: Its Structure and Effects." *Discussion Papers in Environmental Philosophy* 16 (1987). Canberra: Philosophy Program (RSSS), Australian National University.

Hobbes, Thomas. *Leviathan.* Edited by Richard Tuck. Cambridge: Cambridge University Press, [1651] 1991.

Hooker, Brad. "Is Moral Virtue a Benefit to the Agent?" In *How Should One Live? Essays on the Virtues.* Edited by Roger Crisp. Oxford: Oxford University Press, 1996.

Hospers, John. *Human Conduct.* 3rd ed. Fort Worth, Tex.: Harcourt Brace, 1996.

Hume, David. *Enquiry Concerning the Principles of Morals.* Edited by L. A. Selby-Bigge, rev. P. H. Nidditch. Oxford: Clarendon, [1751] 1975.

——. *A Treatise of Human Nature.* Edited by L. A. Selby-Bigge, rev. P. H. Nidditch. Oxford: Clarendon [1740] 1978.

Hurka, Thomas. *Virtue, Vice and Value.* Oxford: Clarendon, 2001.

Hursthouse, Rosalind. *On Virtue Ethics.* Oxford: Oxford University Press, 1999.

——. "The Virtuous Agent's Reasons: A Response to Williams." In *Aristotle and Moral Realism.* Edited by R. Heinaman. London: University College London Press, 1995.

Hussain, N. J. Z. "The Return of Moral Fictionalism." *Philosophical Perspectives* 18 (2004): 149–87.

Irwin, Terence. "Splendid Vices? Augustine for and against Pagan Virtues." *Mediaeval Philosophy and Theology* 8 (1999): 105–27.

——. "Stoic Naturalism in Butler." In *Hellenistic and Early Modern Philosophy.* Edited by Jon Miller. Cambridge: Cambridge University Press, 2003.

Jeffrey, Richard C. *The Logic of Decision.* 2nd ed. Chicago: University of Chicago Press, 1983.

Jones, Daniel F. "Diagnosis and Character." In *Handbook of Interpersonal Psychoanalysis.* Edited by Marylou Lionells et al. Hillsdale, N.J.: Analytic, 1995.

Joyce, Richard. *The Myth of Morality.* Cambridge: Cambridge University Press, 2001.

——. "Expressivism and Motivation Internalism." *Analysis* 62 (2002): 336–44.

——. Review of *Moral Reality*, by Paul Bloomfield *Mind* 112 (2003): 94–99.

——. "Moral Fictionalism." In *Fictionalism in Metaphysics.* Edited by M. E. Kalderon. Oxford: Oxford University Press, 2005.

——. *The Evolution of Morality.* Cambridge, Mass.: MIT Press, 2006.

Kagan, Shelly. *The Limits of Morality.* New York: Oxford University Press, 1989.

Kalderon, M. E., ed. *Fictionalism in Metaphysics.* Oxford: Oxford University Press, 2005a.

——. *Moral Fictionalism.* Oxford: Oxford University Press, 2005b.

Kamm, Frances Myrna. "Harming Some to Save Others." *Philosophical Studies* 57 (1989): 251–56.

——. Review of *The Limits of Morality*, by Shelly Kagan. *Philosophy and Phenomenological Research*, 51 (1991): 904–5.

——. *Morality, Mortality, vol.* 2. New York: Oxford University Press, 1996.

Kant, Immanuel. *Groundwork of the Metaphysics of Morals.* Translated by H. J. Paton. New York: Harper, [1785] 1964.

——. *Grounding for the Metaphysics of Morals.* Translated by J. Ellington. Indianapolis: Hackett, [1785] 1981.

——. *The Metaphysics of Morals.* Translated by Mary Gregor. Cambridge: Cambridge University Press, [1797] 1996.

——. *Religion With the Bounds of Mere Reason.* Edited by Allen Wood and George di Giovanni. Cambridge: Cambridge University Press. 1998.

——. *Lectures on Ethics.* Edited by P. Heath and J. B. Schneewind. Cambridge: Cambridge University Press, 2001.

Kavka, Gregory. "The Reconciliation Project." In *Morality, Reason and Truth.* Edited by D. Copp and D. Zimmerman. Totowa, N.J.: Rowman and Allanheld, 1984.

Ketelaar, T., and W. T. Au. "The Effects of Feelings of Guilt on the Behavior of Uncooperative Individuals in Repeated Social Bargaining Games: An Affect-as-Information Interpretation of the Role of Emotion in Social Interaction. *Cognition and Emotion* 17 (2003): 429–53.

Knox, R. A. *Enthusiasm.* Oxford: Oxford University Press, 1950.

Korsgaard, Christine. *The Sources of Normativity.* Cambridge: Cambridge University Press, 1996.

Kripke, Saul. *Naming and Necessity.* Cambridge: Harvard University Press, 1972.

Kupperman, Joel J. *Ethics and Qualities of Life.* New York: Oxford University Press, 2007.

Laplanche, J., and J. B. Pontalis. *The Language of Psycho-Analysis.* Translated by D. Nicholson-Smith. New York: Norton, 1974.

Leiter, Brian. *Nietzsche on Morality.* London: Routledge, 2002.

Lewis, D. K. "Dispositional Theories of Value." Reprinted in *Papers in Ethics and Social Philosophy.* Cambridge: Cambridge University Press, [1989] 2000.

Lewis, Helen Block. *Shame and Guilt in Neurosis.* New York: International Universities Press, 1971.

Louden, Robert. *Morality and Moral Theory.* New York: Oxford University Press, 1992.

Luther, Martin. *Luther's Works.* St. Louis: Concordia, 1955.

MacIntyre, Alasdair. "Why Is the Search for the Foundations of Ethics So Frustrating?" In *Hastings Center Report* (1979): 15–22.

Mackie, J. L. *Ethics: Inventing Right and Wrong.* Harmondsworth: Penguin, 1977.

——. *The Miracle of Theism.* Oxford: Clarendon, 1982.

Mandeville, Bernard. *The Fable of the Bees.* In *British Moralists.* Edited by D. D. Raphael. Oxford: Oxford University Press, 1969.

McClennen, Edward F. "The Rationality of Being Guided by Rules." In *The Oxford Handbook of Practical Rationality.* Edited by A. R. Mele and P. Rawlings. Oxford: Oxford University Press, 2004.

McDowell, John. "Are Moral Requirements Hypothetical Imperatives?" *Proceedings of the Aristotelian Society* 52 supp. (1978): S12–S29.

——. "The Role of Eudaimonia in Aristotle's Ethics." Reprinted in *Essays on Aristotle's Ethics.* Edited by Amelie Rorty. Berkeley and Los Angeles: University of California Press, 1980.

McGinn, Colin. "Why Not Be a Bad Person?" In *Moral Literacy.* Indianapolis: Hackett, 1993.

McKeever, S. Review of *The Myth of Morality,* by Richard Joyce. *Ethics* 114 (2003): 182–84.

Mill, John Stuart *"On Liberty" and Other Writings*. Cambridge: Cambridge University Press, 1989.

——. *Utilitarianism*. Oxford: Oxford University Press, 1998.

Millgram, Elijah. "Was Hume a Humean?" *Hume Studies* 21 (1995): 75–93.

Moran, Richard. *Authority and Estrangement: An Essay in Self-Knowledge*. Princeton, N.J.: Princeton University Press, 2001.

Morris, Christopher, W. "A Contractarian Defense of Nuclear Deterrence." *Ethics* 95, no. 3 (April 1985): 479–96.

——. "Punishment and Loss of Moral Standing." *Canadian Journal of Philosophy* 21, no. 1 (March 1991): 53–79.

——. "Moral Standing and Rational-Choice Contractarianism." In *Contractarianism and Rational Choice: Essays on David Gauthier's* Morals by Agreement. Edited by Peter Vallentyne. Cambridge: Cambridge University Press, 1991.

——. "A Contractarian Account of Moral Justification." In *Moral Knowledge? New Readings in Moral Epistemology*. Edited by W. Sinnott-Armstrong and M. Timmons. New York: Oxford University Press, 1996.

——. "Justice, Reasons, and Moral Standing." In *Rational Commitment and Social Justice: Essays for Gregory Kavka*. Edited by J. L. Coleman and C. W. Morris. Cambridge: Cambridge University Press, 1998.

——. "The Trouble with Justice," *Philosophy and Public Policy Quarterly* 24, no. 3 (Summer 2004): 14–20.

Morris, Herbert. "Guilt and Punishment." *The Personalist* 52 (1971): 305–21.

——. *On Guilt and Innocence*. Berkeley and Los Angeles: University of California Press, 1976.

Morrison, Andrew. *Shame: The Underside of Narcissism*. Hillsdale, N.J.: Analytic, 1989.

Mossner, Ernest. *Life of David Hume*. Oxford: Clarendon, 1970.

Nagel, Thomas. *The Possibility of Altruism*. Oxford: Clarendon, 1970.

——. *The View from Nowhere*. New York: Oxford University Press, 1986.

——. "La valeur de l'inviolabilité." *Revue de métaphysique et de morale*, vol. 99, no. 2 (1994): 149–166.

Newman, J. "The Fictionalist Analysis of Some Moral Concepts." *Metaphilosophy* 12 (1981): 47–56.

Nielsen, Kai. *Why Be Moral?* Buffalo: Prometheus, 1989.

Nietzsche, F. *Kritische Studienausgabe*. 2nd ed. Edited by Giorgio Colli and Mazzino Montinari. Berlin: Gruyter, 1988.

——. *On the Genealogy of Morals*. Cambridge: Cambridge University Press, 1994.

Nolan, D., G. Restall, and C. West. "Moral Fictionalism Versus the Rest." *Australasian Journal of Philosophy* 83 (2005): 307–30.

Nozick, Robert. *Anarchy, State, and Utopia*. New York: Basic, 1974.

Nussbaum, Martha. *Hiding from Humanity*. Princeton, N.J.: Princeton University Press, 2004.

Oakeshott, Michael. *Rationalism in Politics*. Indianapolis: Liberty, 1991.

O'Neill, Onora. "Duty and Obligation." In *Encyclopedia of Ethics*, 2nd ed. 2 vols. Edited by L. Becker and C. Becker. New York and London: Routledge, 2001.

Overvold, Mark. "Self-Interest and the Concept of Self-Sacrifice." *Canadian Journal of Philosophy* 10 (1980): 105–18.

Paley, William. *Principles of Moral and Political Philosophy*. In *British Moralists*. Edited by D. D. Raphael. Oxford: Oxford University Press, 1969.

Papineau, David. "The Rise of Physicalism." In *Physicalism and Its Discontents*. Edited by Carl Gillett and Barry Loewer. Cambridge: Cambridge University Press, 2001.

Parfit, Derek. *Reasons and Persons*. Oxford: Clarendon, 1984.

Pfannkuche, Walter. "Supererogation als Element moralischer Verantwortung." In *Analyomen 2, Volume 3*. Edited by Georg Meggle. Hawthorne: de Gruyter, 1997.

Phillips, David. "Butler and the Nature of Self-Interest." In *Philosophy and Phenomenological Research* 60, no. 2 (March 2000): 421–38.

Phillips, D. Z. "Does It Pay to Be Good?" *Proceedings of the Aristotle Society* 65 (1964–65): 45–60.

Piers, Gehart and Milton Singer. *Shame and Guilt: A Psychoanalytic and a Cultural Study*. Springfield, Ill.: Charles C. Thomas, 1953.

Pius V. *Errores Michaeli Baii*. In *Enchiridion Symbolorum*. 36th ed. Edited by H. Denzinger and A. Schönmetzer. Freiburg: Herder, 1976.

Plato. *Theaetetus*. Translated by Levett, revised by Burnyeat. Indianapolis: Hackett Publishing, 1990.

——. *Republic*. Translated by R. Waterfield. Oxford: Oxford University Press, 1993.

——. *Symposium*. Translated by R. Waterfield. Oxford: Oxford University Press, 1994.

——. *Republic*. Translated by G. M.A. Grube, rev. C. D. C. Reeve, in Plato Complete Works, ed. John M. Cooper. Indianapolis: Hackett, [1974] 1997.

Postema, Gerald. "Conflict, Conversation, and Convention: Reflections on Hume's Account of the Emergence of Norms of Justice." (unpublished).

Prichard, H. A. "Does Moral Philosophy Rest on a Mistake?" *Mind* 21 (1912): 21–37.

——. *Moral Obligation*. Oxford: Oxford University Press, [1949] 1968.

Putnam, Hilary. *Philosophy of Logic*. New York: Harper & Row, 1971.

Quine, W. V. *Word and Object*. Cambridge, Mass.: MIT Press, 1960.

Quinn, Warren S. "Actions, Intentions and Consequences: The Doctrine of Doing and Allowing." *Philosophical Review* 98 (1989): 287–312.

Rand, Ayn. *The Virtue of Selfishness*. New York: New American Library, 1964.

Raphael, D. D., ed. *The British Moralists*. Oxford: Oxford University Press, 1969.

Rawls, John. *A Theory of Justice*. Cambridge: Harvard University Press, 1971.

Raz, Joseph. "Permissions and Supererogation." *American Philosophical Quarterly* 12 (1975): 161–68.

——. *The Authority of Law*. Oxford: Clarendon, 1979.

——. *The Morality of Freedom*. Oxford: Clarendon, 1986.

——. "A Morality Fit for Humans." *Michigan Law Review* 91 (1993): 1297–1314.

——. *Practical Reason and Norms*. Oxford: Clarendon, [1975] 1999.

——. *Engaging Reason: On the Theory of Value and Action*. Oxford: Oxford University Press, 1999.

——. "The Central Conflict: Morality and Self-Interest." In *Well-Being and Morality: Essays in Honour of James Griffin*. Edited by Roger Crisp and Brad Hooker. Oxford: Clarendon, 2000.

Richardson, John. *Nietzsche's New Darwinism*. Oxford: Oxford University Press, 2004.

——. *Nietzsche's System*. Oxford: Oxford University Press, 1996.

Risse, Mathias. "Origins of *Ressentiment* and Sources of Normativity." *Nietzsche Studien* 32 (2003): 142–70.

——. "The Second Treatise in *On the Genealogy of Morality*: Nietzsche on the Origin of the Bad Conscience." *The European Journal of Philosophy* 9 (2001): 55–81.

Rogers, Kelly. "Beyond Self and Other." *Social Philosophy and Policy* 14, no. 1 (1997): 1–20.

———. *Self-Interest: An Anthology of Philosophical Perspectives*. New York: Routledge, 1997.

Rorty, Amélie. "Moral Complexity, Conflicted Resonance and Virtue." In *Philosophy and Phenomenological Research* 55 (1995): 949–956.

Ross, W. D. *The Right and the Good*. Oxford: Clarendon, 1930.

Sachs, David. "A Fallacy in the *Republic*." In *Plato II*. Edited by Gregory Vlastos. Notre Dame, Ind.: University of Notre Dame Press, 1971.

———. "Notes on Unfairly Gaining More: Pleonexia." In *Virtues and Reasons*. Edited by R. Hursthouse, G. Lawrence, and W. Quinn. Oxford: Clarendon, 1995.

Sartre, Jean-Paul. *Being and Nothingness*. Edited by Hazel Barnes. New York: Philosophical Library, 1956.

Sayre-McCord, Geoffrey. "On Why Hume's 'General Point of View' Isn't Ideal—and Shouldn't Be." *Social Philosophy and Policy* 11 (1994): 202–28.

Scanlon, T. M. "Rights, Goals, and Fairness." In *Public and Private Morality*. Edited by S. Hampshire. Cambridge: Cambridge University Press, 1978.

———. *What We Owe to Each Other*. Cambridge, Mass.: Harvard University Press, 1998.

———. "Reasons, Responsibility, and Reliance: Replies to Wallace, Dworkin, and Deigh." *Ethics* 112 (2002): 507–28.

Schafer, Roy. "Ideals, The Ego Ideal, and the Ideal Self." *Psychological Issues* 18 (1967): 129–74.

———. "The Loving and Beloved Superego in Freud's Structural Thought." *Contemporary Psychoanalysis* 15 (1979): 163–88.

Schecter, David. "The Loving and Persecuting Superego." *Contemporary Psychoanalysis* 15 (1979): 361–79.

Scheffler, Samuel. *Human Morality*. New York: Oxford University Press, 1992.

———. *The Rejection of Consequentialism*. New York: Oxford University Press, 1982.

Schmidtz, David. "Scheffler's Hybrid Theory of the Right." *Nous* 24 (1990): 622–27.

———. *The Limits of Government: An Essay on the Public Goods Argument*. Boulder, Colo.: Westview, 1991.

———. "Reasons for Altruism." *Social Philosophy and Policy* 10, no. 1 (1993): 52–68.

———. "Choosing Ends." *Ethics* 104 (1994): 226–51.

———. *Rational Choice and Moral Agency*. Princeton, N.J.: Princeton University Press, 1995.

———. "Self-Interest: What's In It for Me?" *Social Philosophy and Policy* 14, no. 1 (1997): 107–21.

Scotus, Duns. *Duns Scotus on the Will and Morality*. Translated and edited by A. B. Wolter. Washington, D.C.: The Catholic University Press of America, 1986.

———. *Opera Omnia*. 12 vols. Edited by L. Wadding. Lyons: Durand, 1639.

Shaftesbury (Anthony Ashley Cooper, 3rd Earl of Shaftesbuy). *An Inquiry Concerning Virtue or Merit*. Manchester: Manchester University Press, [1714] 1977.

———. *Characteristics of Men, Manners, Opinions, Times*. Edited by Lawrence Klein. Cambridge: Cambridge University Press, 2003.

Shapiro, David. *Neurotic Styles*. New York: Basic, 1965.

———. *Autonomy and the Rigid Character*. New York: Basic, 1981.

Sherman, Nancy. "Aristotle on Friendship and the Shared Life." *Philosophy and Phenomenological Research* 47, no. 4 (1987): 589–613.

———. "Common Sense and Uncommon Virtue." *Midwest Studies* 13 (1988): 97–114.

Sidgwick, Henry. *Outlines of the History of Ethics*. 3rd ed. London: MacMillan, 1896.

——. *The Methods of Ethics*. 7th ed. Chicago: University of Chicago Press, [1907] 1962.

Singer, Peter. *How Are We to Live? Ethics in an Age of Self-Interest*. Amherst, N.Y.: Prometheus, 1995.

Smith, Michael. *The Moral Problem*. Oxford: Blackwell, 1994.

Smith, Tara. *Viable Values*. Lanham, Md.: Rowman and Littlefield, 2000.

Sreenivasan, Gopal. "What Is the General Will?" *Philosophical Review* 109 (2000): 545–81.

Stanley, Jason. "Hermeneutic Fictionalism." *Midwest Studies in Philosophy* 25 (2001): 36–71.

Stocker, Michael. "The Schizophrenia of Modern Ethical Theories." *Journal of Philosophy* 73 (1976): 453–66.

——. *Plural and Conflicting Values*. Oxford: Clarendon Press, 1990.

Strom, Stephanie. "An Organ Donor's Generosity Raises the Question of How Much Is Too Much." *New York Times*. August 17, 2003.

Swain, M., ed. *Induction, Acceptance, and Rational Belief*. Dordrecht, Holland: D. Reidel, 1970.

Swanton, Christine. *Virtue Ethics, a Pluralistic View*. Oxford: Oxford University Press, 2003.

Tangney, June Price, and Ronda L. Dearing. *Shame and Guilt*. New York and London: Guilford, 2002.

Tangney, June Price, D. Mashek, J. Stuewig, P. Magaletta, et al. "Working at the Social-Clinical-Community-Criminology Interface: The GMU Inmate Study." *Journal of Social and Clinical Psychology* 26 (2007): 1–28.

Taylor, Gabriele. *Pride, Shame, and Guilt: Emotions of Self-Assessment*. Oxford: Oxford University Press, 1985.

Taylor, Michael. *The Possibility of Cooperation*. Cambridge: Cambridge University Press, 1987.

Telfer, Elizabeth. "Self-Respect." *Philosophical Quarterly* 18 (1968): 114–21.

Thomas, Laurence. *Living Morally*. Philadelphia: Temple University Press, 1989.

Thomson, Judith Jarvis. "Normativity." In *Oxford Studies in Metaethics* 2. Edited by R. Shafer-Landau. Oxford: Oxford University Press, 2007.

——. *The Realm of Rights*. Cambridge, Mass.: Harvard University Press, 1990.

Thornton, J. C. "Can the Moral Point of View Be Justified?" In *Readings in Contemporary Ethical Theory*. Edited by K. Pahel and M. Schiller. Englewood Cliffs, N.J.: Prentice Hall, 1970.

Tiberius, V., and J. Walker. "Arrogance." *American Philosophical Quarterly* 35 (1998): 379–90.

Timmons, Mark. *Morality without Foundations*. New York: Oxford University Press, 1999.

Toulmin, Stephen. *An Examination of the Place of Reason in Ethics*. Cambridge: Cambridge University Press, 1950.

——. "The Logic of Moral Reasoning, and Reason and Faith." In *Readings in Contemporary Ethical Theory*. Edited by K. Pahel and M. Schiller. Englewood Cliffs, N.J.: Prentice Hall, 1970.

Urmson, J. "Saints and Heroes." In *Essays in Moral Philosophy*. Edited by A. Melden. Seattle: University of Washington Press, 1958.

Vaihinger, H. *The Philosophy of "As If."* Translated by C. K. Ogden. London: Routledge & Kegan Paul, 1935.

Velleman, David. "What Happens When Someone Acts?" Reprinted in *The Possibility of Practical Reason*. New York: Oxford University Press, 2000.

Vlastos, Gregory. "The Argument in the *Republic* That 'Justice Pays'." *Journal of Philosophy* 65, no. 21 (1968): 665–74.

Wallace, R. Jay. "Scanlon's Contractualism." *Ethics* 112 (2002): 429–70.

———. Review of *The Myth of Morality*, by Richard Joyce. *Notre Dame Philosophical Reviews* (November 2003).

———. "The Rightness of Acts and the Goodness of Lives." In *Reason and Value: Themes from the Moral Philosophy of Joseph Raz*. Edited by R. J. Wallace, P. Pettit, S. Scheffler, and M. Smith. Oxford: Clarendon, 2004.

Wedgwood, Ralph. "Choosing Rationally and Choosing Correctly." In *Weakness of Will and Practical Irrationality*. Edited by S. Stroud and C. Tappolet. Oxford: Oxford University Press, 2003.

———. "The Normativity of the Intentional." In *The Oxford Handbook of the Philosophy of Mind*. Edited by B. McLaughlin and A. Beckermann. Oxford: Oxford University Press, forthcoming.

Williams, Bernard. "A Critique of Utilitarianism." In *Utilitarianism: For and Against*. Edited by J. J. C. Smart and Bernard Williams. Cambridge: Cambridge University Press, 1973.

———. "Justice as a Virtue." In *Essays on Aristotle's Ethics*. Edited by A. Rorty. Berkeley and Los Angeles: University of California Press, 1980.

———. *Moral Luck*. Cambridge: Cambridge University Press, 1981.

———. "Persons, Character and Morality." Reprinted in *Moral Luck*. Cambridge: Cambridge University Press, 1981.

———. *Ethics and the Limits of Philosophy*. Cambridge, Mass.: Harvard University Press, 1985.

———. *Shame and Necessity*. Berkeley and Los Angeles: University of California Press, 1993.

———. "Acting as the Virtuous Person Acts." In *Aristotle and Moral Realism*. Edited by R. Heinaman. London: University College London Press, 1995.

Wiltshire, Roderick. "The Wrong and the Good," unpublished.

Wittgenstein, L. "Lecture on Ethics." *Philosophical Review* 74 (1965): 3–12.

Wolf, Susan. "Moral Saints." *Journal of Philosophy* 79, no. 8 (1982): 419–39.

———. "Happiness and Meaning: Two Aspects of the Good Life." *Social Philosophy and Policy* 14, no. 1 (1997): 207–25.

———. "Morality and the View from Here." *Journal of Ethics* 3 (1999): 203–23.

Wollaston, William. *Religion of Nature Delineated* [1722] Delmar, N.Y.: Scholars' Facsimiles & Reprints, 1974.

Wray, K. B. "Collective Belief and Acceptance." *Synthese* 129 (2001): 319–33.

Wright, C. *Truth and Objectivity*. Cambridge, Mass.: Harvard University Press, 1992.

———. "Truth in Ethics." In *Truth in Ethics*. Edited by B. Hooker. Oxford: Blackwell, 1996.

Zhong, C. and K. Liljenquist. "Washing Away Your Sins: Threatened Morality and Physical Cleansing." *Science* 313 (2006): 1451–52.

Ziff, Paul. *Semantic Analysis*. Ithaca, N.Y.: Cornell University Press, 1960.

Zimmerman, Michael J. "Supererogation and Doing the Best One Can." *American Philosophical Quarterly* 30, no. 4 (1993): 373–80.

Index